Public Finance in Theory and Practice
Second edition

The events of the 1990s have challenged the contemporary neo-classical synthesis in all branches of economics, but particularly public finance. The most notable feature of the second edition of *Public Finance in Theory and Practice* is the infusion of behavioral economics throughout the text, with an end-of-chapter section with questions inviting the student to apply a behavioral lens to some question or issue. There continues to be an emphasis on the importance of the institutional context, drawing on examples from many countries and emphasizing the role of lower-level governments in a federal system. The first five chapters establish this context by reviewing the role of government in a market system, the description of government structure from an economic perspective, the basic data about revenue and expenditures, the elements of public choice, and the distributional role of government.

Public Finance in Theory and Practice has been substantially reorganized to put more emphasis on public expenditure. Expanded treatment of public goods includes common property resources and congestible or club goods. Expanded discussion of budgeting and cost-benefit analysis provides some practical application of the theory. Updated discussions of social security, public education and health care address these three major contemporary public finance issues. The traditional emphasis on revenue (taxes, fees and grants) has been retained but follows rather than precedes the discussion of expenditures.

To ensure the text is totally accessible, theory is conveyed primarily with diagrams, assuming only a basic knowledge of microeconomics. Appendices provide the mathematical formulation of public goods and externalities for the interested reader, while case studies provide some particular applications of the theory. This is a readable and comprehensive textbook that forms the perfect introduction to public finance.

Holley H. Ulbrich is Alumni Distinguished Professor Emerita of Economics at Clemson University and Senior Fellow at the Strom Thurmond Institute, USA. She is also the co-author on four of the six editions of *Principles of Economics* with Ryan C. Amacher.

Public Finance in Theory and Practice

Second edition

Holley H. Ulbrich

Routledge
Taylor & Francis Group

LONDON AND NEW YORK

First edition published
by South Western College Publishers, Mason, OH, 2003

Second edition published 2011
by Routledge
2 Park Square, Milton Park, Abingdon, Oxon OX14 4RN

Simultaneously published in the USA and Canada
by Routledge
711 Third Avenue, New York, NY 10017

Routledge is an imprint of the Taylor & Francis Group, an informa business

British Library Cataloguing in Publication Data
A catalogue record for this book is available from the British Library

Library of Congress Cataloging in Publication Data
A catalog record has been requested for this book

ISBN: 978-0-415-58596-5 (hbk)
ISBN: 978-0-415-58597-2 (pbk)
ISBN: 978-0-203-81701-8 (ebk)

Typeset in Times New Roman
by RefineCatch Limited, Bungay, Suffolk

MIX
Paper from
responsible sources
FSC
www.fsc.org
FSC® C004839

Printed and bound in Great Britain by
TJ International Ltd, Padstow, Cornwall

Contents

List of figures

List of tables

Preface to the second edition

Much has changed in the world of public sector economics since the first edition of this book came out eight years ago. Tax protests and battles over Social Security and health care have escalated, while massive budget deficits have become one of the most critical public issues of our time. The core theoretical foundations of public sector economics, however—the theory of public expenditure and the principles of taxation—remain both intact and relevant, and they receive due treatment in this book.

Users of the first edition will notice many changes in both organization and content in response to reviewer comments and my own experience in teaching from this book. Issues of income distribution now form a part of the five foundation chapters, along with two chapters on the size and structure of governments and an expanded treatment of public choice. It is impossible to address either expenditures or taxation without first considering the pervasive issues of income distribution on public sector decision-making processes.

A deeper treatment of the theory of public expenditures resulted in splitting the single chapter on public goods and externalities into two chapters, followed immediately by three chapters on applied issues in public expenditure—budgeting, borrowing, and cost-benefit analysis. The structure of the revenue and taxation chapters is largely unchanged, but the content has been updated and expanded. The chapters on competition and government and on infrastructure have been deleted, with some of the material moved to other chapters and some available on the web site. The final three chapters on issues in public expenditure revisit the issues in providing public education, Social Security, and health care in the light of the experience of the past decade.

In both the first and second editions, we emphasize that government includes all levels of government—federal, state, and local. The United States is one of a handful of countries with a federal form of government (Canada, Germany, Switzerland, and Australia are among the others). Most nations have a unitary structure with only central and local governments. But at the same time, the European Union has expanded not only its membership but also the responsibilities that are carried out by the EU rather than its individual member countries, presenting a new challenge to our understanding of federalism as a fiscal issue. Within nations, the respective roles of different levels of government have changed greatly in just the past two decades. Much more of the "action" in terms of service delivery and revenue-raising is now concentrated at the state and local level. So this challenge of fiscal federalism appears throughout the book.

In a global economy, it is no longer adequate to study public finance from the perspective of one particular country. Considering the institutions and practices of many nations is an important reminder that the way in which the economics of public finance works out in practice in one particular country is the result of an encounter of a general theory with a specific history and set of institutions. Differences between countries reflect the same theory at work in different cultures with different histories, resources, and values. Different nations might reasonably make different choices that are more suited to their size, income levels, history, and preferences. These other experiences will serve as a reminder that economic theory and policy analysis rarely produce a single solution to a particular question or problem, but rather a number of possible solutions with different attributes. That emphasis not only remains but is strengthened in this second edition especially with the addition of end-of-chapter questions that invite the student to "think globally."

Behavioral economics has been around for a long time but has received much more attention in the past ten years, and it receives more attention in this book. The only Nobel Prize in economics to go to a psychologist was given to Daniel Kahneman in 2002 for his work in understanding how people make decisions. Behavioral economics helps us to understand why policy decisions often do not have the impact that theoretical models would predict. Behavioral economics does not replace the standard theory, but rather enriches it.

There are two basic premises of behavioral economics: the motivational and the cognitive. Humans are motivationally more complex than is adequately described by the self-interest model. They are also social and relational beings who are influenced by social norms and by concern for others, especially those closest to them. At the same time, humans are generally not as good or as fast at acquiring, processing and applying information to their choices as the rational choice model implies, an idea pioneered by Herbert Simon with his description of bounded rationality. Behavioral economics is introduced in the first chapter and applications, including end of chapter questions, are found throughout the book.

Economists rely heavily on descriptive statistics to flesh out the theory. So do politicians and economic journalists. Numbers give concrete reality to ideas. It is important for students to learn to tease the story out of the statistics, to be able to describe situations in concrete terms, to spot trends and look for patterns. For that reason, along with all the descriptive statistics in the chapters, there is an end-of-chapter question in each chapter that invites students to explore the world of descriptive statistics as it applies to the material in that chapter.

Finally, economics is a policy science. Its original name was political economy, and the political referred not to politics but to policy. So each chapter also offers the student a policy application question to address.

Acknowledgments

I want to acknowledge the contributions of my colleagues at the Strom Thurmond Institute, Ellen Saltzman and Lori Dickes; five anonymous reviewers who offered many helpful suggestions; my students in public administration and policy studies who were helpful guinea pigs and critics of both the first edition and this revision; Robert Langham at Routledge, who encouraged me to undertake a second edition; graduate student Patrick Tandoh-Offin and undergraduate economics student and computer artist Corey Allen, who prepared the illustrations; and Joyce Bridges and Kathy Skinner who helped to prepare the final manuscript. I also acknowledge the support of my patient and encouraging husband, Carlton Ulbrich, during this long process of revision.

I hope that this textbook will provide the student a solid foundation in the theory and practice of public finance or public sector economics that will enable him or her to be a more informed citizen, and perhaps encourage a career in public policy that is based on a solid understanding of the economic foundations.

Holley Ulbrich
Clemson, South Carolina

Acknowledgements

Part 1

Government and the market

Like other branches of economics, public finance or public sector economics combines a body of theory with a set of institutions to describe, analyze, and interpret the workings of government in a predominantly private economy. The theory is more or less universal, but it works out differently in different institutional contexts. Policies that work well for a small, homogeneous, highly centralized nation or in highly competitive markets may have very different effects in a nation that is larger, heterogeneous, and decentralized, or in an economy with a substantial concentration of private economic power. While much of this book is written from an American perspective, that viewpoint is heavily qualified by frequent comparisons with experience in other countries, particularly but not exclusively other English-speaking industrial and post-industrial countries.

From before recorded history, human societies have felt the need to have governments. Very small societies may get by with relatively little government, but once societies become large, complex, and technologically sophisticated, they need a referee, a rule setter, an authority for resolving disputes. Many of those rules and disputes are economic in nature.

Some governments, like the American government in the words of the Declaration of Independence, "derive their just powers from the consent of the governed." Others exist by force of arms, or tradition, or external imposition, or other sources of power. Governments come into being to balance the desire of the individual for autonomy and freedom with the need for citizens to find ways to work together to address common concerns, manage shared resources, protect themselves from each other and external enemies, and resolve the boundary problems that separate one household from another.

In many countries, the powers and limitations of government are laid out in formal documents. Among the major English-speaking countries, those documents are a more or less continuous series, beginning with Magna Carta in 1215; the US Articles of Confederation in 1781, superseded by the US Constitution of 1787; the British North America Act of 1867 that is the core of the Canadian Constitution; the 1900 Constitution of the Commonwealth of Australia; and the 1949 Constitution of India, just to list a few.

However limited the original mandate—and in the United States, the original mandate, the Articles of Confederation, was very limited indeed—sooner or later, the role of government begins to expand. Much thought and discussion goes into determining what government should be permitted to do when the central vision is a private society that is largely governed by individual choice, with government intervening only when necessary. However, the opportunity to use the government to get others to pay for your pet project or to restrict your pet annoyance tends to expand both the budgetary and regulatory reach of government.

The paragraph above describes a distinctly American (and to a lesser degree, British) view of government. Most Americans assume that this individualistic interpretation of the role of government—as an intruder into primarily market and private decisions—to be "the way it is," rather than one interpretation among many possible ones. Many nations have no such hierarchy of activity, with the market as primary and the government as secondary. Instead, there may be a fluctuating blend of public and private activity, with the assignment of tasks to one or the other determined on an *ad hoc* basis. Western and Latin American countries have shifted back and forth between a larger public role and a larger private role in an effort to balance competing demands of equity and efficiency, individual security and work incentives, public infrastructure, and private capital.

Still other countries have undergone a public/private sorting-out process in reverse. In the former Soviet Union and Eastern Europe, the challenge has been to transition from a system in which the community took precedence over the individual to one that provides a much larger sphere for private, individual decisions. It has been a slow and confusing road, from a system in which the government managed almost all economic activity to an alternative model in which individuals, markets, and private voluntary associations play important roles in organizing economic activity. One of the biggest needs was the creation of the social infrastructure that supports the market, such as financial institutions, regulatory agencies, property rights, and contract law.

Reflecting on the transition experience of Eastern and Central European countries in the past two decades suggests that there is no single "right" balance between individual and community, public and private, government and the market. Different societies can and do settle at different points along the continuum from minimum government, maximum market/private sector to the opposite extreme. The point of settlement is always a moving target.

Mindful of diversity, we nevertheless attempt to distill the common ground of public sector economics across many different cultural and institutional contexts. The five chapters in Part 1 address some fundamental issues about government that provide the background for a closer examination of the revenue and expenditure dimensions of public sector activity. Chapter 1 reviews basic understandings about the division of responsibility between governments and markets. Chapter 2 provides a quantitative measure of the size and scope of government—how much revenue flows into public coffers and from what sources, and which services those revenues are used to provide.

Chapter 3 addresses the structure of governments, which is particularly important in federal systems with three levels of government, such as the United States, Canada, and Australia. In a federal system, authority and responsibility are sometimes shared and sometimes divided across levels of government. While most countries have local governments with varying degrees of autonomy, there is a more limited number of countries with three levels of government with their own defined spheres of activity. In such countries, the structure must address such questions as: Do the benefits from government programs stay local (or within the state or province), or do they spill over to other areas? Which taxes are suited to local use? What responsibilities are national in scope? Understanding the interplay between theory and context, including the formal and informal division of responsibility between state, local and federal, between government, market and the nonprofit sector is an essential part of one's education as a policy economist.

The decision-making process in the public sector is of necessity different from that of the private sector. While decisions in the private sector are made by voting with dollars, public sector decision-making is more complex, involving both economic and political considerations such as agenda-setting, monitoring and incentives, and incomplete information. The branch of political economy that addresses that decision-making process from an economic perspective is known as public choice, the subject of Chapter 4.

Everything the government does (or fails to do) affects the distribution of income and wealth. Some of it is intentional—the progressive income tax, welfare, Social Security. Some redistribution is a byproduct of government decisions made for other reasons. More often, decisions about public goods and services and the distribution of their costs and benefits are made simultaneously. Chapter 5 examines the impact of public sector activities on the distribution of income, resources, wealth and opportunities among citizens.

1 Government in a market system

Introduction

Once students get past their introductory course in economics, they probably find that their university or college offers a fairly standard package of upper division courses in economics. This package almost always includes intermediate macroeconomics, intermediate micro-economics, statistics and/or econometrics, money and banking, and labor economics.

Note that even in this short list there are several courses in which the government plays a central role. One is macroeconomics, and another is money and banking, two courses taken by most economics majors. Monetary and fiscal policy, debts and deficits, stimulus packages and bank regulation are very much the stuff of both daily headlines and courses in macroeconomics and money and banking. Students may also have an opportunity to take courses in government and business, environmental economics, economic development, urban economics, public choice and, of course, public finance or public sector economics. All of these courses cover some substantial role of government in directing economic activity.

Breaking the subject matter of economics down into individual courses is a challenging task. There is substantial overlap between one field and another. Which parts of the role of government in a market system are included in a course in public sector economics, and which are reserved for other courses? The answer to that question has evolved considerably in the past 30 years.

One of the best-known twentieth-century economists in the field of public finance, Richard Musgrave, divided the economic role of government into allocation, distribution, and stabilization. **Allocation** refers to anything the government does that affects the mixture (quantity and quality) of goods and services that the economy produces, from direct government production to regulation to tax incentives to penalties for illegal activities. **Distribution** refers to anything the government does that affects the distribution of income and wealth. Just about everything the government does, from locating roads to tax cuts to school vouchers and college scholarships to mortgage insurance guarantees, affects the distribution of income and wealth, intentionally or otherwise. Finally, **stabilization** covers those government actions that influence the overall level of employment, output, and prices. To do justice to all of those aspects of government involvement in the economy would require several volumes and span several courses. So courses and textbooks in **public sector economics** or **public finance** have developed some boundaries that have narrowed the subject matter.

Although public sector economics has been displacing public finance as the preferred title of the field, the older title of public finance does have an advantage in defining its scope. The finance in public finance refers to the budgeting, taxing, and spending activities of government. Most activities of the government that are not primarily budget-related (such as regulatory activities) are left to other courses.

A second way in which public finance/public sector economics has narrowed its scope in the past two decades was to assign the stabilization function to courses in macroeconomics and money and banking, along with government policies that encourage or retard economic growth. So technically speaking, a course in public sector economics or public finance is focused on the microeconomics of government revenue and spending. Except for some limited discussion of the size and management of the public debt and budget deficits and surpluses, stabilization policy is largely absent from public finance courses and textbooks. This narrower definition, tying public finance to microeconomics and to budget-centered issues of taxing and spending, provided the central focus for the economic sub-discipline of public finance for several decades.

More recently, as public finance has evolved into public sector economics, the scope of the field has broadened beyond the components of the budget.[1] The use of taxes, fees, and charges as instruments to achieve social or regulatory objectives has led to much more analysis of issues in public sector pricing, such as the design of congestion fees and effluent charges, demand measurement for public goods, and setting prices for publicly provided goods and services.

The relatively new field of public choice that has developed over the past 30 years has also exerted considerable influence on economists' understanding of how decisions are made in the public sector. **Public choice** is a partially separate field of economics that analyzes the behavior of elected officials and bureaucrats in the public sector and explores the policy implications of government failure. Sometimes public choice is taught as part of a course in public sector economics or public finance. In other cases, public choice commands a separate course of its own.

Governments, markets and efficiency

In a market system, private individuals and organizations (including corporations) in pursuit of their own self-interest make most of the economic decisions. The widespread preference for markets as the decision-making tool is grounded in microeconomic theory. Microeconomics demonstrates that under ideal conditions, the market will be more efficient than any alternative system at providing the maximum social welfare out of available resources.

Economic efficiency is measured by the quantity and variety of goods and services that its members produce, consume, and distribute out of their limited available resources. The market is more efficient at determining which combination of goods and services people want and delivering that combination. The market is more efficient in ensuring that goods are produced at the lowest possible resource cost and sold at the lowest possible price. The market is more efficient at rewarding those who heed market signals and punishing those who pay no attention. If efficiency in the use of scarce resources is the sole or primary objective, the market is the ideal tool to achieve that goal.

In its strongest form, this ideal efficient outcome of markets is referred to as **Pareto optimality**. An economic situation of production or distribution or both is Pareto optimal when it is not possible to make at least one person better off without making one or more persons worse off. In a Pareto optimal world, all prices are equal to marginal cost, all products are being produced with the most efficient resource mix, all inputs are paid the value of their marginal product, and all consumers have allocated their budgets so that the satisfaction that they receive from the last unit of each good purchased is just equal to the price, which is in turn equal to the marginal cost of producing it. Costs and prices reflect social as well as private costs. In such a Pareto optimal world, there would be little need for government.

What should government do?

Because a perfectly functioning market system would lead to a Pareto optimal allocation of resources, such a system would limit government's role to those functions that the market cannot perform at all. The list is surprisingly short. Almost all of the activities that people have come to associate with government—providing for defense, controlling the money supply, ensuring law enforcement, building highways, and educating the next generation—can be and have been produced privately by either non-profit or for-profit firms at some time. Private security guards can protect life and property. Hired mercenaries can defend citizens from foreign enemies. Private toll roads were the norm in colonial New England and continue to exist along public highways in some places. Scrip in company towns in the nineteenth and early twentieth centuries served as private money. Private schools continue to educate large numbers of students. Is there anything the market cannot do? Is there any essential, indispensable function for government in a market system?

It is true that just about every function of government can be, or has been, performed by private groups, but often the market does not perform those functions very satisfactorily—or even very efficiently. Why? Perhaps one or more of the ideal market conditions that are needed to ensure efficiency do not hold. Students should recall from earlier courses what those conditions are, because they are the same assumptions that underlie the perfectly competitive model:

- large numbers of individuals and firms;
- little or no concentration of market power;
- perfect information;
- free mobility of resources and products;
- no spillover effects in either production or consumption so that private and social costs and benefits are the same.

When any of these assumptions are violated, there is a possibility of **market failure**. When the market delivers less than satisfactory outcomes, there is a case to be made for turning to government for improved results.

When the market fails to produce desired goods and services, or to produce them in sufficient quantity/quality, or when it produces undesirable goods and services, or produces too many goods with harmful spillovers, then governments may intervene to try to restore production to something closer to optimal levels. There are a number of tools that the government can use to encourage or discourage production of particular goods and services. These tools include:

1   Subsidies (reducing seller costs or net price paid by the buyer, e.g., subsidizing higher education with grants to students and/or to colleges and universities) in order to encourage private production or consumption of goods and services with broad public benefits.
2   Tax incentives (e.g., tax deductions for educational expenditures or charitable contributions) to encourage private production/consumption of specified goods and services that are believed to provide broad public benefits.

3   Guarantees that reduce risk (e.g., disaster insurance, crop insurance, mortgage loan guarantees, student loan guarantees, bank deposit insurance) and thus encourage private production and/or consumption of specified goods and services.
4   Penalties in the form of taxes, charges, fines, etc. for excessive production of goods or services that are believed to impose costs on others.
5   Mandating production/consumption of a particular good or service (e.g., seat belts in cars, safety helmets on motorcycles, required school attendance).
6   Forbidding production/consumption of a particular good or service (e.g., cocaine, tobacco or pornography to people under age 18, firearms in public places).
7   Public production (e.g., national defense, law enforcement).
8   Private production with public financing.

Each of these eight tools will appear in later chapters as policy options available for responding to various issues.

Government as rule-maker and referee

A market system is based on private ownership of the means of production—land, labor, capital, and enterprise. The use of those resources, and the products produced by those resources, are bought and sold in the marketplace. In order to engage in exchange or negotiate contracts with strangers or over long distances or time periods, buyers and sellers need some assurances that the seller really owns what is being sold, that buyers know what rights are being conveyed with purchase, and that contracts are enforceable. A market system requires a clear definition of these kinds of property rights and a guarantee that those rights are protected. A primary function of government has always been the creation, protection, definition, interpretation, and enforcement of property rights.

The government-provided system of courts and law enforcement exists in order to ensure that people who owe money can be compelled to pay, that sellers are liable for defective products, that the car you bought was really owned by the seller, or that the title to the lot you sold did (or didn't) include mineral or water rights. Because of the central importance of property rights in a market system, the rule-making and rule-enforcing function of government is its primary economic responsibility. These rules include the Constitution, laws, and the interpretation of the laws by the executive branch, the courts, and the various administrative agencies.

When people fail to abide by some kinds of rules set by the government, they can be arrested and charged with various kinds of crimes against the state, ranging from illegal parking to high treason. People can also be charged with crimes against other individuals, such as murder, theft, embezzlement, or assault. But the government also establishes rules and procedures for resolving non-criminal disputes between private individuals, over such matters as ownership of property, trespass, enforcement of contracts, and divorce. There are also courts and enforcement procedures for these civil matters. (The word civil, derived from the Latin *civis* or citizen, refers to cases between private citizens, including corporations as well as individuals.)

Government as manager of risk

In the past decade, citizens in many countries have become increasingly aware of yet another important role of government as an insurer against disasters of various kinds. For Americans, the wake-up call to this role came as a result of Hurricane Katrina in 2005 and the financial system crisis of 2007–09. When government provides insurance against disaster by subsidizing flood insurance, regulating and insuring bank deposits, and providing relief funds for banks, borrowers, and disaster victims, the risk is spread across the entire population.

Certainly there is an ample role for private firms in providing insurance against death, property losses, liability, and medical emergencies, although all of these private kinds of insurance are usually subject to government regulation to protect consumers. But some forms of insurance do not lend themselves to pure market solutions. The first flood insurance company in the United States was located on the Mississippi River, famous for annual flooding. The first year, the firm suffered significant economic losses. The second year, the firm's headquarters washed down the river along with most of its remaining assets. Mortgage lenders are reluctant to make loans to homeowners buying property in flood-prone areas, so in recent decades flood insurance has been subsidized by the federal government in the United States.

The role of government in risk management extends far beyond natural disasters to a broad range of economic activity where the risks are unknown, or where individuals cannot obtain the kind of information they need in order to make a wise or informed decision. In the United States, these kinds of government insurance include mortgage guarantees (by the Veterans' Administration and later Freddie Mac and Fannie Mae), federally subsidized flood insurance, the Federal Emergency Management Administration (FEMA), the Department of Homeland Security, protection of bank deposits by the Federal Deposit Insurance Corporation, guaranteed student loans, unemployment insurance, and Social Security. Most other modern nations would add health insurance to that list. Regardless of the division of activities between public and private sectors, there are countless examples of the government acting as an insurer in areas where private guarantees are not available or not adequate.

Insurance encourages individuals and firms to take risks. That may be a good thing, or it may not. Risk-taking is vital to a dynamic economy, but foolish risks are expensive, and no one wants the government to bail out every person or firm who makes foolish choices just because they are insured against loss. So public insurance requires that there be regulation limiting the amount or kind of insurable risk that people can take on, and like private insurers, public insurers usually want the insured to cover some of the cost through a deductible, co-pay, insurance premium, or other contribution that is related to the degree of risk. A significant part of the regulatory function of most governments is related to that particular role as the rescuer of those in economic distress through insurance guarantees of various kinds.

Government, markets and equity

A second reason for calling on the government to modify market outcomes is that the objective function—that is, the desired goals and objectives of economic activity—may include additional considerations besides economic efficiency. Most often, those additional considerations involve **equity**. Equity means some agreed-on notion of fairness in the distribution of the costs and benefits of government among groups of citizens at the current time, or in balancing the needs of present and future generations.

The market can create extremes of wealth and poverty. Households with limited productive resources may not earn enough to attain a decent standard of living. Some are unable to earn anything. In the United States, market signals have resulted in much more production of luxury homes than basic affordable housing, resulting in widespread homelessness. A largely market-driven health care system has left a large share of the population without health insurance. Market forces have favored private over public transportation and have made it difficult for lower-income households to have transportation to work, shopping, health care, and education.

The government can and does intervene in the market-determined distribution of income in many ways, principally through taxes and transfer programs that put more of the cost of public services on higher-income households and provide food stamps, unemployment insurance, Medicaid and housing vouchers at the bottom of the income ladder.

Equity between members of the same generation or between successive generations is very difficult to define in a way that will result in broad agreement. Despite the challenge of definition and measurement, however, equity has been a central concern of philosophers of the public sector since Plato's *Republic* more than two thousand years ago gave central place to justice in the design of the perfect society. The equity issue recurs throughout this book, but gets particular attention in Chapter 5.

The short-term perspective: who is responsible for the future?

One frequent criticism of the market system is its tendency to focus on the short-run, although there are exceptions. Management of corporations is rewarded for performance, defined as increases in shareholder wealth. Investors are notoriously fickle in selling stocks that are underperforming in order to buy others that hold more hope of profits, preferably in the near term. As the price of the stock falls, the firm becomes vulnerable to a takeover, which may threaten the position of the current management and board of directors.

The emphasis on changes in shareholder wealth (stock prices and/or dividends) can force management to adopt strategies that are more profitable in the short-run but contribute less to the long-term viability or success of the firm. Performance pressures may also lead to abuses of relationships with workers and communities in the drive to improve the bottom line. Putting a very high value on present and near-term performance at the possible expense of long-term results is called over-discounting the future.

Ideally, government can offset this private sector emphasis on the short term by anticipating needs farther into the future. Many major projects were undertaken by governments when the private market failed to think that far ahead, particularly in highway and rail systems, public pension funds, and the creation of higher education systems. Governments can also place regulatory constraints on firms that ensure protection of workers and communities even at some cost in shareholder wealth. By imposing the same constraints on all firms (wage and hour regulations, environmental and health regulations, pension requirements), the government levels the playing field among competing firms so that no one firm would gain an advantage by at least some forms of over-discounting the future.

However, government has its own limits in time horizons. Most governments are elected, and voters, like shareholders, are interested in short-term results. If public officials are constantly running for re-election, it is difficult for them to think of long-term needs and challenges. In addition, the power of the government to regulate the private sector in the interests of the long-term future is constrained by competition from other governments in a global economy. Multinational firms can easily shift operations offshore to a location with a more stockholder-friendly government if the government demands threaten the bottom line.

Shareholder activism by institutional investors, such as mutual funds, pension funds, and large nonprofits with endowments, can help to mitigate the short-term perspective in the private sector. Privately owned firms can and sometimes do take a longer-term perspective because the management and owners are one and the same and are not accountable to share-holders. Some public officials are also relatively secure in their positions and can afford to take a longer-term perspective and concern themselves with such issues as economic sustainability, environmental quality, and intergenerational commitments for health care and public pensions. Ultimately, however, it is citizens and shareholders who must accept a responsibility for thinking about long-term issues and hold both managers of investor-owned firms and elected officials accountable for doing so as well.

Government failure: efficiency in the public sector

Two central differences between market processes and government processes should be noted at the beginning. First, citizens vote in the market with their spending choices. Unequal incomes mean that people have very different abilities to make purchases in the market. Second, in most markets, buyers all pay the same price and consume different quantities of goods and services. When it comes to making choices through government, however, citizens cast their votes at the ballot box, and each person has one and only one vote. Citizens also try to influence legislators in other ways—with letters, phone calls, paid lobbyists, and campaign contributions. So money sneaks back into the political marketplace in other ways.

When it comes to consuming services provided by government and financed by taxes, citizens pay different prices (taxes) but are all allowed to consume the same quantity of goods and services. Clearly, some citizens will be happier with market processes and outcomes, others with government processes and outcomes. In fact, the same citizen may be happier with markets for some services and government for others.

When governments intervene to correct market failure, they may create new forms of inefficiency and inequity that are equal to or even greater than the inefficiencies and/or inequities they were intended to address. These risks are not just theoretical. There are certain characteristics of governments, even the best-designed governmental systems, which make them prone to **government failure**. Like market failure, government failure means that intervention by government results in less than optimal or efficient outcomes—sometimes even less efficient or desirable than the unsatisfactory outcomes these interventions were intended to correct.

Government workers and agencies are not normally disciplined by the competition of the marketplace. Government workers often have more job security than workers in the private sector and consequently have less incentive to please their "customers." Government procurement practices designed to circumvent graft and corruption are often cumbersome and inefficient, resulting in government paying more for their purchases than would a private sector firm.

Even a well-intentioned government finds it difficult to determine exactly what the public wants and what price the public is willing to pay for shared goods and public services. They are not motivated by profit or threatened with the fear of losses that keeps private firms on their toes. For a private firm, the owner or owners (including shareholders) are the **residual claimant** who receives any profit or bears any loss, although stockholders are limited in their liability to the value of their stock holdings. Government has no residual claimant to keep a wary eye on efficiency matters.

Although economies can be designed with very diverse spheres for the public and private sectors, the market system has become the dominant form of economic organization at the beginning of the twenty-first century. While governments undertake some activities that are quite similar to what markets do, there are also fundamental differences that will be explored more fully in later chapters.

Behavioral public finance: rational economic man or just muddling through?

Models of both market and government decisions are based on the rational, self-interested, autonomous individual who knows what he/she wants and works to maximize satisfaction both in the private sector as a worker, consumer and investor and in the public sector as a citizen-voter. Recent work in behavioral economics has challenged that assumption.

New developments in understanding how people actually make economic decisions are the foundation of **behavioral economics**. Some of the insights of behavioral economics come from allied disciplines such as psychology and sociology, which investigate how people actually make individual and collective choices. Psychology in particular has encouraged economists to think about two important aspects of decision-making, motivation and cognition.[2] Motivation is the "why" of our actions, some blend of self-interested maximizations and concern for the well-being of others. Cognition is the process by which we acquire, process and act on information.

Among the relevant findings from those two disciplines are the importance of framing (how an issue or choice is presented) and the existence of strong biases toward the status quo and the present rather than the future. Another important finding is that people are frequently less self-interested and more altruistic than economic models of rational, self-interested behavior would predict. Perceptions of options and policies are highly imperfect, the more so when the options are complex and difficult to comprehend. Herbert Simon taught economists long ago that people operated within **bounded rationality**. Given limited time and information, the typical firm or individual cannot possibly include all the options in their choice set, so they focus on a narrower subset of choices (Simon 1957). The implications of his work are still being explored in contemporary economic theory and policy.

Behavioral economics is both very new and very old. Many of the insights into the behavior of real human beings rather than rational economic actors have been known (but ignored) for decades, going back as far as Adam Smith's *Theory of Moral Sentiments* (1759). When people do not behave according to the expectations of traditional economic models, markets can fail to generate optimal results and government policy changes will not have the intended effect. In later chapters, we will explore some specific insights from behavioral economics that are important in public finance.

Summary

- In some countries, the economy is regarded as largely a private matter with government intervening where needed. In other countries, the division of responsibility between the government and the market is more fluid and more varied.
- Public finance or public sector economics combines a body of theory with a set of institutions to describe, analyze, and interpret the workings of government in a predominantly private economy.
- Two relatively recent developments in public finance are public choice and behavioral economics. Public choice analyzes the behavior of elected officials and bureaucrats in the public sector and explores the policy implications of government failure. Behavioral economics explores the effect of behavior that is not always rational and self-interested on the outcome of both private and public economic activity.
- For most economic activity, well-functioning markets are more efficient than government. Markets will achieve peak efficiency if they are competitive, have large numbers

of individuals and firms, perfect information, free mobility of resources and products, and no spillover effects. If any of these conditions do not hold, there will be market failure.

- Governments may intervene in market processes if the outcomes are inequitable or if the market fails to produce certain goods and services or produces non-optimal amounts. Possible tools for the government to use in correcting market failure are subsidies, tax incentives, guarantees, penalties (including tax penalties), mandates or prohibitions of certain items, public production, or private production with public financing.
- Fundamental differences between markets and governments include the expression of preference through voting rather than buying or spending, and the fact that citizens pay different prices but all consume the same quantity of public services. In the market, citizens usually pay the same prices and choose to consume different quantities.
- The most basic function of government in a market system is to act as a referee in defining and enforcing property rights, because market systems are based on private property. Such a social infrastructure is essential in order for markets to function. Governments also play a role in the management of shared risk.
- Both governments and markets have failed to adequately balance long-term concerns with the demand for immediate performance for the benefit of stockholders or particular groups of voters.

Key terms

Allocation, distribution, stabilization
Behavioral economics
Bounded rationality
Economic efficiency
Equity
Government failure
Market failure
Pareto optimality
Public choice
Public finance, public sector economics
Residual claimant

Questions

1   The US government has been actively involved in providing flood insurance to people along rivers and coasts at risk from floods and hurricanes, along with efforts to reduce potential damage and discourage building in the highest risk areas. Why do you think the private sector failed to meet this need? Do you see any drawbacks to government intervention in this area?

2   Suppose that your local government is trying to decide whether to commit additional funds to more police protection (more patrols) or to more tennis courts. In what way is this choice an efficiency question? In what way might it be an equity question?

3   How does the absence of a residual claimant tend to make governments less efficient than private firms?

4   **By the numbers**. Using data from *The Survey of Current Business* (http://www.bea. gov.scb) or other public sources, find the ratio of government consumption to GDP for

the current year and for the previous 20 years. How has it changed? Using the same source, which areas of government spending have shown the most increase? How else might you try to measure changes in the economic importance of government relative to private activity?

5   **Policy application**. Assume that studies have demonstrated that your state is lagging in economic development because too few students go on to post-secondary education, whether technical or academic. Review the list of eight tools for responding to market failure and consider whether and how each is or could be used to address this problem.

6   **Behavioral economics**. In private transactions, bounded rationality means that the individual only considers a limited number of choices—a few makes and models of cars, for example. How might bounded rationality come into play in voting for public officials? In deciding how to spend unexpected additional revenue in a city? Whose job is it to narrow the choices that are presented to voters or city officials?

7   **Thinking globally**. Transportation is an important dimension of our private and public lives. One of the big choices is between private cars and public transit such as buses, trains, and subways. How is the mix of various kinds of passenger transportation different between countries? Why do you think that is the case? If you live in the United States, pick another country for comparison purposes. If you live in another country, you can compare your country to the United States, or to a third country.

2 Measuring the size and scope of government

Introduction

Since the early 1980s there has been a strong constituency in many countries, but especially in the United States, lobbying for smaller government so that more economic activity takes place in the market and less in the public sector. Just how big is government? What kind of indicators can be used to measure it?

The full economic impact of government is hard to measure, because its scope goes beyond simply taxing and spending. Regulations impact on the quality and the cost of everything people buy from meat inspection and food labels to the safety of automobiles and baby cribs. The government plays a role in the rate of pay that people earn in the private sector, the safety conditions of their workplaces, and the freedom of expression on the airwaves they listen to and the newspapers they read. While these effects are important, in public sector economics the efforts to measure government focus mainly on the fiscal dimensions, the flow of money through government.

Here are some of the questions most frequently asked by policy-makers, politicians and interested citizens who are trying to get a handle on the size of government. How much money does "the government" collect, and what do they do with it? Where does the money come from? How much comes from taxes, and how much from other sources? How much of it is collected and spent by each level of government? And how do these answers compare with what government was doing last year, 10 years ago, half a century ago? How does what *our* government (federal, state, or local) is doing compare to what other governments are doing in other countries, states, counties, or cities?

For the United States, answers to these questions can be mined from a rich source of descriptive data, the Bureau of the Census. The Bureau of the Census collects financial data on governments from a variety of sources. Other good sources of current and historical fiscal data are the annual *Economic Report of the President* and the monthly periodical *Survey of Current Business*, issued by the U.S. Department of Commerce.

The challenge of comparisons

Numbers in isolation are meaningless. The fact, for example, that state and local governments in the United States spent $478 billion on public education in 2007 does not provide much information unless it is combined with a few more facts. How many pupils did that account for, i.e., how much was spent per pupil? That answer gives a little bit of sense of educational quality. Is per pupil spending increasing or decreasing over time? Is that measurement before or after adjusting for inflation? That answer may help citizens decide whether it is poor administration or inadequate resources that are the source of unsatisfactory performance by their children in readings, math, and standardized tests.

How much did the average citizen have to pay in taxes to support the public schools? What percentage of his or her income did it take to pay for education, and is that percentage rising or falling over time? Those answers may help determine how burdensome it is to support public education, and whether that burden is increasing or decreasing. How does spending by this state or school district compare to that of other states or school districts? This comparison is always of great interest, because taxpayers in those districts that spend more expect to see better results in terms of learning, graduation rates, and college entrance examination scores. How unequal is the spending between rich states and poor states, or rich districts and poor districts? This question is of interest to policy-makers who want to ensure that a child's chances of getting a decent education are not unduly affected by geography. How does education spending in the United States per pupil, or as a percentage of GDP, or as a percentage of total government spending, compare to what other nations spend? This answer may help policy-makers to grapple with differences in academic performance by comparing inputs and seeing to what extent they are connected with outputs.

Population growth and inflation

Comparative numbers must be used with caution. The most obvious caution is to be careful with comparisons over time, because these figures have to be adjusted for inflation and for increases (or decreases) in population. Adjusting for inflation ensures that you are comparing the same amount of real resources in different years. An indirect method of adjusting for inflation is to compare the growth of revenues or spending to the growth of personal income, since both are affected similarly by inflation.

The inflation adjustment is often based on the Consumer Price Index or the GDP deflator, but a more accurate adjustment would use the GDP deflator for the government sector, which is available in the *Survey of Current Business*. This deflator, or price index, is based on the kinds of things that governments buy—labor, supplies, materials, and other inputs to government production.

Adjustment for increases in population can be done directly, by putting all figures in per capita terms, or indirectly, by expressing all years as a percentage of personal income or of GDP. Since income or GDP grows at least as fast as population and usually slightly faster, either method will make some correction for population growth. The direct method of computing per capita values makes a more precise correction, because personal income is subject to fluctuations over the course of economic expansions or recessions.

Differences in income, wealth, or special conditions

Comparisons of national, state, or local governments with each other during the same year suffer from a different set of hazards. Suppose that you were told that State A collected only $520 per capita in income taxes while state B collected $750 in the same year. What could you conclude? Less than you might think. It may appear that State B has higher income tax rates, but it may just have a higher per capita income. A poor state will raise less money per capita with the same tax at the same rates than a wealthier state.

Suppose, instead, taxes are compared as a percentage of personal income; in State A income taxes took 4 percent of personal income while in State B they took only 3.5 percent.

Now are taxes higher in State A? You can answer yes with a little more confidence in this case, at least for the income tax. State A may have higher tax rates, but perhaps it has fewer households, or an income that is more unequally distributed. State B may have low income taxes but high sales or property taxes, so that the overall tax burden is not particularly low. Finally, like Alaska and Texas, State B may enjoy substantial revenues from mineral extraction that fall largely on nonresidents and do not burden its own citizens.

Per capita taxes or expenditures are useful in comparing revenue and expenditure statistics for nations, states, or cities with similar incomes in the same year. Per capita measures offer a reasonable indication of what government costs and what government can provide in the way of services to the average resident. Percentages of income data are better for comparing over time within a state or nation and between states and nations, because both the numerator and the denominator are affected equally by inflation, and because population growth is closely related to income growth. The percentage of income figure is not distorted by inflation and is much less sensitive to population growth. However, tax revenues as a percentage of income figures are very sensitive to fluctuations in income and output. During a recession, the percentage of income going to taxes and public services will rise just because the denominator (personal income) is falling, while during rapid expansion the percentage of income passing through government is likely to fall even though governments are collecting and spending more.

Data limitations

A final hazard of comparisons is the limited data that are available. Few figures are available on a timely basis. After the fiscal year ends, it takes time to compile and collect and check the data. Local government data are particularly likely to be several years out of date. The data that are available have other shortcomings that limit their usefulness for comparisons. For example, many of the international data sources only report central government data. In unitary countries, with no middle level, per capita spending may appear to be relatively higher because the central government is responsible for functions carried out by two levels of government in federal countries, only one of which is reported. Likewise, in comparing states (or provinces), it is important to include both state and local revenues and spending in the comparison, because some states are more fiscally centralized than others and different states divide spending responsibilities differently.

US federal government revenues and spending

Most of the revenues and spending of the US federal government pass through the government budget, which takes effect on October 1st each year. This budget pays for general operations of government. Each federal **fiscal year** is referred to by the ending date: for example, fiscal year (FY) 2011 refers to the 12-month period that ends September 30th, 2011. In addition to budgeted funds, there are also off-budget funds, the most significant of which are the Social Security Trust Fund and the Medicare Trust Fund. When these off-budget funds are lumped together with the budgeted funds, the result is called the **unified budget**. The unified budget is the most important one for purposes of fiscal policy. The deficit or surplus reported each year refers to the unified budget, including the revenues and expenditures of the trust funds.

However, the debates in Congress and in the Executive Branch about changing tax laws, raising or lowering taxes, and how to allocate the federal revenues among various spending priorities refer to the budget that is ultimately passed by Congress and signed by the President each year. This legislated budget does not include the trust funds. The deficit looks smaller when the trust funds are included because these funds have been running surpluses for several decades. However, starting in 2017, the trust funds will be running deficits that will add to any deficits in the operating budget approved by Congress and signed into law by the president.

Trends in federal revenue: levels and composition

In FY2009, a particularly bad budget year because of the financial crisis and recession, the US federal government took in $2,105 billion in revenue, of which $1,451 billion was "on budget" (available to pay for Congressional appropriations) and $654 billion was "off budget," primarily to various trust funds such as the Social Security Trust Fund. This unified budget revenue represented 14 percent of GDP in 2009 (see Table 2.1). Individual income taxes are the mainstay of the federal operating budget, contributing $915 billion or 64 percent of the on-budget total. Corporate income taxes contributed another $138 billion. Taxes on products—mainly excise taxes on gasoline, cigarettes, automobile tires, and other items—accounted for most of the remaining revenue, along with modest contributions from estate and gift taxes, customs receipts from tariffs on imported goods, and fees and charges for federal government services.

Has the US federal government been taking an increasing share of the nation's income over time? The answer to this question is not affected by the rate of inflation, because both federal revenue and GDP are measured in current dollars. The answer is no for the last half-century. But in the period since 1960, federal revenue has been a relatively stable share of GDP, ranging from a low of 15 percent in 2009 to a high of 20.6 percent in 2000, with most years in the 17–18 percent range. (The high year was the end of a long boom, and 2009's low was affected both by tax cuts and by recessions.)

The mixture of federal government revenue sources shown in Figure 2.1 for FY2009 has changed relatively little also. Individual income taxes have accounted for 40–50 percent of all federal revenue in every year but four for more than half a century. Corporate income taxes have shown a steady decline in their share of the total from more than 20 percent in the 1950s and 1960s to 6.6 percent in 2009. That decline reflects not only the recession but also a longer-term trend toward less corporate activity in the GDP and lower rates. Corporate income taxes are also much more sensitive to fluctuations in economic activity, so there are greater swings in receipts from year to year.

Table 2.1 Federal government revenue, FY2009

	$ billions	*Per capita*
On budget revenues	1,451	4,696
Individual income taxes	915.3	2,962
Corporate income taxes	138.2	447
Excise taxes and other	160.5	519
Trust fund revenue	890.9	2,883
Total, unified budget	2,104.9	6,812

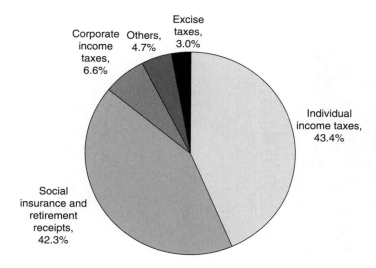

Figure 2.1 Federal revenues, unified budget, FY2009.

Trends in federal spending

Spending figures do not even come close to matching revenue figures on an annual basis because the federal government, unlike most state and local governments, is not obligated to balance its budget. For most of the last half of the twentieth century, until the very end, the federal government's spending consistently exceeded its revenue. In 2000, there was actually a budget surplus of $237 billion. Federal spending that year accounted for only 17.8 percent of GDP, the smallest share since 1974. Since that time, however, federal spending has risen relative to GDP. In 2009, federal spending in the unified budget accounted for just over 25 percent of GDP.

There are many ways to sort federal spending—by cabinet department or agency, by direct spending or grants and transfers. Three major categories in the unified budget accounted for 83 percent of federal spending in 2009—national defense, human resources including Social Security benefits, and net interest. Figure 2.2 shows federal spending patterns for FY2009, and Table 2.2 shows the dollar figures for total and per capita federal spending by category.

While the revenue mix has been relatively stable, the makeup of federal spending has changed dramatically in the last half-century. Defense spending has been particularly volatile. In 1950 (after World War II but early in the Korean War), national defense was 32 percent of the federal budget and 5 percent of GDP. Defense spending rose sharply during the Korean War and remained over 40 percent of federal spending (and 7–10 percent of GDP) until 1971, when it began to decline. By 1980, defense spending had fallen to 23 percent of the federal budget and 5 percent of GDP. President Reagan emphasized rebuilding defense in the last decade of the Cold War, and defense spending surged to 28 percent of the budget (1987) and over 6 percent of GDP before starting a steady decline to a 17 percent share of federal outlays and a 3 percent share of GDP in 2000. With the wars in Afghanistan and Iraq, defense spending was back up to 19 percent of the unified budget and not quite 5 percent of GDP in 2009.

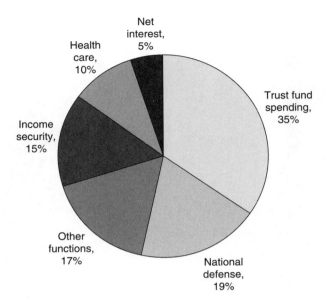

Figure 2.2 Federal government spending, FY2009.

Table 2.2 Federal government spending, FY2009

Source	$ billions	Per capita
On budget spending	2,305	7,458
National defense	661	2,139
Health care	668	2,386
Income security	334	1,082
Net interest	187	605
Other functions	589	1,907
Trust fund spending	1,213	2,883
Total federal spending	3,518	11,384

Income security is a broad category that has come to be dominated by more than $1.2 trillion in Social Security as the largest single item. Even in 1950 this category accounted for one-third of the budget, with veterans' benefits (mostly from World War II) accounting for the largest share of the spending at that time. By 1956, Social Security surpassed veterans' benefits and has been the dominant share ever since.

The growth in this category reflects a shift in the role of the federal government from being primarily a producer/provider of services to being primarily a guarantor of income security through **transfer payments**. Transfer payments collect taxes from citizens in general and give them to selected groups of citizens, not in payment for services but because they are believed to be needy, deserving, or entitled to such payments (including payments of Social Security benefits to retired workers who have contributed to the system).

Net interest is determined by two factors: the growth of the government debt, and the prevailing market interest rates. As the economy and the budget "grew into" managing the accumulated debt from World War II, the share of the budget going to net interest fell from 11 percent in 1950 to the 6–8 percent range. This decline reversed in 1979, when high interest rates and increasing deficits drove its share upward to over 14 percent in 1988 and 15 percent in 1995. Low interest rates in the first decade of the century partly offset the debt service effect of growing budget deficits. In 2009, net interest payments took only 5 percent of the unified budget, but are projected to increase in the near future with rising interest rates and persistent budget deficits.

Finally, there is the category of other expenditures—which include most of what we think of as the primary activities of government, but which account for less than 17 percent of the budget—infrastructure, international affairs, science, space and technology, agriculture, administration of justice, and general government. These functions cost about 4 percent of GDP but have declined in relative importance with the rising share of the budget that goes to transfer payments.

Trends in federal debt and deficits

The budget surpluses of 1998–2000 are a distant memory as tax cuts, recessions, and increased spending for transfer payments and defense resulted in increasing deficits starting in 2002, with a deficit of $148 billion. By 2009, that deficit had risen to $1.4 trillion, and is expected to only recede gradually as the economy recovers. In 2017, the effect of the Social Security trust funds on the unified budget will begin to change as the last of the baby boomers (those born between 1946 and 1964) reach retirement age. At that point, the Social Security Trust funds will begin to present the IOUs that have been accumulating for several decades to the Treasury, and it will be necessary to run on-budget surpluses in order to redeem those IOUs. Figure 2.3 shows the trends from 1990 to 2009 in unified budget revenue and expenditures, with the gap between them measuring the deficit or surplus.

State and local revenue and expenditures

State and local governments have a very different mix of revenue sources and spending obligations from the federal government, as is appropriate in a federal system. While most of the federal government's revenue comes from individual income taxes and Social Security

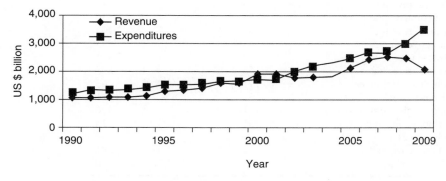

Figure 2.3 Federal unified budget revenues and expenditures, 1990–2009.

taxes, state and local governments rely on a fairly even mix of income taxes, retail sales taxes, and property taxes. Like the federal government, state and local governments also receive some revenue from corporate income taxes and excise taxes, but unlike the federal government, they receive substantial and increasing revenue from fees and charges of various kinds ranging from dog tags to business licenses to tuition at public colleges to highway tolls. On the spending side, education and welfare are the big ticket items, with substantial outlays for health and hospitals, highways, and law enforcement and corrections.

Patterns of revenue and spending vary greatly from state to state. Forty-five states and the District of Columbia have retail sales taxes, 41 have broad-based individual income taxes, and one state—New Hampshire—has neither. Excise taxes on tobacco are very high in the north-east, very low in the tobacco-growing states of North Carolina, South Carolina, Virginia and Kentucky. Lotteries are now a minor source of revenue in a majority of states, a significant change since the first state (New Hampshire) adopted its lottery in 1964. Spending patterns tend to be a little more uniform, since there is fairly widespread agreement that the state, in partnership with local governments, has major responsibilities for education, highways, law enforcement, and public health. But even in these categories there are great variations in per capita spending from state to state as well as within states.

State revenue

Table 2.3 and Figure 2.4 summarize state revenue patterns. Note that states distinguish between total revenue, general revenue, and own-source revenues. **Total revenue** includes the earnings of state-operated enterprises such as public utilities, liquor stores, and insurance trust funds. **General revenue** includes intergovernmental revenue—revenue from other governments, federal to state, state to local, federal to local, sometimes even interlocal—as well as **own-source revenues**, which are those raised by that particular level of government by imposing taxes, fees, and charges. The pie chart makes it quite clear that sales taxes (both

Table 2.3 State government revenue, FY2008

Source	Total $ billions	Per capita
State revenue		
Total	1,096	4,059
General revenue	865	3,024
Government enterprises	231	856
General revenue	865	3,203
Intergovernmental	241	893
Own-source	624	2,311
General sales taxes	156	578
Selective sales taxes	71	263
License taxes	30	111
Individual income taxes	161	596
Corporate income taxes	31	115
Other taxes	26	99
Current charges/fees	76	281
Miscellaneous	73	270

Source: U.S. Bureau of the Census, *Census of Governments*.

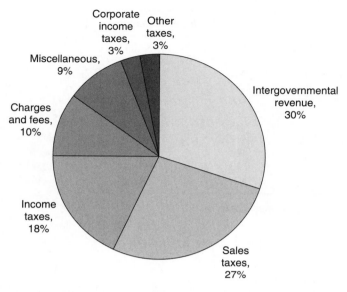

Figure 2.4 State government general revenue, FY2008.

general and selective) and individual income taxes are the main revenue sources of state governments. Government enterprises include insurance trust funds as well as state liquor stores and other enterprises. Inter-governmental revenue remains a significant source for states at almost one-third of general revenue in 2009, reflecting the stimulus package enacted to combat the recession.

There is great diversity among the states in taxes and in services. State tax collections per capita, for example, ranged from nearly $3,000 in Connecticut to less than $900 in New Hampshire in 2008. There are significant differences in the mix of taxes used, the quality and variety of services provided, and the division of revenue collections and expenditure responsibilities between state and local governments that make comparisons very difficult.

States experienced strong revenue growth during the 1990s, enabling many of them to reduce taxes while expanding the quality and variety of services. With the bursting of the dot.com bubble and the recession that began in 2001, state revenue dropped sharply. They recovered from 2004 to 2007, only to be hit hard again by the financial crisis and recession that began in late 2007.

Local revenue

Table 2.4 and Figures 2.5 and 2.6 present a summary of local government revenue and expenditures in the United States in 2007. (Local government data come in more slowly than state data.) As you can see, local governments depend even more heavily on intergovernmental funds (more than one-third of general revenue) than states. Most of these local funds originate at the state level, although some come from the federal government. Property taxes and charges (and miscellaneous) provide 84 percent of local own-source revenue, with the rest coming from a variety of smaller taxes.

Table 2.4 Local government revenue, 2007

Source	Total $ billions	Per capita
Total revenue	848	3,200
Less: Government enterprises	101	381
Equals: General revenue	747	2,819
Intergovernmental	287	1,083
Own-source	460	1,736
Property taxes	209	789
Sales/excise taxes	45	170
Individual income taxes	14	53
Corporate income taxes	3	11
Other taxes	13	49
Charges and miscellaneous	177	668

Source: U.S. Bureau of the Census, *Census of Governments*.

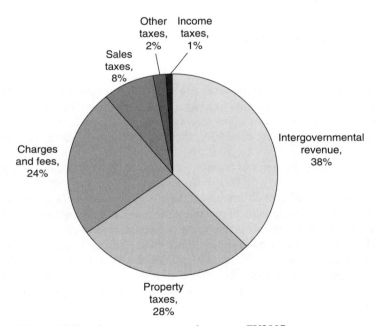

Figure 2.5 Local government general revenue, FY2007.

Retail sales taxes and individual income taxes are clearly the workhorses of state governments, while local governments rely primarily on property taxes, intergovernmental aid, and fees and charges for specific services. The low revenue figures for local sales and income taxes reflect both very low rates (typically 1 percent for both taxes) and the limited number of local governments that use such taxes.

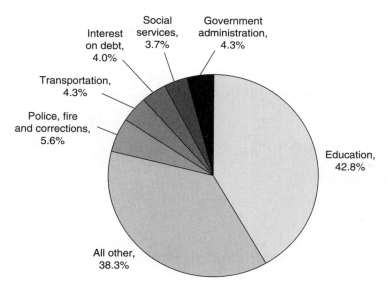

Figure 2.6 Local government general expenditures, FY2007.

State and local expenditures

Education is the overwhelming driver of state and local spending. Public welfare has historically been a significant spending area for states also, although it has declined in recent years after welfare reform. State and local governments share responsibilities in many areas but particularly highways, with the state paying about two-thirds of the cost and the locals the other one-third. In public safety (police, fire, correction), local governments spend nearly as much as state governments. Parks and recreation, sewerage, and solid waste management are primarily local. Within education, states assume most of the responsibility for higher education and share responsibility for the public schools.

State government expenditures are described in Table 2.5, and local government spending in Table 2.6. As you can see, education and social services account for more than half of state spending, with the other major areas transportation and public safety. Education and social services are also the two biggest categories for local government, followed by public safety. Public safety at the state level has a large component of prisons and courts, while at the local level more of the spending is for police and fire protection.

How big should government be?

The extended debate in the United States and elsewhere over the size and growth of government can be viewed as a search for "right-sizing." How much government—how much tax burden, how much in the way of services, how much borrowing—is "enough"? This question goes beyond the kinds of taxes used and the kinds of spending decisions made, or the mix of revenue sources and outlays, to the issue of overall size.

Some people argue that if government's share grows, the share of the private sector must shrink, and the private sector offers significant advantages in terms of greater efficiency and

Table 2.5 State government expenditures, FY2008

Source	Total $ billions	Per capita
State expenditures		
Total	930	3,321
General	828	2,957
Government enterprises and insurance trusts	102	364
General expenditure		
Intergovernmental	279	996
Direct	549	1,961
Education and libraries	295	1,054
Social Services/Income support	272	971
Transportation	64	229
Public Safety	39	139
Government administration	31	111
Interest on general debt	27	69
Other	83	296

Source: U.S. Bureau of the Census, *Census of Governments*.

Table 2.6 Local government expenditures, 2007

Source	Total $ billions	Per capita
Total expenditure	837	2,886
Intergovernmental	9	30
Direct	828	2,856
Education	314	1,162
Social Services	98	363
Public Safety	76	281
Transportation	46	170
Sewer/solid waste	39	144
Government administration	39	144
Interest on debt	36	133
All other	180	667

Source: U.S. Bureau of the Census, *Census of Governments*.

responsiveness. Others see the public and private sectors as having different and complementary roles, so that some kinds of growth in the public sector may enhance rather than subtract from private activity. In either case, the issue of size of government is an important topic of debate, one with few easy answers. Efforts to impose constitutional or statutory limits on the size and growth of government at all levels are a response to such concerns about efficiency, responsiveness, and uncontrolled growth.

There are various ways to measure how much government is enough. One is the level of satisfaction of the representative citizen with his or her tax burdens relative to services received. If the marginal value of the last unit of government services is just equal to the pain of parting with the last few dollars of tax money to pay for that service, then the level of government activity is optimal. However, there is no good way to make such measurements. Elections give some very rough and general guidance to the level of citizen satisfaction or dissatisfaction, but often non-economic issues dominate the races, or the choices are not clear enough for voters to send an unambiguous message.

So policy-makers turn to some less satisfactory indicators. One is how fast government is growing, absolutely and relative to population and/or GDP. The other is to compare the size of our government, per capita or as a share of GDP, to the size of government in other nations, especially other nations at similar levels of economic development.

Share of GDP

US government consumption was 17 percent of GDP in 2009. Until 2008, the federal government's share of GDP had been relatively stable, particularly on the revenue side. State and local revenue and spending as a share of GDP have grown considerably over the last half-century, from 6–7 percent in the 1950s and early 1960s to over 10 percent in the 1970s. That growth leveled off in the late 1970s, but picked up again since the mid-1980s in spite of deliberate efforts to limit the growth of government through tax and spending limitations.

International comparisons

A valuable indicator of the size of government is its rank relative to other nations of a similar level of income and wealth. The World Bank groups the United States with 25 other nations as high-income countries, ranging from Portugal to the United Arab Emirates. Excluding the four nations that are very small and/or oil-based (Kuwait, Hong Kong, Singapore, United Arab Emirates), there remains a "peer group" of 20 countries to which the United States can reasonably be compared. In 2007, according to the World Bank's *World Development Report*, central government tax receipts in these 21 countries ranged from 17.8 percent of GDP (Japan) to 44.7 percent (the Netherlands), and total revenue from 20 percent of GDP (Japan, the United States) to 48.5 percent (the Netherlands).

The United States was second lowest in tax revenue at 18.5 percent and tied with Japan for lowest in total revenue at 20 percent. Similarly, on the spending side, the share of GDP ranged from 23 percent in the United States to 52.9 percent in the Netherlands. It should be noted, however, that three of the four countries with exceptionally low ratios of revenue and spending to GDP are federal countries—the United States, Switzerland, Canada and Australia. In the United States, 10.8 percent of all revenue in 1994 was for state and local governments, which would raise the US revenue/GDP ratio to 30.8 percent. Similar adjustment would be likely for other federal countries, including Germany, but such corrections would still leave government in the United States toward the lower end of the size spectrum.

The inclusion of state and local government (which are particularly important in the United States) raises the 2007 US revenue figure to 29.2 percent of GDP. This percentage is considerably higher that the federal-only figure but still below central government revenue as a percentage of GDP in 16 of the other 18 industrial nations. Both of the peer nations— Switzerland and Australia—that report lower shares of GDP going to the central government are also federal countries with substantial state and local sectors. In both cases, their central government revenue was higher than US central government revenue as a share of GDP. It is fairly clear from these data (and the patterns do not vary greatly from year to year) that by any measure the United States has a lower share of economic activity passing through its public sector than most other industrial nations.

What does this comparison mean? Probably not too much. It means that Americans have chosen to produce or provide a larger share of what they consume through the market or through private, voluntary groups. Health care, for example, is almost universally run through government in these other 18 nations, but the private sector still dominates the provision and financing of health care in the United States. Low-income households are more likely to depend on private voluntary organizations. A significant number of American students are served by private schools from pre-kindergarten through college. These differences represent a combination of conscious choices and historical patterns for Americans. There is no "right" share for government, but it is clear that proponents of smaller government will have to base their arguments on something other than international comparisons.

What makes government grow?

The dramatic growth of government, and especially state and local spending in the last half-century has not only sparked discussion of what size is optimal but also led to a search for explanations about what made it grow. Is it some insatiable monster—a Leviathan that will continue to demand larger and larger shares of the economic pie unless it is somehow constrained? And if so, why? Is government growing in response to citizen demand for more services? Is it growing because elected officials and bureaucrats like to create programs that they can control and are able to sneak them by an inattentive public? Is it growing because the revenue system continues to generate rapid growth of revenues to state and local governments which legislators choose to spend rather than return in the form of tax cuts? Is some of the growth reflective of the fee-for-service approach to many public services in which beneficiaries pay to use public campgrounds, boat launches, roads, and other services? At the federal level, has the absence of a meaningful budget constraint (the ability to run deficits at will) allowed runaway growth of federal spending? Let's consider each of these explanations in turn.

Citizen expectations

At least at the state and local level, some of the spending does seem to be driven by the expectations and desires of citizens. Back in the 1950s, economist John Kenneth Galbraith crafted a memorable and often quoted description of an imbalance between private consumption and the public infrastructure and services to go with it in *The Affluent Society*:

> The family which takes its mauve and cerise, air-conditioned, power-steered and power-braked automobile out for a tour passes through cities that are badly paved, made hideous by litter, blighted buildings, billboards, and posts for wires that should long since have been put underground. They pass into a countryside that has been rendered largely invisible by commercial art . . . They picnic on exquisitely packaged food from a portable icebox by a polluted stream and go on to spend the night at a park, which is a menace to public health and morals. Just before dozing off on an air mattress, beneath a nylon tent, amid the stench of decaying refuse, they may reflect vaguely on the unevenness of their blessings.
>
> (Galbraith 1958: p. 253)

Galbraith might not have written that paragraph 50 years later, when billboards are more restricted, newer communities have underground utilities, pollution is more tightly controlled, and better efforts are being made to dispose of trash, although the complaints about the conditions of roads and blighted buildings still have some validity. As consumers become more affluent, they do expect better infrastructure and better public services, whether it is recreation, better schools, roads, trash collection, or law enforcement. Some citizens retreat to gated communities and private schools and purchase these services privately, but others pressure state and local governments to provide more and better public services to complement their higher standard of private consumption. Often they are willing to pay for those services at least partly through fees, which are one of the faster-growing components of state and local revenues.

At the US federal level, a significant part of spending is on two very popular programs: Social Security and Medicare. National defense spending rose sharply during the Reagan years, declined in the 1990s, and picked up again with the wars in Iraq and Afghanistan. Most of the growth in the past few decades is concentrated in those two areas. Thus, while citizen demand is not likely to be the whole explanation, it certainly plays some role—particularly for federal transfer payments and local public services.

Driven by bureaucracy

Public choice economists developed this explanation for government growth. Combine the desire of elected officials to increase their chances of re-election by enacting popular programs and getting "pork barrel" projects for their districts with the desire of government bureaucrats to keep their jobs and enhance their power and prestige by the growth of their agencies, and it is easy to see that the forces for growth are strong. Apathetic citizens, knowing that their individual votes have little impact, are a weak constraint against these pressures. Some of the models that attempt to explain why citizens get more government than they might consciously choose are described in Chapter 4.

Elastic revenue sources

Yet a third explanation for this growth is that at least some of the revenue sources in place at all three levels—federal, state, and local—have been able to generate steady growth of revenue—faster than population growth, faster than personal income growth, most of the time without requiring an increase in tax rates. The automatic growth of revenues, keyed to the growth of the tax base (income, spending, and wealth), could lead to an automatic and uncontrolled growth of the public sector without a conscious decision about how much of economic activity citizens want to have run through or managed by government.

The problem with explaining growth of government as driven by elastic revenue sources is that the income elasticity also reduces revenue sharply when there is a slowdown in economic activity. If elected officials, especially at the state level, have been using revenue growth to fund programs that will require future annual appropriations, or to justify permanent cuts in tax rates, then they run the risk of sudden budget shortfalls. State governments have taken two big revenue hits since the year 2000, one in 2001–03 and another beginning in 2008. Many legislatures had enacted permanent tax cuts during the boom times. When the recession struck and revenue began to drop, it dropped more dramatically than it would have if the tax cuts were temporary.

Fees for services

Increasingly, governments at all levels, but especially state and local, have shifted some of the responsibility of paying for government services to those who benefit directly from those services. Whether it is building inspection fees, access to parks, airports paid for with fees on both airlines and passengers, highway tolls, trash pickup fees, or recreation charges, citizens have come to expect that many services provided by government will be funded partly through taxes and partly through user fees. These fees have made it possible for government to provide some services that are unprofitable for the private sector to undertake but desirable from the social standpoint. Such fee-financed services represent at least part of the expanded size and scope of government activity.

Lack of a budget constraint

During the 1980s, the fact that Congress could pass unbalanced budgets and run deficits without any meaningful constraints was considered the primary culprit in growth of federal spending. After several unsuccessful attempts to legislate a budget constraint in the 1980s, a combination of steady economic growth, declining inflation and interest rates, and bipartisan agreements to hold the line on spending brought the budget under control at the end of the century.

The 1990s did not see a significant slowdown in government revenue growth, but expenditure growth was limited until it finally matched the revenue available to pay for it. Deficit spending resumed in the 2000s after 9/11, tax cuts, recessions, and two wars ended the brief period of surplus. In 2010, Congress adopted a "PayGo" approach to budgetary changes that required that any tax cuts or spending increases be paid for by adjustments elsewhere in the budget.

Lack of a budget constraint may help to explain federal spending growth, but state and local spending is almost always subject to a balanced budget requirement. In 49 states and the District of Columbia, a balanced budget is required by law. For local governments, the balanced budget is a practical issue of limited ability to borrow to fund operating deficits over more than a year or two at a time.

Summary

- The size of government is measured by revenue, spending, deficits, and debt. In order to make comparisons between time periods, or between states, cities, and countries, data can be adjusted by correcting for inflation, dividing by population (per capita), and/or expressing revenue or spending relative to GDP or personal income.
- Federal revenue and spending are presented in both the budget and the trust funds, which are called the unified budget when they are combined. Reported deficits usually refer to the unified budget.
- Total federal revenue has been growing at about the same rate as personal income, more slowly if the trust funds are not included. Federal revenue as a share of GDP has been relatively stable over the past 50 years. The individual income tax and social security taxes are the main sources of federal revenue.
- Major categories of federal spending are national defense, human resources, physical resources, interest on debt, and other. The composition of federal spending has changed, with a decline in the share of defense spending more than offset by transfer payments. Deficits in most years of the past half-century have resulted in growth in the national debt.
- State and local governments have a very different mix of revenue sources and spending obligations. States rely heavily on income and sales taxes, local governments on property taxes and state aid, and both on fees and charges of various kinds. Education and

welfare are the main spending categories, along with health and hospitals, highways, and law enforcement and corrections.

- There is no simple way to measure the "right" size of government. Reasons why government might grow rapidly include citizen demand, bureaucracy behavior, elastic revenue sources, increased use of fees and charges, and at the federal level, lack of an effective budget constraint. Indicators include how fast government is growing, absolutely and relative to population and/or GDP, or comparisons of the size of our government among nations at similar levels of economic development.
- In the United States, the federal government's share of GDP has been relatively stable, particularly on the revenue side. State and local revenue and spending as a share of GDP have grown considerably over the last half century. International comparisons find the United States near the bottom in share of GDP going through government relative to other developed industrial countries.

Key terms

Fiscal year
General revenue
Own-source revenue
Total revenue
Transfer payments
Unified budget

Questions

1   What are the advantages and drawbacks of presenting the surplus or deficit on the basis of the unified budget rather than the operating budget passed by Congress that excludes the trust fund revenue and spending?
2   Suppose you are employed by a politician who is getting ready to make a speech, and he asks you to tell him how fast government has been growing in your state. What kind of answer would make growth look slowest? What kind would make it look fastest? What kind of answer would be the most honest representation of actual growth?
3   If government revenues are very elastic with respect to GDP or personal income, what would tend to happen to government revenue over the course of a business cycle? How would they track growth of income over the long term? How does that make budgeting difficult for state governments that are required to balance their budgets?
4   **By the numbers**. Using the *Survey of Current Business* or the *Economic Report of the President*, find answers to the following questions:

   (a) What was the federal budget deficit or surplus in 2011? In 2012?
   (b) How much did spending for highways by state and local governments increase between 2000 and 2010 before and after adjusting for inflation? What happened to per capita spending for highways?
   (c) Which states were highest and lowest in per capita property taxes? Were they the same states that were highest and lowest in property taxes as a percent of personal income? If not, explain the difference.
   (d) What has happened to federal defense spending—total, inflation-adjusted, and per capita—since the early 1980s?

5   **Policy application**. If you worked for a Congressional committee that was considering an across-the-board tax cut, what kinds of aggregate revenue, spending and debt data, both for the United States and for other countries, might you muster in support of the tax cut? What kinds of data might you use to argue against it?

6   **Behavioral economics**. Some economists argue that individuals suffer from fiscal illusion—that is, they underestimate the cost of government because they are less aware of the sources of revenue than their direct experience the benefits of government spending. (This theory was first developed by Italian economist Amilcare Puviani in the 1940s.) How might fiscal illusion help to explain citizens' willingness to let government activity grow faster than the economy as a whole? Looking at spending data, does the trend in the U.S. at the federal level over the last 50 years support the idea of fiscal illusion?

7   **Thinking globally**. What kinds of country-specific influences might explain the great diversity in government spending as a share of GDP among industrial nations? Choose two countries with very diverse spending patterns and offer some possible explanations for the difference.

3   The structure of governments

Introduction

Before analyzing the economic role of government, it would be helpful to have a clearer picture of how it is organized. There are two useful ways to describe governments. The previous chapters provided a financial description—the amount of money flowing through governments and the sources and uses of those funds. The other way to describe governments is structural—the number of governments, their sizes, their relationships to one another, and their areas of authority and responsibility. Organizational structure of governments is the focus of this chapter. That may not sound very exciting or very economic in nature, but it certainly was both of these things to the authors of the U.S. Constitution more than two centuries ago and the leaders of the European Union today.

At first glance, structure of governments may seem like political science rather than economics. Structure is one of several areas in which these two disciplines overlap. Larger governments may enjoy economies of scale. Some of the spillover effects (both positive and negative) that smaller governments create for their neighbors will be internal to a larger, more regional government. For example, industrial wastes from community A may affect the water supply in community B, but if they are part of a larger regional government that is responsible for the entire watershed, the decisions about effluents and water treatment are internal to the larger government.

On the other hand, if there are more, smaller governments, it may be easier for citizens to match their preferences for taxes and services to a particular community and to make their voices heard, so that public officials have some measure of demand. One of the two 2010 Nobel Prize winners in economics, Elinor Ostrom (actually a political scientist by training), explored ways in which overlapping governments can and sometimes do offer the best of both worlds—small, responsive, specialized local units combined with contracting certain services to a higher-level government serving multiple local units.

Multiple state and local governments introduce some competition into what would otherwise be monopoly government. These issues of scale economies, spillover effects, accommodating diversity, the benefits of competition, and expressing demand for public services are economic in nature. The economic response to these issues cannot be separated from the institutional framework of the structure of governments.

Organizing public service delivery

There are many ways to organize delivery of public services within the public sector. In many countries, especially smaller countries but some larger ones as well, the central government plays the primary role in everything from roads and prisons to health care and education. Local governments may have limited powers to raise and spend revenues, often under rules set by the central government. Sometimes, as in China, local governments are responsible for raising the revenue and sending it to the central government, which keeps most of it and sends a small amount back.

In other countries, there may be an intermediate level of government, most often a state or province with its own government, its own elected officials and its own revenue resources and service responsibilities. The former arrangement, where the central government is primary, the local government is subsidiary (created by and accountable to the central government), and there is no independent in-between authority, is called a **unitary state**. Those arrangements involving more than two levels of government (most often three levels) are called **federalist**.

In economics, the particular aspects of federalism that are of interest are the assignment and coordination of revenue sources, service responsibility, and regulatory authority. The first two aspects are grouped together as **fiscal federalism**, which describes the ways in which revenues and responsibilities are divided, assigned, or shared among different levels of government within a given country.[1]

Throughout history, there has been an unending search for balance between the uniformity imposed by a central authority and the benefits of local diversity and flexibility in deciding which level of government should collect what kinds of revenues and carry out what kinds of service provision. Likewise, there has been a search for the balance between central control and local autonomy. There is no single right answer for all countries and all times, or for all kinds of revenues and services.

Small, homogeneous countries like Bulgaria, Sri Lanka, Taiwan, or Costa Rica can function fairly well with a strong central government, local governments with limited autonomy, and selective delegation of powers and responsibilities. Large and/or culturally heterogeneous countries such as Russia, Canada, India, Brazil, Australia and the United States have to provide services to populations that are much more diverse in terms of income, culture, language, climate, and density of population. The model of an Education Ministry in Paris controlling a highly standardized French public school system would not work in Canada where harsh weather inside the Arctic Circle, one French-speaking province, a multi-ethnic population, and very lightly populated areas on the prairies create different educational needs in different provinces.

Depending on the revenue sources used, one level of government may have an advantage over another in ability to raise funds. That advantage may derive from economies of scale in collecting taxes, or from a degree of monopoly power that makes it difficult to avoid the tax by moving property, purchases, or production activity to another location. In the United States, the federal government has generally enjoyed such an advantage. In other countries, particularly developing countries, raising revenue is most successful at the local level, where personal knowledge of individuals' assets and income and direct personal contact play an important role in tax collection. On the spending side, some services are highly local in their benefits (street lights), others national (defense), while still others have both a national and a local aspect (roads and highways, environmental protection, higher education) with the effects of policies and programs spilling over from one jurisdiction to another.

Various countries and even states within a country make different choices about the assignment of both revenue sources and service responsibilities. Education through high school is a national function in France, a primarily state function in Hawaii, primarily local in New Hampshire. The sales tax, in the form of a value-added tax, is a central government tax in most of Europe and Latin America, while in the form of a retail sales tax it is the exclusive possession of state and local governments in the United States.

Fiscal federalism: multiple levels of government

In the 2007 *Census of Governments*, the United States had 89,476 governments. Citizens paid taxes and received services from federal, state and territorial governments, counties and parishes, cities, towns, and townships, school districts, and special districts. Fortunately, individual American citizens only have to deal with a small subset of those thousands of governments. Everyone is linked to the federal government, their state or territorial government, and a county, parish, or township government. In some states, there may also be a separate school district. Some citizens are served by the government of a city or town if they live in an incorporated municipality, or perhaps one or more special districts. So the average citizen deals with at least three and perhaps as many as six or seven governments, which is still a large number. The same is true of other federal systems. In countries with a unitary structure, the average citizen may only have to deal with two governments: the central and the local government.

The optimal number of governments, particularly the number of levels of government, depends both on the size (population and land area) of the country and the kinds of diversity (cultural, linguistic, climatic, etc.) that must be taken into consideration. That number also depends on the nation's particular history as well as its values reflected in whether its citizens prize uniformity more than diversity or direct more than representative democracy, and how important it is to have clearly visible links between taxes and fees paid and services received.

The question of size

The size of a government can be measured in at least three ways. One measure is land area—the number of square miles under its control. A second measure is population—the number of residents from whom revenues can be extracted and to whom services must be provided (and who want to have their voices heard by elected officials!). The third measure, which was discussed in the previous chapter, is its level of fiscal activity—how much revenue it takes in (total and per capita), how many dollars it spends, how much it owns in the way of public sector capital, and how much debt it has accumulated.

Once a nation's boundaries are defined, its land area is more or less fixed (subject to reclamation, erosion, and other natural forces). Its population may grow due to natural increase or immigration, and its economic activity may grow because of conscious choices by its citizens or public officials. But there is also a set of choices to be made about smaller governments that take responsibility for some subset of that total nation, whether it is a rural village or the state of California. How big (or small) should those second and third tier governments be? Do they all need to be about the same size, or is it necessary (or desirable) to have different sizes? And, most important, which revenue sources and which service responsibilities should be retained by the central government, and which should be delegated or assigned to state or local governments?

Two countries could have the same population and the same number of governments at each level and still have very different systems, because different countries do not make the same defining choices about **centralization**, or concentration of authority and responsibility at higher levels or in larger governmental units. A highly centralized governmental structure is one that concentrates much of the authority, power, decision-making, and tax collection at a higher level of government. When lower levels of government enjoy more autonomy, authority, and independent sources of revenue, the system is more decentralized.

Advantages of centralization

The principal economic advantage of centralization is that the level and variety of public services that each citizen receives do not depend on whether that person lives in a rich state or a poor state, a wealthy suburb or an urban ghetto or a dying prairie town. All citizens receive roughly the same quality of education and other public services. Rich communities pay more in taxes than poor communities (or states), so there is indirect redistribution between rich and poor communities (as well as individuals) in that they pay different amounts according to ability to pay but receive the same services.

A second economic advantage of centralization is that some services have substantial economies of scale; that is, the average cost curve continues to decline with a larger population or service area up to a very large number. Economies of scale have been found in services such as water, sewerage, and garbage collection. In the case of fire protection, economies of scale are found up to populations of 400,000.

A third economic advantage of centralizing at least some services arises from the existence of externalities or spillovers in the provision of public goods and services. If citizens of British Columbia were providing their own defense against foreign enemies, they would inadvertently also be providing some protection to Alberta. But there is no way for the government of British Columbia to force the citizens of Alberta to pay for those benefits, so those spillover benefits would not be taken into account in British Columbia's decision about how much defense to provide. (The problem of deciding how much of a public good to provide is discussed in Chapter 6.)

Likewise, if Georgia draws too much water from the Savannah River, it will affect the water supply and the recreational use of the river by downstream cities on the opposite bank in South Carolina. Spillovers of benefits (or costs) of activities from one jurisdiction to another mean that some beneficiaries are not made to pay and some people who are negatively affected by certain decisions have no voice. By having the largest possible jurisdiction, more of the affected parties (both those who benefit and those who incur costs) are included in paying their fair share as well as in making their voices heard.

Finally, centralization is one way to prevent competition among states from reducing the economic benefits of having a large national market for goods and services, capital and labor. When workers and owners of firms know that they will pay the same taxes and receive pretty much the same services regardless of where they are located in the country, their location decisions will not be distorted. They will make economically optimal decisions based on factors such as access to markets, availability of complementary resources (business services, suppliers, raw materials, water, inexpensive land, climate) and personal preferences. Buyers of goods and services will not seek out the state with the lowest sales tax, but will look for the best deal wherever it can be found (including the cost of transportation and search time).

Advantages of decentralization

There are at least three advantages to decentralization that must be weighed against these advantages of centralization. The first is that decentralization is better suited to accommodating diversity. Different groups of citizens have different needs, preferences, and desires. Spending on highways is more important to Montana than to Delaware, where the distances are short and there are fewer miles of highway per resident. Heat assistance in the winter may be crucial to survival for the poorest citizens of Maine and Minnesota, but help with fans, air conditioning or other defenses against extreme heat may be more important to their low-income counterparts in Arizona or Mississippi. Homelessness is a largely urban problem, while transportation is more likely to be a major need for rural areas.

Citizens also have different service demands. Some communities may be more interested in public recreation, others in public transportation, still others in quality public schools. By allowing citizens to make different choices in different communities, it is possible to accommodate, if not individual, at least smaller group preferences.

Second, and closely related, is the positive value of competition, which can be used as an argument for either centralization or decentralization. If communities offer different service (and tax) mixes, citizens can migrate to those communities that most mirror their preferences—and they do. Some citizens may opt for high tax/high service communities, others for less of both. Seniors may choose retirement communities that offer more recreational amenities and services to the elderly but spend little on public schools.

Creating relatively homogeneous communities in terms of these kinds of preferences increases citizen satisfaction. Citizens who are mobile can threaten to leave if they get no satisfaction of their preferences clearly from elected officials. The threat of losing desirable residents and the taxes they pay forces local public officials to be more sensitive to the needs and preferences of current and potential residents.[2]

Third is the value of innovation and experimentation. Many of the features of the welfare reform of the late 1990s were adapted from experimental programs developed in Massachusetts, Wisconsin, and other states. The Obama health care plan passed in 2010 owes much to an earlier state health care plan initiated in Massachusetts by Republican governor William Weld. It is less costly to experiment and possibly fail in one state than in all 50. States (or cantons, or provinces, or *Länder*) can serve as laboratories of federalism, with the good ideas propagated or even adopted by the central government and the unsuccessful ideas discarded without the high cost of trying them out everywhere.

States also learn from each other. The Georgia lottery, drawing on criticism of how lottery-based education financing was handled in other states such as New York and Florida, was carefully designed to segregate lottery funds for some specific educational purposes, providing a new model that other states could copy. Georgia, in turn, benefited from being one of the later states to implement a lottery, so that it could learn from the successes as well as the mistakes of others.

These same arguments for and against centralization at the federal level play out again at lower levels of government, in debates over state versus local control of education or prisons or highways. At the local level, the argument about centralization re-emerges as a question of optimal size for a city or county.[3] How much land area can a local government effectively serve? (In parts of the Southern United States in the nineteenth century, the answer was: a county seat needs to be no more than a day's drive by horse and buggy round trip from the farthest point in the county.) How many citizens can a local government effectively listen and respond to? How big, in land area and/or population, does a city have to be to enjoy economies of scale in its service provision?

If a city (or county) is too small, more of the benefits of the services it offers or the costs of its activities (pollution, congestion) are likely to spill over to adjacent cities or counties, to people who have no voice and pay no taxes. But as it grows larger, the population within a city is likely to become increasingly diverse, and it is harder for elected officials to find a tax/service mix that will satisfy those very different preferences. Finding a satisfactory size means weighing these two opposing considerations.

States and counties usually have fixed boundaries. Whether they are the "right" size or not, their land areas rarely change, and their populations change only through births, deaths, and migration. The same is not true of cities. In many countries, including the United States, cities can expand through annexation. When cities look to expand, or when citizens of outlying areas are consulted about being annexed, both parties need to weigh these costs and benefits. What is the value/cost of the services provided? How much tax burden/revenue can be expected of new households? Can the city get so large that it begins to experience diseconomies of scale, i.e., an inability to manage the level and diversity of functions it has to carry out?

Weighing all of these considerations, there are three important questions about the structure of government that each nation must address:

1   How many levels of government will there be?
2   How much autonomy will each level have?
3   To what degree will functions and revenue sources be separated by levels of government, and to what degree will they overlap and require coordination?

How many levels of government?

This question is usually the easiest of the three, since the answer is rarely one, usually either two or three, and almost never more than three, although there may be several co-existing and/or overlapping governments at the local level. Small, fairly homogeneous countries can usually manage with two levels—central and local. There may be regional divisions for administrative purposes, but most functions can be satisfactorily designated as either local (few spillovers to the rest of the country, amenable to local control, lack of uniformity is not a problem, services can be financed through local revenue sources) or central (requiring a uniform national program, affecting all citizens equally, and requiring a financial contribution from all segments of the country). Switzerland is one of a kind, a small but ethnically and linguistically diverse nation that is genuinely federal in its structure, with the cantons exercising considerable independent authority.

While it is not true that each nation gets the government it deserves, there is a tendency for larger nations to adopt some modified federal system and for smaller nations to have two major levels, central and local. Countries with multiple levels of government, particularly where the middle level is genuinely separate and somewhat independent rather than just a convenient administrative division, were often formed by the union of those middle levels to form a larger whole. Such was the case in the United States and Germany, which wrote constitutions specifying a federal structure with substantial state autonomy.

Australian unification of its six colonies (Fiji and New Zealand were also invited, but declined) did not take place until 1901. Although the territories were originally expected to exert considerable independence, in practice, power gravitated to the central government over time. Canada also chose a federal system not only because of its large land area but also because of potential conflict among citizens of French descent and British descent. These genuinely federal countries have a greater challenge in figuring out which level of government does what.

How much autonomy?

Some countries that appear to be federal are really less so than they appear, because the middle level (state or province) has relatively little independent authority and serves largely as an administrative division of the central government. If there is a constitution (which most modern nations have), it usually spells out some division of responsibilities. In Germany, the *Länder* exercise authority both in the second chamber of the national legislature and in their separate spheres of responsibility, particularly education and culture. In Canada, all authority not granted to the provinces is reserved to the central government, while in the US Constitution (Article 10), all powers not delegated to the central government are reserved to the states. Ironically, in practice Canada has seen a gradual shift of authority to the provinces, while until recently in the United States power gravitated toward Washington, DC, rather than to the 50 state capitals.

There are two keys to autonomy for state and local governments. One is access to independent revenue sources, so that the state and local government is not primarily dependent on the central government to collect and dispense funds. The other is some defined independent sphere(s) of service provision. For example, state governments might be assigned exclusive authority (and responsibility) to regulate banks and insurance companies, or to provide highways and public education. Constitutional provisions that explicitly either permit state governments or forbid the central government from certain activities provide the strongest safeguards for state autonomy.

As new kinds of government activities develop, the process of sorting out continues to evolve. Ideally, provision for a particular service or use of a particular revenue source would be assigned to that level of government for which it was most suited in terms of scale economies, internalizing potential spillovers, competitive effects, and other considerations. In practice, such sorting out has rarely been done on the basis of economic efficiency. The assignment of general (retail) sales taxes to state and local governments in the United States, for example, was not a deliberate act but an accidental result of a sudden need for a new revenue source by states during the Great Depression.

Separation, overlap and coordination

It is virtually impossible to find a country that does not assign responsibility to the central government for foreign affairs, national defense, international commerce, fiscal policy, and issuing currency. Beyond that limited range of consensus, there is considerable diversity among countries on both the revenue and spending side. Sales taxes are primarily state and local in the United States, usually national (as value-added taxes) in most other countries. Education and health care are national responsibilities in many countries, but much more of a state and local responsibility in the United States.

While it appears to be easier to divide up responsibilities (e.g., defense is national, education is state, police are local) than to share them between levels of government, in practice, assignment of functions is never that clear-cut. For example, police are primarily local in the United States, but the effects of criminal activity spill over from one community to another, and some kinds of police activity enjoy significant economies of scale. Every state has some kind of state Bureau of Investigation or Law Enforcement Division and a State Highway Patrol. Some crimes, like treason, espionage, and kidnapping, may be classified as federal crimes. Even for state crimes there is a need for coordination in access to records and investigative resources. Unlike many other nations, the United States does not have a genuinely national police force, but there is the Federal Bureau of Investigation, which works closely with state and local police on cases that require their assistance and that call for federal intervention as well as pursuing cases involving federal crimes on their own.

Similar overlap occurs in most government functions. Even national defense in the United States is complemented by state National Guards that are under the control of state governors, who can call them out in emergencies. Banks, insurance companies, and public utilities are subject to a mix of state and federal regulation. National parks are supplemented by a second tier of state parks and recreation areas. Interstate highways are a joint federal–state undertaking that links state (and local) roads into a national network.

The chief advantage of a clear separation of responsibilities is to offer citizens or voters better accountability. If services are good, and taxes are low, they know who deserves the credit. They vote to retain the incumbents, or move into well-run local communities. If services are bad, and taxes are high, they can boot the rascals out, or move to a better managed locale. When services and revenue sources are commingled, partly federal, partly state, partly local, it is more difficult to assign credit or blame. These signals of voter satisfaction or dissatisfaction are one useful way to provide direction to public officials.

However, there are also some advantages to sharing responsibilities across levels of government. Suppose, for example, that most of the benefit of education in the lower grades accrues to the locality where the students live. They stay in the area and become adult workers and citizens, and the quality of both the public and private sector is enhanced when they are better educated. But some of them, inevitably, move elsewhere. The benefits of their education accrue to other jurisdictions. If every jurisdiction spent the same, and there was no migration or balanced migration, the costs incurred in educating young people would be roughly balanced by the benefits of educated adult workers and citizens, whether locally raised or migrating in.

But these conditions rarely hold. Some of the benefits of educating children in Albany, Georgia, or in the neighboring states of Alabama and South Carolina, are likely to bear fruit in the magnet city of Atlanta that attracts young workers from all over the Southeast. So the cost of educating those young people should be primarily local, but also shared to some degree by those other areas of the state or nation that also benefit.

Finally, there are big differences in the ability of state governments and especially local governments to generate revenues to finance public services. If citizens are entitled to a certain basic level of public services wherever they live by virtue of being part of one nation, then state and federal governments will have to redistribute resources toward low-income communities in order to ensure that level of services.

Interlocal competition and the Tiebout hypothesis

Lower levels of government frequently compete with one another for high-income residents and commercial and industrial development. This competition can be beneficial, but it can also be destructive, a race to the bottom as tax breaks, worker training, and infrastructure construction cost the state or locality more than the benefits of new jobs, income, and tax revenue.

Tax differences do factor into the choice of a state location for both mobile individuals and firms, although they are rarely at the top of the list. Within a state, however, the individual or firm will zero in on a particular region, perhaps because of its interstate highway access, training facilities, labor availability, or other factors. Within that region, there are likely to be a variety of suitable locations. Consequently, competition for residents and industrial and commercial facilities can become very intense at the local level.

The fiscal package of taxes and services offered by competing cities, counties/townships, and/or school districts is often an important consideration in pinpointing a site on which to build a house, an industrial facility, a shopping center, or a recreational facility. Making those choices, moving between localities because of the relative attractiveness of the tax and service packages, is called "voting with one's feet."

The classic description of the workings of interlocal competition was that of regional economist Charles Tiebout (Tiebout, 1956). The **Tiebout hypothesis** has been one of the most fruitful ideas in regional economics. It has led to considerable empirical testing as well as further refinements of our understanding of the effects of locational decisions and capitalization of fiscal surplus on the prices of land and homes.

Tiebout's basic concept was quite simple. It was based on the assumption that both workers and firms not only engage in the usual informed, self-interested decision-making processes that lie at the heart of economics, but also that workers and firms are mobile. They can move to one community to another, or if relocating in a particular region, they can choose from several competing communities that offer alternative tax and service packages. Communities, in turn, are trying to attain some optimal population in order to reach an efficient size that will minimize the average cost of providing public services. Under these circumstances, people will tend to cluster in communities in which tastes and preferences for public services and taxes are relatively homogeneous. There will be high-service, low-service, and medium-service (and tax) communities from which to select.

This model suggests a monopolistically competitive model of many similar communities differentiated by the offerings of the public sector as well as other amenities that influence people's locational choices. It also accords with what is observed in the real world. Real estate agents consistently note that the questions about a community always zero in on taxes and school quality as two key decision factors—and schools are generally the largest and most expensive local public service. Firms, likewise, take into account both taxes and those public services that are important to them (such as transportation and fire protection) in choosing between alternative locations.

Not all communities are in an intense Tiebout-type competitive situation. Some are too isolated. Others have attractions (such as the state capitol, access to the ocean, or location at the intersection of two interstate highways) that overpower the importance of the fiscal package. But in the suburbs of large cities, or in areas where many small to medium-sized cities are clustered together, the Tiebout hypothesis suggests that mobility gives voters much more voice and clout in the decisions of the local public sector. When residents and firms are mobile, the threat of losing residents and/or commercial and industrial facilities because of mobility is a powerful device for getting the attention of politicians and bureaucrats.

Fiscal surplus or deficit

While any decision by a household or firm to relocate has many aspects, most will take into account the **fiscal surplus** or **fiscal deficit** in each alternative location. The concept is simple: just add up the value of government services received, and subtract the value of taxes paid (including any fees or other nontax obligations).[4] If the difference is positive, the taxpayer has a fiscal surplus; if negative, a fiscal deficit.

Notice that while taxes are easily determined and would represent the same calculation for the taxpayer and the taxing jurisdictions, the value of services received is highly subjective, so that two taxpayers with the same tax burden may have different fiscal surpluses because they value services differently. Often there is a big difference in the size of the fiscal surplus between families with school-aged children, for whom the quality of the public schools is of paramount concern, and childless families for whom other services or lower taxes are more important.

Taxpayers can generally gather information about tax burdens and service quality from realtors, local public officials, prospective employers and other sources so that they can compare the package of taxes and services. Often local governments distribute that kind of information to visitors and prospective residents, packaging their tax/service package as attractively as possible in order to get the most desirable residential-commercial-industrial mix.

Fiscal impact

Fiscal impact represents the opposite side of the coin, subtracting service costs from revenues to determine whether the impact of new residents, commercial developments, or industry is a net addition to or a drain on local (and/or state) public sector resources. The government compares the cost of providing services for the additional resident to the amount of revenue that resident would be expected to generate. If the new resident or firm will generate more revenue to the government than the cost of providing the additional services, the fiscal impact is positive.[5] In the case of a pure public good, where adding another user does not diminish the amount available to existing users, the service cost of an extra resident is zero while the value of the service remains positive. The government can afford to offer this taxpayer a favorable tax service package because an extra resident will result in a revenue increase while expenditures are unchanged.

The revenue side is the easier part of the calculation. The cost of serving a particular additional household may depend on its size, income level, and location. Infill developments that put homes on vacant lots are usually less expensive to serve than new homes built in more isolated locations where the cost of running services (roads, utilities, street lights, police and fire protection, trash pickup, etc.) will be much higher per household. High density housing, such as apartment complexes, can be less expensive to serve with transportation, street lights, and trash pickup, but often generate much higher demand for police protection and recreation services. Industry is usually attractive to local governments not only because of jobs but also because it tends to have lower service demands than households. Commercial development lies somewhere in between. Because the most expensive local public service is education, mobile home parks with their many children and low tax revenue per household are often actively discouraged by local governments.

Homogeneous communities?

The Tiebout hypothesis suggests that market-type forces will result in communities that are relatively homogeneous in terms of preferences for public services and the willingness to pay for them. Will these communities also be homogeneous in terms of income? They might, because tastes for public services are likely to be related to income levels. But there are other factors at work, particularly the attraction of being a low-income resident in a high-income community.

Remember, for local governments the property tax is usually the primary source of local revenue. Thus, a household's tax burden will be related to the value of taxable property that household owns—most likely a house, and perhaps one or two cars. But the service level is the same for everyone in the community. People who own less taxable property (smaller houses, older cars) will have larger fiscal surpluses than those who live in more expensive houses or drive newer, pricier cars. No one will want to be the biggest property owner in town, especially a town with high service levels.

So communities that raise their taxes too high, or communities that have only a few high value properties and a large number of low to medium value properties, face the threat of losing some of their wealthier residents. As those residents depart, they sell their houses at depressed prices, because prospective buyers are deterred by the high tax burden associated with that house. When the price falls, so does the tax burden.

Higher-income residents are likely to seek out communities that are homogeneous not only in taste for public services but also in income levels and housing values so that their fiscal surpluses are not diminished by having to support services for occupants of lower-valued homes. Thus, one conclusion of the Tiebout hypothesis is that there may be some tendency for communities to become segregated by income levels.

At the other end of the scale, a high-service community might be very attractive to someone looking to buy a small, inexpensive house, because the tax burden will be relatively small, both in comparison to services received and in comparison to the average tax burden on residents. Demand for a limited supply of such houses will drive up their price and their value for tax purposes.

So this high-service community is likely to attract residents seeking smaller, lower-valued homes and discourage those looking for larger and more upscale residences. But in the process, the tax burden on smaller houses rises and that on larger houses falls, reducing some of the disparity in the fiscal surplus enjoyed by residents with very different housing choices. These market-like forces mitigate the inflow and outflow of residents attracted or driven away by relative tax burdens.

Fiscal capitalization

The process by which present and future fiscal surpluses are reflected in the prices of houses is called **fiscal capitalization**. Capitalization refers to the process by which a stream of future income flows or expected costs is incorporated into the present value of an asset, in this case a house or other real estate. Recall that the present value of any series of future payments, positive or negative, is the sum of the discounted value of each of those future payments. If, for example, in the sixth year from now the tax bill is expected to be $500, and the interest rate used is 6 percent, then the present value of the tax liability in six years is $500/(1.06)^6$, which works out to $352.49. The present value of future tax liabilities is given by the present value formula

$$PV = \Sigma FV_i/(1+r)^i$$

Where PV is present value, FV is future value, r is the interest rate, and *i* is the number of years. If the tax bill will be $500 for the next ten years, then the present value of ten years of tax liabilities is $500\ *(1/1.06 + 1/(1.06)^2 + (1/1.06)^3 +. . .(1/1.06)^{10}$, or $3680. $3680 is the amount that one would have to set aside right now at 6 percent interest in order to make that total of $5,000 in future tax payments at a rate of $500 a year.

The same calculation can be made for the value of public services in future years. They may be the same, or they may be different. Perhaps the household will only have children in schools for some of those years. Perhaps they are presently using wells and septic tanks and on a gravel road, but have assurances of city water, city sewer and paved roads in the near future. Combining the two calculations yields the present value of future taxes and services.

If one of those factors changes, the present value will increase or decrease. If the fiscal surplus on a property increases, the value of the property should increase by the same amount, other things being equal. If the fiscal surplus decreases, either because the expected future tax burden increases or the expected value of services decreases, the value of the property should decline, other things being equal. The change in the stream of future obligations and benefits is incorporated into the value of the property, or capitalized.

An important implication of fiscal capitalization is that any changes in taxes or service levels impacts primarily those who own the property at the time, not future owners. If, for example, a tax increase in one community results in a decline in the fiscal surplus associated with residences in that town relative to neighboring towns, then housing prices will decline. Current owners not only have to pay the higher taxes, but if they attempt to escape them by relocating, they will find that the (lower) price they receive for their property will reflect the higher tax burdens. The next buyer will have to pay the higher taxes, but he or she will also be able to purchase the house at a lower price that reflects that disadvantage.

Fiscal zoning

Another implication of the Tiebout hypothesis is that cities and even counties can attempt to defend themselves against some of the undesirable effects of citizen mobility through zoning designed to limit in-migration of low tax, high service demand residents. When zoning regulations set high minimum lot sizes or minimum square footage requirements in order to protect the value of the fiscal surplus of established and higher-income residents, that community is engaging in **fiscal zoning**. Lower-income households cannot move in and buy or build small houses to enjoy larger fiscal surpluses at the expense of high tax burdens on larger, more valuable properties. Again, the result of fiscal zoning tends to be communities that are homogeneous not only in tastes and preferences but also in income and wealth.

Behavioral economics: do people vote with their feet?

Some people do vote with their feet. They move to states and communities, or choose among communities when relocating anyway, based on many factors, but the fiscal surplus or deficit is often one of them. Realtors are aware that different state or local tax and service packages are an important factor in buying a home. However, once located, it is costly to relocate, so changes in tax and service packages may keep some dissatisfied residents in place. Renters are somewhat more flexible, but a very high percentage of American households own their homes.

In addition, people's motivations are complex. They may wish to be close to family, or become attached to neighbors, friends, and organizations in a particular community, which will make them less mobile. If they stay, they may instead choose to try to influence the tax and service package by expressing their concerns to local officials, or even running for public office.

However, the Tiebout hypothesis does not require that everyone be mobile. People do relocate for many reasons. When they move, they do consider tax and service packages, because good schools and other local services are important to them and to the value of their home, which is usually the household's largest asset. Taxes affect their monthly payments. Some communities are isolated, and therefore in a less competitive situation. Others, like the District of Columbia and the five surrounding counties in Virginia and Maryland, are in intense competition. So the competition among communities to attract business firms and residents does influence the tax and service packages offered, even if that influence may not be quite as extensive or pervasive as the Tiebout hypothesis implies.

The state/local relationship

The relationship between a state (or province, or other intermediate level of government) and its local governments is quite different from that between the central and state governments. In the United States, the existence of states is specified in the Constitution, along with some indication of their powers and the procedures for admitting new states to the union, but there is no mention of local governments. Each state makes its own rules for local governments. While there are many similarities between states in the form and sphere of local government, there are also some striking differences.

Home rule

Home rule refers to the degree of autonomy or independence that local governments enjoy in making all kinds of decisions. For our purposes, a particularly important dimension of the state/local relationship that varies greatly from state to state is local **fiscal autonomy**. Fiscal autonomy refers to the degree of freedom that a city, county, or school district has to set its own property tax rate, use nonproperty tax revenue sources, and decide what quantity and variety of services to offer. Most states have some involvement in the administration of the property tax, particularly in overseeing the assessment process and determining what kinds of property should be subject to the tax. In 17 states, the state determines different assessment rates[6] for different classes of property (residential, commercial, agricultural, etc.) that are subject to the local property tax. Many states also determine which properties will be exempt, and some states compensate local governments for the lost revenue. Local governments may have total freedom in setting the tax rate or mill rate, although in the 1980s and 1990s many state governments imposed some limits on increases in property tax millage in response to taxpayer protests.

The state may specify other revenue sources (including permissible rates) that local governments are allowed to use, but not limited to local income taxes, local sales taxes, fees, business licenses, and accommodations taxes (taxes on motels, hotels, and other short-term rentals). Some states give local governments (most often just cities) free rein in tapping revenue sources, or least limit their direction to a list of revenue sources that local governments may *not* use, leaving them free to explore those sources that are not forbidden.

On the spending side, the state may mandate certain kinds and levels of spending to a surprisingly fine degree, e.g., how many minutes to spend on biology each week in the 7th grade, what grade of paving material to use on the highway, or how many square feet of space to provide in the circuit judge's courtroom. These specific directives are known as mandates. When these spending responsibilities come without the money to pay for implementing them, they are known as unfunded mandates, fighting words to most local public officials. Some states are much more controlling of local spending than others. In some cases the state spells out what kinds of services a city or county may provide, in other cases which ones they are not to provide.

A more indirect way in which state governments influence local government activity is through revenue sharing and/or state grants to local governments. Local governments derive about one-third of their revenue on average from state grants and state-shared revenues.

Some of the funds with specific spending directives attached, some going into the local general fund to be spent according to local directives.

Structure of local government in the United States

In general, US states are divided into counties, parishes (Louisiana), or townships (mostly in the northeast). Similar divisions exist in other federal countries. The important feature of this kind of local government is that every resident is located in a county, parish, or township. Counties and their counterparts in other states almost always rely heavily on the property tax for revenue and usually have responsibilities for highways, law enforcement, and a variety of other functions. They may or may not also have responsibility for schools.

In some states, counties are primarily regional agents of state government, while in other states they have significant independent authority. In urban areas, in some states it is possible for a county (or counties) to merge with its primary city or cities to form a single metropolitan government that carries out both municipal and county functions and exercises the powers of both.

The other universal form of local government is the city or town, which differs from a county or parish or township in having defined boundaries that can be changed by annexation. Unlike counties, cities and towns do not include the entire landscape; many citizens live in unincorporated areas or "out in the country" without enjoying or paying for municipal services. A city is more like a club, which citizens join by buying or renting residential property inside the city limits or by being annexed to an existing city.

Cities are also heavy users of property taxes as a revenue source, although they tend to be more diversified in their revenue sources than counties. Since residents of cities and towns are packed into less land area than those in counties and rural areas, many of their service demands are related to density: more traffic management, solid waste collection services, more police patrols, sidewalks and street lights. Cities and towns are responsible for schools in some states, while, in other states, school districts are separate from both cities and counties.

Creation and growth of cities

One major way in which states differ in their treatment of cities relates to the process of forming or expanding cities. Cities come into being through incorporation and expand through annexation or consolidation (the former being the addition of unincorporated areas to the city, the latter a merger with another city). Residents of suburbs reap benefits from being close to the city but often contribute little if anything to the cost of maintaining that city. In other words, cities generate spillover benefits or positive externalities for their neighbors. Also, citizens in unincorporated areas may rely more heavily on county services (such as the sheriff or county recreation programs) than those in the city, who have municipal services. But in many states people living outside city limits pay the same county taxes as city-dwellers and no city taxes—a situation that seems very unfair to those living inside city limits, a clear case of "free-riding."

Incorporation is very easy in some states and difficult in others. States often may impose requirements of population size, density, or tax base on incorporation in order to ensure that a city will be viable, i.e., able to support the provision of basic municipal services out of its revenue base. Incorporation may involve petitions, votes, or other procedures specified by the state.

Annexation, likewise, is usually governed by state rules. In some states, such as North Carolina, annexation is relatively easy, done largely at the initiative of the annexing city, often despite protests from the areas being annexed. These liberal annexation laws have made it easy for cities like Charlotte, Asheville, and Greensboro to grow and expand by taking in their growing suburbs, whether or not those suburbs want to become part of the city. In other states, such as Connecticut, annexation is more difficult. Connecticut's older cities like Hartford and Waterbury have seen suburbs spring up around them that use the city as a commercial and service center but contribute little to its revenues.

Both incorporation and annexation involve important economic issues of balancing costs and benefits. From the city's point of view, do additional citizens add more to revenue than they do to cost? From the viewpoint of those being annexed, does the value of the services provided by the city justify the additional taxes they will have to pay and the additional regulations (like no open burning, or keeping a dog on the leash) with which they will have to comply? Economists would expect there to be some optimal size for a city that precisely balances the marginal cost (broadly defined) of adding another citizen with the marginal revenue that citizen generates.

Matching resources and responsibilities: redistribution among governments

State (and local) governments have similar responsibilities and demands but very different resources for meeting those demands. Local governments are more limited than state governments in their ability to raise revenue, state governments more so than the central government. These two kinds of inequality lead to redistribution of revenues between levels of government, between states, and between local governments within a state in order to provide a better match between needs and resources. Redistribution between levels of government in order to match revenues with responsibilities is known as **vertical equalization**; redistribution among governments at the same level in order to ensure citizens of equal access to services regardless of the wealth of their communities is known as **horizontal equalization**.

Vertical equalization can go in either direction. In China and in Russia and Eastern Europe under communism, revenue was collected locally and sent to the central government. In the United States and many Western countries, the pattern is normally the reverse. Funds collected by the central government are shared with state and local governments, and some of the funds collected by state governments are redistributed to local governments. However, the funds rarely return to state or local governments in proportion to the revenue originating in each place, so there is some horizontal redistribution between states and between local governments in the process. If that kind of redistribution also reduces the inequality between states or between local governments, then horizontal equalization is also taking place.

State aid to local governments

In 2007, local governments across the country received an average of 37.3 percent of general revenue from higher levels of government, of which 4.1 percent was federal and 33.2 percent was from the parent state.[7] On the surface, state aid to local governments—counties, cities, school districts—has some similarities to **General Revenue Sharing** (with a much longer history). But in fact, there is an important difference. States have considerable autonomy in the US federal system, while local governments are created by and dependent on their state governments.

Court decisions, particularly related to education funding, have forced states to play an increasingly important role in ensuring that the quality of a child's education is not too heavily dependent on the wealth of the school district in which that child resides. Increasingly, the burden of paying for public education (kindergarten through grade 12) has been shifting to the state level. States also often mandate that county or municipal governments offer certain services or meet certain standards, and there is pressure on states to fund those mandates so as not to overburden smaller and/or poorer communities with limited taxable wealth.

Another factor in justifying state aid is the extremely competitive situation facing local governments in attracting or retaining both residents and commercial/industrial taxpayers. No local government can afford to let either its tax rates or its service quality (especially schools) get too far out of line with its neighbors. Yet a city or county or school district with very little taxable wealth requires a much higher tax rate to generate the same amount of revenue and provide the same quality of public services as a wealthy neighbor. To protect poorer communities from the consequences of the tax competition game, states either partially fund certain local services or redistribute tax revenues from wealthier to poorer areas.

Fiscal federalism in the European Union

The European Union began its life as the European Economic Community (EEC) with the Treaty of Rome in 1957, signed by six countries (Germany, France, Italy, Belgium, the Netherlands, and Luxembourg). It was preceded by a much more limited organization, the European Coal and Steel Community, organized in 1953 to coordinate these nationalized industries in the six countries. In the beginning, the EEC was primarily a customs union, eliminating tariffs and other trade barriers within the community while negotiating as a group on tariffs with other countries, primarily the United States. But from the beginning the intent was something more comprehensive, sometimes referred to as the United States of Europe.

At the same time that the EEC was creating an internal common market with a free flow of labor and capital between countries and a harmonized tax system based on the value-added tax as a primary revenue source, it was also adding member countries. To join the EU, a country must have a stable democracy that respects human rights, a market economy, and willingness to accept the obligations of membership. Today there are 27 member countries. The biggest step toward greater unification was the 1992 Maastricht Treaty, which created a monetary union (common currency) and EU citizenship. Common institutions were created—a European Parliament and a European flag, and finally, a common currency, the euro. Under the Lisbon Treaty, which took effect in 2009, there is now an EU-wide president as the chief executive.

Some of the same tensions that framed the US Constitution were present in the formation and evolution of the European Union. How much sovereignty are member states willing to surrender for the benefits of being part of a larger force on the world stage politically and the economic power that comes with a huge internal market and free movement of labor and capital? The 2010 financial crisis involving crushing debt burdens and pending bankruptcy in Greece and Portugal was the first major test of the union's centralized monetary policy, which represented a significant surrender of autonomy by member countries.

Today the 27 member nations are moving closer to a relationship to the EU that is quite similar to the relationship of American states and Canadian and Australian provinces to their central governments—a broad sphere of activity that is carried out by the central government with certain revenue sources and responsibilities, such as roads and education, reserved to the member states or countries.

Summary

- The structure of governments, or the number of governments, the number of levels and types, and the sizes, responsibility and autonomy of each level or type are the institutional framework within which public economics operates. The choice of a structure involves such economic concerns as scale economies, internalizing externalities, measuring demand, and the benefits of intergovernmental competition.
- The appropriate choice of structure will depend on the country—its size, diversity, values, culture, and level of economic development. The United States is one of a relatively small number of countries with a federal structure, consisting of three levels with a significant amount of independent authority at the middle (state) level.
- Larger or more centralized governments may enjoy greater economies of scale and be able to include most of the beneficiaries of their services within the taxing jurisdiction (internalizing externalities). A large, centralized government will be able to offer the same level of services to all citizens and control destructive competition by lower levels of government seeking to lure businesses or high-income residents. However, decentralization allows for diversity of citizen preferences, beneficial competition, and innovation and experimentation.
- A structure of governments must address the number of levels of government, how much autonomy to allow each level, and to what degree functions and revenue sources will be separated or coordinated between levels of government. Most countries have either two or three levels.
- Autonomy means that lower levels of government have independent revenue sources and separate service responsibilities, although both may overlap. Separation of responsibilities means greater accountability. Sharing of responsibilities makes it easier to assign the cost to those who benefit from the services. Also, different levels of government have different abilities to raise revenue, which may not match up to their service responsibilities.
- Local governments in the United States include counties, parishes, or townships, sometimes separate school districts. Some citizens live inside corporate cities or towns, others outside. Counties are created by the state and cover the entire state, while cities are created by incorporation and grow by annexation.
- In some states, local governments enjoy a high degree of independence in raising revenues and providing services, while in other states local governments are more closely monitored and regulated by the state.
- The fiscal surplus offered by competing cities, counties/townships, and/or school districts is often an important consideration for individuals and firms in choosing a location. The Tiebout hypothesis suggests that mobile workers and firms will be more inclined to select a community that offers the most attractive fiscal package.
- Capitalization is the process by which changes in taxes or service levels are translated through fiscal surplus into appreciation or depreciation in home prices. One consequence of tax capitalization is that the wealth effect of a change in tax or service levels falls on those who own property at the time of the change and not on subsequent owners.

- Fiscal zoning restricts the ability to construct smaller homes for less affluent families and creates relatively homogeneous communities, generally of higher-income residents.
- Redistribution between levels of government in order to match revenues with responsibilities is vertical equalization; redistribution among governments at the same level in order to ensure that citizens have equal access to services, regardless of the wealth of their communities, is known as horizontal equalization.
- The federalism challenge to the European Union has been to integrate multiple nations into one entity that respects autonomy while still ensuring mutual responsibility and shared economic and fiscal institutions, including a common currency.

Key terms

Centralization
Federalist
Fiscal autonomy
Fiscal capitalization
Fiscal federalism
Fiscal impact
Fiscal surplus (deficit)
Fiscal zoning
General Revenue Sharing
Home rule
Horizontal equalization
Tiebout hypothesis
Unitary state
Vertical equalization

Questions

1 Is structure of state (or provincial) and local government where you live highly centralized compared to other states? How would you measure the degree of centralization?

2 What are the principal services provided by your local government? How much of the benefits accrue to strictly local residents, and how much to visitors and others? Who should pay for those services?

3 What might be the benefits/costs to existing residents in expanding the size of the city? To those being annexed? Based on your analysis, do you think it should be easy or difficult for cities to annex the surrounding areas?

4 Which of the following government services seems most suited to national or central rather than local provision? Why?

   (a) environmental protection
   (b) public welfare (aid to the poor)
   (c) lighthouses
   (d) innoculations for preschool children

5 In which of the following kinds of new development do you think that fiscal impact on local government is likely to be negative, as opposed to moderately or even highly

positive? Why? What strategies are implied from the perspective of local government in order to minimize adverse fiscal impacts?

(a) mobile home parks with large numbers of children
(b) upscale residential communities for wealthy retirees
(c) low density suburbs of moderate-prices households on fairly large lots, with much open space
(d) a large, dense commercial district with shops, restaurants, and service firms
(e) an industrial park with light, high-tech industry

6 While local governments are supposedly "closest to the people" and therefore more responsive than higher level governments, in the past 25 years many state governments in the United States have imposed increasing restrictions on the ability of local governments to raise taxes and/or borrow money. Why (or why not) would it be appropriate for state governments to put such restrictions on local governments?

7 **By the numbers**. Using the U.S. Bureau of the Census data on state and local governments, find the amount of state aid to local governments from 1997 to the most recent available year and calculate the amount of aid as a percentage of general revenue. Do the same for your state. Graph the result. How has it changed?

8 **Policy application**. What are some of the ways that states can engage in horizontal equalization between cities and counties? What criteria might they use for distributing funds/resources? What are the advantages and disadvantages of each of the following methods?

(a) direct state provision of certain services
(b) sending money to local governments to provide the same services, with relatively more per capita going to cities and counties with a smaller tax base or a higher percentage of poor people
(c) sending the same amount per capita to all cities and counties to provide the similar levels of local services

9 **Behavioral economics**. Based on both motivation (concern for people you know well) and cognition (how much information you can access and process and visibility of taxes and services), how might citizen attitudes toward local government taxes and spending be different from attitudes toward the federal government?

10 **Thinking globally**. Externalities occur not only within countries but across countries, particularly in matters of environmental spillovers. But there is no higher level of government above the national level to address such concerns. Using the internet, research how nations have dealt with this problem of sovereignty and spillovers in terms of some issue such as acid rain, climate change, or overfishing the oceans.

4 Decision-making in the public sector

Introduction

There are two conflicting views of how decisions are made in the public sector about taxing and spending, borrowing and regulating. One view might be described as the benevolent dictator or good public servant model. That person, or group of persons, attempts to maximize collective welfare by making decisions in the best interests of the general public. For a long time, that view of government was the dominant view among economists.

The other view, which developed largely in the middle to the end of the twentieth century, has a less sanguine perspective on government. This other view extends the traditional economic view of individuals as rational, self-interested and maximizing their own well-being into their public sector activity, whether as elected officials, civil servants, or citizens.

As you might expect, the two approaches lead to very different conclusions. The benevolent dictator or good public servant model suggests that governments will attempt to determine what citizens want and what they are willing to pay, and will model their policies on that basis. The second view suggests that public officials, elected or appointed, will pursue their own interests and only serve the perceived interest of the public to the extent necessary to retain power. The relatively new field of behavioral economics finds that human motivation is more multi-dimensional and human behavior is often less rational than economists might expect. So perhaps the truth lies somewhere in between.

In the past three decades an extensive economic literature has grown up attesting to the problems of government failure and the challenges of making good decisions in the public sector. Much of this literature crosses the boundaries between economics and political science in order to look at the interaction between the institutions of government, the self-interested behavior of individuals in both the public and private sectors, and market or quasi-market forces. The intersection of markets, self-interested and public-spirited individuals, and governments determines what government produces, directly or indirectly, and how the responsibility for paying for that production is distributed.

This chapter has two aims:

1   to explore how decisions are made in the public sector and how that process is similar to and different from the private sector, and
2   to explore some of the dimensions of and possible remedies for the problem of government failure.

Differences between the public and private sectors

There are five important differences between the private sector and the public sector that can make the public sector less efficient and less responsive than the market:

1   Much of public sector production is designed for collective rather than individual consumption, so clear price signals are lacking.
2   Unlike the market, the public sector has no clear residual claimant for the surplus or deficit (profit or loss).
3   The incentives facing public officials are different from those facing managers in private for-profit firms.
4   It is difficult to get "consumers" (citizens) to clearly reveal their preferences.
5   It is harder to measure and value output in the public sector.

These five properties of public sector production, taken together, often result in poor communication from citizens and lack of responsiveness from public officials and bureaucrats. When government officials either don't know or don't care what citizens want, there is a problem of **government failure**. If market failure means that the market fails to provide the socially optimal level and combination of output, government failure in turn means that intervention designed to correct market failure can either fail to provide better results or actually provide worse results than the private market. Understanding these unique features of government production identified above should provide some insight into the problem of government failure.

Collective versus individual consumption

Some goods are private goods. They are consumed exclusively by one person or household. Think of shoes, sandwiches, skateboards, and sandpaper. If one person is using, eating, or wearing that item, it is not available to another person. Other goods may be shared, like highways, buses, parks, or concerts. More than one person can consume the same good at the same time without reducing the consumption of others, at least to the point of congestion. The difference between public and private goods is described in greater detail in Chapter 6, but the important issue for right now is that collective consumption does not lend itself to payment for services in the way that private goods do.

The challenge is how to apportion the cost among the users. The most common solution is to charge a single price for access to the collective good, and let all those who value it at least that much have access to it. But this solution is likely to be inefficient. If the price is greater than zero while the marginal cost of another user is zero, the amount consumed will fall short of the optimal level. Potential users will be excluded even though the cost of serving more users is zero. So the more common solution is to levy taxes on everyone, based on some measure of ability to pay, and use that revenue to pay for public goods for everyone, whether they consume them or not. The link between payment and product or service characteristic of private market is broken.

Lack of a residual claimant

The presence of a **residual claimant**—a person or group that is entitled to what is left over from revenue after costs have been paid—is an important part of what makes the private market work. In a privately owned company, the hope of profit or fear of loss puts pressure on entrepreneurs, owners and managers to improve their responsiveness to consumers and their efficiency in using resources. If their prices or costs are too high or their product is of poor quality or not responsive to changing consumer tastes, those bad decisions will be reflected in the company's bottom line. In a company whose stock is publicly traded, the pressure for profit comes from stockholders (especially large stockholders or institutional investors), who are likely to throw out the management if performance is poor. Or the pressure may come from other companies who seek to acquire a firm when its stock is cheap because of poor past performance, hoping to shape it up and resell it at a profit.

Public sector managers, along with managers of nonprofit organizations, rarely have such clear-cut measures of success or failure or such immediate and direct pressures for efficient performance as managers of private firms. The only stockholders are the citizens, and their interest, knowledge, and involvement are generally very diffused. Public agencies do not usually sell their product or services; their revenue stream comes from appropriations and is not tied directly to product quality, output levels, or customer satisfaction. If an agency runs a surplus, its budget is likely to be cut the following year, so there is a powerful incentive to spend it all before the end of the fiscal year!

Obviously, there are exceptions. City water and sewer managers, state park operators, ports authorities, the postal service, and other public agencies that sell their services directly to customers have to be somewhat attuned to customer needs, preferences, and complaints. But as a general rule, customers of the government—better known as citizens—find it more difficult to communicate effectively with or enforce responsiveness from their supplier of defense, law enforcement, and highways than it is to send clear signals to firms that provide them with food, clothing, and entertainment.

Bureaucrats and incentives

William Niskanen and other public choice economists have developed economic models of the behavior of bureaucrats that reflect this different environment (Niskanen 1971). **Public choice** is the area of economics (and political science) that addresses the processes by which decisions are made in the public sector. Typically, these public choice models begin by exploring the self-interested behavior of the bureaucrat.

Since the bureaucrat cannot enhance his or her well-being by making profits, Niskanen assumes that self-interested behavior will take the form of seeking more power and influence, perks and compensation, and opportunities for advancement in the bureaucracy. Such motivation would lead the bureaucrat to try to maximize his or her budget, number of employees, sphere of influence, and level of activity. Chances for success are greater when the "boss" is a large number of citizens with relatively little interest in any particular agency and no good channels of protest. The result is likely to be uncontrolled growth of government.

Other public choice economists, most notably James Buchanan, borrowed from sixteenth-century British philosopher Thomas Hobbes the name **Leviathan** for this tendency toward excessive growth of government. Leviathan, which was originally the name of a Babylonian sea monster, describes a monster—a monster that gobbles up resources and threatens our economic well-being. The debate over whether government is a Leviathan and what steps can be taken to bring it under control has been going on for several decades.

Behavioral economics: rational ignorance and revealed preference

But isn't the citizen the residual claimant—the one who benefits from any increases in efficiency? Yes, theoretically, but in practice, citizens often find that the costs of asserting their claims exceed the benefits. Citizens will free-ride on others. They may count on the Sierra Club, the Heritage Foundation, the League of Women Voters or other organized think tanks and citizen interest groups to do their homework for them. As a result, there is a lack of information conveyed from citizens to government.

The idea that there is a lack of effective communication about the desired size and scope of government activity follows logically from the self-interested model of citizen/voter behavior. Citizens are more likely to get involved in the political process—vote, lobby, make campaign contributions, even run for office—when they are affected immediately and substantially by a policy decision. Citizens for whom the effect of a proposed policy is modest or inconsequential are much less likely to get involved, because the cost of their efforts is greater than the benefits they will receive. The economist's model of self-interested behavior suggests that a democratic society is likely to suffer from voter apathy. Public choice economists have labeled the intentional lack of effort and involvement by voters **rational ignorance**.

Voters not only choose not to participate but also to avoid making the effort to acquire the information needed in order to participate intelligently in the political process. Rational ignorance is a choice based on weighing the costs of acquiring and acting on relevant information versus the expected benefits. Most people, consciously or not, choose to be rationally ignorant about many aspects of their lives from purchasing pencils to knowing the ingredients of foods to auto safety.

In some cases, they are engaging in a form of free-riding behavior, assuming that enough other consumers have checked the prices of pencils, the crash safety reports on cars, and the fat content of food. Alternatively, citizens may be assuming that government agencies are at least monitoring private activity to ensure auto and food safety. But in both public and private decisions, there is a choice about the amount of effort to invest in acquiring and processing information about all kinds of decisions. For public sector decisions, the benefit to an individual citizen/voter from being better informed is often very small relative to the cost or effort.

Rational ignorance has been a very fruitful hypothesis in explaining some forms of government failure. Rational ignorance makes it more likely that a policy with overall costs that exceed benefits can nevertheless be enacted if the benefits are immediate and concentrated on a small number of citizens, while the costs are either delayed or diffused thinly among a large number of citizens. A new missile system is of immediate interest to defense contractors, their employees, and the communities in which their facilities are located. With more than 300 million Americans, even a $3 billion price tag comes to only $10 per citizen, hardly enough for most people to go to the effort of becoming informed and writing to their member of Congress. Even if the sum of the costs exceeds the value of the benefits, such a policy is likely to win simply because the intensity of preference among the few big gainers swamps the apathy of the many small losers.

Is there no hope that public policy will ever reflect citizen preferences? Fortunately, there are some forces countering the harmful effects of rational ignorance. In many cases, there is a counter-coalition of those whose feelings or valuations are equally intense in the opposite direction. The anti-missile coalition could include groups trying to divert military funding to other projects as well as pacifists and even groups covertly supported by foreign governments. Whatever the issue, there is always the potential to mobilize a group strongly in favor and a group strongly opposed and to pit them against one another in a battle for money and votes fought with letters, lobbyists, position papers, and campaign contributions. The outcome may fall short of optimal, but the clash of coalitions will usually push the outcome toward the middle rather than the extremes.

In addition to apathy, citizens have another problem. They have no incentive to truthfully reveal their preferences about public goods. Suppose that citizens think that the price they will be expected to pay individually will be based on the value that they admit the good has for them, i.e., their marginal benefit. Then they will actually have an incentive to hide their true demand in order to increase their opportunity to use the public good without contributing much (if anything) to its cost. This self-interested behavior of citizens gives the impression of less demand than actually exists, so the public good may be under-produced.

In private transactions, citizens reveal their preferences by the prices they are willing to pay and the quantities they choose to purchase. In the public sector, even if voters choose to be truthful, they still must send these signals through indirect methods: voting, lobbying, responding to polls, and campaign contributions. None of these methods are very effective as far as letting policy-makers know what people think about specific programs or services. Voting is primarily for candidates, and each candidate represents a "package" of positions rather than a specific choice about a new missile system or single-payer health care. Lobbying represents the most intense preferences, but rarely the most numerous—the vocal minority is heard, while the silent majority is not. Polls are sometimes a useful technique, but it is difficult to elicit clear responses to complex questions about resource allocation by this method. Campaign contributions, like lobbying, give a louder voice to the minority who benefit most directly.

The problem of revealed preference is compounded by those governments that are not bound by a balanced budget constraint. If governments can borrow to finance current operations rather than collect taxes and fees, the opposite error will occur, and public goods will be overproduced. If citizens are doing even a rudimentary job of balancing costs and benefits, but the benefits are immediate and the costs are deferred, they are likely to demand too much in the way of public production.

Measuring and valuing output

As already noted, most of the services provided in the public sector are financed partially or entirely from taxes or general revenue rather than by specific payments from users. This lack of direct payment makes it difficult to measure and value output. How much would people have purchased if they were confronted with a price and a choice? It is not possible to answer that question for goods and services with a strong element of collective consumption, or goods with substantial social benefits.

There are three measures of production in the public sector that are used for various purposes. One is inputs, or the cost of producing goods and services in the public sector. This set of numbers is used to value public sector output in the national income accounts. It does not measure consumption, or the value of that production to citizens.

These inputs are used to produce intermediate and final outputs. Intermediate outputs measure activities—streets patrolled, students attending, park visitors, prison inmate days, etc. Intermediate outputs cannot be priced and valued either, because they are not sold, but they at least provide a quantitative measure for comparison purposes. For example, one state can be compared to another in terms of prison expenditures per inmate day to see if costs are unusually high or low for some reason.

Final outputs represent what citizens want—educated children, safety, clean water, a prompt and responsive police and fire department, a reasonable travel time and travel access between locations. These final outputs represent the purpose of public sector production, but they are also the most difficult to measure. Water quality is testable. Students' test scores are at least a partial indicator of what the public schools are doing, as are employer satisfaction surveys of the performance of graduates of public high schools and technical colleges. Insurance ratings give some measure of the quality of a local government's fire department.

But all of these measures are just indicators of performance that cannot be added in the way that prices and quantities in the private sector can be totaled. Evidence of satisfaction or dissatisfaction with public production is difficult to obtain and interpret, making it even more difficult for policy-makers to make good choices about how to allocate public sector resources.

Voting and public choice

Citizens have many ways to try to influence or convey their desires to public officials. They can lobby, individually or as part of organized interest groups, writing letters, providing information, offering persuasive arguments, and helping draft legislation. They can make campaign contributions. Running for public office is very expensive, especially at the federal level, and politicians are inclined to listen more closely to those big contributors whose resources they will need to tap in the next election.

Because voting is the most widely available method for influencing public officials, economists have paid a great deal of attention to voting: why people vote, how people vote, how different voting schema influence outcomes, and how voting might be better designed to convey more precise information. The study of voting is one of several areas where economists and political scientists meet. The classic study of the economic dimensions of voting and voting systems is *The Calculus of Consent* (Buchanan and Tullock 1962), which provided a foundation for many later studies of the role of voting in public sector decision-making.

One person, one vote

Voting is usually done on the basis of one person, one vote, whether it is to elect a mayor or Member of Congress, pass a referendum or vote on a new ordinance in a city council. This system has the attraction of equality among citizens.

People "voting" on what goods and services to produce in the private sector have very unequal amounts of dollars with which to vote. In the public sector, however, each citizen is endowed with exactly the same amount of voting power, although income inequality still means unequal ability to influence the political process through lobbying and campaign contributions. However, equal numbers of votes do not necessarily produce "better" outcomes. People with equal voting rights often have different intensities of preferences, but those people who feel more strongly cannot buy an extra vote to cast. The most they can do is to try to influence the outcome with campaign contributions and/or efforts to convince others to vote the same way.

Ranking preferences, inconsistent results, and the voting paradox

Either/or, up/down, yes–no voting takes place on issues as well as candidates, and with similar ambiguous results. One famous demonstration of how such bilateral/polar choices give dubious results was spelled out by Nobel prize-winning economist Kenneth Arrow. Arrow posed an interesting challenge to public sector decision-making by way of voting, namely that in a group of three or more options there may be no clear-cut first choice—a demonstration known as the **voting paradox**. Consider the simplified situation in Table 4.1 involving three voters (or equal-sized groups of voters) contemplating three options for spending $1 million in Central City, USA, with their preference ranking for the three options:

Table 4.1 The voting paradox 1

Group/option	Children's park	Fire station	Road improvements
A	1	2	3
B	2	3	1
C	3	1	2

Suppose that voters are asked to choose between the children's park and the fire station. A and B vote for the park, C for the fire station, and the park wins. Suppose, however, that the choice is between the park and the potholes. Voters B and C vote for road improvements, A for the park, and the potholes win. Finally, suppose voters get to choose between the fire station and road improvements. Voters A and C vote for the fire station and B for the road improvements. It appears that the park is preferred to the fire station, the fire station is preferred to the road improvements, and the road improvements are preferred to the park! You may have learned in either mathematics or logic that such a rank ordering violates the transitivity principle, which states that if A>B and B>C (or in this case, A is preferred to B and B is preferred to C), then A>C (A is preferred to C).

What this example points to is the difficulty in making efficient and responsive public sector decisions through simple voting. The problem with simple yes–no, either–or voting is that there is no way of measuring the intensity of those preferences. Voter A may strongly prefer a park to any alternative. Voter B may weight the park and road improvements almost equally with no interest in a fire station. Voter C may be largely indifferent with all three options being moderately attractive but the fire station just barely edging out the other two on his preference scale. A simple yes–no, either–or vote does not convey the same wealth of information as prices offered and accepted, quantities bought and sold in the private marketplace.

There is a second lesson in this model as well, which is the importance of controlling the agenda. If the city manager's preference is for the park, she will make sure that it is matched against the fire station in the budget deliberations, while the road improvements are not listed among the options. By excluding certain choices from the set under consideration, there appears to be a clear preference among voters or the city council for the park option when in fact the outcome would be different if the choices were paired differently.

Parties and platforms

While many countries have multiple political parties and form coalition governments, the United States has historically had two major parties and a series of minor ones that have had relatively little impact. Parties have platforms, or sets of positions on a variety of policy issues ranging from abortion and school choice to tax reform and trade policy. With only two major parties, each party must design its platform to appeal to a broad spectrum of voters.

Voters, in turn, have to buy package deals—much like going to the supermarket and being offered a choice between two pre-filled grocery carts with a different mix of foods in each. A two-party system is a classic case of the **duopoly** model in microeconomic theory, a special case of oligopoly with only two suppliers.

There are a number of models of duopoly in economic literature, but one in particular that is relevant to the political system. Consider the owner of two mobile refreshment stands along a mile of beachfront. The sole owner would locate them strategically ¼ of a mile from each end of the mile-long stretch. But suppose that, tired of operating two refreshment stands, the owner sold one of his franchises to a competitor. Now there is a duopoly—a market supplied by only two firms. The refreshment stand on the north end of the beach has the exclusive custom of all the surfers to the north of her stand; the only way to increase patronage is to move toward the middle and capture more customers to the south. The owner of the refreshment stand on the south end reasons the same way. Over time, the two migrate to the center, side by side.

So do political parties. When there are only two parties, one of two things happens. In some cases the far end of the beach controls the nomination for one or both parties, so that the nominee is farther from rather than closer to the center of the political beach. But many times, both parties will wind up very close to the center of the distribution of preferences among citizens. These two parties are both trying to capture the populous center while holding on to their fringes in each direction who have no viable alternative. Both are in search of the median voter.

The median voter model

If government cannot be precise in assigning costs and benefits to citizens, and if voting is a clumsy form of communication, is there a usable substitute? One useful model of how communication occurs, one with good predictive power in terms of the behavior of both citizens and politicians, is based on the concept of the **median voter model**. The median voter is not the median citizen or resident. Public officials are responsive primarily to those who participate in the political process. They vote, they contribute to campaigns, they lobby, they write letters. The median voter, then, is the person right at the center of the distribution of preferences among that subset of people who will actually go to the polls and who must therefore be courted by politicians seeking election.

The median voter probably represents a different person or collection of persons on different issues. The median voter also probably doesn't have a median income or a median family size. Younger people, both single and married, with or without children, are less likely to vote and therefore are underrepresented in determining the preferences of the median voter. Older people, particularly retired, are generally overrepresented because they are more likely to vote.

The median voter is also a moving target. People's preferences change as their incomes change, as they have children, children grow up, they retire. Preferences also change in response to external stimuli of both information and persuasion. Another source of change is the influence of different cohorts of people born in different decades as they move into the voting population. The "young-old" (60–70) of the last decade were born during the Great Depression and grew up in the 1940s, periods of economic and social and political upheaval. The Baby Boomers, a very large cohort born between 1946 and 1964, began to exert influence through their parents from the time they were born. From the late 1970s until well into the twenty-first century, the boomers have been and will continue to be a dominant share of the voting population. They now range in age from mid-30s to mid-50s, and are particularly concerned about issues that impact on their lives, ranging from child care to health care to retirement and the future of Social Security.

The distribution of preferences

This notion of a distribution of preferences rather than an either–or, yes–no, polar choice mirrors what occurs in the private sector, where people choose houses of different sizes, clothing in various quantities and qualities, and trade off between hamburger and steak, beef and chicken. In the public sector, the choice is often not simply park/no park, but what kind, what size, what location, how much to spend on improvements and facilities.

You are probably familiar with the normal distribution—also known as "the curve" when it comes to grading student performance. If people's preferences are normally distributed, as in Figures 4.1 and 4.2, then most people are clustered around the middle of the distribution. The vertical axis, F(x), measures the number of people whose preference lies at that point on the horizontal axis. The median voter is the person who lies at the peak of the distribution, i.e., at the x-bar. The horizontal axis may represent the quantity of the public good in dollars, space, or capacity, or it may represent some other measurable attribute of the public good.

In Figures 4.1 and 4.2, the horizontal axis represents dollars spent on park acquisition and improvements. There are a few people at one end of the distribution who want very little spending on parks, and a few on the other end who want a lot, but most voters are clustered toward the middle, balancing their tax burden and their desire for parks.

In order to be elected and re-elected, public officials need the support of at least 50 percent of the voters. The easiest way to get that support is to concentrate on that large block of voters who are found within one standard deviation (sigma) either side of the mean. In a normal distribution, the mean plus or minus one standard deviation will include about ⅔ of

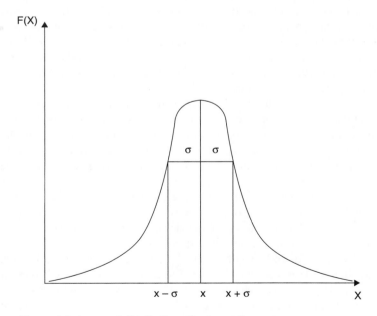

Figure 4.1 A normal distribution of voter preferences.

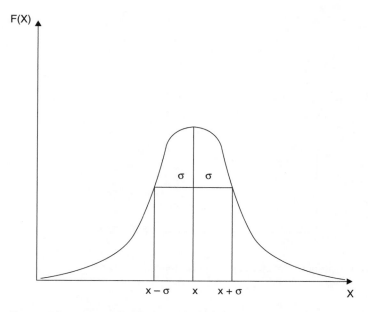

Figure 4.2 A normal distribution with a larger standard deviation.

all voters, a solid majority. So a key element in the signaling of preferences from voters to politicians and bureaucrats is to pinpoint that center of the distribution and aim close to it.

Politicians will attempt to locate the median voter through polling, focus groups, meetings with constituents and other methods. Voters who are outside that center of the distribution will attempt to muddy the waters through letter-writing campaigns, turning up in large numbers at meetings, and other methods. The purpose of all this activity is to convince elected officials that the mean of the distribution is in fact quite far to the right (or left) of where it actually is.

Normal distributed may be fairly sharply peaked with a small standard deviation, as in Figure 4.1, or rather flat with a large standard deviation, as in Figure 4.2. In Figure 4.1, it is easy for politicians to obtain a stable majority of support for the middle-of-the road position, because so many voters are tightly clustered around the mean. In Figure 4.2, the majority will include more voters whose preferences are somewhat farther from the mean and who will be more dissatisfied with the outcome—too much or too little spending on parks.

Other distributions

Not all preferences are distributed according to the normal distribution, or bell curve. Figures 4.3 and 4.4 show two of the many possible alternative distributions. Figure 4.3 is a one-tailed distribution with a peak near the origin (known as a Poisson distribution). Again, the x-axis represents desired spending on parks, while the vertical axis represents the percentage of all citizens wanting to spend a particular amount. This distribution of preferences suggests that that most citizens want to spend very little on a park. There is a tail to the right of people who strongly support spending on parks, but the strong majority is clustered closer to the origin.

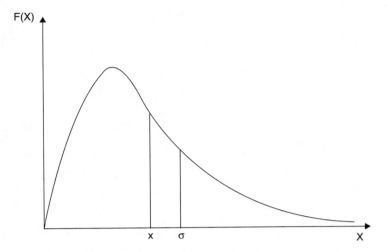

Figure 4.3 A Poisson distribution of citizen preferences for park spending.

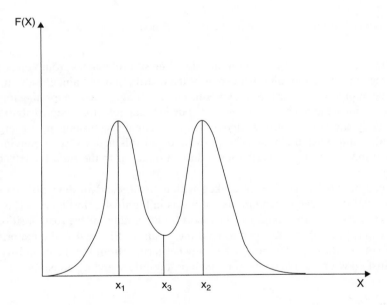

Figure 4.4 A bimodal distribution of preferences for park spending.

Figure 4.4, which shows a real challenge to politicians, is one that often occurs—a bimodal distribution. In this case the median voter lies between the peaks. One peak consists of a large and vocal group of voters who want very little spending on parks (clustered around spending level x_1). The other peak reflects a second, equally large and vocal group, who wants more parks, bigger parks, better parks (clustered around spending level x_3).

Satisfying the median voter, who is at x_2, will leave the great majority of the population dissatisfied. This situation has occurred in disputes over public school spending in areas with large populations of retirees. In at least one instance, steps had to be taken to exclude a retirement community from the school district in order to pass a bond referendum to meet the urgent demands of families with children.

With a bimodal distribution, it is difficult to find satisfactory compromises. Campaigns to change tastes and preferences (often disguised as "educational" campaigns) are often focused on issues for which the distribution of voter preferences is bimodal. Sometimes these campaigns center around finding common ground. Other times they are addressed at moving a critical mass of voters from one group to the other to create a working majority clustered around one of the two poles. Still a third strategy is to refocus the question. Instead of park spending in general, suppose that the issue is more narrowly defined as recreational opportunities for all age groups. Alternatively, the focus may be on parks as part of a plan for green space, which would enhance the attractiveness of the community and increase property values even for citizens not interested in the parks for recreational purposes. Each time the question is redefined, citizens will distribute themselves a little differently along the continuum.

If the distribution of preferences is normal, and the government manages to satisfy the preferences of the median voter, would the results pass the test of economic efficiency or Pareto optimality? Probably not. Recall that the efficiency test in microeconomic theory requires that the marginal tax price paid by the buyer be equal to the marginal benefit received from the last unit of the public good. But in a society in which income is distributed unequally, the median voter is likely to have less than the median income. If tax prices are allocated (as they most often are) in proportion to income, then the marginal tax price for the median voter is less than it is for the citizen/voter with the median income. If the median voter and the person with the median income have the same preferences, the median voter will demand a higher level of public production/provision of services than the citizen with the median income, because his or her marginal tax price is lower.

Taken by itself, this model implies that government production or provision of goods will in general exceed the socially optimal level. Of course, if wealthier citizens are able to impress elected officials more strongly with their preferences because of their campaign contributions or hired lobbyists, they could turn the tide in the opposite direction. Alternatively, if the demand for public services rises with income levels, then the median voter will have both a higher marginal tax price and a higher quantity of public services demanded than the person with the median income.

Behavioral economics and public choice

The models derived from a public choice perspective operate on the basic model of *Homo economicus* described in Chapter 1, transporting that autonomous, self-interested individual into the public sector to engage in the same rational, maximizing behavior that serves his or her needs as a private citizen. But psychology and sociology suggest that people are more complex than that model implies, both in their motivation and in their cognition, or thought processes. Humans are social animals, responding to social norms and expectations, as well as the desire to meet their own needs and wants.

There have been numerous studies of the degree of altruistic behavior in laboratory settings with mixed results. At least some of these studies suggest that concern for the welfare of others is a part of our complex psychological makeup. Not wishing to bear the cost of public goods and services and redistribution alone, the government is often perceived as the best available means to address that concern, however imperfect the process and/or the outcomes. Citizens may also be motivated to engage in public policy debates not merely out of narrow self-interest but also out of genuine concern for the impact on the society in which they live.

Human beings are also subject to limitations in their ability to acquire and process relevant information, especially about complex public issues. Both citizens and policy-makers are influenced by framing, or the way an issue is presented, that may lead to choices that might have gone differently if the matter was framed in a different way. Think about "welfare queens," the phrase "death tax" instead of the more neutral "estate tax," and emotional appeals about "our children are our future" used to support requests for more education funding. All of these techniques and other catch phrases influence how we respond to the informational content of a speech or document.

The failure to clearly reveal their preferences is not merely a strategy by voters to avoid being taxed, but also an inability to articulate those preferences in the face of bewildering and complex choices. Rational ignorance is a choice made in the face of limited time and information, even though the internet has made information more accessible and participation in the political process much faster and simpler. It is certainly true that those who stand to gain or lose the most from a particular government action will be more vocal and more involved in trying to influence the outcome. But there are also organized public interest groups that reduce the cost of participation on issues of particular interest to scattered citizens, giving them voice and visibility at relatively low cost per participant.

Addressing the problem of government failure

Even if people are not all rational actors in matters of public policy, the insights of public choice economics over the past 35 years have nevertheless made it clear that government intervention in cases of market failure will not always improve outcomes and may, in fact, result in less efficient allocation of resources. Public choice economists believe that the error is most likely to take the form of excess production of public goods and other government services relative to the socially optimal level, either because of the problem just described, or because of the incentives facing politicians and bureaucrats, or because of rational ignorance on the part of voters.

This conclusion does not mean that government should be eliminated in favor of anarchy. Rather, public choice economics, combined with practical innovations in the past two decades, have pointed out some ways in which government's role in the economy can be made both more constructive and less inefficient. Among the proposed and actual strategies for increasing the efficiency and responsiveness of government decision-making are privatization and devolution, balancing rules versus discretion, and making more decisions through direct citizen participation making via town meetings, initiative, and referenda. All of these strategies involve either increasing the use of market incentives, providing more effective channels of citizen participation, or both.

Privatization

The many privatization initiatives of the past 30 years are one response to government failure. From the Great Depression of the 1930s through the late 1970s there was a steady expansion in both the size and scope of government activity at all levels. Some of the activities undertaken by government lend themselves to private production or at least private provision. For those activities, there is an opportunity to use the beneficial effects of market prices, competition, and the profit motive to ensure that suppliers are listening to their customers in more effective ways than bureaucrats and politicians are able (or willing) to do.

Devolution

Devolution is another trend of the past 30 years. Devolution means shifting responsibility for providing (and sometimes financing) certain government activities from the central government to state and/or local governments. Where there are no significant externalities involved (with costs or benefits spilling over to adjacent jurisdictions), there can be some real efficiency gains from placing the provision and financing of services at the lowest possible level of government.

These gains come from two sources. First of all, with smaller numbers, there is less rational ignorance or free-riding on the revealed preferences of others. One person's participation or failure to participate, whether in voting or in contributing to the cost of a local public good, will make a measurable difference. It is also easier for citizens to convey their opinions and preferences (lower signaling costs).

Second, many small, competing jurisdictions rather than a few large ones make it more likely that preferences will be more homogeneous within each jurisdiction. People will be attracted to communities offering the mix and level of services that they prefer, as described by the Tiebout hypothesis discussed in Chapter 3. The distribution of tastes and preferences for smaller communities tends to look more like Figure 4.1 than Figure 4.2. Because people have had an opportunity to select from several residential locations offering alternative features, including local tax levels and services, there will be fewer citizens whose preferred packages of public services are far from the mean. In any normal distribution of preferences, the mean plus and minus one standard deviation will always contain about ⅔ of the citizens, but the size of the standard deviation (i.e. the degree to which the not-quite-average citizen is dissatisfied) can vary greatly from one normal distribution to another.

Rules versus discretion

Yet another response to government failure is to limit the discretionary authority of both elected officials (politicians) and appointed or civil service government workers (bureaucrats). Many rules have been passed which tie the hands of judges (truth in sentencing), future legislatures and city councils (tax and spending limitations), regulatory agencies (the ban on cancer-causing substances), and the executive branch (requiring 49 of the 50 governors to submit a balanced budget). When the federal budget deficit was large, there was considerable pressure to add an amendment to the US Constitution requiring a balanced budget.

The advantage of rules is that they offer certainty for the citizen, the business firm, and the politician. Rules make it easier to make difficult or unpopular decisions, pointing to the rule as limiting one's ability to make the decision being sought. Rules make it harder for big contributors or organized lobbies to use the government for their own purposes. Rules can be effective in slowing the growth of government beyond the optimal level.

The drawback of rules is that they make no allowance for special circumstances. Jails are full of first-time drug offenders caught in the wave of mandatory sentencing laws. Improved ability to detect carcinogens has made the Congressional ban on cancer-causing substances a formidable barrier to development of new pharmaceuticals and processed foods. An unbalanced budget as a temporary measure might be the wisest policy in a catastrophe, a war, or a major depression. Economists would like to see us weigh the costs and benefits and balance at the margin for every question. Rules rarely allow such balancing processes to happen.

Citizen decision-making

Finally, there are still places where citizens are directly involved in making decisions—about legislation, about budgets, about rules. One form of direct citizen decision-making is the town meeting, still popular in New England's small towns but also used in other places. Annual (or special) town meetings may approve the budget, approve ordinances, and take other actions, leaving the local governing body (the city council or board of selectmen) to run the town's affairs between meetings. The use of town meetings has not increased, but it does provide an effective channel of communication between voters and elected officials in a small town setting.

The other forms of citizen decision-making that are in fairly widespread use are initiative and referendum, both of which have seen increased use in recent decades. **Initiatives** place issues on the ballot at the request of a group of citizens, usually with some minimum number of signatures. Initiative is not an option in every state, and only a few states use it freely. California's numerous citizen initiatives have dealt with such hot-button issues as second-hand smoke, ending affirmative action, and most famous of all, Proposition 13 limiting the property tax.

A referendum is a question referred to the voters by the state legislature or other governing body. Referenda frequently deal with fundamental questions such as changing the state constitution or approving bond issues, although less weighty matters can appear on the ballot as well. Some referenda are binding, others advisory. In a system of representative government most decisions are still made by politicians and bureaucrats, but initiatives and referenda do offer an alternative form of expression of citizen preferences.

Summary

- Significant differences between the public and private sectors include collective rather than individual consumption of much of its production, bureaucratic incentives, the lack of a residual claimant, the difficulty of getting "consumers" (citizens) to clearly reveal their preferences, and problems of measuring and valuing output. When government production/provision of goods and services deviates substantially from the socially optimal level and mixture, there is government failure.
- Incentives facing politicians, bureaucrats, and citizens lead to excessive government spending and poor signals about citizen preferences or demand. The existence of a residual claimant to any surplus provides a measure of success or failure and/or a monetary system of reward and punishment that are the driving forces for self-interested individuals in the private sector to be responsive to the preferences of their customers.
- Self-interested behavior of voters tends to result in low participation in the political system because of rational ignorance. Voters only get involved if they have a direct, immediate, personal interest at stake. Government actions are likely to benefit the few at the expense of the many. Sometimes countervailing forces will check this tendency as lobbyists on opposite sides of an issue force the outcome toward the middle.

- Signals are also unclear because of collective consumption and the opportunity to free-ride. Voters may conceal their true preferences in order to escape paying for a good that they hope to be able to consume without contributing.
- One person, one vote does not take account of different intensity of preferences among voters. Single-member districts and winner-take-all systems also limit the ability to translate voter preferences into a representative elected body.
- The Arrow impossibility theorem demonstrates that it is possible for each of three (or more) alternatives to be selected depending on the way they are paired in an either–or choice. This theorem not only points to the difficulty of making such choices for collective consumption but also highlights the role of agenda-setting in determining outcomes.
- A two-party system shares some of the characteristics of duopoly in the private sector in that both parties aim at the center of the distribution of voters and offer very similar platforms and programs.
- The median voter model offers an explanation of how politicians seek voter support in their positions on issues and their votes on legislation. The median voter is the one at the center of a distribution of tastes and preferences of those who are actually likely to vote, a subset of the larger population.
- Possible solutions to the problem of government failure include privatization and devolution, relying on rules rather than discretion, and expanding the role of citizen participation in decisions.

Key terms

Devolution
Duopoly
Government failure
Initiative
Leviathan
Median voter model
Public choice
Rational ignorance
Referendum
Residual claimant
Voting paradox

Questions

1   Suppose that your class has the opportunity to vote on the format of an exam. The options are multiple choice, essay, or a combination of the two. Suggest at least two voting schemes to make this decision and evaluate the advantages and drawbacks of each.
2   You are an elected official who is up for re-election. How is your strategy likely to differ on a particular issue for the four different preference distributions in the median voter graphs in this chapter (Figures 4.1–4.4), steep normal, flat normal, Poisson, and bimodal?
3   Why and how is government likely to fail? What can citizens (or writers of constitutions, or even politicians) do to minimize government failure?

4   **By the numbers**. Suppose that the voting population consists of 5,000 people. The median voter would like to have a police budget of $650,000. The standard deviation is $50,000. You support a policy budget of $600,000. What percentage of voters are with you on that decision? (Hint: 66 percent of the population is within one standard deviation of the mean and 95 percent of the population is within two standard deviations of the mean, so your supporters fall within two standard deviations to the left and one standard deviation to the right.) How would your answer be different if the standard deviation was only $15,000?

5   **Policy application**. What happens to the voting paradox when there are more choices and/or more voters or voting groups? Try a simple experiment. Add to the table of preferences (Table 4.1) a fourth choice, new school buses, with the same three voters or groups of voters (Table 4.2)

Table 4.2 The voting paradox 2

Group/Option	Children's park	Fire station	Road improvements	School buses
A	1	2	3	4
B	2	3	4	1
C	3	4	1	2

Is there now a clear dominant choice, or a clear rejection, i.e. one choice that loses in any pairwise comparison? What do you think would happen if you increased the number of voters while holding the array of choices the same?

6   **Behavioral economics**. What kind of behavioral model of public officials suggests that they respond to incentives in ways that are not consistent with the desires and preferences of voters? What kind of behavior by voters might make it more likely that public officials will be more responsive to signals from voters?

7   **Thinking globally**. While the United States has a separation of powers between the Congress and the Executive Branch, elected separately for terms of different lengths, many other countries do not. In many countries the prime minister is a member of the legislative body, and so are the members of his cabinet. How might such an arrangement make the problem of responsiveness to the preferences of voters weaker or stronger?

5 Equity, income distribution, and the social safety net

Introduction

For economists, the two desired outcomes of market and government activity are efficiency and equity. The next two chapters will concentrate heavily on efficiency, or the allocation of resources among competing uses so as to obtain a given level of output (or utility, or satisfaction) at the least cost.[1] Efficiency is a more or less positive or objective idea that often, but not always, lends itself to measurement and evaluation by agreed-on standards.

Equity, however, is openly normative in nature. Equity means "fairness" in the distribution of wealth, income, and resources. Equity does not mean simple equality, but in a society in which resources are distributed very unequally, a movement toward less inequality is generally interpreted as a move in the direction of equity. Such movements can occur through market forces, private voluntary redistribution, or government, but the major player in redistribution is usually government.

While markets get high marks for efficiency, they do not perform as well on most measures of equity. The distribution of income and wealth that results purely from market processes tends to be highly unequal. Most societies expect their governments to make at least some effort to address that inequality, with a focus on the alleviation of poverty and its effects rather than on simply reducing inequality by taking from the rich and giving to the poor in some form.

Government is inherently redistributive

Redistribution through government does not simply consist of taking money in the form of taxes from the rich and giving it either in cash or in services to the poor. Everything the government does is redistributive, and much of that redistribution does not benefit the poor and needy. Corporate handouts, farm subsidies, special tax breaks for some of the rich, and tax structures that favor the voting majority in the middle class are among those other kinds of redistribution.

Think about any government program and ask yourself who pays for it and who benefits from it. Rarely do the two match one-for-one, except in the case of a fee for service operation, like Amtrak or the Post Office (and even these services involve redistributive effects). Suppose that the Corps of Engineers develops a new recreational lake facility in Missouri that also provides flood control and hydroelectric power. The initial cost is paid with federal funds. Operating costs come from the federal and state governments, revenues from the electricity wholesaler, and recreational user fees.

Where is the redistribution? Taxes come from citizens across the country and are levied unequally according to various measures of ability to pay (income, family size, wages, etc.).

Benefits go to local landowners in the form of increased property values (especially along the lake front) and reduced flood risk, to power customers who may experience lower costs per kilowatt hour, and to recreational users, most of whom live in Missouri.

But not everyone who lives in Missouri benefits equally. Missourians who fish, swim or sail for recreation benefit more than those who hunt, bowl, or play video games. Missouri residents who live closer to the lake benefit more than those farther away. Residents of Missouri and surrounding states who get electricity from this source benefit more if they use electricity for heating instead of oil or natural gas. Even in this relatively simple case, the distribution of costs and benefits is complex and difficult to track.

Redistribution is not limited to taxing and spending programs. Regulatory actions also redistribute income and wealth among citizens. Remember the controversy over logging in the habitat of the endangered spotted owl in the Pacific Northwest? Who were the gainers and losers (besides the spotted owls)? Loggers lost directly in terms of jobs. New home prices rose with the higher prices for lumber, affecting the construction industry as well as would-be home buyers. As new homes became more expensive, they pulled up the values of existing homes as well. Higher real estate values generated more commissions for realtors and more property tax dollars for local governments. Environmentalists gained in terms of achieving their desire to preserve not only spotted owls but also old-growth forests. Lawyers, as they often do, gained because of the demand for their services in extensive litigation.

Because government is such a powerful tool for redistributing income and wealth, it is always tempting for small, well-organized groups to attempt to use government for that purpose. Lobbying, campaign contributions, and media campaigns are often directed at pressuring either legislators or bureaucrats to make decisions that redistribute income and/or wealth in favor of particular groups. Being able to identify and quantify these redistributive effects is an important part of the function of a public policy analyst. This chapter, however, focuses on a subset of the redistributive activities of government for which the primary purpose is to create a more equitable distribution of income, resources, and/or opportunities.

Concepts of equity

Equity is rooted in the ethical concept of justice. Justice comes in three forms: distributive justice, retributive justice, and restorative justice. Distributive justice refers to access to the necessities of life, however defined. Distributive justice may involve a minimum income or access to certain services regardless of ability to pay. **Retributive justice** requires an appropriate penalty for engaging in actions considered harmful to others or to society. **Restorative justice** means making a person whole for harm or injury inflicted on them. Our focus in this chapter is primarily on distributive justice.

Economists find it difficult to formulate an acceptable definition of distributional equity because it would require interpersonal comparisons of utility. Ideally, a tax system would require equal sacrifice, not of dollars, but of utility from each citizen in order to support shared public services. If A is very poor and B is very rich, it seems reasonable that a smaller contribution from A and a larger contribution from B would meet this standard of equal sacrifice.

To simplify the equity question, suppose that, instead of taking $1 from A and $2 from B to finance a public service that A and B can share equally, the government simply takes a dollar from B and gives it to A. Is equity (and social welfare) increased, decreased, or unchanged by this action? If A is poor and B is rich, the initial response is to say that equity has increased, and that in the opposite case equity would have decreased. But to arrive at that judgment implies some comparison of the marginal utility of income (or wealth) between persons A and B.

In order to make such comparisons, some assumptions have to be made about whether income or wealth as a whole (as distinct from a particular kind of consumption) is subject to diminishing marginal utility, and whether the marginal utility declines at similar or different rates for different people. If the marginal utility of income declines as income rises, and does so at about the same rate for everyone, then a transfer from A to B would indeed increase utility, because the gain to B would be greater than the loss to A. But what if income or wealth is not subject to diminishing marginal utility?

Or suppose that A, while wealthier, also has a greater capacity to enjoy income due to her cultured tastes, while B is an ascetic with limited needs and wants. A's greater capacity for enjoying income could mean that the utility she sacrifices is greater than the utility B gains. In either case, there is nothing that can be said about net gains and losses in utility to society as a whole.

Yet another way to approach the question of equity is through the idea of **entitlement**. An entitlement is something for which we qualify or become eligible by meeting certain criteria. In the US Declaration of Independence, the entitlements (or inalienable rights) that Jefferson specified were "life, liberty, and the pursuit of happiness." Since that time, the concept of entitlement in the United States has included adequate food, shelter, education, and more or less health care. In other developed countries, entitlements are often both broader in scope and more generous in content.

Equity is a central issue in public sector economics and in public policy. It is at the heart of almost all economics policy debates. Is there a way out of this impasse that might make it possible to define equity? This question has engaged some of the best minds in economics in the past two centuries, resulting in some creative if not always definitive answers.

Rawls' theory of justice

Equity, fairness, and justice are all closely intertwined. Justice may be thought of as more structural in nature, the rules of society that determine the rights, privileges and obligations as well as the opportunities, income, and wealth that each of us is entitled to as a member of society. In his landmark 1971 book *A Theory of Justice*, John Rawls set forth a theoretical model for how those rules might be developed for a particular society (Rawls 1971). In his more recent work, *Political Liberalism*, Rawls answers some of his critics and extends his model (Rawls 1993). The rules that Rawls developed in both of these works that are of particular concern to public sector economics are those that pertain to distribution of resources, including income and wealth.

Suppose that you were given the charge to design a system to distribute opportunities, resources, and rewards among workers and non-workers, old and young, productive and unproductive, skilled and unskilled, without any prior knowledge of where you will find yourself in the system you have designed? Rawls described this decision framework in his earlier work as the **"veil of ignorance."** The reader is asked to think about how to design a system of incentives and rewards without knowing where he or she will be located in the system once it is in place.

As you might expect, the outcome of such a thought experiment is usually a system of rules and practices that provide more protection for those who find themselves most disadvantaged in a market system—those with few skills, little education, or other handicaps that affect their productivity. In particular, Rawls suggests that the rules of society that result from such an experiment are likely to reflect the "maximin principle" from game theory. The maximin principle is short for maximizing the value of the worst (minimum) outcome in the system.

In his later work, Rawls attempted to extend his theory to address the specific challenge of a pluralistic society. Markets are particularly efficient in addressing the diverse material needs of a pluralistic society, but the challenge Rawls attempted to address is that different values among different groups make it difficult to develop an agreed-on set of rules by which society should operate. Those different values among different groups are described by Rawls as "reasonable comprehensive doctrines" (Rawls 1993).

Rawls suggested that it would be necessary to identify the areas of agreement or overlapping consensus among those competing comprehensive doctrines (of the goals of society, or the nature of the good), and to base the rules for distribution of society's income, wealth, and opportunities on those areas of agreement. Among the areas of agreement that Rawls thought might emerge from such a process are some basic personal liberties guaranteed to all, and a set of rules that guaranteed equality of opportunity in competing for offices and positions with different rewards. In addition, Rawls believed (as in his earlier work) that any rules that allowed inequality in income and wealth must be designed so as to be of the greatest benefit to the least advantaged members of society.

While Rawls' philosophical system is more general than the specific distributional issues of concern to a modified market economy, it does raise some important questions about the existing distribution of income and wealth as well as the distribution of the increases in income and wealth that result from innovation, risk-taking, skill improvements, and other factors. These actions result in increased output per worker in a firm (micro) or economic growth (macro). How much of the additional income and wealth should go to those responsible for creating it as an efficiency incentive and how much should be shared with fellow workers and owners (micro) or with others in the economy (macro)? Rawls' notion of the veil of ignorance is also a useful way of thinking about proposals to modify reward and incentive systems for groups such as those retired on Social Security or welfare recipients being encouraged (or pressured) to find paid employment.

Horizontal equity

One partial answer to the dilemma of defining and measuring equity is the concept of **horizontal equity**, which means treating people alike if they are in the same or similar economic situations—making them pay the same taxes and/or providing them with the same public services. Implicit in the notion of horizontal equity is an assumption that people's capacity to enjoy income is similar, at least within a given range of incomes.

Economic situation does not simply mean income. It could include the concept of permanent or lifetime income rather than simply current annual income. It might take into account wealth, family size, age, or special circumstances such as disability or chronic health problems. As a result, a generally accepted measure of horizontal equity can be difficult to find. Instead, it is defined differently in specific contexts; charges for admission to national parks are by the carload, all income up to a certain level is taxed at the same rate, all children are entitled to 12 years of free public schooling. Much of the complexity in the federal income tax arises from attempts to define equal economic situations for purposes of horizontal equity.

Vertical equity

A second and even more challenging concept of equity is **vertical equity**. Vertical equity means treating people differently according to the differences in their income, wealth, or other measure of need or ability to pay. Vertical equity appears in many different contexts. Progressive income taxes, discussed in Chapter 13, are often justified on the basis of some concept of vertical equity. Vertical equity is also reflected in the use of **means testing** for many public programs, including free or reduced price school lunches, subsidized housing, and Medicaid. Property tax relief at the state and local level is also means-tested in many cases.

Means testing refers to determining eligibility for a public program or service on the basis of having an income that is less than some threshold level. Sometimes means-tested programs involve a threshold or a cutoff point. Subsidized child care, for example, might be available to households with incomes up to 150 percent of the poverty level. Once the family reaches that level, they are no longer eligible. Other programs gradually reduce the benefits as family income gets higher, and at the threshold level the benefit finally reaches zero.

One difficulty with using vertical equity as a guide to public policy is in measurement. How unequal should the treatment of people be in relation to their unequal ability to pay? In a famous work on the progressive income tax, a nineteenth-century economist argued that once we depart from the notion of proportionality in taxation "we are at sea without rudder or compass" (McCullough 1845). Does having twice as much income mean twice as much ability to pay taxes, or three times as much? Does a family of four with an income of less than $15,000 deserve food stamps, but the same family should no longer be entitled when their income reaches $15,001? Using cutoff income levels as a tool for vertical equity create notches in eligibility for benefits or services that create new inequities between those just under the notch and those just over the notch. Attempting to determine vertical equity also raises the serious problems discussed earlier that are associated with interpersonal comparisons of utility.

The compensation principle

Finally, a third route out of the thicket of interpersonal comparisons of utility lies in the theory of the second best and the compensation principle. Economists define Pareto optimality as a state in which no change can be made that makes some people better off without making at least one person worse off. (We will explore this concept further in Chapter 10.)

Strictly interpreted, the concept of Pareto optimality is heavily loaded in favor of the status quo. Most policy proposals—tax cuts, highway programs, sentencing guidelines, or almost anything you can imagine—will involve both winners and losers. A criterion of Pareto optimality would rule out such changes. The inability to make interpersonal comparisons of utility makes it very difficult to justify any policy change for which there are losers as well as gainers. Pareto optimality becomes a strong endorsement of the status quo, whatever that status quo happens to be.

Recognizing this problem, economists have searched for some criteria for policy decisions where Pareto optimality is not attainable. These criteria provide a guide to making "second-best" decisions. One of the most useful criteria is the **compensation principle**,[2] which offers a rough guide to choosing between alternative policies on the basis of which one does more to increase social welfare.

The principle goes something like this: If, in moving from state A to state B, the gainers from the move can compensate the losers for their losses and still be better off, then the move is desirable from the standpoint of total social welfare. Conversely, if those who lose by moving from state A to state B can bribe the gainers not to make the change and still have some welfare gain remaining, then the change should not be made.

Note that the compensation does not actually have to be paid. Actual compensation is a political rather than a theoretical question, whether the "bribe" is actually either required to get legislation passed (or other change approved) or desirable from the standpoint of income distribution (e.g., gainers are rich, losers are poor). And even if there is compensation, it doesn't necessarily have to be in cash. When the nuclear plant at Barnwell, South Carolina, was built to process nuclear weapons materials in the 1970s, the federal government helped to build a new town and relocate the people in the town of Ellington to that new site, now known as New Ellington. That kind of compensation comes closer to restorative than distributive justice.

The compensation principle has been particularly visible in trade policy. The gradual reduction of barriers to international trade throughout the mid- to late twentieth century benefited consumers and exporters at the expense of workers and owners in import-competing industries. Losers were compensated with trade adjustment assistance as well as gradual implementation of policy changes. (Gradual implementation of new policies, giving time to adjust, is one form of compensation.) But almost any proposal for spending or changing tax rules or choosing a site for a new prison or building a new highway creates both winners and losers. There is always an opportunity to negotiate compensation for at least some of the losers as a condition for persuading politicians to vote for such legislation.

Measuring inequality

While alleviating poverty has been a primary focus of government policy in redistribution, there are also concerns about the shape of the overall distribution of income. The most widely used measure of income distribution is the Lorenz curve, which shows the cumulative percentages of income accruing to various percentages of population. Usually the population is sorted into quintiles, or fifths, so the graph shows the percentage of income received by the lowest fifth (20 percent), the lowest two-fifths (40 percent), and so forth. If income were distributed with complete equality, the Lorenz curve would be the straight line from the origin to the northeast corner of the box. The greater the deviation of the actual curve from the diagonal line, the greater the degree of inequality.

Figure 5.1 shows the US income distribution in 2008. The lowest 20 percent of the population received only 3.4 percent of the income; the lowest 40 percent, 12.0 percent of income; and the lowest 60 percent, 28.6 percent, leaving 71.4 percent for the top 40 percent and 48.5 percent for the top 20 percent. Inequality has increased in the United States over the past three decades.

To provide a numerical comparison, the area between the diagonal line and the curve is divided by the total area of the lower half of the diagram (below the diagonal). This number is called a Gini coefficient. The higher the Gini coefficient, the greater the degree of inequality.

The Lorenz curve is used as a comparative tool in measuring changes in income distribution over time and differences in income distribution between different countries. However, the Gini coefficient is often a more convenient way to compare across multiple countries. In the mid-2000s, the United States had a relatively high degree of inequality, with a Gini coefficient of .38. Other developed countries ranged from .23 (Denmark, Switzerland, Sweden) to .35 (Italy), as indicated in Table 5.1.

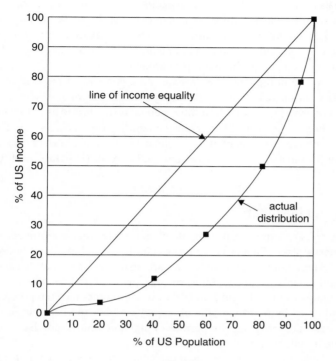

Figure 5.1 US income distribution in 2008.

Table 5.1 Gini coefficients of developed countries

Country	Gini coefficient	Country	Gini coefficient
United States	.38	Australia	.30
Austria	.27	Canada	.32
Denmark	.23	France	.28
Germany	.30	Italy	.35
Japan	.32	New Zealand	.34
Norway	.28	Sweden	.23
Switzerland	.23	United Kingdom	.34

Source: Gini coefficients are from Organization for Economic Cooperation and Development (OECD 2008).

Measuring poverty

In the United States, measures of poverty were developed in the 1960s as part of President Johnson's War on Poverty. The original measure was based on the cost of food for a family of four for a year, which was estimated at $1,000 in 1965. Since food typically took about one-third of a low-income household's budget, the poverty level for a family of four was set at $3,000.

Since that time the figure has been regularly adjusted for inflation, and adjusted for family size, rural–urban cost of living differences, and other considerations. In 2009, the poverty level of income was $22,025 a year for an urban family of four. Information on income is then used to compute the percentage of the population in poverty or near poverty (e.g., 150 percent of poverty is the ceiling income for eligibility for certain programs).

In 2008, the official poverty rate in the United States was 13.2 percent, an increase over the 11.7 percent in 1999. 2008 was a year of high and rising unemployment and recession, which always drives up the poverty rate. About 40 million people were classed as below the poverty threshold (or other thresholds for single persons or families of varying size). The highest poverty rate was for children: 19 percent of those under 18 years of age were poor in 2008, while the poverty rate for those over age 65 was only 9.7 percent (US Bureau of the Census 2008).

Policy issues in poverty and inequality

In a market system, household are expected to earn their income by making productive resources available in the marketplace. That assumption is valid for most but not all households in a market economy. There are always people who are unable to earn at all because of age, disability, lack of skills, lack of opportunities, or other barriers. Others are able to work but cannot earn enough to sustain a decent standard of living. Sometimes the problem is temporary and can be addressed by improving the efficiency of labor markets and/or by **unemployment insurance** and other programs for periods of high unemployment. But even in robust economic times, there will be households in need of support.

The challenge of a market economy is to ensure that those who cannot earn or cannot earn enough are adequately provided for while at the same time retaining strong work incentives and limiting the amount spent on supporting low-income households. A system that is too restrictive will leave many people undernourished, badly housed, and without access to essential services such as health care, transportation, and education. A system that is too lavish will have to impose high tax burdens on those who do work in order to support those who do not, creating poor work incentives and inadequate work effort at both ends of the spectrum. A well-designed social safety net must be broad enough to catch those who fall in, but not so attractive as to invite people to jump in.

Some economists regard poverty as a form of market failure, or at least some kinds of poverty. When poverty results from intentional choices—to be a starving artist, to drop out of the labor force and do nothing—then there is no particular need or justification for providing assistance. To do so would weaken the incentives to work and contribute that lie at the heart of a market-driven economy. The concern about poverty deals, rather, with two groups of people who do not fare well under a pure market economy.

Some people are unable to work because they are too old, or disabled in some way. A second group suffers from lack of access to jobs because of their location, lack of skills, or lack of access to transportation or child care. This group includes the underemployed, who may be working part-time but would prefer full-time, or who work full-time but earn too little to lift them out of poverty.

Social Security is intended to protect the elderly and those with disabilities. Reforms in the welfare system in the 1990s addressed some of the problems represented by the second category, but not all. The problem of those who are young and physically able to work but cannot find enough work or work that pays adequately accounts for a great deal of poverty among children.

For the most part, poor children live in poor families with adults who fall into one of the following categories:

- Those who work but who lack the skills, training, or experience to earn a wage that will pull them and their families above the poverty level. The responsibility for addressing this source of poverty falls heavily on the states in such programs as school-to-work, technical and community colleges, job training programs for industries, and other activities that link economic development with getting people ready to fully participate in the labor force.
- Those with special circumstances such as poor health, large family size, or special responsibilities to care for dependents (e.g., aging parents, family members with disabilities) that make it impossible either to work or to maintain an above-poverty standard of living on their earnings, even though such earnings might be adequate under more normal circumstances. For those who work at all, the primary policy response to this source of poverty is the Earned Income Tax Credit. Other responses include **Temporary Assistance to Needy Families (TANF)**, food stamps, and direct provision of services such as health care (Medicaid and State Children's Health Insurance Program (SCHIP), both of which are funded jointly by federal and state governments.

Is poverty a form of market failure?

In what sense does this kind of poverty constitute market failure? One argument that these cases represent market failure is that the existence of poverty among some individuals reduces the well-being of others (because of empathy with the suffering of others) and therefore has the same kinds of spillover effects as water pollution, noise, litter, or other familiar negative externalities.

A second argument is also based on negative externalities. Poverty can diminish the quality of life of the community. Poverty may breed drug addiction, blight, crime, and other social ills that impact on more prosperous households. Children who lack homes where their brains are stimulated early are likely to have difficulties in school, requiring more resources and holding back the rest of the students. Poor children who lack basic health care and skills may grow up to be unproductive workers and/or dependent on society. A little prevention or correction of these social ills will benefit others besides the target population. This different type of externality argument still treats the consequences of poverty as a form of market failure.

Yet a third argument is that social safety nets are a form of insurance that catch those who suffer from economic reversals outside their control. Even the non-poor may think that this could happen to them as well, and they would like to ensure the existence of a social safety net in case they should ever happen to need one.

Some kinds of insurance lend themselves better to private provision than others. Disasters that strike unexpectedly at identifiable target groups, such as floods, hurricanes, or earthquakes are least suited to purely private (unsubsidized, non-mandatory) insurance. Unemployment, prolonged illness, or disability have some of the same characteristics as natural disaster. Those most at risk may be willing to buy insurance, but the premiums are prohibitively high because of the high probability of loss. Those least at risk see no need for the insurance and opt out of the pool, leaving only the high-risk applicants.

If those who are at risk of unemployment, prolonged illness or disability are not only high risk but also low income, as they often are, the private market will not be able to resolve their need for a social safety net with affordable private insurance.[3] For this reason, social insurance has been one of the fastest growing categories of government activity in the United States and other nations in the last century. Since the market fails to provide insurance against these types of hazards, it could be argued that the absence of such a market constitutes a form of market failure, and the provision of this service has some attributes of a public good.

Redistribution and free-riding behavior

Few people will argue that there should be no redistribution, but it is often argued that redistribution should be voluntary rather than through government. There is some voluntary redistribution through churches, nonprofit agencies, and individual charity that alters the distribution of income and wealth determined solely by the market. If voluntary redistribution could do the job, there would be no need for government intervention. But can society rely on individual decisions to ensure that the total amount of redistribution is socially optimal? Probably not. It is too easy to free-ride on the charity of others, even more so in larger communities than in smaller ones where your failure to contribute is more likely to be noticed.

If Mrs. Jones is a widow with six children and unable to work because of lack of child care, lack of opportunity, and health problems, most people would feel charitably disposed toward her and the six children. But because each of their contributions would likely be a very small part of the total needed, they are likely to free-ride, feeling that the amount of aid going to Mrs. Jones will not be significantly altered by their small share of the total required. If everyone reasons this way, Mrs. Jones is out of luck.

In very small communities, shirking one's due share of the obligation is too visible and has too much impact on the outcome to allow free-riding to dominate. But in a highly mobile society, and a society in which most people live in large urban areas where the poor and needy are often less directly visible, free-riding is likely to predominate. With free-riding, the amount of private voluntary redistribution will fall short of the socially optimum level.

Administrative cost and fraud

While some economists and policy-makers are opposed to any intentional redistribution of income through government, there appears to be some degree of social consensus that at least some aid to designated groups (such as the elderly or disabled, or abandoned children) is a desirable activity for government to undertake. Once it is agreed that it is appropriate for the government to undertake some direct redistribution, the challenge becomes one of finding a way to do so with maximum efficiency.

However, there is another kind of efficiency in redistribution: targeting aid to those who "deserve" it, with minimal expenditures for administration and minimal diversion of revenues to those who are perceived as "undeserving" (including those who obtain assistance via fraud or misrepresentation). If the goal is to minimize administrative costs, then the limited resources for oversight may make it difficult to exclude the undeserving. If an extensive cross-checking system is created to root out fraud and abuse, then administrative costs will be much higher.

The two most successful programs of redistribution in terms of minimizing fraud while operating with very low overhead expense are the Social Security retirement program and the **Earned Income Tax Credit (EITC)** on the federal income tax. The success of Social Security rests on two important features: near-universal participation, and no means-testing.[4] Near universal participation means that Social Security enrollment is simple and automatic.

Much of the burden of getting revenue into the system with the accompanying documentation falls on employers and the self-employed. For the pension part of Social Security, the only test is a simple one of age and years of participation in the system, both of which are easy to verify.

In the case of the Earned Income Tax Credit, which provides refundable credits for working individuals and families, the tests are again fairly simple and straightforward because they rely on information provided for income tax purposes. Other forms of income transfers, such as Temporary Assistance to Needy Families, housing vouchers, and food stamps, require a complex verification process to determine eligibility and are much more costly to administer. Most of that higher cost is a result of efforts to prevent fraud.

It is quite possible that, for some kinds of redistribution, the cost of monitoring to prevent fraud would be greater than the savings from preventing or detecting fraud. That is, it could very well be cheaper to operate a system that is 90 percent fraudproof and allow 10 percent to get away with cheating, because the benefits paid to that 10 percent would cost less than the additional monitoring effort required to screen cheaters out.

That argument may be valid in the short run, but in the long run the negative effects on the system as a whole may outweigh the short-run cost savings from tolerating a certain amount of fraud and abuse. It does not take long for rational, calculating people to figure out how to "game" the system for their own benefit if the risk is perceived as low (because of lack of monitoring) and the payoff high. In the long run, a system that is vulnerable to fraud and abuse because of inadequate safeguards will attract cheaters. This long-run effect will not only increase costs but also decrease faith in and support for the system of redistribution.

Efficiency and work incentives

Another important efficiency issue in redistribution is the effect of these programs on incentives to work, invest, and take entrepreneurial risks. These negative incentive effects impact both those who "contribute" the tax monies and those who receive the aid. The tax wedge between the gross earnings of the worker, investor, and entrepreneur and the after-tax earnings can result in a diminution of effort below the optimal level. The combined effect of state and federal income taxes and Social Security taxes can push the marginal tax rate on a highly productive worker above 40 percent, discouraging overtime, freelancing, moonlighting, or other forms of extra effort.

When redistribution of one's earnings to others reduces the return to work or investment effort, many rational, calculating members of society will respond by making less effort than they would otherwise have done. Workers will substitute leisure, which is not taxed, for income from working, which is taxed.

Figure 5.2 shows a representative citizen balancing the choices between work and leisure. With no taxes on earnings (line A_1B), this individual would choose OX_1 of earnings and OY_1 of leisure. If a tax is placed on earnings while leisure is untaxed, the budget line rotates to A_2B. The worker is forced to accept less of both earnings and leisure, but the drop in earnings (to OX_2) is greater than the drop in leisure (to OY_2). If the tax became severe enough (A_3B), the worker might respond by increasing leisure to OY_3 at the expense of earnings (now only OX_3).

The availability of public assistance, and the likelihood of losing that assistance when moving into paid employment, can also create disincentives to work. In the past, prior to welfare reform, recipients of aid who compared the returns to working 40 hours a week at the minimum wage or slightly above, after adjusting for the costs of working (child care,

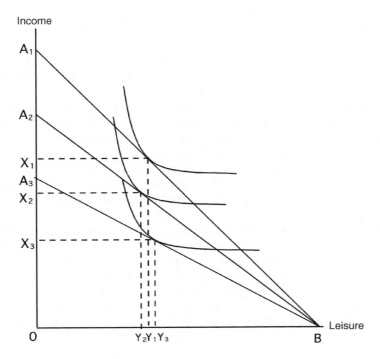

Figure 5.2 Income, leisure, and taxation.

transportation, etc.) and the loss of benefits, might well have concluded that there would be little or no increase in economic well-being as a result of entering the workforce. A major goal of US welfare reform in the 1990s was to provide support services and delay the cutoff of benefits to those who do enter the labor force, while at the same time imposing time limits on benefits and other penalties on those who do not respond to work opportunities.

Equality of opportunity or equality of results?

Beyond the earlier debates over whether there should be any governmental redistribution at all, there is a secondary debate among both economists and policy-makers over whether the goal of any intentional redistribution should focus on equality of opportunity or equality of results. **Equality of opportunity**—providing education, health care and other services that allow people to develop into and remain productive, contributing adults—is a philosophy more in accord with a market system.

   For a large share of the population, equality of opportunity represents the primary form of redistribution, especially in the form of free, compulsory public education and low-cost, state-sponsored post-secondary education and training programs. These services are available to all, more or less irrespective of ability to pay. Even access to post-secondary education is heavily subsidized with grants, low-cost student loans, and work-study opportunities. In other countries, including Canada and Western Europe, the extent of such services is much greater, including universal health care and day care for preschool children regardless of ability to pay.

Equality of results emphasizes reducing disparities in income and immediate alleviation of poverty, rather than on "investing" in poor people. The difference in strategy is captured in the old proverb, "Give a man a fish, he can eat for a day; teach a man to fish, he can eat for a lifetime." Often the need is too immediate and direct to be addressed by longer-term strategies of education and training. Ideally, both strategies would be pursued simultaneously, but usually budget limitations push legislators toward responding to the immediate problem rather than the long run.

One component of equality of results in the United States and elsewhere is the progressive income tax, which takes a larger share of income in taxes from higher-income households than from lower-income ones. Since World War II, when the top bracket on the income tax rose to 98 percent during the war, there has been a series of reductions in federal income tax rates across the board. Bigger reductions in top bracket rates have made the system less progressive. Although the EITC and larger personal exemptions have also favored lower-income households, a variety of specialized tax breaks have also reduced tax burdens on middle- and upper-income taxpayers.

Other programs that aim at equality of results are payments, direct or indirect, to low-income households in the form of cash, food stamps, housing subsidies, and other forms of income support. Social Security, another results-oriented program, has been particularly successful in reducing poverty among the elderly.

Behavioral economics: in-kind or in-cash?

Another issue that is often viewed differently by donors and recipients is the form that redistribution takes. Recipients prefer cash, which gives them more flexibility in how they use the funds. Donors, however, are often looking for specific outcomes and want to impose their preferences rather than those of recipients on the use of funds. Donors may want to see the money earmarked for food, or housing, or child care, or health services. Implicit in the donor preferences is the expectation that recipients are not rational, responsible, thoughtful people who will use those resources effectively. Donors think of themselves as *Homo economicus*, but they are not so sure about the motivations and the cognitive abilities of those who receive assistance.

Both groups vote, lobby, and exercise political influence in various ways. In general, donors are more interested in creating equality of opportunity and in making sure that funds are spent in particular ways. Recipients are more interested in equality of results and in having some flexibility in how to use the resources that come their way. While in-kind payments may satisfy donor (or taxpayer or legislator) preferences about how funds are spent, they usually cost more to administer than cash payments.

The easiest way to earmark funds is to provide the services directly rather than cash payments. Health clinics and education programs are examples of direct service provision. A second substitute for cash, increasingly popular in recent years, is a **voucher**. Vouchers are written claims, issued by government, that can be exchanged for housing, education, food (food stamps), or other designated uses. The voucher is presented to the seller as the equivalent of cash, but only for the designated use. Vouchers are not supposed to be convertible into cash, which can then be spent on other purposes.

Which level of government?

Should redistribution be the responsibility of the central government, state (or provincial) government or local government? Or should it be shared between them? Until the 1930s, addressing poverty in the United States was primarily the responsibility of local governments, with workhouses for families with employable members and "outdoor relief" (outside of poorhouses or workhouses) for widows and orphans. Private charity took care of some problems.

With the advent of the Great Depression, first local and later state governments were overwhelmed with the magnitude of the problem of poverty resulting from widespread unemployment. In the 1930s, the combination of a worldwide depression and the aftermath of a major conversion from small town, agricultural economies to an industrial age with population concentrated in large urban centers, the capacity of local governments to take care of the poor, the elderly, the sick, and others who were unable to earn a living in a market system was overwhelmed. Central (and in the United States and Canada, state or provincial) governments became increasingly involved in providing a social safety net.

In the United States, a major part of the New Deal was a series of programs designed to relieve poverty among the aged, the disabled, widows with small children, and the unemployed. The two primary underpinnings of that social safety net were created simultaneously in 1935. One was the Social Security system for those who worked, and the other was the welfare system (Aid to Dependent Children, Aid to the Aged, Aid to the Blind, etc.) for those who were unable to work because of age or other disabilities. With many modifications in the intervening years, these two pillars of the social safety net remained intact in the United States until the 1990s.

The enlarged federal role relative to state and local governments may have been a pragmatic response to necessity, but there is some economic justification as well for locating some of that responsibility at the central level in a federal system. Poorer states tend to have larger concentrations of low-income people with a greater need for assistance and fewer tax resources with which to provide that assistance. If they raise benefits, they have to raise taxes, making them less competitive to attract or retain industry and higher-income residents. Wealthier states that can afford to offer more generous benefits are hesitant to do so for fear of attracting welfare recipients from other states. This kind of competitive environment is less likely to encourage support for the poor than a system where welfare benefits are more uniform across states. If the benefits of antipoverty programs spill over state boundaries to affect nearby states and even the nation as a whole, then the cost should be shared in a similar manner.

All of these reasons offer support and economic justification for the ultimately practical decisions of politicians during the Great Depression who designed and implemented both the welfare system and the social insurance system that are still with us in modified form today.

Even in the 1930s, however, there continued to be a state and local role in poverty relief. Federal aid consisted primarily of cash payments to the poor with some state-matching funds. The required match varied from state to state depending on income and poverty levels in each state. These programs continued to exist, expand and evolve until 1996 when welfare reform significantly reduced this kind of federal aid to individuals mediated through state social service agencies.

The case for centralizing redistribution rests on competition among states. If one state offers more attractive benefits to persons in need than another, it risks becoming a haven for migration of those persons. Faced with the threat of attracting the needy and overburdening the welfare system, states will reduce their benefit levels below what they would offer in the absence of migration. Uniform national standards (adjusted for differences in the cost of living) remove that incentive to migrate between states in search of better benefits.

The case for localizing redistribution rests on the arguments offered above for regarding poverty as a form of market failure. Both the empathy and the social blight arguments for poverty relief suggest that the benefits from relieving poverty are very local in nature. In addition, there is the need to monitor eligibility and control fraud, which is much easier to do effectively at the local community level. Despite repeated efforts to sort out responsibilities and assign responsibilities for poverty relief to a particular level of government, it is as it has been since the Great Depression a shared function of federal, state, and local governments.

Poverty relief and work incentives

The design and reform of programs to alleviate poverty are based on certain assumptions about why people are poor. The stereotype of the welfare queen buying prime steaks with food stamps (now renamed SNAP) persists despite the reality of welfare programs and welfare recipients. Certainly there are people who are poor because they are unwilling or unable to work, but most welfare recipients are willing to work if they can overcome the obstacles, which may include lack of skills, lack of mobility, lack of opportunities, or problems with transportation and child care.

Many programs, especially in the United States, encourage work by increasing the financial rewards from working and helping people to overcome obstacles to paid employment. Both Temporary Assistance to Needy Families and the Earned Income Tax Credit are designed on that basis. However, these programs require case workers and programs to help low-income households overcome these obstacles, including access to education and training programs, transportation, and help with child care.

In addition, many people who work, even full-time, do not succeed in escaping poverty, and the work they can find often does not include fringe benefits and health care. Food stamps, housing subsidies, Medicaid, and other health care programs are intended to address these dimensions of poverty.

Major poverty relief programs in the United States

In general, the social safety net of programs and services to support families in the United States is more restrictive in coverage than in many other countries. One strategy used more often elsewhere is to make certain services available to all, regardless of income, which itself is a form of poverty relief. The United States has chosen the route of targeting those in need and imposing eligibility requirements for most services.

Although there has been some movement in the direction of universal health care in 2010, the United States is the only major industrial country without such a program. Publicly funded programs for day care and early childhood education and subsidized housing are more limited than in other countries. There are no family allowances for children such as citizens have in Canada and Europe, although the income tax does include dependent allowances.

In addition to Social Security, which is covered in Chapter 19, there are five significant anti-poverty programs in the United States. Two of them—food stamps and the Earned Income Tax Credit (EITC) are federal programs. The other three, Supplemental Security Income (SSI), Temporary Assistance to Needy Families (TANF) and Unemployment Compensation are shared state–federal responsibilities.

Food stamps

The Food Stamp program, initiated in 1965, was recently renamed SNAP (Supplemental Nutrition Assistance Program). Eligibility is based on income, assets, and family size. People who are able to work and are between age 18 and 60 must register for work to qualify, and may be required to take part in an employment or training program. Monthly benefits in 2010 range from $200 for a single person to $1,202 for an eight-person family. SNAP is the largest of the federal non-cash welfare programs. In 2009, almost 40 million people received about $4.3 billion in SNAP benefits.

The Earned Income Tax Credit (EITC)

One of the most important redistribution programs for working individuals and families is the Earned Income Tax Credit (EITC). Working couples without children receive smaller EITCs than those with dependent children.

EITC is a modest version of the negative income tax first proposed in the 1970s by Nobel laureate Milton Friedman (Friedman 2001). EITC has replaced traditional welfare as the major form of federal aid to low-income households, but it is aimed at working households rather than households on public assistance. In addition to the federal program, 24 states also offer some form of Earned Income Tax Credit.

There are three design elements in a negative income tax: an acceptable minimum income (benefit to those with no earnings), a rate of decline of benefits as household income rises (the marginal tax rate), and the cross-over income level at which all benefits are phased out and the recipient becomes a positive taxpayer.

When two of these numbers are determined, the third one is automatically set. For example, if the minimum guaranteed income for a family of four is set at $10,000, and the benefit loss rate is 25 percent as income rises from zero, then the crossover income level becomes $40,000.

If the minimum guaranteed income is too low, there will be large numbers of people still in poverty. If the crossover income is set too high, the government will face a severe revenue drain. If the benefit loss rate is too high, there is a severe disincentive to work and earn more for low-income households.

The EITC is a less global program than a negative income tax. It offers workers whose income is below a certain level a refundable income tax credit that increases with earnings up to a peak and is then phased out as income continues to rise. Refundable means that workers receive the money even if they pay no federal income taxes.

Figure 5.3 shows the EITC credit in 2009 for families of various sizes. The subsidy for a four-person family, up to an income of about $18,000, provides a work incentive. However, the phaseout range beyond that point creates a work disincentive, which is the reason why the phaseout rate is lower than the subsidy rate (note the flatter slope of the curve on the right). Combining the reduction in the subsidy with Social Security taxes of 7.6 percent and a federal marginal income tax rate of 15 percent, a worker in the $20,000–$50,000 income range would be facing a combined marginal tax rate of 42.6 percent, not including any state income taxes.

In addition, other benefits are phased out at different rates for those transitioning from welfare to work. Fortunately for work incentives, the EITC benefit increasing over the lower-income range where benefits to former welfare recipients for food stamps, child care, and Medicaid begin to be phased out.

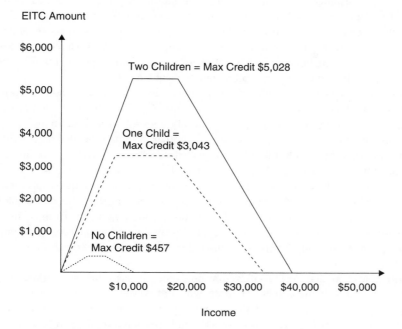

EITC Amount

Figure 5.3 The federal earned income tax credit in tax year 2009.

Source: Center for Budget and Policy Priotities (www.cbbp.org)

EITC is one of the few factors countering the trend toward greater income inequality and toward declining real incomes among families in the lowest two quintiles (fifths) of the income distribution (Greenstein and Shapiro 1998; Ellwood 2000). In 2009, the EITC lifted an estimated 6.6 million people out of poverty, half of them children. Work is the ultimate antipoverty strategy for those able and willing to work. Many entry-level workers are paid at the federal minimum wage of $7.25 an hour. For a year-round, full-time worker, that wage translates (at 40 hours a week, or 2,000 hours a year), to an income of $14,500. In 2009, the official poverty threshold for a family of four was $22,025. A year-round minimum wage worker with a spouse and two children would qualify for the maximum credit of $5,028, bringing the family's income to $19,528, still below the poverty level. However, with a wage just moderately above the minimum, a four-person household would cross the poverty threshold.

Welfare: from AFDC to SSI and TANF

Historically, the term welfare in the United States was interchangeable with **Aid to Families with Dependent Children (AFDC)**, which was replaced in 1996 by Temporary Assistance to Needy Families (TANF). The term welfare in the United States has in the past included Aid to the Aged (now part of **Supplementary Security Income**, or **SSI**) and Aid to the Disabled/Blind (now also under SSI, unless the person qualifies for Social Security). All of these programs date from the New Deal era.

SSI is a program of assistance to the blind, disabled, and/or elderly who do not quality for Social Security. Eligibility is limited by the person's income and assets. Although SSI is administered by the Social Security Administration, it is funded out of general tax revenues, not the Social Security Trust Fund. Some states offer supplementary assistance. Almost 8 million people were receiving benefits in 2010, with an average benefit per month of about $500. Ninety percent of the recipients were blind and/or disabled.

AFDC was based on a typical household of a male breadwinner and a wife/mother whose responsibility was to maintain the home and raise the children. If the male breadwinner was absent, this program would provide for the family, largely widows with children and a few divorced women as well. Over the years, however, the number of female-headed households has increased dramatically, the result not only of higher divorce rates but also more unmarried women (especially teens) having children. More and more mothers of children of all ages and from all economic levels were working outside the home, raising questions about supporting some mothers on welfare with tax dollars from other mothers who placed their children in day care or after-school care in order to support their families. Both of these factors began to erode public support even as the cost of providing assistance rose. In 1960, income security accounted for only 8 percent of the federal budget; by 2009, that figure had risen to 15 percent.

Many economists argued that AFDC offered strong incentives to choose welfare over low-wage work and strong disincentives for those who left welfare for the labor market. Most welfare payments were modest. At the beginning of reform, the average monthly payment to a family of four in 1996 ranged from $435 in Mississippi to $833 in New York. However, that payment was accompanied by Medicaid benefits and food stamps. Mothers who stayed at home did not incur the cost of transportation, work clothes, and day care. Many single parents on welfare had limited education and skills and could only hope to qualify for minimum-wage jobs. It would make no sense to commit to a 40-hour week of difficult, often boring, low-paying work when the loss of health insurance and the cost of child care and transportation might well leave the family no better off than before.

The challenge of reform was to identify and encourage those who could be prepared for and supported in transition to work while continuing to help those unable to work. There were still many people on welfare with health problems or addiction challenges, people in areas where job opportunities, day care, or transportation were limited. Any reform needed to recognize that no solution would address all situations, and some provision needed to be made for those who would be unable to leave welfare and find a place in the labor market.

Powered by not only the arguments of economists, but also changed expectations for women's labor force participation, the changing mix of families, and the rising cost of welfare, the 1990s saw dramatic changes in the form, nature, and level of assistance to the non-elderly, non-disabled poor. President Clinton was elected on a platform of "ending welfare as we know it," and together with a Republican Congress, made dramatic changes in the welfare system starting in 1996. Even the name was changed. Temporary meant maximum time limits on public assistance for a large share of households, with some exceptions and some discretion granted to states. In particular, states were allowed to exempt up to 20 percent of their cases.

From matching grants to states to encourage more generous levels of public assistance, the form changed to block grants and the emphasis toward supporting the transition from welfare to work with day care, with retaining eligibility for Medicaid and food stamps, and with training and assistance in job placement. In a strong economy with low unemployment rates and a relatively small cohort of new workers coming into the market, conditions were ideal for getting these hard-to-place workers into the labor market. A final element of the comprehensive program emphasized stronger enforcement of child support obligations by absent parents, mostly fathers.

Unemployment compensation

The federal–state unemployment compensation program was created along with the original welfare program and Social Security as part of the New Deal in 1935. Unemployment compensation is a social insurance program that provides benefits for workers who lose their jobs through no fault of their own. Funding comes from a payroll tax on employers, and the program is administered by the states, with different benefits, eligibility requirements and taxes. Beneficiaries must be looking for work while receiving benefits. In 2010, 16.3 million people received benefits totaling $157.1 billion. Normal maximum duration of benefits is 26 weeks, but during the prolonged high unemployment in the recession that began in 2008, benefits were extended to longer periods.

Welfare programs in Canada and Australia

Programs of assistance to the non-elderly in the United States are somewhat more limited than in many other developed countries. Most developed countries have universal health care rather than the patchwork coverage provided in the United States that, even after the 2010 reforms, still leaves many people uninsured or under-insured. Most of these countries, like the United States, offer free public education and subsidized post-secondary education. Other countries, including Canada, have adopted some variant of the EITC and also have unemployment insurance.

Children's allowances and/or subsidized daycare are widely available elsewhere. In Canada, for example, there are both federal child tax credits and, in some provinces, a per child benefit for low-income families. Much of the Canadian welfare program is administered and supplemented by the provinces. Australia, similarly, has study payments for full-time students and apprentices, caregiver allowances for those caring for a person with a disability, maternity allowances, and parenting payments to help with the cost of raising children. In general, income support programs are more extensive in other countries than they are in the United States, and taxes to support such programs are higher.

Summary

- Government is inherently redistributive; every action, whether taxing, spending, or regulating, changes the distribution of income and/or wealth. Most changes in public policy involve gains and losses to different groups, redistributing income and/or wealth.
- The purpose of redistribution is to create a more equitable distribution of income, resources, and opportunities. There are many different concepts of distributional equity. Horizontal equity means treating people alike if they are in the same or similar economic situations. Vertical equity means treating people differently according to the differences in their income, wealth, or other measure of need or ability to pay.
- The compensation principle offers a guide to incorporating equity and income distribution considerations into policy evaluation. A policy change is desirable if the gainers from the change can compensate the losers for their losses and still be better off.
- The poverty threshold in the United States is adjusted each year for inflation and other considerations. In 2009, the poverty level of income was $22,025 a year for a family of

four. In a market system, where income is based on contributions to the economy, inability to work, lack of skills, training, or experience to earn an adequate wage are the main sources of poverty.

- Poverty is sometimes classed as market failure because (1) poverty among some individuals reduces the well-being of others; (2) poverty breed drug addiction, blight, crime, and other social ills; (3) a social safety net has attributes of a public good; and (4) private redistribution will be less than adequate because of free-riding behavior.
- Redistribution can be aimed at equality of opportunity or equality of results and can be done either in cash or in kind. Equality of opportunity means providing education, health care and other services that allow people to develop into and remain productive, contributing adults. Equality of results is aimed at immediate and direct relief of poverty with programs such as the progressive income tax, food stamps, housing subsidies, and Social Security.
- There are good arguments both for centralizing and for localizing redistribution. If it is decentralized, beneficiaries are likely to migrate to states with more generous benefits. Localized redistribution is justified by the local impact of poverty relief within the community: local control also makes it easier to monitor eligibility and control fraud.
- Historically, welfare has included Aid to the Aged (now part of Supplementary Security Income, or SSI), Aid to the Disabled/Blind (now part of SSI and Social Security), General Assistance, and Aid to Families with Dependent Children (AFDC). AFDC was replaced in the 1990s with Temporary Assistance to Needy Families (TANF). Welfare also includes SNAP (formerly food stamps), a federal program, and unemployment insurance, a joint federal-state program. The expanded Earned Income Tax Credit (EITC) an important form of poverty relief for working families.

Key terms

Aid to Families with Dependent Children (AFDC)
Compensation principle
Distributive justice
Earned Income Tax Credit (EITC)
Entitlement
Equality of opportunity
Equality of results
Horizontal equity
Means testing
Restorative justice
Supplementary Security Income (SSI)
Temporary Assistance to Needy Families (TANF)
Unemployment insurance
Veil of ignorance
Vertical equity
Vouchers

Questions

1   Try a Rawls-type thought experiment based on his *Theory of Justice*. Consider a situation where a group of employees at a plant are all receiving the same pay. An outside

efficiency expert concludes that if five employees at key points in the process work harder than the others, output can increase by a significant percentage. Should those five workers be paid more? How much more? Should they get all the increase in the company's net income since they created it, or should it be at least partly shared with other workers? What considerations influenced your answer?

2   What are the efficiency, equity, and administrative advantages and disadvantages of a means-testing system that phases out eligibility as household income approaches a certain limit instead of just saying that every household below that limit is eligible and those above it are not?

3   Using Figure 5.2 as a starting point, separate the income and substitution effects of the tax on income and leisure. Hint: The income effect is measured by drawing a line parallel to AB but tangent to a lower indifference curve. The combination chosen with this budget line represents the income effect. The further changes to the income/leisure combination represent the substitution effect. Label the size of each effect on your diagram.

4   **By the numbers**. Look at the budget for the United States for the last 20 years and find the amount going each year to income support. How has it changed? Separate that amount into Social Security, Medicare/Medicaid, and other. What are the fast growing parts of income support?

5   **Policy application**. You work for a Congressional committee that is reviewing the Earned Income Tax Credit. They would like you to look at Figure 5.3 and make recommendations about increasing the maximum credit going to families with two or more children. What are some of the ways to do that? What are the advantages and drawbacks of each method?

6   **Behavioral economics**. The debate over retaining work incentives underlies both TANF and the EITC. What model of human motivation underlies those two programs? How might the programs be designed differently if part of people's motivation for working was not just earning an income but also a matter of dignity, self-expression, feeling like a useful and productive part of the community, etc.?

7   **Thinking globally**. Many other countries, such as Canada, address the problem of eligibility for certain programs such as children's allowances by providing them to everyone and then recapturing more of the cost from higher income households with higher taxes, especially income taxes. What are the advantages and disadvantages of this approach? What do you think would be the objections to that approach in the United States?

Part 2

Government expenditures and budgets

For much of the history of public sector economics, the focus of attention was almost exclusively on the tax or revenue side of the ledger. The expenditure side was mostly about justifying public spending to produce public goods, encouraging production of goods with positive externalities, and controlling negative externalities. It is only in the past 30 years that detailed attention has been paid to the spending side of the budget equation.

We begin Part 2 with two chapters that explore the nature and production of public goods and the challenge of externalities as a form of market failure. Taken together, these chapters constitute the basic theory of public expenditures. Public expenditures lead directly into consideration of public budgets in Chapter 8. Budgets are the framework within which decisions about both revenue and expenditures are made. A budget involves both revenues and expenditures simultaneously—a plan for spending and a plan for paying for it. Budgeting depends on the foundation we have built in the preceding chapters—the nature and structure of governments, the desired size of the public sector, the process of public sector decision-making on the distribution of income, and the rationale for providing certain goods and services through the public sector.

Budgets raise two particular additional policy challenges: borrowing, including multi-year financing of capital projects, and choosing among competing projects. Budgets may or may not be balanced, with revenue equal to expenditures. When expenditures exceed revenues, the difference is financed by issuing debt. With the massive growth of public debt in many countries, in recent years, the issue of managing public debt and the consequences for future budgets and future generations have become a significant public finance issue. The processes of providing of multi-year financing and setting priorities for capital projects are different from budgeting for regular, recurring annual outlays for operating ongoing programs and making transfer payments. Chapter 9 describes the issues involved in government borrowing, debt and debt service, and capital project financing. Chapter 10 explains one of the most important and widely-used methods of analyzing a proposed public expenditure, cost-benefit analysis, which is grounded in Pareto optimality and the theory of the second best.

6   Public goods

Introduction

Efficiency is the major achievement that the market has to offer. The market is, as a general rule, very good at allocating resources to their "highest and best" uses and distributing output to those who desire it the most, as measured by the prices people are willing to pay. The market is also good at ensuring that, under favorable conditions, goods and services will be produced at the lowest possible resource costs, and that changes in consumer preferences or resource availability will call forth a rapid response in terms of input or output combinations.

The relationship between government and efficiency in a market economy has several aspects. One connection is that the government is expected to ensure that the conditions under which the market operates are indeed favorable to efficiency, particularly in terms of competition. A second connection is that the government itself should strive for some of the same kinds of efficiency in terms of cost and desired output mix as the private sector. A third relationship lies in the reason for government production of goods and services. There are certain kinds of goods and services demanded by consumers/citizens that the market fails to produce in the right quantities, or sometimes fails to produce at all. It is this third kind of efficiency that is the subject of this chapter and the one that follows.

Public goods and private goods

In casual use, the term public goods and services is used to describe whatever it is that governments provide, from street lights to defense to a system of courts. Economists, however, use the term **public good** in a more precise sense to describe goods (or more often, services) that have two key characteristics: **non-rivalry** in consumption and **non-excludability**. These two characteristics must both be present in significant degree for something to qualify as a public good.

Non-rivalry

A good that is non-rival in consumption can be consumed by any number of people simultaneously, without diminishing the amount available to be consumed by others. A beautiful sunset is a pure public good. A pair of shoes is a private good; if you are wearing them, no one else can use them at the same time. Between shoes and sunsets lies a whole spectrum of nearly private and nearly public goods. At the public end of the spectrum are national defense and lighthouses, because the same army and the same lighthouse that afford you protection can simultaneously protect others without in any way diminishing your safety.

Note that non-rivalry does not mean that all consumers value the public good equally, only that they share consumption in a noncompetitive way. Nearer to the private end of the spectrum in rivalry are such traditional publicly produced services as garbage pickup and early childhood education. As more consumers are added, the frequency of garbage pickups and/or the amount of attention given to the individual child is likely to diminish.

It has probably occurred to you that this non-rivalry characteristic also applies to activities or products that would not be described as "good," i.e., desirable. There are also "public bads"—environmental deterioration, blight, or crime that makes large areas unsafe at night. In fact, many activities of the public sector can be viewed less as provision of public goods than reduction of public "bads." This problem in semantics is easy to address; the elimination or reduction in a public bad can be defined as a public good. Improved environmental quality, neighborhood revitalization, and increased public safety would be the flip side of the public bads.

Non-excludability

Non-excludability is the second dimension of publicness. It describes the difficulty of keeping people, specifically non-payers, from consuming the good or service. A sunset and a lighthouse also qualify on this criterion, because it is difficult to locate and collect payment from all those who benefit. National defense suffers from the same problem. Even if a citizen refused to pay taxes, it would be very difficult for the government to single her out as an acceptable target for enemy forces to attack without endangering her neighbors as well.

Exclusion is not an either/or issue, but a question of the costs of exclusion relative to the benefits. If the cost of excluding non-payers is low relative to the payment that would be received, then it makes sense to undertake the effort to exclude. In many parts of the United States, for example, public recreation areas charge a fee with a gatekeeper during peak seasons (when the revenue generated exceeds the cost of collection). But they allow free admission during the off-season, when the receipts would not cover the cost of staffing the gatehouse.

It is the problem of excluding non-payers rather than non-rivalry that is often the determining factor in calling for public production. When innovations in technology or just more imaginative solutions reduce the cost of excluding non-payers, it becomes possible to shift some activities from the public sector to the private sector. For example, it is much cheaper to have automatic toll booths or subway entries than it is to staff them with human toll collectors. An electronic readable device on cars that records their highway use and collects payments by electronic funds transfer is another new exclusion technology. Likewise, new methods of identification such as voiceprints and handprints can bypass the human gatekeeper in ensuring access only to those who are entitled by membership and contribution.

Some new techniques make exclusion more difficult rather than easier. Internet technology has made it more difficult for owners of intellectual property rights to charge users. It's too easy to share music files or other kinds of intellectual property. The loss of newspaper circulation, likewise, was the result of problems of blocking access on-line to non-payers, although newspapers are working on solutions to that problem. The Napster case for downloading and sharing music was followed by the Google case for downloading and sharing copyrighted documents. With the internet, previously excludable private goods lost some of the essential quality that made private production profitable, although the courts have been seeking remedies to protect creators from unauthorized access to their work.

Balancing probabilities with penalties is another useful exclusion technique. Parking regulations or beach access restrictions can be enforced with infrequent checks but high fines for violation. The higher fines and less frequent enforcement will have a similar effect on compliance to lower fines with more frequent checks because the expected cost of violation will be similar. The expected cost of illegal or expired parking is equal to the probability of being caught multiplied by the amount of the penalty or fine. A low probability, such as 5 percent, can be combined with a high penalty, say $200, so that the expected cost of illegal parking or accessing a restricted beach is $10. The same expected cost could be the result of frequent patrols that raised the probability of being caught to 50 percent but only imposed a $20 fine. But the lower probability (less enforcement effort) and higher fine for violation greatly reduce the enforcement cost of excluding non-payers.

Free-riding and public goods

The primary reason why it is difficult to rely on the market to produce public goods is the **free-rider** problem. The term free-rider comes from the labor union movement. Labor unions produce a limited public good. They negotiate on behalf of all the workers in their plant or trade group, members or not. Nonunion workers benefit from those negotiations whether or not they pay their union dues. There is an obvious incentive to obtain the benefits without paying. If a large number of people decide to free-ride, there will not be enough dues paid to keep the union going or enough members to make the union a recognized bargaining agent.

In the case of a public good, free-riding means that there will not be enough payers to cover the costs of private for-profit firms undertaking production. Since it is easy to consume while avoiding payment, many users would refuse to pay, and a private firm could not recover its costs. Where the number of users/residents is large, free-riders know that the availability of the public good is largely independent of their small contribution to its cost. One person reasoning this way will gain the benefit of having the public good and not bearing any of the cost. Large numbers of people reasoning this way will make it impossible to finance the public good, and it will not come into being. It is for this reason that goods and services with both very low rivalry AND very low excludability are usually provided through the public sector and paid for with compulsory taxes.

A case study in free-riding: street lights

In the outskirts of the small town of Clemson, South Carolina, in the 1960s, there were few sidewalks and even fewer street lights. These outskirts were fairly densely populated but not a part of the nearby small town. The only local government was the county, but the county didn't provide street lights, which were regarded as a municipal (city) service. Some citizens took the initiative to pay the electric company $30 a year for a street light, but most fumbled along in the dark with flashlights. As a result, walking at night was a chancy venture, even though the crime rate was too low to worry about. It was ditches and potholes that threatened pedestrians after dark.

In one particular neighborhood, Mrs. G. had undertaken to have a street light installed in front of her house, and some of her neighbors, when they remembered, would chip in toward the annual payment to the electric company. But not many did, because they knew that the street light would shine whether they kicked in or not, and it was easier to free-ride on Mrs. G's public-spiritedness. Unfortunately, the free-riders were in the majority, and street lights were few and far between. One dark Hallowe'en night one of Mrs. G's neighbors took his little daughter out for trick-or-treat. With only the light of a flashlight to see by, the little girl fell in a ditch with burning leaves and burned her hand—an accident that could have been prevented with a few well-placed street lights.

The next year, this neighborhood along with many others was annexed into the city. One of the first actions of the city council of the enlarged community was to extend the public provision of street lights throughout the city, paid for with taxes. Free-riders could no longer free-ride, children had a little more protection from ditches and burning leaves, and even strangers to the city could bask in the glow of street lights as they sought to find addresses in the subdivisions around the city.

Although this story may sound like an edifying moral tale for the ears of little children, it is based on an actual incident. A street light is a local public good. Most of its benefits accrue to local residents, especially within neighborhoods, but people travel from one neighborhood to another, so the benefits of a street light are shared throughout the city. It is easy to free-ride if street lights are privately provided, difficult to exclude non-payers from benefiting from the light. A street light is largely non-rival in consumption; it shines on the rich and poor, payers and non-payers alike. It has the two defining attributes of a public good that suggest that private provision will be difficult at best. Since most of the benefits accrue to local residents rather than visitors passing through, a street light is a local public good. Non-rival in consumption and highly non-excludable, street lights are a clear candidate for local public production.

Is the result efficient and equitable?

Was the level of street light production optimal (marginal social cost = marginal social benefit) after this intervention? Perhaps, perhaps not. It is fairly clear that before government intervention, the level of street light production was below optimal, but whether the after-intervention level of production was still below optimal, optimal, or beyond optimal is difficult to determine. Depending on whether government intervention moved the output level closer to the optimum or beyond the optimum, the effect of intervention could have increased or decreased economic efficiency.

And what about equity? Was pricing perfectly allocated among taxpayers? Probably not. Some taxpayers go out at night frequently, others not at all. Pedestrians value street lights more than automobile passengers, families with children more than those without. The street lights were funded with property taxes. The tax price is based on the value of property owned, which is not perfectly correlated with demand for street lights. Thus, an imperfect private outcome was replaced with an imperfect government intervention.

Behavioral economics: does economics encourage free-riding?

In a classic article, Marwell and Ames attempted to answer this question by the use of economic experiments (Marwell and Ames 1981). They compared free-riding behavior among economics students and those in other majors in 11 different experiments. They found significant differences in their willingness to contribute to provision of a public good, with the more self-interested behavior emerging among the economics majors.

Their work has generated a number of subsequent studies, some confirming and others contradicting their findings. One of the unanswered questions is whether people self-select into economics because it affirms their existing behavior pattern or whether the study of economics encourages more self-interested behavior. But the policy implications are significant. If economists make policy recommendations based on their profession's widely shared self-interest model of human motivation, and if that model does not accurately describe a substantial part of the population, then those recommendations need to be reconsidered in the light of a different understanding of how people make choices.

Production and provision

Just because something meets the two tests of publicness does not mean that it is, or should be, produced in the public sector. Public provision is not the same as public production. For example, a significant amount of national defense, a public good, is produced by private contractors in the United States and other countries. Some kinds of public goods are produced by private nonprofit organizations. Medical research is often funded and carried out by private nonprofit organizations using voluntary contributions, and the results benefit many people who did not contribute.

Finally, there are some public goods that are not produced in the economic sense, such as integrity and trust, that are essential for the workings of markets and for the general health of society. Integrity and trust are non-rival and non-excludable. Each of us benefits from being able to trust the integrity of others, from the dependability of their word and their promises. As a society, we can try to "produce" more integrity, trust, and other qualities that benefit everyone else through education and example. We rely heavily on what sociologist Peter Berger calls mediating structures—churches, schools, service clubs, scouting, other voluntary associations—to do the work of promoting these values and qualities of character that constitute public goods if we produce enough. There will certainly still be free-riders who are untrustworthy and lacking in integrity who take advantage of others, but we can also monitor such activity and, if their actions violate the law, we can exclude free-riders from society by putting them in jail!

Identifying public goods

The biggest difficulty in distinguishing public goods from private goods is that both of the defining characteristics of public goods exist in varying degrees. It is not easy to draw a clear dividing line between pure public goods, pure private goods, and goods with varying degrees of publicness. There are very few pure public goods, like a sunset, where consumption is totally non-rival and exclusion virtually impossible. Likewise, there are relatively few purely private goods, because most consumption (and production) have at least some shared aspects and some difficulty in exclusion. Your consumption of a T-shirt with a provocative slogan has an impact on those you encounter. Once you put the T-shirt on, it is difficult to exclude passers-by from seeing it, whether you want them to or not. The smell of your burger, the sound of your motorcycle, the sight of your answers on a test all have an impact on those who share your company on a given day. You may seek out an isolated corner in which to eat the burger, put a muffler on your motorcycle, or cover your test paper, but exclusion is not costless even for these essentially private goods.

Figure 6.1 categorizes a variety of goods and services on two axes. The horizontal axis ranges from highly excludable (to the left of the origin) to virtually impossible to exclude. The vertical axis ranges from the highly non-rival in consumption (at the top) to the highly rival (at the bottom). Goods and services in the northeast quadrant are, in varying degrees, public goods. Those in the southwest quadrant are mostly private goods. Those in the northwest quadrant are "**club goods**" or **local public goods**, jointly consumed by club members or residents but easily kept from nonmembers or nonresidents. Club goods are non-rival but

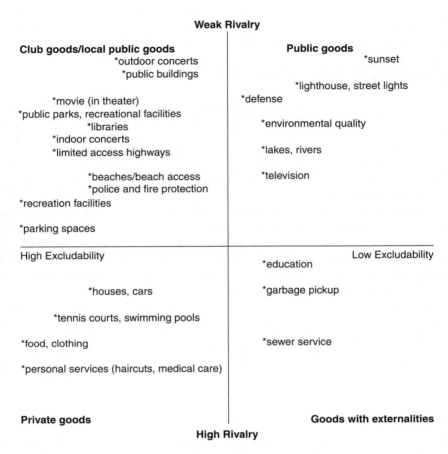

Figure 6.1 Classifying goods and services by rivalry and excludability.

excludable. This quadrant also includes **congestible goods**, which are non-rival in consumption until capacity is approached. Once that point is reached, competition for parking spaces, seats on the subway, or space on the freeway make congestible goods rival in consumption.

The upper right and lower left quadrants represent the extremes of public and private goods. The upper left corner, which includes local public goods, club goods, and congestible goods, is discussed later in this chapter, while goods with **externalities** are covered in the next chapter. Those goods and services in which one person's consumption is not diminished by sharing it with another (low rivalry) and where exclusion is difficult or costly (low excludability) are clearly public goods.

If a private producer attempted to produce such goods, she would find that she cannot easily keep non-payers from sharing in their consumption. Nor is there any good economic reason to exclude them, since consumption is noncompetitive. Goods and services with high rivalry and excludability (southwest quadrant), in contrast, lend themselves readily to market production and distribution. Consumers are readily identified and can be excluded for nonpayment, and consumption is competitive.

Managing public goods

Determining what should be produced in the public sector, how much, and who should pay is one of the most difficult challenges to public finance. Decentralized decision-making in the market place, responding to sales and profit opportunities, is pretty easy to understand. But the signals from consumers, or voters, are not nearly as clear in the public sector. We can draw some "idealized" versions of how to decide what and how much to produce and what price to charge for public production, but in practice, it is very difficult to get those numbers right.

Demand, price, and the level of output

Figures 6.2 and 6.3 illustrates the difference in how we aggregate demand curves for public and private goods in a society of only two individuals (or, more realistically, two groups of individuals), A and B. In Figure 6.2, which represents private goods with high rivalry and high excludability, the demand curves of person A (D_A) and person B (D_B) are added horizontally to create a market demand curve. The combined curve, D_T, has a kink in it, because it runs along B's demand curve until the price is low enough so that A enters the market. Beyond that kink, the points on the combined demand curve are added by choosing a price (any price) and adding the quantity demanded by A at that price to the quantity demanded by B at that price. The intersection of that market demand curve with the supply or marginal cost curve determines the equilibrium price P_1 and the equilibrium quantity Q_T. The total quantity is divided between A and B on the basis of the quantity each wishes to purchase at market price P_1, which is Q_A for person A and Q_B for person B.

However, in Figure 6.3, the situation is quite different. Because these goods are non-rival in nature, the amount available for A to consume is always the same as the amount available to B, even if they benefit from it to greater or lesser degree. If A has a 100,000-soldier army, so does B, even if B is a pacifist and totally opposed to war. If A has a lighthouse and 20 traffic lights, so does B, even if B does not own a ship or a car. In this case, what can vary

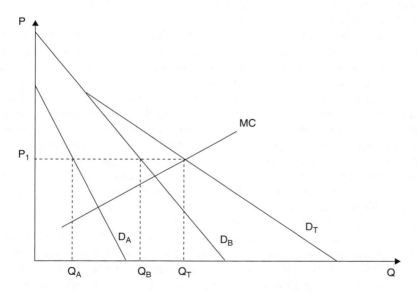

Figure 6.2 Market demand and optimal output for private goods.

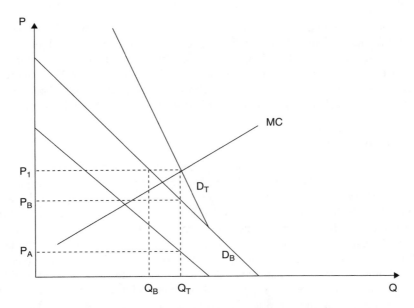

Figure 6.3 Demand, supply, and equilibrium in the market for a public good.

is not the quantity each person consumes (as for private goods) but rather the marginal benefit to each consumer and (with appropriate price discrimination) the prices paid by the two consumers of this shared good. In fact, there is a quantity for which A's marginal benefit is zero—she doesn't want more at any price—and only B is willing to pay a positive price. This quantity creates the "kink" in the total demand curve, beyond which the only demand for more units of the public good comes from B.

Think about national defense, for example. A may want just enough defense spending to protect us from a "traditional" war fought with armies and navies, while B may want a much higher level of protection such as what the "Star Wars" missile shield might provide. A is not willing to contribute a single dollar toward the missile shield.

Because of the peculiar nature of public goods, we add the demand curves vertically rather than horizontally. For private goods in Figure 6.2, we added the two demand curves by choosing a price and summing the quantities that A and B each want to consume at that price. For public goods, the quantity consumed is the same for both A and B, but the prices that A and B are willing to pay are different, because they value the public good differently. So we choose a particular quantity and add the price each is willing to pay for that shared quantity. In Figure 6.3, B's demand for this particular public good is much stronger than A's, as indicated by the higher prices B is willing to pay for any given quantity.

Both diagrams identify a socially optimal price and quantity. For the private good, everyone pays the same price and consumes a different quantity. For the public good, everyone pays a different price and consumes the same quantity. But in both cases, the price and quantity answer we are looking for is found by setting marginal benefit (measured by the prices A and B are willing to pay) equal to marginal cost (the MC curve). The optimal amount, where marginal benefit equals marginal cost, occurs in Figure 6.3 at Q_T, with a combined price of P_1. Of that total price, person A is willing to pay only P_A, while person B is willing to pay a much higher price P_B.

Who pays for public goods?

Two problems are readily apparent in the situation shown in Figure 6.3. First of all, there is the challenge of finding out how much A and B each value the public good so that each of them can be charged the appropriate price. The second problem is determining the optimal quantity when it is not possible to exclude non-payers or free-riders. It is very likely (in the absence of any intervention) that A will choose to pay nothing and just enjoy the benefits of the public good that B chooses for his or her own consumption, since that would still be a generous plenty (by A's standards) of Q_B. A has every incentive to be a free-rider in this instance. Ensuring production of the optimal amount and assigning payment to beneficiaries is much more difficult when citizens have widely different demand curves for a public good.

In Figure 6.3, the appropriate prices to charge are P_A for person A and P_B for person B. These prices, each representing the marginal benefit to the consumer, are called **Lindahl prices**. Optimality requires not only that total marginal benefit (measured by the combined demand curve) be equal to marginal cost, but also that the **marginal tax price** paid by each citizen be equal to the marginal benefit received. That challenge is much harder.

Price discrimination by means of Lindahl prices makes it more likely that the public sector will produce the optimal amount of the public good. If all citizens paid the same price, then in Figure 6.3 each person would pay a price of $P_1/2$. A would complain about high taxes for too much of a public good that she does not care that much about, and B would complain about too little of the public good being produced (but probably not about his taxes being too low). To placate A, production would be reduced so that each person would pay the lower price A is willing to pay. The result would be a level of production that is less than optimal in terms of marginal benefit and marginal costs.

Public goods are usually financed through broad-based taxes such as income, sales, and property taxes. Suppose, for example, that the city of Smallville decides to build a public park and finance it through an increase in the property tax levied on the value of property in the city. The marginal tax price is the amount of additional tax a particular citizen has to pay in order to finance this park. In Smallville, the new park costs an amount P, which is financed by a property tax at rate $t = P/V$ on all the value of the property (V) in the community. If the nth taxpayer owns property with a value of v_n, then the marginal tax price facing the nth taxpayer for another unit of the public good is

$$MTP = P/V * v_n = t * v_n.$$

Let the cost of the park be \$500,000, and the value of all the property in town \$200 million. A park would require a tax rate of \$500,000/\$200,000,000, or 0.25 percent. If you are taxpayer n, and you own a house worth \$75,000, your share of the cost of the park is .25 percent of \$75,000, or \$187.50. It is this value that the citizen compares to the additional benefit of having the park in deciding whether or not to encourage or discourage public officials from building the park.

Sometimes citizens get to vote directly on additional tax levies, but more often public officials must make these decisions with limited information about how citizen preferences match up with cost shares in new ventures. The decision may be made on the basis of rough proxies, such as assuming that the desire for public parks rises with income and that value of property owned is a good proxy for income. Or officials may focus on balancing the tax burden and service demands of the median voter whom we encountered in Chapter 4.

If there is reason to believe that demand for a public good, like national defense, is similar from one household to another, then a tax that collects the same amount from each household is an appropriate way to pay for that good from the perspective of efficiency. (Equity may be another matter.) If demand is closely related to income, as it might be for education or cultural facilities, then a proportional tax that rises as income rises would be a suitable way to raise the revenue, because it would come fairly close to matching tax prices to benefits.

In a few cases, those who benefit most are a defined subset of the population, who can be assigned their share of the cost through a **benefit tax**. Taxes on gasoline to finance highway construction and maintenance ensure that those who drive more (using the highways more and causing more wear and tear) pay a larger share of the cost through gasoline taxes. Special assessment on property taxes for improvements that only benefit one part of the community ensure that those who benefit are the ones who pay. The property tax in general, because it pays for services whose value is linked to the value of property (police protection, garbage collection, sidewalks, fire protection, etc.) has some claim to being a benefit tax.

In general, the challenge to governments in attempting to implement Lindahl pricing has two parts. The first challenge is to measure or estimate differences in demand from different individuals or groups within the population. The second challenge is to devise ways of collecting revenue that approximate those Lindahl prices for different segments of the population. Some public goods lend themselves more easily than others to such a strategy. If a lighthouse benefits primarily commercial fishing boats, then a property tax or other levy that applied only to boats would ensure that those who obtained most of the benefit would incur most or all of the cost.

Quasi-public goods: local public goods, club goods and congestible goods

In some cases, the most efficient method of providing a public good may be to locate production elsewhere with central government financing. One place to go is a lower level of government. It is often easier to monitor exclusion of non-payers, determine citizen preferences, and/or prevent free-riding at the local level, which is one of the rationales for devolution of responsibilities from central to state governments and from state to local governments. In other cases, the responsibility is shifted to the local nonprofit sector—churches, private schools, or civic organizations. The US Head Start program for preschool children is funded by the central government but actually provided mostly by private nonprofit groups.

Goods that fit this model are called local public goods if they are provided through the public sector or funded by government but produced by a nonprofit organization. They are called club goods if they are provided only to members of a private voluntary group, such as a sailing club or a neighborhood association.

Free-riding is much harder to do and easier to monitor in small groups, such as clubs, small towns, and neighborhood associations. With small numbers, one person's contribution—time, money, or votes—does make a difference to the outcome. Participation or non-participation becomes visible and personal, making free-riding more difficult. The northwest quadrant of Figure 6.1 identifies some of these local public goods and club goods, which are characterized by low rivalry but also by lower costs or fewer obstacles to excluding non-payers than public goods.[1]

Many of the goods and services listed in this quadrant are congestible goods. A congestible good is one where consumption is non-rival up to a point at which crowding begins to diminish the enjoyment of all users. Beyond that point, the good becomes more rival in nature and more like a private good. While local public goods and club goods are usually produced by local governments or private associations such as neighborhood associations, sailing clubs, and nonprofit groups, congestible goods can be found in all three producing sectors—public agencies, private for-profit firms, and private nonprofit-voluntary organizations.

A highway, an outdoor concert series, a library, a beach, and downtown parking are all congestible goods. All of them have periods of low demand and peak demand depending on the time of day, the season of the year, or the reputation of the concert performer. For those low-demand periods, as noted above, it may be less expensive to allow free usage than to incur the cost of a gatekeeper to collect admission. The problem of when to exclude non-payers and what price to charge to discourage congestion is illustrated in Figure 6.4.

Peak-load pricing

Most people have probably noticed that there are differential tolls on highways and rates on subways for peak periods and off periods, as well as periods when parking is charged for (weekdays) and periods when it is free (weekends, Sundays). This same peak-load pricing strategy is found in the private sector, where different prices are charged for matinee and evening movie seats and afternoon and evening bowling. The strategy of making the service free during periods of low demand and charging only during periods of higher demand is appropriate when the marginal cost of another user is essentially zero during off-peak periods. Up to a point (about where D_2 crosses the MC curve), additional users create only a very low and constant marginal cost (sometimes even zero)—so low that it may not be worth the trouble to try to collect a payment from them.

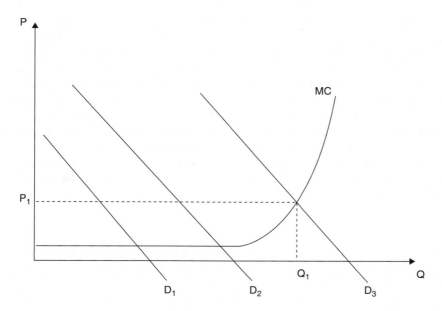

Figure 6.4 Supply, demand, and price for a congestible good.

Parking in a downtown area with lots of empty spaces, riders on a nearly empty subway train, drivers on a largely vacant stretch of highway, extra listeners at a lightly attended outdoor concert all impose very low marginal costs either on other users or in wear-and-tear or other marginal costs on the supplier. But at periods of peak demand, additional users require extra cars on the subway train, cause congestion and accidents on the Beltway, or compete for scarce parking spaces. In this case, there are at least five reasons why the producer should be charging a peak-period fee.

1   The fee rations a scarce good among competing users, assuring that the parking space, the spot in the subway car, or the space on the highway goes to the person who values it the most.
2   Revenue collected relative to the cost of collecting it rises sharply, so that it is worth incurring the cost of posting a gate-keeper to enforce payment and exclude non-payers.
3   Additional users or would-be users—drivers, parkers, riders—are imposing significant costs on others in terms of congestion and delay.
4   In the absence of a fee, public demand would pressure the authorities in charge of the facility to expand the available "slots" up to the point where the demand curve crosses the horizontal axis, i.e., up to the point where marginal benefit is equal to the zero price.
5   The price difference for congestion and non-congestion times offers an incentive for some would-be users to consider alternate times, alternative routes, or other substitutions, thus reducing peak-load demand and pressure to expand capacity.

Any time it is possible to enclose the good or service and put a ticket-taker, a toll booth, a security guard, or a pass code at the entryway at a moderate cost, the free-riding problem can be overcome. The key to payment in such cases, however, is not usually a per-use charge. Instead, these local public goods, club goods, or congestible goods are often financed by a membership fee or local tax that entitles the user to access the facility or service. Examples include a municipal swimming pool, a county library with a library card, or a beach with a membership sticker or local-resident sticker or nonresident pass displayed in the car. The single payment for unlimited access reflects the non-rival characteristic of local public goods, while at the same time identifying beneficiaries and assigning the cost of construction, maintenance and operations to those who choose to use the facility.

Often local government will assume that most residents will choose to use the facility to some degree and simply pay for the facility with taxes, issue identification cards to local residents, and only charge nonresidents. Because the marginal cost of an additional user or an additional use is equal or close to zero, users should be encouraged to use the good or service up to the point where the marginal benefit is equal or close to zero. Users will only expand their consumption to that point if the price of an additional swim in the pool or day at the beach is zero. In this case, a flat membership fee with no per-use charge is both efficient and equitable.

The two-part tariff

Still a third strategy combines the flat rate with a per-use charge. A two-part pricing schedule is often appropriate for local, club, and congestible goods, particularly if the fixed costs are relatively high and the marginal cost of additional units is relatively low. In this case, setting price equal to marginal cost—the efficiency ideal—will result in losses, because marginal cost is less than average cost (see Figure 6.5). But setting price to cover average cost

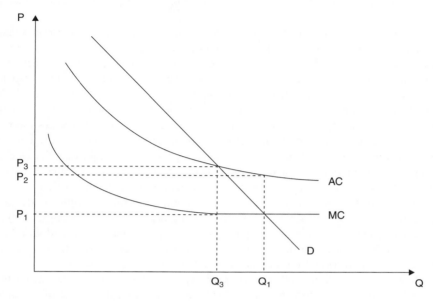

Figure 6.5 A two-part tariff.

will discourage consumption and result in less than an optimal level of production and consumption.

If the cost of excluding non-payers is not too high, an alternative strategy called the **two-part tariff** can be borrowed from utility pricing. A two-part tariff sets a charge for users with two components, a flat rate independent of quantity consumed for membership or access and a price per unit for each actual use. For example, you may have a boat at a marina with an annual charge for boat storage and a small dock fee for each time you actually use the dock. Or you may have an annual pass to a city park that entitles you to free entry, with an extra charge if you want to use certain specified services like the volleyball court or the tennis court or the pool. The fixed fee is intended to ration the available capacity among a limited number of persons with the right of access, while the per-use charge covers the variable costs of cleanup, maintenance, or other services that are positively related to the number of times the facility is actually used.

In Figure 6.5, the price that results in the socially optimal level of output Q_1 is P_1, but at that price, the total revenue is less than total cost by the amount of the shaded area. A price that covers average cost would be P_3, but it would result in output that is only Q_3. Instead, each member of the group or household in the community is charged a flat membership fee or annual charge of the shaded area divided by the number of residents, plus a price of P_1 for each unit consumed.

Common pool resources

Closely related to the provision of public or quasi-public goods is the challenge of managing **common pool resources**. These shared goods include production inputs where the property rights are held in common and consumption capital such as parks and recreation facilities.

The defining characteristic is that the resource is held in common and the use of the resource is jointly determined.

Economist Yoram Barzel argues that property rights to such resources are more complex than simple "own–don't own." Assets, including common pool resources, have many attributes. Some of the rights to those attributes belong to one person, some to another, and still others live in the public domain. For example, if you rent a car, you have certain rights of use (and responsibilities), the rental company has certain rights (a full tank of gas, return the car promptly in good condition), and certain rights remain in the public domain, like driving on the right side of the road and stopping for stop signs and red lights. Land in the eastern United States follows riparian law, which gives the owner of land access to ground and surface water contiguous to the property. Land in the western United States, where water is scarcer, follows a doctrine of prior appropriation that more clearly and narrowly defines property rights to water. Buying a piece of land in the West may or may not come with any rights to water (Barzel 1997)!

Barzel further notes that many assets remain in the public domain with rights undefined until demand for them rises for some reason—increasing population, for example. Public hunting grounds by common consent can quickly become privatized and posted with "no trespassing" signs. Beach access is in the public domain in some places, privatized in others, restricted to certain groups (like local permanent residents) in still other places.

The classic work on the subject of common property resources is Garrett Hardin's 1968 article on the tragedy of the commons (Hardin 1968). Hardin used the image of a shared grazing area in a village. Each resident would like to graze as many cows as possible, but the grazing area is limited in size, and overuse will lead to its destruction. Yet each person thinks that one more cow will make little difference to the commons, but a great difference to his income and wealth. So the temptation to overuse the shared resource is difficult to resist.

One way to deal with the management of common pool resources is to privatize the commons, so that each square foot of it belongs to someone who can use it for his or her own purposes or lease or sell it to others. However, there are problems with this approach. Succeeding generations each get smaller and smaller individual shares, and newcomers to the community find it difficult to get access to what was once a common resource. The other alternative is to manage the commons and control the terms of use. That task usually falls to the local or regional government, sometimes to a private co-operative group.

Elinor Ostrom won (shared) the Nobel Prize in Economics in 2009 for her work in exploring the many ways in which we manage common pool resources. Ostrom argues that there are intermediate options between fragmenting the commons into privately owned pieces and government control and ownership. She explores many systems around the world for managing natural resources, such as water or grazing land, that are managed by cooperative ownership. If the size of the group and the commons is small enough, there will be no opportunity for anyone to get away undetected with free-riding. What is required is ways to exclude external parties, rules about the use of common property resources, broad participation in decision-making, effective monitoring, sanctions, and methods of conflict resolution (Ostrom 1990).

Summary

- The public sector faces the same challenges of efficiency and equity as the private sector. Governments take responsibility for producing those goods that the private sector fails to produce, or to produce enough, because of the free-rider problem in the private sector.

- Public goods are characterized by non-rivalry in consumption and non-excludability of those who do not pay. There are few pure cases of public goods, but many goods with little rivalry and high costs of exclusion.
- All goods can be classified according to the degree of rivalry and excludability into four classes. Low rivalry, low excludability goods are public goods; high rivalry, high excludability goods are private goods; low rivalry, high excludability goods are local public goods or club goods; and high rivalry, low excludability goods are those that create positive or negative externalities.
- For public goods, demand is added vertically rather than horizontally to determine the optimum quantity. When each person pays the price that reflects their marginal benefit, they are being charged Lindahl prices. In the absence of government intervention, the market will produce too little of the public good and charge a price that is too low for optimality.
- Optimality requires not only that sum of the marginal benefits (measured by the combined demand curve) be equal to marginal cost, but also that the marginal tax price paid by each citizen be equal to the marginal benefit received. The marginal tax price is the citizen's share of the additional taxes required to pay for the public good. Shifting production of local public goods from the central to the local level, with or without central government funding, is one way to provide a better match between the tax cost and the benefits of those goods.
- A local public good or a club good is shared by members of a group or community on the basis of shared membership. Free-riding is avoided because the good is excludable.
- Congestible goods are a special case of local public goods (or private or club goods) in which the marginal cost is very low up to a capacity point at which the marginal cost of additional users begins to rise sharply. Peak load pricing or two part tariffs are two methods for pricing congestible goods.
- Common pool resources are shared goods that include production inputs where the property rights are held in common and consumption capital such as parks and recreation facilities. One way to deal with the management of common pool resources is to privatize the commons, The other alternative is to allow a local government or private co-operative group to manage the commons and control the terms of use.

Key terms

Benefit tax
Club goods
Common pool resources
Congestible goods
Externality
Free-rider
Lindahl prices
Local public goods
Marginal tax price
Non-excludability
Non-rivalry
Public goods
Two-part tariff

Questions

1   For each of the following goods or services, would you classify it as a public good, a local public or club good or congestible good, or a private good (with or without externalities)? Explain your choice. Could some of them fall in one or another category depending on the assignment of property rights?

    •   the Supreme Court
    •   a local magistrate's court
    •   the interstate highway system
    •   college education
    •   a beach
    •   the stars at night viewed from outdoors
    •   the stars viewed at a planetarium

2   Your neighborhood association manages a swimming pool that is open to both neighborhood residents and a limited number of outsiders who pay a fee (members of the association have a fee included in their association dues). How many outsiders do you want to accept? How would you determine a charge? Would it be per use, a flat fee, or a combination? What factors would influence your choice?

3   Suppose you are charged with financing the construction and operation of a lighthouse. Who benefits? Do some groups benefit more than others? Make your case for some kind of financing with any combination of general taxes, taxes on specific activities or goods, or fees to particular identified groups.

4   **By the numbers**. Suppose you operate a parking lot. The marginal cost of an additional customer is only 50 cents, but the fixed cost of the whole operation in the short run for space rent, maintenance, and a ticket taker is $1,000 per day. The average daily number of customers is 200. What is the appropriate price to charge? Does the answer differ if marginal cost is falling instead of rising at that level of demand?

5   **Policy application**. Suppose that you live in a small, self-contained neighborhood that has a neighborhood association. The association automatically counts all property owners in the neighborhood as voting members. The association owns a vacant lot, and the members are divided about its use. One group wants to leave it undeveloped as green space, a quiet buffer against outside noises; the other group wants to develop it into a picnic area and a playground for the children. You, as president of the association, have to help them find a solution. How might you determine the highest and best use of this property?

6   **Behavioral economics**. What characteristics or qualities in human motivation might make people more likely to free-ride? What characteristics or qualities might make them less likely to free-ride? What kinds of social institutions or practices (such as values, education) might influence human motivation and behavior so as to reduce free-riding?

7   **Thinking globally**. Common pool resources extend beyond national boundaries—the oceans, the atmosphere, rivers that flow through multiple countries. How does national sovereignty limit our ability to manage common pool resources appropriately? What role, if any, can markets and prices play in the management of these common pool resources?

Appendix: the mathematics of public and private goods

Private goods

The mathematical determination of the price and quantity in a market with (for simplicity) just two consumers or groups of consumers is as follows. The expressions

$$Q_a^x = f_a(P^x), \ Q_b^x = f_b(P^x) \tag{6.1}$$

represent the quantities of good X that persons A and B will purchase at various alternative prices.

In the private sector, the market demand curve is simply the horizontal (quantity) sum of these two demand curves, i.e.

$$Q_m = Q_a^x + Q_b^x = f_a(P^x) + f_b(P^x) \tag{6.2}$$

For example, consider two linear demand curves for good x for persons A and B:

$$Q_a^x = A_0 - a_1 P^x \text{ and } Q_b^x = B_0 - b_1 P^x \tag{6.3}$$

which sum to

$$Q_m^x = Q_a^x + Q_b^x = A_0 - a_1 P^x + B_0 - b_1 P^x = (A_0 + B_0) - (a_1 + b_1) \, P^x \tag{6.4}$$

This equation can be solved for price as a function of quantity:

$$P^x = \frac{(A_0 + B_0) - Q_m^x}{(a_1 + b_1)} \tag{6.5}$$

The market supply curve is the marginal cost curve, also expressed with price as a function of quantity:

$$MC = P^x = C_0 + c_1 Q_m^x \tag{6.6}$$

These two equations can be solved for the unique equilibrium values of P^x and Q_m^x expressed in terms of the six parameters A_0, B_0, and C_0 and a_1, b_1, and c_1. Once P^x is determined, consumers A and B can substitute that value into their demand curves to determine their individual shares of the total market purchases of good X. Each consumer pays the same price and chooses a quantity for which his or her marginal benefit, as reflected in the demand curve, is equal to the price of the good.

Public goods

Mathematically, the problem is similar to the one posed above, except that in this case the solution is for a market-clearing quantity and different prices paid by the two buyers. Let A and B, as before, have demand curves

$$Q^x = A_0 - a_1 P_a^x \text{ and } Q^x = B_0 - b_1 P_b^x \tag{6.7}$$

which must be inverted before adding them to get the sum of the prices that the two buyers will pay:

$$P_a^x = \frac{A_0 + Q^x}{a_1} \text{ and } P_a^x = \frac{B_0 + Q^x}{b_1} \tag{6.8}$$

Since the price paid is the sum of the contributions of A and B,

$$P^x = P_a^x + P_b^x = A_0/a_1 - (1/a_1)Q^x + B_0/b_1 - (1/b_1)Q^x$$
$$= (A_0/a_1 + B_0/b_1) - (1/a_1 + 1/b_1)\, Q^x \tag{6.9}$$

This equation can be rewritten so that the shared quantity, Q^x, is expressed as a function of the price and the parameters or constants A_0, B_0, a_1, and b_1:

$$Q^x = \frac{(A_0/a_1 + B_0/b_1) - P^x}{(1/a_1 + 1/b_1)} \tag{6.10}$$

The supply curve (or marginal cost curve) for the good,

$$MC = P^x = C_0 + c_1 Q^x \tag{6.11}$$

must also be rewritten with Q^x as a function of price:

$$Q^x = -C_0/c_1 + (1/c_1)P^x \tag{6.12}$$

Equations 6.10 and 6.12 can be solved to find P_x, which can then be substituted into either equation to determine Q_x. The two equations 6.10 and 6.12 will yield unique equilibrium values for Q_x and P_x that can be expressed in terms of the six parameters A_0, B_0, and C_0 and a_1, b_1, and c_1. This value of Q_x can then be substituted back in the demand Equations 6.8 to determine the (different) prices that A and B are willing to pay for that quantity of the shared good. Q_x is optimal because the marginal benefit (A's plus B's) is equal to the marginal cost at that quantity.

7 Externalities
Dealing with spillover effects

Introduction

In the previous chapter, we explored the difference between public goods and private goods and also looked at the hybrid case of club goods or congestible goods. That left just those goods and services in the lower right quadrant of Figure 6.1: goods and services that create positive **externalities**, or spillover effects. Services with positive spillover effects, or social benefits, include education, garbage pickup, and sewer service. In each case, the production or consumption by one person benefits other people who are not paying for the good or service. Negative externalities are costs imposed on or benefits received by third parties outside the market transaction, costs that they cannot impose on their creators or benefits for which they are not charged.

Externalities can result from either production or consumption. Consumption (production) externalities occur when a second person is affected by your consumption (production) of a good or service, either positively or negatively, even though that person (or often, many persons) is not a party to the transaction leading to your consumption (production).

Typically, when there are positive externalities from either consumption or production, it is very difficult to exclude non-payers from receiving those benefits. That's why externalities appeared in the high rivalry, low excludability part of Figure 6.1. Externalities typically result from what we think of as basically private activities with side-effects (costs or benefits) that we cannot easily prevent from spilling over to others.

Both consumption and production activities can also generate negative externalities. Examples of negative spillover effects include poorly maintained yards and houses that detract from the neighborhood and property values, sewage discharge into waterways that affects downstream residents, and litter discarded along the sides of highways. Reducing negative externalities poses the same kind of challenge as the encouragement of positive externalities.

An important characteristic of externalities, positive or negative, consumption or production, is that they are reciprocal in nature. A firm may impose externalities on its neighborhood residents by creating traffic congestion or odors. On the other hand, the firm may consider its neighbors' demands for less traffic or aroma as imposing costs on it. There are costs regardless of whether there is more or less traffic or more or less smell.

The real question is who bears the costs (or reaps the benefits, in the case of positive externalities). Much of the debate about externalities is about the distribution of costs and benefits. The economist's concern is to distribute the costs and benefits in ways that move production toward the level at which marginal cost is equal to marginal benefit, when all costs and benefits are taken into account. As we shall see, there are many ways to achieve that objective.

Positive externalities

A child's education not only benefits the child and her family but also other people in the community. Others in the community benefit from being a part of a more educated, productive community. Educated citizens are more productive, more informed citizens, and more likely to have a taste for consumer goods and services (upscale restaurants, bookstores, concert halls, etc.) that require a critical mass of educated citizens to support them. Similarly, when your neighbor's garbage is collected regularly, your health risk is reduced and the value of your property is enhanced. When a street light is located half a block from your house, paid for by the resident there, you can walk in greater safety at night. When one household remodels their home or landscapes it attractively, benefits accrue particularly to neighbors but also to those who walk or drive through the neighborhood. All of these examples involve goods or services with positive consumption externalities.

The optimal level of output

Figure 7.1 illustrates a situation of positive externalities, also known as social benefits. Note that the curve labeled MSB (marginal social benefit) looks very similar to the demand curve for one of the two individuals in the case of a public good. **Marginal social benefit** is a measure of the value of positive externalities at various levels of output or consumption.

In both cases, the benefits are added vertically rather than horizontally, because the same quantity of output that produces a given level of private benefits will also generate social benefits. However, in the case of positive externalities, the demand curve D_A represents the preferences of only the direct beneficiary or beneficiaries—the buyers of the good or service.

MSB represents marginal social benefits to all of those who are indirect beneficiaries of the purchase of the same quantities of this good. Most of the benefits accrue to the direct buyers and most of the cost rightly should fall on them in a world that is both efficient and

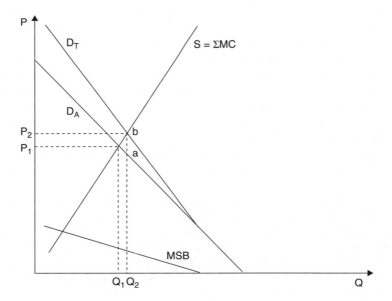

Figure 7.1 Optimal output for a good with positive externalities.

equitable. The sum of the two curves, D_T, reflects both private demand and social benefits. D_T is sometimes called a **shadow curve**, because it exists simultaneously with the private demand curve. The seller perceives D_A as his demand curve. Unless some action is taken to make the seller respond to D_T rather than D_A, the good or service with positive externalities will be under-produced.

The problem associated with relying solely on private production and sale of goods with positive externalities is that these private transactions do not reflect social benefits. Because those who benefit are not easily excluded from the spillover effects of A's consumption, they can free ride rather than contribute to its purchase. Without the contribution *ab* from those enjoying social benefits, the sole force in the market on the demand side is D_A, and the quantity purchased will be Q_1 at a price of P_1—both lower than the socially optimal quantity Q_2 and price P_2. The appropriate price to charge the primary user or direct customers is measured in Figure 7.1 as the lower price P_1.

In order to induce more production of goods with positive externalities, the seller will require a higher price P_1 to cover his increasing marginal costs. The difference between the price received by the seller and the price paid by the buyer is the appropriate contribution per unit from all the would-be free-riders who experience social benefits (or positive externalities), measured by the distance *ab*.

Correcting positive externalities

The fact that there are external benefits does not necessarily mean under-production will occur. If most of the benefits are private, and social benefits are small relative to private benefits, the total benefit curve may intersect the marginal cost curve at a point below where social benefits "kick in" (the kink in Figure 7.1). For example, post-graduate education does create external benefits, but the private benefits are usually so substantial relative to the externalities (particularly for MBAs, law school and medical school) that a subsidy is not necessary in order to produce the socially optimum level of output. When intervention is needed, however, the question is how to fill in the *ab* gap. What prices, taxes, subsidies, or fees will distribute the burden of payment efficiently and equitably while giving the appropriate amount of encouragement to production of goods with positive externalities?

Among the methods of addressing positive externalities are producing the good or service in the public sector, paying with taxes; providing public subsidies to private production; or mandating the consumption of the good or service. Mandating became controversial in the Obama health care legislation in 2010 because it required people to buy health insurance. The cost of providing the social benefit is imposed on the consumer unless it is accompanied by some kind of **subsidy**, such as a tax credit or voucher.

Public production distributes the total cost of the good or service among all taxpayers even though the benefits accrue primarily to a smaller subset of principal users, whether the good is education, parks, or garbage pickup. Heavier users will enjoy benefits in excess of their costs, while light users or nonusers who only get external benefits are likely to pay more in taxes than the benefits they receive.

Public subsidies for private production can be a little more successful in distributing the cost between primary and secondary beneficiaries, so that the primary consumers still pay the bulk of the cost and the subsidy from general tax revenues only covers the difference between private and social benefits. But the distribution of the tax burden may be very different from the distribution of the external benefits. So an important consideration in the choice of a method to move from Q_2 to Q_1 is the effects on the distribution of income and wealth.

Positive production externalities

It is easier to come up with examples of positive **consumption externalities** than positive **production externalities**, but there are some. One of the forms that positive production externalities take is called economies of agglomeration. When firms in the same industry are located in the same area (from Detroit in the past to Silicon Valley), they benefit each other. They attract and share a pool of talent, enjoy economies of scale, and challenge each other to stay on the cutting edge. They attract suppliers, reducing shipping costs.

On a smaller scale, commercial development has the same agglomeration effect if there is a critical mass of diverse but complementary retail stores, restaurants and service firms in a given area. They compete with each other, but they also create a destination that attracts more customers that patronize several establishments at once.

Case study: positive externalities and bus service

Using public transportation generates significant social benefits for others. There is less highway congestion and air pollution, less competition for parking spaces or pressure to create additional parking at commercial areas and workplaces. At the local level, the most common form of public transportation is the bus. But riding the bus is not always the most convenient way for people to get around. Buses operate on fixed schedules, so that there is a time cost in waiting for the bus. There is a convenience factor in having your own car if you have errands to run or children to pick up. So people need to be encouraged to ride the bus because of the social benefits or positive externalities they create.

Private bus companies have been unable to compete with the lure of the personal car as a way to get around, so most of them have gone out of business, been taken over by local governments, or operate with a subsidy. The question is not whether there should be a subsidy, but how much of a subsidy and how should it be distributed among potential riders?

Different cities have come up with different answers. College towns often have free bus service, or at least "free" for students (the cost is usually buried in tuition), in order to reduce the amount of scarce and valuable campus space that must be devoted to parking. Often these buses also shuttle commuting students and faculty from remote parking lots to the center of campus. Sometimes, but not often, the free bus service is extended to others as well. If most of the riders are entitled to free service, it may be less expensive to let everyone ride free than to collect small fees from non-qualifying customers. Often those most in need of transportation are those least able to pay, so there is a distributional issue as well in deciding whether to charge a fee.

Most bus services do charge customers a fee, but the charge is usually less than the average cost, perhaps closer to marginal cost. If the bus is going to drive a route anyway, then at least in the short run the marginal cost of an additional rider is very close to zero. However, if the route is popular, there will be a demand for more frequent service, requiring additional buses, drivers and fuel, so it is appropriate to make some charge in order to manage demand. Using tokens, fare cards, or other methods of quick and convenient payment minimizes the time and effort expended in collecting, with only the odd out-of-town user offering actual cash for riding the bus.

Distribution of the cost is an issue when a fee is charged. Some cities might offer bus passes to low-income residents. Often senior citizens are entitled to a lower fare, which may be because they are assumed to be poorer, or because there is a desire to get them off the road! Buses also often offer amenities to entice riders, such as a bicycle carrier to connect bike riders with public transportation, or wheelchair access capability with a lift. These additional costs without additional charges are also a form of public subsidy.

Negative externalities

External social costs can result from either production or consumption. Second-hand smoke from cigars and cigarettes or air pollution from driving a car are examples of consumption externalities, while water pollution from factory effluent or health care costs from pesticide residue on food are examples of production externalities.

The optimal level of output

Figure 7.2 illustrates negative externalities, or external social costs. When goods are produced and sold (and consumed), the seller's supply curve (or marginal cost curve, S_P) only reflects the explicit costs that he or she has to pay in order to produce the good. If costs fall on others because the production (or consumption) of the good creates noise, pollution, hazards, or other social costs, market forces will not take those external effects into account in determining the equilibrium price (P_1) and the quantity (Q_1). In the absence of intervention, producers and consumers will strike a bargain at a price that is too low and a quantity that is too high, because they have failed to take into account all the costs of producing the good, including the social costs.

Because production externalities are on the cost side of the supply–demand relationship, they impact on the supply curve. The additive process is the same, but the interpretation and the outcome are different. Social costs are taken into account by adding the cost of the spillover effects to the cost of raw materials, labor, capital, and other inputs to the firm's marginal cost/supply curve. Spillover effects are measured graphically on the marginal social benefit

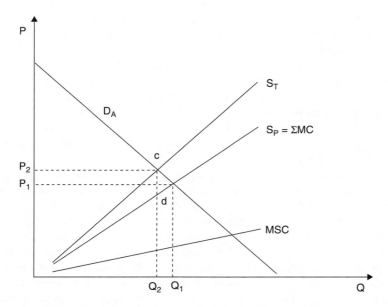

Figure 7.2 Optimal output for a good with negative externalities.

curve, which shows the value of negative externalities experienced by all parties at various levels of production or consumption. These curves are added vertically because the combined cost is the sum of two kinds of costs for the same quantity of output. If social costs are reflected in the supply curve, consumers will face higher prices and choose a smaller quantity, so that the equilibrium will occur at the higher equilibrium price P_2 and the lower equilibrium quantity Q_2.

Internalizing externalities: taxes or regulation?

Somehow the additional cost cd has to be reflected in the costs incurred by the producer so that it will be reflected in the market price, a process known as **internalizing externalities**. There are many techniques for internalizing externalities. Regulations can force producers to use methods of production that increase worker or product safety, reduce emissions, effluents, or noise, or raise costs in other ways. In recent years, however, there has been increased reliance on market-like mechanisms of fees, fines, taxes and charges that are set so as to shift the cost curve to S_T, internalizing the externalities and moving market choices toward the socially optimal level of output

How are the externalities internalized? Most commonly, a tax, fee, or effluent charge is used in the case of air (emissions) or water (effluents). If the amount of the fee per unit can be set at a value approximately equal to cd in Figure 7.2, then production of the externality-causing good or service will be reduced to the socially optimal level. Effluent charges have been used for many years in France, Germany, and the Netherlands in order to ensure acceptable levels of water quality (Hahn 1989). Their use in the United States is more recent.

Case study: the garbage dilemma

One of the biggest problems facing local governments is the collection and disposal of household solid waste. Environmental regulations to protect groundwater from leakages out of landfills have made it expensive to build landfills, and land at a convenient location for disposal is hard to find, especially since very few people want a landfill sited in their back yards. By the 1990s, local governments had begun to recognize that, while solid waste (including its shadow companion, litter) was an unavoidable negative externality in a consumer society, the production of solid waste appeared to be exceeding the socially optimal level. Faced with the unpleasant prospect of raising local taxes, local officials felt that the savings in collection and disposal costs by reducing solid waste going into the landfill would exceed the inconvenience, higher prices, restricted choices, or other negative incentives that citizens would have to endure.

The "old" style of dealing with negative externalities would have been a regulatory approach that simply limited the amount of waste a household could have picked up and imposed severe penalties on other forms of disposal (like dropping it by the side of the road). But that approach would have penalized large households, or households with children. Instead, local governments have adopted a mixed bag of carrots and sticks designed to reduce household wastes, often under pressure from their state governments to meet specific targets. Recycling programs, including educational efforts and programs to make it easier and more convenient (like curbside pickup and convenient collection stations) succeeded in reducing the amount of trash that found its way into the landfill. Many local governments even made money reselling recyclables!

Pay-as-you-throw programs were another incentive system, in which garbage had to be put out in bags purchased only from the local government. The more bags you put out, the more you paid. Sorted recyclables, however, were picked up at no charge. While results are mixed, this blend of recycling incentives and higher marginal cost of more waste has been widely adopted. It may not have resulted in the optimal level of trash, but the pile of garbage was at least reduced, a move in the correct direction.

Marginal social cost and marginal social benefit

An alternative approach to analyzing negative externalities is to focus on the externality itself rather than the good whose production or consumption creates the externality. Whether the externality is pollution, congestion, noise, beauty, ambience, or the sound of beautiful music, this approach focuses only on the **marginal social cost** and marginal social benefit of creating or experiencing the externality. In both cases, unless the externalities are extremely severe in their social costs, the optimal level of a negative externality is not likely to be zero, because zero externalities would also shut down the production and consumption of desirable goods and services. Figure 7.3 illustrates this approach to analyzing social costs.

This approach emphasizes the reciprocal nature of externalities. Reductions in externalities are subject to diminishing marginal benefit. People may want cleaner, safer water, but absolute purity is not essential. Each additional step in making water cleaner costs more. It is easy to filter out the trash, and more expensive to treat water with chemicals, and prohibitively expensive to make it absolutely pure. At some point, the cost of an additional step in purifying water exceeds the benefits. So there is an optimal level of pollution at which the marginal benefit of the last reduction in impurities just equals the marginal cost of

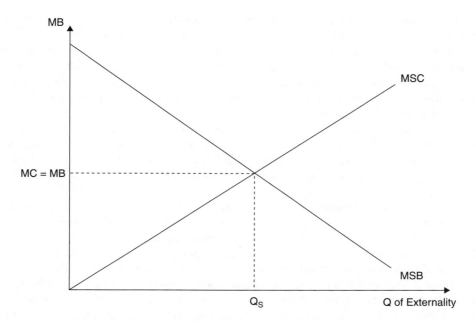

Figure 7.3 Marginal cost and marginal benefit.

elimination. That optimal level of pollution in this diagram is Q_s. Beyond that point there is not enough additional benefit to further reduction to offset the higher cost.

Creative solutions

Determining the optimal level of public good production and allocating the cost appropriately among users is a real challenge to public officials. So is measuring externalities and designing and executing appropriate interventions to move output to the appropriate level and assign the costs to beneficiaries to the extent possible. In the 1950s and 1960s, the standard response to this form of market failure was for the government to produce public goods or goods with substantial positive externalities. For negative externalities, the response was to regulate, forbid, or restrict the production of those externalities, either directly (limits on discharges into the air or water, for example) or through limits on the production and consumption of goods that cause negative externalities (safety regulations, restrictions on access to alcohol, etc.).

In recent decades, much attention has been given to identifying existing mechanisms for correcting externalities as well as devising new techniques. They include:

- assignment of property rights (the Coase theorem);
- tax incentives and vouchers;
- educational/informational programs to encourage or discourage certain types of production;
- the development of markets in permits for emissions;
- shifting production to a lower level of government or a nonprofit provider.

Property rights and the Coase theorem

The Coase theorem, developed by Nobel prize winner Ronald Coase, suggests that some externality problems could be resolved through assignment of property rights. Specifically, this theorem says that, where small numbers of participants are involved, property rights can be assigned to one of the parties for a contested resource (such as the use of a lake or waterway), and subsequent negotiations will result in the socially optimal use of the resource. This outcome is independent of which of the two parties is given the property right, although the distributional effects can be an important consideration (Coase 1960).

For example, suppose that an industrial firm and a group of nature lovers are interested in using a small lake, the former for discharging wastes, the latter for swimming, boating, and fishing. These two uses are not compatible. Which is the best and highest use of the lake? If it is assumed that both parties have enough resources to express their effective demand, then the lake should be used by the party who is willing to pay the highest price for the use of the lake. Suppose that the industrial firm is assigned the right to use the lake as it sees fit. The group of nature lovers could make the firm an offer to restrict its effluent below a certain level that would make the lake still usable for recreation. If the cost of disposing of its effluent in another way was less than the amount offered by the nature lovers, the industrial firm would agree, and the lake would be used for fishing, boating, and swimming.

Suppose, conversely, that the right to control the use of the lake was assigned to the nature lovers group. The industrial firm could approach them with an offer of a price at which a given amount of effluent could be discharged into the lake. If that amount is sufficient for the nature lovers to either restore the lake to their desired use or make satisfactory other arrangements for their outdoor recreation, then the lake will be used for industrial discharge. If not, it will be used for recreation. The cost always falls on the group which did not receive the initial distribution of property rights, so the distribution of costs and benefits is very different, but the outcome in terms of the use of the resource is the same in both instances.

The Coase theorem obviously applies only to cases where there are relatively few affected parties. However, it has considerable potential for resolving local disputes or neighborhood conflicts if the equity issue can be addressed. The great advantage of this approach is that it forces participants to reveal their demand or preferences by bidding for the use of the contested resource. However, as the affected parties increase in number, there is still a potential for free-riding. If you are a nature lover and it appears that your side will win either by bidding the rights away from the industrial plant, you can remain quiet, hoping that you will get to use the lake for recreation without having to contribute. In some cases, exclusion mechanisms exist that limit the use of the contested resource to those who paid. In other cases, exclusion is difficult. But certainly a Coase solution is one recourse for addressing some problems of externalities.

Property rights and equity

Equity questions also arise in the recent trend toward seeking market-based solutions to conflicts by assigning property rights. The Coase theorem is often considered to be a method of attaining efficiency, but its implications for equity are at least as important as its usefulness in promoting efficient outcomes. As Nobel Prize-winning economist Ronald Coase has ably demonstrated, the outcome of a conflict over how certain resources are to be used is likely to be the same regardless of which of the conflicting parties are initially assigned the property rights. There will, however, be major differences in the distribution of income and wealth.

Suppose, for example, once more that the common property in dispute is a small lake. The property adjacent to the lake is owned by ten private homeowners and one factory. The homeowners' association wants to use the lake for boating, swimming and fishing, while the factory wants to use the lake as a source of water for its operations and a way to dispose of industrial wastes at a point beyond that intake. The latter use is in conflict with the desires of homeowners. The government could intervene in this dispute in a regulatory fashion by restricting the rights of either or both parties, or it could simply assign property rights to either the factory owner or the ten homeowners and let market forces resolve the dispute. If the property rights to the lake are assigned to the factory owner, he or she will use the lake for disposal purposes. But if the value of the lake for recreation is high enough for the ten residential property owners to band together and bribe the factory owner to find another method of waste disposal, the lake will be used for recreation.

Conversely, if the right to determine the use of the lake is assigned to the residential property owners' association, it will be used for recreation, unless its value to the factory owner for disposal purposes is so high that he or she can pay the owners' association to take their recreation elsewhere. In either case, the use of the lake will go to the party that values it the most. The only difference between assigning rights to residents versus the factory owner is the distribution of wealth between the two parties, because the one who receives the initial property rights either gets to control the use of the lake or gets paid to have it used otherwise.

Once property rights are assigned, the Coase theorem states that the property in dispute will tend toward its highest and best use as valued by market prices as long as the number of parties involved is small enough. While the outcome of assigning property rights is likely to be efficient, however, it is not necessarily perceived as equitable, because the conflicting parties do not have equal resources with which to bid for the use of the disputed property. When the government addresses conflicts over use of resources by assigning property rights, it is important to take such equity considerations into account.

Tax incentives and vouchers

Tax incentives (deductions, exclusions or credits, usually on the income tax) and vouchers are two techniques used to encourage the production and consumption of goods that generate positive externalities. In both cases, these instruments are intended to roughly approximate the value of the marginal social benefits in order to increase consumption of such desirable goods and services as education, beautification, energy-efficient housing, and private social welfare agencies (through the charitable deduction). The value of the tax revenue forgone in order to promote certain kinds of production or consumption is known as a tax expenditure. Vouchers (typically for housing, education, or health care services) allow individuals to purchase those goods or services free or at a reduced price. The service provider redeems the vouchers for payment from the government that issued them.

   The appeal of these two techniques is that the decision about whether and how much to consume and which supplier to patronize is transferred from the government to the consumer. By utilizing the private sector, there is more opportunity for competition, which may hold down costs and make suppliers more responsive to consumers. The drawback is that both methods can be somewhat inefficient in terms of the amount of consumption that they stimulate per tax dollar spent, relative to the amount of spending for those purposes that would have taken place without the incentive or voucher. The tax credit or voucher goes to all consumers who qualify, including a substantial number of those who would have made the purchase without the incentive. Targeted vouchers or tax breaks, limited to those below a certain income level, above a certain family size or age, or other criteria, may reduce this inefficiency.

Behavioral economics: Shifting the demand curve

Yet another approach to encouraging the consumption of goods with positive externalities, such as education, is to attempt to stimulate a stronger preference for those goods through educational and informational methods. Likewise, it is possible to discourage the consumption of goods with negative externalities—alcohol, cigarettes, tobacco—through advertising and educational campaigns. Shifting the private demand for goods with positive externalities to the right and those with negative externalities to the left can reduce the relative importance of social costs and/or social benefits in determining the optimal level of output and make the private market output closer to the optimal level.

Marketable emission permits: cap and trade

Frustration with the rigidity of regulatory approaches to environmental quality has led to the development of markets in permits for emissions and other methods of allowing firms or groups of firms to allocate the "right to pollute" based on market forces. If the ultimate goal is a certain level of air quality or water quality, or a target maximum level of emissions, that goal can be attained in many ways. Some sources can be reduced more cheaply than others.

By using markets to allocate a limited number of emission permits, the goal will be attained more efficiently than by regulations which do not differentiate between pollution sources that can reduce emissions easily and others that can only do it at high cost.

In the United States, this approach of **cap and trade** was used successfully starting in 1990 to reduce "acid rain," a consequence of emissions of sulphur dioxide and nitrous oxide. There are severe penalties for excess emissions. A cap was set on allowable emissions, and firms emitting SO_2 and NO_x were required to have permits equal to the amount emitted. Firms that require more permits can purchase them from other firms in an open market, but the amount of emissions allowed is reduced annually. From 1990 to 2008, sulphur dioxide emissions dropped 52 percent. Nitrous oxide emissions fell by 51 percent over the same period.[1]

In 2005 the European Union began using a similar program to reduce carbon emissions, which scientists generally believe contribute to global warming. Initially permits were given away, and the permits available were too generous to result in much carbon reduction. Now the permits are sold and the number is more restricted, resulting in reduced carbon emissions. The fear that companies would relocate to countries with no emissions restrictions does not appear to have been realized as yet, but it is a concern about the effectiveness of a cap and trade system, particularly for non-utility firms which may have more flexibility in their choice of location. The United States is contemplating a similar program. Australia has a somewhat different approach called "fee and dividend," which imposes a fee on the initial sale of fossil fuel and distributes the revenue to the public to help them cope with rising costs of energy use.

Which level of government?

Externalities are a challenge at all levels of government. Some externalities are highly local—the benefits of a local bus system, or reduced waste to haul to the local landfill, for example. These externalities can be addressed by local governments based on the needs and desires of the local community, although often state or national governments will offer positive incentives in the form of grants or penalties for failure to achieve goals as a way of encouraging reductions in externalities that spill over local or state boundaries.

Often the externalities, positive or negative, are spread over a larger area. Most of the students who graduate from public schools remain in the general area, but not necessarily in the locality where they attended, so the social benefits of their education may accrue to other communities. To the extent that they migrate to urban areas, local funding of education is a tax on rural areas with the benefits being felt in urban centers. That situation suggests a larger state role in funding education. Because watersheds cross state boundaries—rivers frequently define state borders—the central government has a role to play in protecting water quality. Issues such as overfishing, pollution of the oceans, and global warming require international collaboration, such as the Copenhagen Treaty on carbon emissions.

In most cases, responsibility for externalities is shared between two or three levels of government, with the lower levels having some flexibility in meeting targets and receiving some financial support for their efforts. Experimentation with different approaches in different states and countries is a useful way to take advantage of federalism as a laboratory for policy. Making it easier for local governments to combine through annexation or consolidation, or to create collaborative bodies may allow the jurisdiction to correspond more closely to the range of the externality in question. In that case, those who cause the externality and those affected by it both have a voice in addressing the externality.

Competition between localities for residents and business firms may result in under-production of positive externalities and overproduction of negative externalities. Positive incentives (such as grants) and negative incentives (penalties) from a higher level of government may be required in order to move the production of externalities toward the social optimum.

Summary

- Externalities are spillover effects from consumption or production that fall on third parties. Goods that create positive externalities or marginal social benefits to someone other than the buyer will be underproduced by the market in the absence of intervention.
- To determine the optimal quantity and price, private demand and marginal social benefits are added vertically. The difference between the demand price and the supply price at the optimal level of output is the required subsidy.
- Goods that create negative externalities or marginal social costs to someone other than the producer or consumer will be overproduced by the market in the absence of intervention.
- To determine the optimal quantity and price, marginal social costs are added vertically to the supply or marginal private cost curve. The difference between the demand price and the supply price at the optimal level of output is the required additional cost that must be paid by the supplier, part of which is passed on to the consumer.
- Total elimination of externalities is prohibitively expensive, even if it is technically feasible. The additional resources required to do so will not generate enough additional benefits to justify the additional cost. Focusing on setting marginal cost equal to marginal benefit is a useful way to think about optimal pollution.
- Traditional responses to externalities include public production, taxes, subsidies, and regulations. Evolving forms of correction for externalities include reducing the cost of exclusion, assignment of property rights, use of tax incentives and vouchers, educational/informational programs to encourage or discourage certain types of production, and development of markets in permits for emissions.
- Assignment of property rights if the number of parties affected is small will result in an optimal allocation of resources, regardless of which party receives the initial assignment of property rights.
- Marketable emission permits have gained in popularity in the past two decades, first for sulphur dioxide and nitrous oxide and more recently for carbon emissions.
- Responsibility for subsidizing positive externalities and discouraging negative externalities is often shared among levels of government because of spillovers across jurisdictions and because of competition.

Key terms

Cap and trade
Consumption externalities
Externality
Internalizing externalities
Marginal social benefit
Marginal social cost
Production externalities
Shadow curve
Subsidy

Questions

1   Figure 7.2 illustrates a negative production externality. It can be adapted to describe the case of negative consumption externalities, in which buyers would consume too much because they failed to take into account the costs their consumption imposes on others. This kind of externality can be visualized with shadow demand curves rather than supply curves. Redraw Figure 7.2 to illustrate the negative consumption externalities associated with smoking. Find the socially optimal level of consumption and the amount of tax or penalty needed to bring it about.

2   How do neighborhood associations and homeowners' covenants control negative externalities and encourage (or require!) positive externalities? What are the advantages and drawbacks of this approach from the perspective of the individual homeowner?

3   How might either the Coase theorem or the compensation principle help in the following situations?

   (a)   One neighbor in a subdivision who does not maintain her property and makes it less attractive to everyone (and reduces adjacent property values)
   (b)   Conflict between those who want more street lights for safety and those who like dark streets at night because the light doesn't keep them awake
   (c)   Access to a limited supply of potable water that households want to use but that farmers would like to have for irrigation
   (d)   Allocating an unexpected increase in local government revenue for street improvements

4   **By the numbers**. Tax deductions and tax credits are one way to subsidize individuals to spend their money in ways that create positive externalities, such as contributions to charities or saving for their children's education. How much did Americans claim in itemized charitable deductions on their federal income tax in the most recent available year? If the average person claiming a tax deduction was in the 25 percent bracket, how much did this subsidy cost the government?

5   **Policy application**. Suggest at least two appropriate ways to address each of the following kinds of externality problems:

   (a)   noise pollution from a neighbor who insists on mowing his lawn at 7 a.m. Sunday morning;
   (b)   rundown houses that reduce property values
   (c)   overcrowding on a public beach
   (d)   underinvestment in post-secondary education
   (e)   higher health costs for everyone to cover indigent care for newborns because mothers in low-income families fail to get adequate prenatal care
   (f)   accidents due to driving under the influence of alcohol.

6   **Behavioral economics**. Suppose the government has determined that we as a society are underproducing preventive health care services. What would the traditional model of rational economic man recommend as a strategy to induce people to take better care of their health? How might a focus on motivation be an alternative or complementary strategy to shift the demand curve?

7   **Thinking globally**. Acid rain is an example of a negative externality that spills across national boundaries. Using the internet, find out what kinds of actions have been taken to correct this negative externality.

Appendix: the mathematics of externalities

Mathematically, the solution to the problem of negative externalities is similar to that given in Chapter 6's appendix for public goods. In this case, however, we will add external costs to the marginal cost or supply curve rather than the demand curve.

$$Q^x = C_0 + c_1 P_c^x \text{ and } Q^x = D_0 + d_1 P_d^x \tag{7.1}$$

where P_c^x and P_d^x represent, respectively, the private costs and the social costs being borne by bystanders to the transaction. Again, these two equations must be rewritten before adding them to get the sum of the costs incurred in the production of this product:

$$P_c^x = \frac{Q^x - C_0}{c_1} \text{ and } P_d^x = \frac{D_0 + Q^x}{d_1} \tag{7.2}$$

Since the total cost, including social cost, is the sum of the cost paid by the firm (P_c) and the cost imposed on others (P_d), along a supply curve that fully reflects both private and social costs the price will be

$$P^x = P_c^x + P_d^x = -C_0/c_1 + (1/c_1)Q^x + D_0/d_1 - (1/d_1)Q^x$$
$$= (-C_0/c_1 + D_0/d_1) + (1/c_1 - 1/d_1) \, Q^x \tag{7.3}$$

This equation can be rewritten so that the quantity, Q^x, is expressed as a function of the price/cost and the parameters or constants C_0, D_0, c_1, and d_1:

$$Q^x = \frac{P^x (C_0/c_1 + D_0/d_1)}{(1/c_1 + 1/d_1)} \tag{7.4}$$

The demand curve for this product is a normal market demand curve of the form

$$Q^x = A_0 - a_1 P^x \tag{7.5}$$

Once again, there is a supply curve with quantity supplied expressed in terms of the full-cost price P_x and a normal market demand curve in which quantity demanded is expressed as a function of the same price. Elimination of quantity between these two equations gives a unique solution for the value of P_x in terms of the parameters A_0, C_0, D_0, a_1, c_1, and d_1. This value can then be substituted back in either equation to determine the socially optimal level of output, which corresponds to Q_2 at a price of P_2 in Figure 7.2.

The solution to determine the equilibrium price and quantity for a good with positive externalities and the appropriate division of the price between the direct purchasers and those who receive spillover benefits is quite similar to the public good problem described in Equations 6.7 to 6.12 in Chapter 6, and adds social benefits to the private demand curve. This computation is left as an exercise for the reader.

8   Budgeting in the public sector

Introduction

Every January, the US President, like many of his foreign counterparts, sends Congress a proposed budget. Congress then parcels it out among various committees, holds hearings, offers amendments, debates, and in good years, actually manages to pass a budget that the President signs in time for the beginning of the new fiscal year on October 1st. (Until 1977, the fiscal year began July 1st, but Congress found it increasingly difficult to develop a budget in that time frame.) In bad years, Congress passes continuing authorizations and the government manages to continue to function until the budget finally is completed sometime before the Christmas recess. In really bad years, the government shuts down for a few hours or days while Congress and the president try to finalize a budget. It's not a pretty process.

As a general rule, the 50 U.S. state governments and the District of Columbia operate on a fiscal year basis that runs from July 1 to June 30, which means that legislatures have to move a little faster than Congress, and are generally able to put a budget together before the beginning of the next fiscal year. The thousands of local governments do the same, some on a calendar year, some on a July–June fiscal year, and some on a schedule all their own. At whatever level of government, no spending can take place without a budget authorization and an appropriation of funds to cover those expenditures. Once the budget is in place, it is difficult to initiate any new spending program until the next budget cycle.

The budgeting process

A **budget**, whether for a school district, the US government, or a household, is a spending plan that is based on expected revenue and setting priorities for the quantity and quality of services to be provided and/or the transfers to be made. The development of budgets involves three elements:

- a revenue plan, including a forecast of revenues available from existing sources and any proposed changes to the revenue system;
- expenditure forecasts and requests from the various agencies and departments for continuing funding and new projects, which must be evaluated and prioritized in some fashion, including the use of cost-benefit analysis and related techniques;
- a procedure for dealing with any gap between revenues and expenditures, how best to use any surplus or how to address any projected deficit.

Revenue forecasting

For a government with a relatively stable tax structure, the first element in developing a budget is to determine how much revenue will be available. The primary sources of revenue for the federal government are income taxes and social security taxes. The primary revenue sources for most state governments are income taxes and retail sales taxes. For local governments, the primary revenue source is still the property tax, although local revenue sources are becoming increasingly diversified.

Revenue forecasting is an art, not a science. Revenue forecasting is also very politically sensitive, because revenue forecasters are telling legislators how much money they will have to spend. There may be pressures to up the estimates to make pet projects feasible, or pressures to estimate conservatively so that legislators can later enjoy the pleasure of allocating a surplus or taking credit for fiscal restraint. Politicians who have endured the pain of having to approve midyear budget cuts when revenue did not come up to projections are apt to prefer caution in making forecasts. Revenue forecasters are often public employees who must respond to the political climate as well as their own best judgment and experience in making forecasts.

At the federal level, US revenue forecasts are made at least twice a year by both the Congressional Budget Office (CBO) and the Office of Management and Budget (OMB), which is an executive agency. One forecast is made at the time that the budget is sent to Congress in January or February, and the second comes in August as Congress nears the end of the budgeting process. These budgets are revised periodically between the two major forecasts based on changes in economic conditions, proposed policy changes that will affect revenue, and technical adjustments.

By the end of the twentieth century, forecasts emerged that predicted growing budget surpluses, based on the expectations of continued healthy economic conditions of steady growth, full employment and low inflation that had been experienced for almost a decade. These optimistic forecasts not only affected the current budget but also the dialogue about the tax structure, new and expanded expenditure programs, and the future of the Social Security program. Clearly, revenue forecasting plays an important role in making economic policy, even though critics point out that revenue forecasting at the federal level has not been exceptionally accurate.

Economic forecasts

Any revenue forecast begins with an economic forecast that projects the next few years in terms of income, output, employment, and inflation. The major sources of public revenue are income taxes (including payroll taxes), sales taxes (retail sales taxes in the United States, value-added taxes in most of the rest of the world, and excise taxes of various kinds), and taxes on assets (property and other kinds of wealth), and excise taxes just about everywhere. All of them are somewhat linked to the performance of the economy.

If personal income rises or falls, income tax revenue will rise or fall more than in proportion to the change in personal income, because the federal income tax and the majority of state income taxes are at least somewhat progressive. If the rise or fall in personal income is related to the unemployment rate, revenue from payroll taxes (mostly Social Security in the United States) will fall when unemployment rises and rise when unemployment falls.

If personal income rises or falls, taxable retail sales will also rise or fall in the same direction, although these sales are less volatile than income, so the tax base is more stable. So the revenue forecaster starts with a forecast for personal income in his or her nation, state, or locality. Some revenue forecasters develop their own income projections, but most rely on the Federal Reserve Bank, academic economists, or professional forecasting firms with large and complex macroeconomic models to provide these forecasts for them.

From economic forecast to the tax base

The next step in revenue forecasting is to link the economic forecast with what is happening to the tax base, i.e., how does the forecast for the US economy translate into taxable personal income, taxable corporate income, and payroll subject to Social Security taxes? Or at the state level, how does the forecast for Missouri's or Nebraska's economic growth translate into changes in taxable personal income and taxable retail sales? Each state's answer will be different, because each state defines the base of its major taxes a little differently.

Table 8.1 shows some estimates of the relationship between personal income and the tax bases for income, Social Security, and sales taxes (Sobel and Holcombe 1996). At the local level, the property tax base is not as closely tied to economic performance as the other tax bases, but because of the time lag between assessment of property and imposition of taxes, local governments generally know the size of the property tax base before preparing their budgets.

In the short term, the retail sales tax base grows (or declines) slightly faster than personal income, but over the longer term, the base lags substantially behind growth of personal income. Retail sales are very sensitive to short-term fluctuations in economic activity as people cut down on big-ticket items whenever they become concerned about their immediate financial future, and respond to good economic times by splurging on cars, boats, appliances, electronics, and home furnishings. But in the long term, the base of the retail sales tax lags behind the growth of personal income, because much of the growth in income goes into the purchase of services (including housing services), few of which are subject to retail sales taxes in most states.

Because corporate net income is roughly the same as corporate profits, which are very volatile in the short run, corporate income is also extremely sensitive to short-run fluctuations. Like the retail sales tax base, growth in the base of the corporate income tax tends to lag behind overall income growth over the longer term. The most income-sensitive tax is, not surprisingly, the individual income tax. Since the reduction in the tax base for personal exemptions and standard deductions changes only slowly, any change in personal income in the short or long run will result in a larger percentage change in taxable personal income than in gross income.

Table 8.1 Elasticity relationship between personal income and tax bases

Tax base	Long-term elasticity	Short-term elasticity
Taxable personal income	1.22	1.16
Taxable corporate income	0.670	3.37
Retail sales	0.660	1.04

From tax base to revenue

The final step in forecasting revenue is to convert expected changes in the tax base into expected changes in revenue. There are several ways in which to carry out this last step. Some forecasters use a moving average of the relationship between tax base and tax revenue over earlier years to make a simple linear projection, after taking into account any changes in the tax structure. Often a board of advisers is involved in fine-tuning revenue projections to take into account other information or influences. Many forecasters use econometric forecasting techniques that develop a statistical relationship between base changes and changes in revenue yield.

Tax expenditures

An important downward adjustment to the revenue forecast must be made for any changes in tax expenditures. Tax expenditures, which will be discussed in more detail in Chapter 12, consist largely of revenue forgone in order to encourage or promote certain kinds of expenditures in the private sector. The target of a tax expenditure might be soup kitchens, land preservation, preventive health care, or enrolling in college. Once these tax expenditure programs are in place and have some history, they can be incorporated into the revenue forecasting techniques described above.

The effect of relatively new programs may be hard to predict, because it is difficult to anticipate how many taxpayers will respond to the incentive and how much they will spend. Tax expenditures are open-ended, like some grant programs. Opportunities to reduce your tax bill because you put money into an Individual Retirement Account, sent your child to college, or made your house more energy-efficient are all open to whoever chooses to respond, and the revenue drain from some of these programs can be substantial.

Budgeting expenditures

The expenditure side of the budget has to address both on-going programs and proposed new programs. Some kinds of expenditures are forecast in ways similar to revenue forecasting, while others are budgeted and limited to the budgeted amount. Unexpended budget funds in the operating budget normally expire at the end of the fiscal year, giving agencies an incentive to "spend it or lose it" toward the end of the fiscal year. If an agency fails to spend most of its budget, not only does it lose the unexpended funds, but there is also a good chance that next year's budget will be reduced. As a result, there is often a frenzy of spending in federal agencies in August and September (May and June in state agencies) in order to use up their budgeted funds and protect their budget for future years.

Expenditure forecasting

Some expenditures are pre-determined by previous legislative actions that created programs called **entitlements**. These programs automatically include every household, firm, or other entity that meets certain criteria. In the United States, entitlement programs include food stamps, Medicare, Medicaid, unemployment benefits, and Social Security. In other nations the entitlement programs are often broader and more inclusive. Many countries offer family allowances, universal health care, and day care for pre-school children as entitlement programs.

Spending for entitlements can be forecast (but not controlled) based on past experience and knowledge about the age distribution and family composition of the population. There is very little flexibility in this category of spending unless the legislature chooses to alter the parameters of the program, for example, the income limits for eligibility for food stamps, or the reimbursement rates for Medicaid and Medicare.

Forecasts for spending on prisons, public education, and health clinics are also based on the expected number of participants, which in turn reflects such relevant data as crime rates, the age distribution of the population, and the number choosing or needing to use public health clinics. Strictly speaking, these outlays are forecast rather than budgeted, because if the amount that must be spent on all those who qualify exceeds the budgeted amount, those additional expenditures will be normally be made. There may be ways to economize at the margin with crowded cells, crowded classrooms, or long lines at health clinics that deter people from coming, but the opportunities to adjust are limited. Unless the legislature is willing to reconsider, there is additional spending that must be made to accommodate these clients of the system.

Because state and local governments are required to balance their operating budgets, they tend to be much more cautious about creating entitlements than the federal government, but a larger share of their spending is for specific services that reflect the size, growth, and age distribution of the population, which drives their budgets in much the same way. Entitlement programs and population-driven services are a major reason for the continuous adjustments in the federal budget surplus or deficit forecast—and it still turns out to be a surprise at the end of the fiscal year!

Expenditure forecasting, like revenue forecasting, lends itself to the development of econometric models and other statistical forecasting techniques. Among the major variables in this forecasting model are expected inflation rates (using some specialized indicator such as the GDP deflator for the federal or state and local government component of GDP) and expected population growth, both in general and in specific age categories. For public schools, the relevant age category is ages 5–18; for prisons, about 18–30 (the prime crime ages); for Medicare, over 65 and especially over 85. Particular categories of expenditures may have other forecasting elements as well, such as heating and cooling costs, construction costs, or even hurricane forecasts for coastal states.

Changes in planned spending

A simple projection of present spending into the future to accommodate inflation and population growth doesn't require a legislative body, only some good accountants and a few economists. The policy part of the budgeting process relies on two useful sets of techniques. One set of techniques is used to re-examine existing spending patterns and make decisions about reallocating resources or accommodating new needs. These budget methods include program budgeting, performance budgeting, and zero-based budgeting. The second technique of budget policy is evaluating new programs and projects using an applied form of marginal analysis called cost-benefit analysis, which is addressed in Chapter 10.

Program, performance, and zero-based budgeting

Prior to the 1950s, many public budgets were **line-item budgets**. A line-item budget sorts spending into categories of the kinds of goods and services that were purchased. There will be line items for salaries and wages, utilities, office supplies, recreational equipment, and auto repair services to public vehicles. Line-item budgets are sorted into the governmental units that are responsible for providing the service. At the local level, for example, there might be a recreation department line-item budget, a garbage collection and disposal line-item budget, and a financial administration line-item budget. Line-item budgets are convenient for accounting purposes, but they only measure inputs. What citizens and public officials need for evaluation purposes is not a measure of inputs only but of intermediate and final outputs. Program and performance budgeting were developed for that purpose.

A **program budget** defines a group of related governmental activities and specifies the funds to be allocated to those activities. For a recreation department, these activities might include a youth sports program, summer camp, outdoor concerts, and water-safety programs. Each of these activities would have a budget as well as an overall administrative budget that covered general management and maintenance of facilities and equipment for these programs. A program budget makes more sense to an economist because the value of the program can be compared to the cost in making decisions about continuing, expanding, or reducing the budget for the program in future years. Program budgets may give managers more flexibility about the allocation of funds within the program than a line-item budget.

Performance budgeting goes a step further and attempts to define outcomes, such as the number of children participating in a recreation program or the number of meals served at a senior center. These outcomes are then linked to the budget allocation to attempt to achieve those objectives. Performance budgeting is more difficult and more complex and therefore not used as often as program budgeting.

Zero-based budgeting was an idea that first became popular in the 1970s. The usual practice is called incremental budgeting, which starts with the previous year's budget for each agency or program and makes a decision about what to increase and what to leave the same. In zero-based budgeting, each agency or program prepares several "decision packages" with different levels of services and spending, which are then collected and prioritized by those who prepare the budget. Because of the enormous amount of documentation required, and the need to get a budget prepared for the next fiscal year in a timely manner, zero-based budgeting has not been used very much in the public sector.

Off-budget and on-budget funds

How big is a government budget? It depends on what you count. The figures reported for the US federal, state, and local governments rarely include all the funds that pass through those governments or all of the expenditures that they make. Rather, the typical public budget consists of an operating or General Fund budget that covers regular operations and a variety of **off-budget accounts** that do not pass through the legislative budget process on an annual basis. Some countries, and many state and local governments, also have a separate capital budget to pay for infrastructure over a longer period than the annual budget. Budgeting for capital spending is addressed in Chapter 11.

Social Security, Medicare, and the combined budget

At the federal level, the most important off-budget accounts are those of the Social Security and Medicare trust funds, which operate independently. While Congress may change the rules under which these trust funds operate, i.e., changing tax rates and benefit structures, the budgets of these trust funds are not part of the legislative package that must be passed by October 1st each year. Many government enterprises that provide services for payment, such as the Postal Service, are also operated outside of the regular budget, but the largest sums of money are those that pass through the Social Security and Medicare trust funds. To further confuse the reader of government statistics, the budget deficit or surplus is usually reported as the sum of the on-budget and off-budget accounts, so that a deficit in the regular budget may be offset by a surplus in the off-budget accounts. For example, in the 2009 US government budget there was a combined deficit of $482 billion, but the deficit in the operating budget was $663 billion, while the off-budget accounts had a surplus of $181 billion. The surplus in the trust funds has been invested in the bonds that fund the operating deficit, resulting in the appearance of a smaller budget deficit or larger surplus than would actually be the case if the trust funds were truly independent.

State and local special funds

State and local governments also have a number of off-budget accounts. Many state or local governments have a separate capital account in which purchases of capital assets are funded by a combination of budgeted appropriations and issuance of bonds. Another large group of special funds are the retirement funds for state and local employees, which are managed separately from the operating budget. Retirement funds receive contributions from workers and from the state or local government as employers, make investments, earn income from investments, and disburse pension payments to retired workers. These retirement funds are quite large; state pension funds, in particular, are major institutional investors in the stock and bond markets.

Finally, governments at all levels usually have **enterprise funds** for those services that are not financed out of budgetary revenue but rather are sustained by user charges. The more common kinds of enterprise funds include water and sewer funds, locally operated electric and gas utilities, public transit services, and higher education institutions. While there are annual budget appropriations for publicly supported colleges, they also depend heavily on tuition and contributions and have independent budgets approved by their boards. The annual government appropriations for US public colleges are only a part of their total budgets.

Government enterprises have been far more numerous in developing nations in the last half century. Many of them were manufacturing firms or services that are normally found in the private sector producing for profit. As part of its program of structural adjustment in the 1980s and 1990s, the World Bank has encouraged nations to privatize many public enterprises so that governments can focus on their core businesses such as education, infrastructure, defense, and health care.

The political economy of budgets: budgeting and public choice

Public choice theory assumes that not only voters but also elected officials and public administrators engage in self-interested, maximizing behavior. Chapter 5 explored the implications of that theory for the behavior of voters, but the model also has some implications for the supply responses of the public sector that are reflected in budget-making. The best known public choice model of agency budget-making is that of William Niskanen (1971).

Bureaucrat and **bureaucracy** are somewhat uncomplimentary terms for the civil servants and agency heads who do the day-to-day work of government, at least nominally under the direction of the elected leadership and their political appointees. Bureaucrats and bureaucracy exist in all forms of government, parliamentary and executive-legislative, market-centered and statists, democracy and dictatorship. Niskanen and others point to the difficulty of evaluating performance and the multiplicity of objectives for public agencies that give administrators considerable discretion in making tradeoffs within their budgets and in persuading elected officials of the need for additional funding. They also note that the incentive structures in the public sector make it unlikely that the interests and preferences of citizens and voters will be clearly aligned with the interests of those who are assigned the task of addressing those interests and preferences. Those desires are transmitted through the voting process to elected officials (executive and legislative) who in turn must translate them to appointed officials, including agency heads. The principal–agent problem in the private sector, wherein stockholders direct boards, and boards are supposed to oversee management as the agent of the owners, has an even less effective counterpart in the public sector in ensuring that the ultimate "owners" (citizens) are well served by their agents.

Niskanen's model views the bureaucrat, or agency director, as a self-interested maximizer whose goals include salary, power, and reputation, all of which are enhanced by increasing the size of the agency. Competition in the public sector takes place between bureaucrats trying to get more funds for their respective agencies. Bureaucrats are aided in their budget-maximizing task by the fact that they have superior access to information about costs and alternatives compared to either legislators or citizens. As a result, there is constant upward pressure on public expenditures that is driven, not by voters' demand for more or better public services, but by the desire of bureaucrats to increase their own well-being and the ability to use their greater information to persuade legislators to grant the desired budgetary increases.

Public choice theorists have suggested several possible policy responses to the challenge of this kind of bureaucracy-driven budgetary growth. Forcing government agencies to compete with suppliers in the private market has been one response, particularly at the state and local level. Public fire protection, solid waste collection, and even schools have had to demonstrate the quality of services and level of costs in competition with private providers. Devolving service responsibilities to lower levels of government that are in more competitive circumstances is another possible response. Competing governments will be under greater pressure to be efficient in order to hold down taxes or else lose business firms and higher-income residents. A third approach is constraints on the rate of growth of government, which are intended to force bureaucrats to compete with one another for a slow-growing pot of resources rather than attempt to increase total resources in the form of a rapidly growing budget.

Tax and spending limitations

The rapid growth of federal, state, and local spending in the United States in the 1970s led to a variety of efforts to put some reins on rising public budgets. The Gramm–Rudman Act in the 1980s put some rather ineffective constraints on the growth of federal spending. Much of the action, however, was in the states, especially those states that provide for legislation via citizen-initiated referenda. Typically these state **tax and spending limitations** put a limit on spending growth, holding budgeted spending growth to the same rate as growth of income or population. Others attempted to limit revenue growth. Some of these limits focus on growth of state revenue and/or spending, while others restrain local governments, especially the property tax.

A typical state tax and spending limitation restricts the growth of state spending to some maximum percentage rate, based on factors such as population growth, inflation, or personal income growth. At the local level, the focus was on limiting the growth of the property tax, in response to rapidly increasing home prices during the inflation-fueled housing boom of the 1970s.

The best known of these efforts was the Jarvis–Gann Amendment in California, passed by referendum in 1978 and better known as Proposition 13. Proposition 13 limited the growth of property taxes in California, both by limiting the percentage of assessed property value that could be collected in property tax (1 percent) and by limiting the increase in assessed value for property that was not sold to 2 percent a year. Property that was sold, however, was reassessed at its actual sales price.

The results of these limitations were a substantial reduction in property tax rates and revenue as well as significant inequities in tax burdens between property that was recently sold and property that was not. Other states soon followed. In 1981, Massachusetts' Proposition 2–1/2 limited municipal revenue to 2.5 percent of assessed value and limited the annual growth of revenue to 2.5 percent, which amounts to a revenue reduction if inflation exceeds 2.5 percent. New construction was not included in the limit, and there was provision for voter override, but this law was still a fairly restrictive limit on local government spending.

The movement to restrict property taxes slowed in the 1990s only to pick up steam during the housing boom of the early 2000s. Some of the side-effects of property tax limits and assessment caps (which are now in effect in 16 states) have been felt by users of local public services, especially public schools. In California, where the property tax limitation movement began, the quality of schools and local public services was initially maintained with an infusion of state funds. But as state budgets became tighter, local governments ran into serious revenue shortfalls and citizens began to experience crowded classrooms, aging infrastructure, crowded public facilities, and more potholes. Massachusetts did not have a state budget surplus when Proposition 2–1/2 took effect, so the adjustment burden fell on local governments from the beginning.

Behavioral economics: responding to limits

Imposing constraints of any kind invariably calls forth a behavioral response of seeking ways to evade or offset some of the negative effect of those constraints. Citizens may want constraints because they have accurately anticipated the benefits (lower taxes) but significantly underestimated the costs (poorer services). In addition, no constraint can fully anticipate all the possible responses that allow the ceiling to be evaded. A tax limitation encourages the use of non-tax revenues, mainly fees. A spending limitation that is based on the budget encourages legislators to create off-budget funds with their own revenue stream to support some kinds of spending. One interesting response to a particularly restrictive limitation took place in the 1980s in Prince George's County, Maryland, a very large county lying just to the east of the District of Columbia.

In 1978, during the great wave of tax and expenditure limitations, Prince George's County passed one of the most restrictive spending limits in the country. While other states and counties were limiting tax rates, or annual rates of revenue growth or spending growth, or tying growth to population and/or personal income, Prince George's County went a step further. The TRIM proposition, which passed in November 1978, put a ceiling on the total tax dollars that the county could collect.

The District of Columbia has five adjoining counties, two in Maryland, three in Virginia. For lower to middle income families trying to move out of the District and into the suburbs, Prince

George's County, which shares a very long eastern border with the district, has long been the most affordable. After the TRIM proposition passed, county population continued to grow at a very rapid rate, and county officials found that they were serving more people, and paying higher prices for labor and materials as a result of inflation, with no more dollars to work with.

It was an untenable situation. Class sizes grew larger, and so did potholes. Police response time became longer and longer. Finally, in 1994 there was an organized revolt against the impossible limitations on county government. A well-orchestrated campaign, complete with bumper stickers, billboards, meetings at public schools, and distribution of flyers at Metro stops, persuaded the citizens of Prince George's County to reverse their decision and repeal the TRIM amendment.

The important lesson in this experience is that an overly restrictive limitation can be worse than none at all, making it impossible for government to do its job. One of the basic skills you learn as an economist-in-training is to balance costs and benefits, to know how far is far enough, or in the words of Gilbert and Sullivan, to make the punishment fit the crime. Making marginal adjustments, fine-tuning, balancing opposing needs and concerns is the bread-and-butter of economics.

An economist, asked to design an appropriate constraint on the growth of government in Prince George's County, would have been much more likely to have limited its rate of growth to that required to maintain real per capita spending, i.e., a rate that reflects inflation and increases in population. This limitation would ensure that real per capita spending and services would not decline steadily under the double hammer of inflation and population growth. Instead of seesawing between an intolerable restriction followed by no restriction at all, the county would have had a workable constraint on growth of government.

TABOR in Colorado

The state tax and spending limitation movement peaked in 1984, and appeared to be subsiding, when Colorado entered the fray with the most restrictive plan to date, passed in 1992.[1] TABOR (for Taxpayers Bill Of Rights) limits the rate of growth of state and local revenues in Colorado to inflation plus population growth. This formula does not allow for any new programs, any expansion of existing programs, or the possibility that service costs in some areas (such as health care) may grow significantly faster than the inflation factor used to control revenue growth. Revenue in excess of that limit must be refunded to taxpayers.

In November 2005, voters suspended TABOR for five years through a referendum, allowing the state to spend all the revenue it collects during that period. However, the impact on public services lingers. Although Colorado is a relatively wealthy state, it dropped from 35th in 1992 to 48th in 2006 in per pupil education funding, and the state ranked 49th in 2007 in teacher pay. Other sharp cuts were in higher education, public health, and medical coverage. Despite the negative experience in Colorado, similar legislation or a referendum has been proposed in other states in recent years.

Summary

- A budget is a spending plan based on expected revenue that sets priorities for the quantity and quality of services to be provided and/or the transfers to be made. It includes a revenue forecast, expenditure forecasts and appropriations for continuing funding of existing projects and outlays for new projects, and a procedure for funding any deficit or allocating any projected surplus.

- Revenue forecasts are based on anticipated economic conditions, which are then incorporated into formal or informal models that related the economic forecast to the tax base and, using elasticity relationship, from the tax base to revenue. These forecasts also reflect any changes in the tax structure including rates and tax expenditures. Expenditure budgeting also involves forecasts that are based primarily on inflation projections and population growth.
- The budget of any government does not usually include all revenue and expenditures. Some revenue and expenditures are recorded separately in off-budget accounts that do not pass through the legislative budget process on an annual basis. Social Security and Medicare are the most important US federal off-budget accounts, while state employee retirement systems are the largest state off-budget account. There are also separate enterprise funds at the federal as well as the state and local level for many fee-financed services such as water and sewerage.
- The form of the expenditure budget may be a line-item budget, which looks at the recipients of payments (e.g., wages, services purchased), or more likely a program budget, which allocates funds to agencies or programs so that the cost of a program can be related to its benefits.
- New or expanded programs or projects go through a variety of evaluative processes. Some budgetary processes also periodically apply such scrutiny to existing budgets. More sophisticated forms of developing expenditure budgets are performance budgeting or zero-based budgeting, but both require a great deal of paperwork and are time-consuming and expensive to implement.
- Past efforts to contain government growth at the federal level include the Gramm–Rudman Act of the 1980s and at the state and local level, tax and expenditure limitations (TELs) such as Proposition 13 in California and TABOR in Colorado. However, some TELs have had a negative impact on the quality of local public services.

Key terms

Budget
Bureaucracy
Enterprise funds
Entitlements
Expenditure forecasting
Line-item budget
Off-budget accounts
Performance budgeting
Program budget
Revenue forecasting
Tax and spending limitations
Zero-based budgeting

Questions

1   Suppose that you are hired, with your economics degree, to forecast revenue and expenditures for a large city in your state. Describe the process by which you would go about developing those forecasts.

2   What are the advantages and drawbacks of creating off-budget funds to which certain revenue streams are directed automatically instead of going through the appropriation process?

3   **By the numbers**. Using the *Economic Report of the President* (http://www.gpoaccess.gov/eop/) as a data source, calculate the per capita, inflation-adjusted level of US federal spending for on-budget items only from 1980 to 2010. How has it changed? What factors might account for that change?

4   **Policy application**. You have been asked to design a tax and spending limitation for a state government that limits excessive spending in years of high revenue growth, creates a cushion of funds to supplement revenue in recession years, and balances constraint with flexibility. What features might you choose to incorporate?

5   **Behavioral economics**. Assuming that the motives of bureaucrats are those of the standard self-interested maximizing individual, what methods might be used to limit growth of government that results from incentives for bureaucrats to try to grow their own agencies? What if their motivations are more complex, and include concern for the well-being of others and/or taking pride in their professionalism and in a job well done?

6   **Thinking globally**. Compare the composition of spending in the US federal budget to the federal budget in Canada, which is similar to the United States in income level and federal structure. How does the spending mix differ? What factors might account for that difference?

9 Borrowing, debt service, and capital financing

Introduction

For the most part, courses in public sector economics leave macroeconomic issues to be addressed elsewhere. Balanced budgets, deficits, and debt are usually addressed in courses in macroeconomics as a matter of fiscal policy to influence the level of output and employment. But borrowing, debt service, and capital financing also have important microeconomic implications for the budget process, the choice of what expenditures to fund, and whether to make changes in the tax system in order to balance the budget. Those are the aspects of borrowing, debt and deficits addressed in this chapter.

The **deficit** is the gap between spending and revenue in a particular year (a surplus if revenue exceeds spending). The **debt** is the cumulative result of past surpluses and deficits, the stock of government IOUs that must eventually be repaid and that generate a debt service obligation in the current year's budget. **Debt service** refers to payments of interest and repayments of principal as an operating expense. Some debt service is part of the regular budget; other debt service is off-budget in special funds, including enterprise funds (like water and sewage) or agency funds (like public colleges and universities).

Microeconomic and macroeconomic concerns about budget deficits cannot be separated from each other, because the state of the economy affects both revenue and expenditures, and changes in the level of revenue and expenditures (especially by the central government) in turn affect the economy. When times are good, higher income and employment generate more income tax and payroll tax revenue, and higher consumer spending generates more sales or value-added tax revenue. Even the property tax is not immune to the effects of the economy, as housing prices tend to reflect changes underlying economic conditions, although property tax revenue is more stable than income and sales tax revenue.

US federal government borrowing

The lack of a balanced budget constraint at the US federal level, as in most countries, means that decisions about spending are often made without considering opportunity cost. With a balanced budget constraint, the opportunity cost of a new program or project is either other spending forgone, or additional tax burdens on citizens to fund the program or project. Those explicit costs provide both a challenge and an opportunity to weigh marginal costs and benefits and allocate resources efficiently. While the federal government needs to have the ability to run deficits during economic downturns, that budget flexibility has often resulted in running deficits during periods when there was no macroeconomic justification.

Federal borrowing impacts many other players in both the public sector and the private sector. High levels of federal borrowing can drive up interest rates and make it more expensive for both state and local governments and private firms and households to borrow (crowding out). Using the projected surplus to pay off part of the accumulated national debt will have the opposite effect, putting downward pressure on interest rates and making it easier for households, firms and state and local governments to borrow.

Lower interest rates helped to prolong the expansions of the 1990s and 2000s, although the low interest rates of the late 2000s were more the result of monetary policy, not low budget deficits. Lower interest rates also reduce the part of US federal spending that goes to pay interest on the accumulated national debt. Interest on the debt currently accounts for only about 5.3 percent of all federal spending, but that figure is expected to rise in the next decade as the Social Security surplus shrinks and interest must be paid on the very large deficits of 2008 to 2011.

Who owns the debt?

According to the US Treasury, the public debt as of December 2009 was $12,311 billion. Of that amount, $5,278 billion was held by federal government agencies, mainly the Federal Reserve and the Social Security Trust Funds. Private entities, including pension funds, insurance companies, mutual funds and individuals, and state and local governments in the United States held another $3,343 billion. The remaining $3,692 billion was held by foreign governments and private investors. Each of those holders represents a different situation.

Most of the government agency funds are held either by the Federal Reserve or the Social Security Trust Fund. There is no pending repayment obligation to the Fed, but as more people retire, the Social Security Trust Fund will have to redeem some of its bonds in order to pay benefits, putting pressure on future federal budgets. Individual holdings in the United States do not represent an immediate demand on the government, but there is concern about foreign holdings of US bonds. Any large-scale attempt to redeem them could put downward pressure on the value of the dollar, making imports more expensive and forcing interest rates upward, both of which could result in inflation.

In a sense, the debt is "owned" by future generations. As long as the cost of servicing the debt—paying interest and redeeming some bonds as they come due—is not an excessive part of the federal budget, or is not growing more rapidly than the overall economy, then the debt is not a burden on future generations. Some of that debt may have been incurred to finance public capital that will benefit those future generations. But if the cost of debt service grows faster than the economy, and faster than government revenue, future generations will have to pay higher taxes or enjoy fewer public services than the generation that incurred this debt. A whole new area of economics called intergenerational accounting has developed in recent decades to try to measure this shift of costs and benefits between generations.

Government debt in the European Union

In 2010, a crisis developed in the European Union as a result of very large budget deficits and accumulated debt in two member countries, Greece and Spain, with problems emerging in a few other countries as well. The United Kingdom was also running large budget deficits, but unlike 16 EU member countries, was not on the euro, so its problems did not represent as much of a challenge to shared monetary management or the value of the euro on international markets.

The debt problem was the first major challenge to the euro since its introduction in 1999. Countries with better fiscal health and the International Monetary Fund have provided assistance, but there is pressure on countries with large deficits to raise taxes and cut spending. The debt crisis raises the question of autonomy versus sovereignty in a federal-type system, as we explored in Chapter 3. With a common currency, which makes it easier to trade and move resources about within the Union, nations have less freedom in managing their fiscal affairs because of the effect of their actions on the value of the common currency.

State and local borrowing

State and local governments generally have to balance their operating budgets, which forces tradeoffs within the budget. Capital projects are often financed by the issuance of debt or municipal bonds, which may be general obligation bonds (backed by the full faith and credit of the issuing government) or revenue bonds (with revenue from fees or other income from the project earmarked for payments of interest and principal). Because the interest on municipal bonds is exempt from federal income taxes, they are attractive to higher income individuals even at lower interest rates. This tax exemption is a form of federal subsidy for state and local capital spending.

State and local governments can also borrow to cover temporary shortfalls when expenditures have to be made before the revenue flows in. This problem is particularly true for local governments that depend on the property tax, because much of that revenue comes in all at once, while expenditures take place at a more steady pace throughout the year.

When state and local governments borrow for capital projects, they issue debt in a variety of forms, but the two most common forms are **general obligation bonds** and **revenue bonds**. (All this borrowing is lumped together in general discussions of financial markets under the single header of **municipal bonds**, which refers to any debt of states or their political subdivisions, the interest on which is exempt from US federal income tax.)

General obligation bonds are backed by the general taxing power of the issuing government, and meeting the payment on interest and principal is a priority obligation for that government. These bonds are valued by securities dealers based on the fiscal health and past performance of the issuing government, with lower interest rates on higher-rated bonds. Revenue bonds are issued for many capital projects that will generate some kinds of fees or other income, such as dormitories, public transit systems, parking garages, and recreation facilities. These bonds are not backed by the full faith and credit of the issuing government, but the revenue from the project is earmarked for payment of interest and principal on the bonds.

States, cities, counties, and school districts borrow in the municipal bond market at favorable rates because the interest income on these bonds is exempt from federal income taxes (and usually from state income taxes in the issuing state as well). For bondholders in higher income tax brackets, the after-tax return on a municipal bond can be very attractive relative to other forms of investment. Demand for such bonds drives their prices up and their yields down so that after-tax yields are roughly equivalent across all financial instruments.

Because the interest on municipal bonds is exempt from US federal income taxes, they are attractive to higher-income individuals even at lower interest rates. The higher one's marginal tax rate, the greater the after-tax return is on a given municipal bond. The investor had to calculate the **taxable equivalent yield (TEY)** in order to determine whether or not the bond is a good buy:

$$TEY = r_n * (1 + t)$$

Where r_n is the yield on a municipal bond and t is the marginal tax rate for the bondholder. For example, if r_n is 5 percent and the bondholder is in the 36 percent tax bracket, the taxable equivalent yield would be 5 percent of 1.36, or 6.8 percent.

After the dust has settled, most municipal bonds will be held by higher-income individuals attracted by the tax break, while nonprofit organizations, lower-income households, pension funds and other institutional investors for whom the tax break has no value will concentrate their holdings in other kinds of financial investments.

Several factors enter into the interest rate that a government must pay on its bonds. Maturity is one factor; the longer the time period, generally the higher the interest rate. But the most important consideration is the evaluation by the bond rating service of the local government's likelihood of repayment of principal and interest in a timely manner. This rating is based on the local government's past track record with debt service as well as its fiscal practices, its reserves, and its tax base, all of which are evidence of ability to repay. In addition, interest rates are different between the two primary kinds of government debt, general obligation bonds and revenue bonds.

This tax exemption of municipal bond interest is a tax expenditure, or a federal subsidy for state and local capital spending. The policy implications of this subsidy have been hotly debated. Supporters see this tax exemption of municipal bonds as an appropriate transfer of resources to local government to help them develop infrastructure. Critics see it as an incentive to excessive local borrowing, often for inappropriate purposes. The low interest rates and ease of borrowing encourage new construction rather than maintenance and renovation. Some state and local governments use their access to cheap capital to subsidize questionable private investments. Competition with private borrowers who have to pay higher interest rates may redirect capital into less desirable public or public–private partnership projects.

Borrowing for capital spending

Much government borrowing, especially at the state and local level, is in order to finance capital projects. No function of government impacts as many people on a daily basis as the only partly visible infrastructure of water and sewer systems, highways and bridges, school buildings and dams. The term **infrastructure** has many meanings, but in public sector economics it usually refers specifically to public sector physical capital. In the narrow sense, infrastructure is generally understood to consist of public physical capital. The largest share of public infrastructure is in the state and local public sector, including offices, courthouses, schools, roads and bridges, parks, jails, hospitals, and water and sewer systems. Federal infrastructure includes national parks, post offices, the interstate highway system, prisons, veterans' hospitals, office buildings, and military bases.

However, none of these assets has to be provided solely in or by the public sector; all of these can be, have been, or are provided in some places by either private for-profit or private nonprofit entities. Private toll roads preceded public highways, citizens may obtain water from a municipal water system or a for-profit water supplier, electric power may be delivered by a public entity, a profit-making firm, or in many rural areas, a rural electrical co-operative. Even if the capital is owned and operated by a government, it was almost certainly constructed by a private commercial contractor.

Efficiency issues: why public capital?

In a market system, the market is the default provider of goods and services. If public provision is to be justified on efficiency grounds, the argument must rely on some form of market failure. For public infrastructure, or physical capital, there may be several kinds of market failure at work. The nature of the market failure often influences the method of financing. The role of the public sector in providing infrastructure and the way that it is paid for reflect both equity and efficiency concerns.

Public sector capital may be a integral component of a larger program of public service that is justified on the usual grounds of public goods (justice/corrections and jails or prisons), merit goods (health clinics), or substantial positive externalities (school and college buildings). It is possible for governments to lease rather than build such facilities, but there are some kinds of buildings and some locations for which a publicly owned building is the only or most feasible option.

Often public sector physical capital has some of the essential non-rival, non-excludability attributes of a public or at least quasi-public good in that the marginal cost of serving an additional user is low to nonexistent. Up to some congestion level, the services of some kinds of public physical capital can be non-rival in consumption. In addition, the cost of enforcing exclusion of non-payers may exceed the benefits. Roads and parks, up to the point of congestion, have such characteristics.

Some kinds of public sector capital may have significant positive externalities, even if it also creates private benefits. Often those externalities accrue to adjacent landowners. The value of a house adjacent to an attractive park, for example, may increase even if the current owner has no interest in the park. These kinds of benefits can be measured and the beneficiary charged more effectively through property taxes (including tax increment financing or special assessments) than through traditional private market prices.

Public infrastructure is generally used to provide services for which most of the cost is in the capital investment, with relatively low operating costs. (School buildings used to provide education services are a notable exception.) This kind of cost structure makes it unlikely that the market would support more than one supplier in a given area, making the sole supplier a monopolist. Because monopolies usually produce less service at a higher price and are unresponsive to consumer demands, many countries choose to place such activities in the public sector. Municipal water and sewer systems are an application of this rationale for public provision.

Finally, in some cases, private financing may be difficult to arrange for new or risky ventures, or when capital is built in anticipation of growth that may not occur. Government backing of such projects, either directly as owner or indirectly as guarantor, can make it easier to raise the needed funds. This role of government as financial guarantor goes far back into US history. The Erie Canal was the most notable of many such nineteenth-century state-guaranteed infrastructure projects that proved to be quite profitable. Such a rationale is still valid today in many developing countries, but much less relevant to modern industrial economies such as those of Western Europe and North America.

Public financing of sports stadiums: a case study in public choice

The past 20 years have seen an explosion of sports facilities built in large and medium-sized cities to accommodate football, baseball, and basketball teams as well as other sports. Most of these stadiums and arenas are built with some infusion of local (and sometimes state) public funds, to the tune of about $10 million per facility per year. Even the federal government is contributing indirectly, because many of these facilities are financed at least in part with municipal bonds, the interest on which is exempt from federal income taxes. Why do cities contribute so heavily to the support of a private, for-profit enterprise? What are the perceived benefits to the city, and how are citizens who may never go to a ball game persuaded to kick in their share of the cost? The burgeoning field of sports economics has attempted to provide some answers to these questions.

The major sports leagues (baseball, football, and basketball) have monopoly power that is protected by a federal anti-trust exemption. These leagues determine how many teams there will be, and where new franchises will be granted. Teams can always threaten (and sometimes follow through!) to relocate if the local community is not supporting them satisfactorily with either subsidies or attendance. Municipalities want sports teams for a variety of reasons, some sounder than others.

Objective studies that attempt to measure the economic impact of sports teams find that the direct, measurable impact on the local economy's income and jobs is quite modest (Noll and Zimbalist 1997). The fiscal impact is likely to be negative, in part because of the subsidies that municipalities now routinely provide to construction, in part because many of the stadiums and arenas are built on prime, municipally-owned land that is lost to the property tax base.

There may be some positive effects that are difficult to quantify. The availability of the park as a recreational opportunity may enhance tourism or may increase citizen satisfaction as a resident of a metropolitan area with a full range of recreational and cultural facilities. The national exposure from televised games may enhance the city's visibility and image. Why, then, do cities routinely cave into pressure to offer or enhance subsidies to team facilities to attract new teams or retain existing footloose ones?

The answer is a case study in public choice. The immediate public benefits are highly visible: new stadium, sometimes a new team, usually new economic activity in the area immediately around the stadium (although perhaps at the expense of economic activity elsewhere in the city).

The costs are spread over a number of years and a number of citizens. Noll and Zimbalist point out that a stadium with a $250 million construction subsidy and a population of 5 million will incur per capita capital costs of $50 spread over the life of the bond financing (Noll and Zimbalist 1997: 58) The benefits are concentrated, accruing to the owners and the players in the form of profits and higher salaries. It is in the interests of the team's owners and players to take advantage of their monopoly position° to extract as many concessions as possible from the local government in order to maximize their own potential economic gain.

In a situation that pits competing local governments against a national sports monopoly, there have been calls for federal intervention to restore the balance of power. Suggestions have ranged from disallowing the federal tax exemption on local revenue bonds used for financing sports stadiums to federal guidelines on stadium financing. But with the powerful hold of televised team sports on the American public, it is unlikely that federal action will be forthcoming. Some municipalities have balked at the demands from sports teams. Cleveland lost the Cleveland Browns to Baltimore when, backed by taxpayer anger, the city refused to comply with the team's demands in the 1990s, although they have since received an NFL expansion team.

Some larger communities, mindful that they too have bargaining power in terms of the size of their potential attendance and support base, have learned to negotiate more acceptable terms. The increasingly visible difference between promised revenue streams and economic impact and the post-construction economic reality in other cities have also strengthened the hand of local governments in reducing the subsidy to sports facilities. As long as Americans are hooked on professional sports, however, taxpayers (sports fans or not) can expect to be subsidizing these teams through their tax dollars for the foreseeable future.

Equity issues: financing public capital

While the federal government does not have a separate capital budget, state and local governments usually separate their capital spending from their operating budgets and borrow for part or all of their capital spending. In addition, states and especially local governments often operate their capital-intensive operations that sell services to citizens as separate **enterprise funds**, so that there is no cross-subsidy in either direction between the enterprise activity and the general fund. For this reason, the primary discussion of financing infrastructure is connected to the state and local sector, although the role of fees and charges is also relevant to federal government infrastructure in some cases (especially parks and museums).

If the primary beneficiaries of new public capital are the residents of the state, county, city, or special district, then equity considerations suggest that those citizens should have primary responsibility for its financing. However, citizens are mobile, and the citizens who are in a county or school district today are different from those who may be using the facilities in five or ten years. Intergenerational and interpersonal equity considerations suggest that such capital should be financed over its useful lifetime rather than on a pay-as-you-go basis so that future residents who use the capital will also have some responsibility to pay for it.

Another alternative to ensure that all users, present and future, pay a fair share of the cost is to impose **impact fees** on new construction and development. Impact fees, which are discussed in Chapter 16, charge the developer (who passes the cost on to the home buyer), a fee per lot that is earmarked for additional capital facilities required to service the newly developed area.

The same trend toward greater reliance on user charges and fees for many public services has also appeared in financing public sector infrastructure. There has been a trend away from general tax financing of infrastructure in favor of identifying beneficiaries and making them pay a reasonable share of the cost. This trend is especially pronounced at the local level because of the property tax revolt.

Many public services that involve infrastructure, such as the police and fire stations and equipment needed to provide fire and police protection, create general benefits in that they meet public "option demand." **Option demand** means paying for a service so that it will be there if needed, even if the payer never actually has to use it—somewhat akin to insurance of various kinds. For such services, general tax financing, or debt financing that is repaid out of general tax revenues, is reasonable on both efficiency (controlling demand) and equity (users pay) grounds. Other kinds of services primarily benefit identifiable users (park and recreation facilities) or adjacent landowners (road improvements). Both equity and efficiency considerations support the notion that these direct beneficiaries of services should pay to the extent feasible.

One technique for assigning costs to beneficiaries is to create special districts whose sole purpose is to fund and maintain or operate particular kinds of infrastructure. Water and sewer districts have been commonplace for many years, but other kinds have increasingly appeared on the scene in recent decades. Texas has pioneered the use of road districts. Montana uses neighborhood rural special improvement districts. The Denver metropolitan area has a special toll road authority.

Such special districts serve some combination of three purposes. First, they can provide residents with some of the benefits, including infrastructure, that come with living in a municipality, without all the additional costs and restrictions. Second, they can allow additional borrowing, and added tax levies to repay that borrowing, when general purpose local governments have exhausted their borrowing or taxing capabilities.

Finally, special districts can ensure that the cost falls on the primary beneficiaries. Special districts are highly diverse in both purpose and financing. Some are entirely tax financed (typically districts providing roads, neighborhood parks, street lights, and beautification) while others are almost entirely financed by user fees (districts providing water and sewers) as well as intermediate cases that use multiple financing sources. What these special districts have in common is a responsibility for providing a particular kind of infrastructure to serve a defined area.

Impact fees on developers, special assessments for improvements, and tax increment financing are increasingly commonplace ways to finance improvements that benefit a particular property, neighborhood, or other defined area. New residents require not only extension of water and sewer lines but also more police cars, fire substations, and public parks. Impact fees cover the additional capital costs imposed by developing vacant lots or adjacent tracts. Special assessments are more likely to pay for infrastructure improvements to serve already developed lots. Tax increment financing seeks to capture the additional property tax revenue from the increase in property value that results from infrastructure improvements, and dedicates that revenue stream to paying the capital costs.

Financing infrastructure through such methods that assign costs to beneficiaries offers at least a partial solution to the problem of measuring and valuing the output of public sector capital, at least that part of the value that is attributable to private benefits. Social benefits must be measured in other ways, such as reduction in congestion or air pollution as a result of an additional investment in public transportation.

In the 1960s and 1970s, the federal government was a significant source of funding for state and local infrastructure. Grants were offered for many projects, but especially water and sewer projects and public housing. Today that source of revenue is greatly diminished. Although federal aid for infrastructure could be defended as a form of fiscal equalization, it has not been a very efficient method. Fiscal equalization can be achieved by other methods that more effectively target poor states and poor individuals.

Capital budgets

State and local governments usually budget separately for operating expenditures and for capital projects. So do most national governments in other countries. The separation of budgets into these two components is considered a good accounting practice. It's also good economics. Just as economists distinguish between stocks and flows, assets and income, debt and debt service, so do both accountants and economists distinguish between the year-to-year recurrent expenditures for providing services and the intermittent acquisition of public capital assets.

The operating budget will probably include appropriations for debt service incurred to acquire assets such as buildings, dams, highways, airports and land, although some assets are acquired through separate accounts by the issuance of revenue bonds (see below). But those assets are usually paid for over their long useful lifetimes just as households (and business firms) acquire homes, cars, factories, and office buildings by paying for them over their useful lifetime rather than up front and all at once. There may be an initial appropriation of some part of the cost, but borrowing is considered the norm for the bulk of asset acquisition in the public sector as in the private sector.

In the case of public assets, this method of payment has the additional advantage of spreading the cost among all the taxpayers who benefit from the asset, a group of people that changes from year to year. Having a capital budget and financing assets at least partly by borrowing means that you, as a mobile worker, will not have to pay up front for the full cost of a recreational facility with a 30-year lifetime for a community that you may only live in for three or four years. Some of the cost will be shifted to the next person to move into town, use the facilities, and pay taxes or fees for debt service.

Some states have assumed some responsibility for helping local governments finance infrastructure, sometimes with grants but sometimes with help in obtaining loans or issuing bonds at more favorable interest rates. State bond banks and revolving state loan funds are two widely used methods. State guarantees can make it possible for local governments to borrow on more favorable terms. States can pool borrowing requests from many small communities, with or without a state guarantee, to get to a critical mass that reduces borrowing costs. Some states borrow on their own credit and use the proceeds to create credit infrastructure banks that lend to local governments.

Does the United States need a capital budget?

The budget that is approved by Congress does not distinguish between ordinary operating expenses, debt service, and acquisition of capital assets. A federal prison or office building is treated as a line-item expenditure just like the payroll for the White House staff or the upkeep of a courthouse or payments for veterans' medical expenses. When debt is incurred, it is simply to provide enough resources to fund the budget and is not tied to any particular capital expense.

Why does the US government not have a similar division into operating and capital budgets? There doesn't seem to be any good answer to that question. Relative to a budget of more than $3 trillion, annual capital expenditures are probably moderate enough to be treated as an operating expense. That is, there will be large capital expenditures every year, and the budgetary impact is going to be about the same whether they are "expensed" (treated as operating rather than capital expenses) or whether they are segregated into a capital account and funded through a combination of borrowing and current appropriations.

Lumpiness of capital expenditures relative to the total budget—years with large capital outlays and years with relatively few big asset acquisitions—is much more likely to happen at the state and local level. In addition, the pool of taxpayers supporting the capital expenditures is much more stable at the national level than at the state or local level. Finally, most state and local governments are required to balance their budgets, but the budget that has to be balanced is the operating budget, which includes annual debt service but does not include capital projects funded by new borrowing. Having a capital budget gives them more budgetary flexibility than they would have with a combined budget. Since the federal government does not have to balance its budget, this reason for a capital budget is not an issue.

The drawback of not having a capital budget at the national level is that there is not much careful thought given to how much federal borrowing is appropriate. Federal borrowing in the past has been justified on the basis of macroeconomic policy, but much of the borrowing of the period from the early 1980s to the late 1990s took place under conditions of relatively full employment when deficits were not needed to stimulate economic activity and federal borrowing drove up the interest rates that private borrowers had to pay.

During periods of relative economic prosperity, a balanced or surplus budget is the appropriate macroeconomic policy. Separate capital budgeting would make it clearer when borrowing was being done for capital purposes or for purposes of stimulatory fiscal policy. Without either of these justifications, Congress would have to work harder to balance the operating budget and set clear spending priorities.

Summary

- The deficit is the gap between spending and revenue in a particular year (a surplus if revenue exceeds spending). The debt is the cumulative result of past surpluses and deficits, the stock of government IOUs that must eventually be repaid and that generate a debt service obligation in the current year's budget. Debt service refers to payments of interest and repayments of principal as an operating expense.
- The federal government does not have any significant constraints on borrowing, but state and local governments usually are subject to a balanced budget requirement. They can, however, borrow for capital spending, primarily for infrastructure, or public physical capital, such as roads, airports, school buildings, water and sewer systems, and parks.
- About 40 percent of federal debt is held by public agencies, with the remainder divided between private domestic investors and foreign governments and investors.
- Most public sector capital is financed by borrowing, or issuing bonds. Interest on state and local government bonds, called municipal bonds, is generally exempt from federal income taxes. General obligation bonds are backed by the taxing power of the government, while revenue bonds are secured by expected income from the capital project.
- Any rationale for public sector capital relies on arguments of market failure, including public goods (low rivalry, low excludability), merit goods, or positive externalities; monopoly characteristics of some kinds of services provided with public infrastructure; or lack of private financing because of risks of various kinds.
- State and local governments use capital financing to spread the cost over the useful lifetime of the capital project and to distribute the burden of payment equitably among present and future taxpayers. Their borrowing is called municipal bonds, with interest exempt from federal income taxes The taxable equivalent yield on a municipal bond is equal to the nominal yield times $1 + t$, where t is the taxpayer's marginal federal income tax rate.
- Public financing of infrastructure raises issues of interpersonal (rich versus poor, users versus nonusers, etc.) and intergenerational equity (present versus future citizens/users). Among the newer methods of financing infrastructure are the use of public–private partnerships, state guarantees and debt subsidies, and creating special districts for the sole purpose of developing and financing infrastructure.

Key terms

Debt
Debt service
Deficit
Enterprise funds
General obligation bonds
Impact fee
Infrastructure
Municipal bonds
Option demand
Revenue bonds
Taxable equivalent yield (TEY)

Questions

1   What are the advantages and disadvantages to a local government of issuing general obligation rather than revenue bonds? What about from the buyer's (lender's) perspective?

2   Many states also exempt interest on municipal bonds from state income taxes if those bonds are issued by that state or its local governments. Suppose that you buy municipal bonds issued in your state, and your federal marginal tax rate is 28 percent and your state marginal tax rate is 6 percent. If the yield on the bonds is 3.5 percent, what is the taxable equivalent yield?

3   **By the numbers.** Suppose that you are in a 27 percent marginal tax bracket and are trying to decide between a municipal bond with a 3 percent yield and a corporate bond of equal maturity and risk with a 5 percent yield. Which one is the better deal? Why?

4   **Policy application.** Financing public capital should take into consideration both inter-personal and intergenerational equity. Consider how you might want to finance the construction and operation of a public recreational facility with an expected 30-year useful lifetime and a capacity to serve about 2,000 persons a day in a community of 25,000 people. Would the availability of competing private recreational facilities be a factor in your financing plan?

5   **Behavioral economics.** The issue of fiscal illusion, introduced in Chapter 4, is particularly important in deficit financing, because citizens will be less aware of the cost of public services if the cost is postponed to some indefinite future time. How would you devise a set of rules that balances the concerns of overspending with the need for flexibility during economic downturns at the central government level?

6   **Thinking globally.** In the formerly Communist nations of Eastern and Central Europe, sorting out public and private capital went in the opposite direction from Western economies. There the challenge was what publicly owned capital belonged in the private sector, how to transfer assets into private hands, and what regulatory role the government would continue to play. How would you decide which assets or businesses to sell and which to keep in public hands? What concerns might you have about foreign rather than domestic buyers?

10   Cost-benefit analysis

Introduction

Economics is all about optimizing—getting the best, the most out of available resources. The most what? Profit for a firm, satisfaction or utility for an individual or a society. The rule for maximizing is always to find that production or consumption point at which the (positive) difference between benefits—revenue, utility, or profit—and the cost of attaining it is the greatest.

That point occurs where marginal benefit equals marginal cost. Why? Because if the additional benefit of one more unit is greater than the additional cost, then producing or consuming that unit increases total welfare. If the additional benefit of one more unit is less than the additional cost, then producing or consuming that unit decreases total welfare. Where marginal cost and marginal benefit are equal, total welfare is maximized.

The term welfare in this context simply refers to the excess of benefits over costs. There is a whole subfield of economics called welfare economics that analyzes various techniques for increasing total welfare and offers some guidance to public policy in trying to maximize social welfare. Two conclusions from that analysis are particularly important. The first is the conclusion stated above, that total welfare is maximized when marginal cost equals marginal benefit.[1] The second conclusion is that there is a decision rule that can guide such decisions. That decision rule is based on the concept of Pareto optimality, or a state of affairs from which no further improvements can be made that will increase social welfare.

Pareto optimality and the compensation principle

Pareto optimality is named for Italian economist Vilfredo Pareto. The decision rule is quite simple. If you can make a change that will make at least one person better off without making anyone worse off, then that change should be made, because it will increase social welfare. However, if anyone is made worse off to any degree, even if many people are made better off, you cannot unequivocally state that social welfare has improved. We cannot make meaningful interpersonal comparisons of utility or happiness or satisfaction, because people have different capacities for enjoyment or satisfaction.

Social welfare in a two-good, two-person world: the Edgeworth–Bowley box

One way to visualize Pareto optimality in a two-person world with fixed resources is a technique called an Edgeworth–Bowley box. You should be familiar with the diagram in Figure 10.1, which shows an individual making an optimal personal choice between two

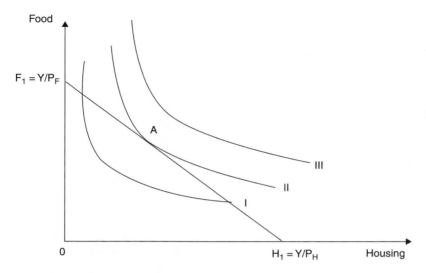

Figure 10.1 Indifference map for food and housing.

goods. This choice is based on two pieces of information: the individual's preferences, represented by an indifference map, and the budget constraint.

An indifference curve shows the various combinations of two goods that give the person the same level of satisfaction or utility. An indifference curve that lies above and to the right of that curve represents combinations that all offer a higher level of satisfaction than those on the lower curve. An indifference map is a set of all possible indifference curves, each representing a different level of satisfaction or utility. Indifference curves are noninter-secting. Otherwise the same combination of goods would lie on two different indifference curves that represented different levels of satisfaction. An indifference curve that lies above and to the right of another one represents a higher level of satisfaction or utility.

The individual whose preferences are represented by this indifference map has a budget constraint, represented by the straight line F_1H_1. That line simply shows what combinations of food and housing this person could buy based on their relative prices and the income available to spend. If the entire budget was spent on food, she could buy a quantity F_1, which is equal to her income Y divided by the price of one unit of food, P_f. If the entire budget was spent on housing, she could buy a quantity H_1, which equals her income Y divided by the price of one unit of housing, P_h. If she wants some of each, the combinations that her budget constraint will allow fall along the line F_1H_1. She chooses combination at point A, which puts her on the highest attainable indifference curve II.

An increase in income would shift the budget constraint out to the right to F_2H_2, while a decrease in income would shift it to the left. An increase in the price of food relative to the price of housing will change the location of the budget constraint on the vertical axis from F_1 to F_3 but would not change H_1. A food price change will rotate the budget line inward if the price of food rose, outward if the price of food fell. Those changes are shown in Figure 10.2.

Now extend that one-person world to a two-person world in which there is a fixed quantity of food and housing that can be divided between the two people, Randy and Susan, in an

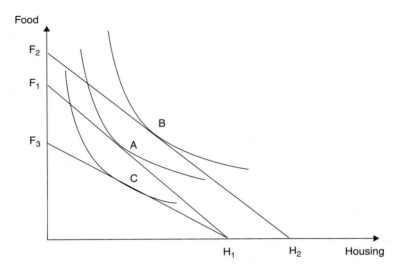

Figure 10.2 Indifference analysis with a budget constraint.

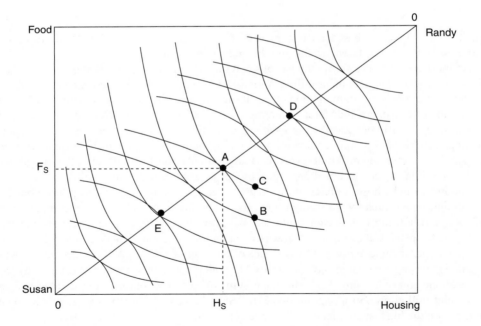

Figure 10.3 An Edgeworth–Bowley box.

infinite variety of ways. We put their worlds together by taking Randy's indifference map and rotating it 180 degrees, then superimposing it on Susan's, in Figure 10.3. So the origin (zero food, zero housing) for Susan's indifference map is also the point where Randy has all the food and all the housing, and vice versa. This two-person diagram makes it possible to explore combinations of food and clothing for both of them that represent potential Pareto optimal points in their world. Those possible Pareto optimal points lie along a contract curve, which connects the points of tangency of their indifference maps. At those points, for whatever particular indifference curve Randy is on, Susan is on her highest attainable indifference curve.

If Randy moves along his indifference curve to a different combination of food and housing, his welfare is unchanged, but Susan's welfare declines. She moves to a lower indifference curve. For example, consider a division of the available food and housing between Randy and Susan at point A. Susan has the quantities F_s of food and H_s of housing. Randy has the rest—F_t—F_s of food and H_t—H_s of housing, where F_t and H_t represent the total available quantities of food and housing, respectively.

If the division of food and housing changes to point B, Randy's welfare is unchanged, because he is on the same indifference curve with more food and less housing, but Susan's welfare has declined. She is on a lower indifference curve with a less satisfactory combination of food and housing. At point C, Susan's welfare is unchanged from point A, but Randy's welfare has declined. So once Susan and Randy settle at point A, there is strong resistance by one or the other to moving from that point. Pareto optimality favors the status quo.

Note that Figure 10.3 does not provide any guidance on choosing Point A as opposed to some other point along the contract curve, such as D or E. In other words, there is no judgment about the initial distribution of goods (or income, or wealth). At point D, Randy has most of the food and housing, and Susan has very little. At point E, the opposite is true. Even the points of origin lie on the contract curve, with either Randy or Susan having everything and the other having nothing. That distribution neutrality is an important limitation of the concept of Pareto optimality as a decision tool.

The second-best and the compensation principle

It is rare but not impossible to find Pareto optimal changes that can be made. Economist Joseph Stiglitz identified some potential Pareto optimal moves, or Pareto improvements, that were discussed but not implemented during his tenure on the Council of Economic Advisers during the Clinton administration (Stiglitz 1998).

It's usually easier to identify such possibilities in small groups, where everyone can express their preferences. But on a larger scale, almost every proposed change in policy will make someone worse off. So the demanding criterion of Pareto optimality strongly favors the status quo. It also rules out some policy changes that we intuitively know should be made. Economists felt the need for a decision rule that offered more flexibility. That rule, variously known as the second-best rule, the **compensation principle**, or the Kaldor–Hicks criterion, offered a way out by considering the possibility of compensation to the losers from the change.

Here is the modified rule. A change should be made if it is possible for the gainers from the change to compensate the losers and still be better off. A change should not be made if it is possible for the losers to "bribe" the potential gainers to agree to not making it, and the losers will still be better off after making the payment.

Note that the payment does not have to actually be made in order for the change to be justified by this criterion. Occasionally policy changes do embody some form of compensation to potential losers, but not often. The health care bill passed by Congress in 2010 will benefit consumers at the expense of health insurers and possibly some providers of medical services, for example. Every action of government has distributional consequences, even when redistribution is not the primary objective. The hypothetical compensation or bribe is merely a way to measure the utility, satisfaction or welfare gains for the affected parties so that it is possible to determine the measure of the change in total welfare. This criterion is independent of the actual resulting distribution of the gains or losses.

Cost-benefit analysis

Cost-benefit analysis and its cousin, cost-effectiveness analysis, are tools for translating the economic theory of Pareto optimality and the theory of the second best into real-world applications. Both techniques attempt to evaluate the effect of alternative choices on social welfare, or utility, of society as a whole.

Cost-benefit (or benefit-cost) analysis is a technique for evaluating proposed programs or projects to determine whether the anticipated benefits exceed the anticipated costs over the lifetime of the program or project. Both costs and benefits should include both monetary and non-monetary costs (e.g., increases or decreases in travel time as a result of a road project). A project may be evaluated in isolation or in comparison to other, competing projects to set priorities for the programs that offer the greatest benefits relative to the costs. Cost-benefit analysis is a complex subject that we cannot adequately explore in the space of a few pages, but it is helpful to have a general idea of how the process works.

The decision rule

Recall from your microeconomics class how individuals and firms make decisions about allocating scarce resources among competing uses. For any given outlay, the decision-maker compares the marginal revenue, marginal utility, or marginal benefit to the price (or marginal cost). Marginal benefit and marginal utility are closely related, but the preferred measure of the value or satisfaction to the user in cost-benefit analysis is marginal benefit. As long as the increase in benefit is greater than the price or cost, the expenditure will increase the total profit for the firm, utility for the individual, or benefit for the organization. So the first form of the decision rule is to purchase a particular good or service up to the point where

$$MB = MC.$$

This decision rule is fine for smaller decisions or decisions where resources are plentiful. Most of the time, however, the decision is among competing alternatives, among making spending decisions between alternatives. Consider a household with a budget constraint B, trying to decide how much to purchase of goods X, Y, and Z, with prices of P_x, P_y, and P_z respectively. If the budget, B, is sufficiently large so that this household can purchase quantities of X, Y, and Z each up to the point where marginal utility equals price, then there is no problem.

But what if the budget is inadequate to get to that point? Then at least for some of these goods, the household will have to buy less than the optimal amount. If marginal benefit (utility) diminishes with more purchases while price is constant (or in some cases, marginal cost is increasing), buying less than the optimal amount means that

$$MB > P \text{ or } MB > MC$$

for at least some goods. For simplicity, we will treat price and marginal cost as the same in order to address the question, how does the household allocate its resources so as to maximize its utility under a budget constraint?

The rule that you should recall is that, in order to maximize utility (or profit, or benefit), resources should be allocated among competing uses so that MU/P or MB/P is the same for X, Y, and Z, i.e.,

$$MB_x/P_x = MB_y/P_y = MB_z/P_z$$

Where the budget constraint, B, is equal to the total spent:

$$B = X*P_x + Y*P_y + Z*P_z$$

The easiest way to demonstrate that this rule maximizes benefit or utility is to consider what would happen if

$$MB_x/P_x > MB_y/P_y.$$

If the next dollar spent on X yields more benefit or utility than the last dollar spent on Y, then total benefit could be increased by reducing spending on Y by one dollar and using that dollar to purchase more X instead. Only when the marginal benefit per dollar spent is equal across all three goods is total benefit maximized within the budget constraint.

This simplified budget model is the foundation for the technique of decision-making known as cost-benefit analysis. Some projects are evaluated simply to determine whether or not the benefits exceed the costs (is MB > or = MC?). More often, proposed projects are evaluated comparatively in terms of the excess of benefits over costs or the ratio of benefits to costs or costs to benefits.

Kinds of cost-benefit analysis

There are two important types of cost-benefit analyses. One kind of analysis begins with a predetermined objective, such as a new elementary school, and evaluates the relative costs and benefits of various proposals to achieve that objective—different locations, sizes, and/or types of construction. Or the objective may be a certain level of public transportation, where the comparative analyses look at bus systems, subways, and other alternatives to find the least-cost method of achieving a particular objective.

Sometimes the objective is an outcome that can be measured but not assigned a dollar value, such as a higher graduation rate, a reduced incidence of AIDS transmission, or a lower vehicle accident rate. In this case, a variant technique called **cost-effectiveness analysis** is used to evaluate alternative strategies to achieve the desired level of outcome. Cost-effectiveness of alternative treatment strategies is often used in health care planning, for example.

The more traditional kind of cost-benefit analysis is a comparative one, which examines different kinds of projects as a way to set priorities for spending. For example, a local government may have limited borrowing and debt service capacity for capital projects. Perhaps the most it can borrow for the next five years is $10 million. The policy analysts would be assigned to evaluate a number of proposed projects, such as a new library, another fire truck, additional neighborhood parks, and a recycling facility and solid waste transfer station. Because the total cost of these projects is likely to exceed $10 million, a cost-benefit analysis will be helpful in ranking these projects from lowest to highest (cost-benefit) or highest to lowest (benefit-cost) to determine which ones will be funded.

Sometimes the traditional method is used simply to determine whether benefits exceed costs. For example, the Federal Emergency Management Agency sponsored an independent study of the future savings resulting from hazard mitigation activities to determine whether the benefits exceeded the costs (Godshalk *et al.* 2009). The authors of the study concluded that each dollar spent in three natural hazard mitigation programs saved an average of $4 in future losses avoided. Because the study did not compare this use of federal funds to alternative programs, it could not be concluded that this was the highest and best use of those funds, but it could be concluded that the program had a substantial net positive impact.

All of these approaches have certain methods in common. All of them start with an objective—a project or product, or an outcome. They all determine present and expected future costs and present and expected future benefits (or sometimes revenue streams) for one or more variants of that project or for alternative methods of bringing about the desired outcome. They all involve some method of adding up present and future costs, present and future benefits, and comparing them.

There are two widely used methods of presenting the results. One method is to subtract costs from benefits to see how big the "surplus" of benefits over costs is. Biggest surplus wins! This method works fine where the projects are of similar size and scale. However, using this method to prioritize among projects of unequal magnitude would favor large projects over smaller ones. In such cases, the alternative is to divide the sum of present and future benefits by present and future costs to come up with a benefit-cost ratio. This number would suggest which project has the highest benefit return on investment, whether it is a large project or a small one.

Present value and cost-benefit analysis

In either case, both the costs and the benefits of a project or program that has a multi-year lifetime must be expressed in terms of present value in order to compare costs to benefits or in order to develop benefit-cost ratios to compare among alternative solutions to a single problem or alternative projects competing for funding. Chapter 7 introduced the present value formula: If a future value FV is the present value PV plus the interest earned on PV at rate r for i years,

$$PV*(1 + r)^i = FV$$

Then this equation can be rewritten to express present value in terms of future value:

$$PV = FV/(1 + r)^i$$

If the future value is a series of benefits or costs rather than a single future amount, then present value of that stream of payments can be written as

$$PV = \Sigma FV_i/(1 + r)^i \text{ for a period of i years.}$$

This computation is made for both future costs and future benefits, so that there are two present values, one for costs, and one for benefits:

PVB = $\Sigma FB_i/(1 + r)^i$ for a period of i years.

PVC = $\Sigma FC_i/(1 + r)^i$ for a period of i years.

The difference between PVB and PVC is the net present benefits of the project, which can be positive or negative. The ratio PVC/PVB is called the cost-benefit ratio. Projects with lower cost-benefit ratios (or higher benefit-cost ratios) are usually given greater priority than those with higher cost-benefit ratios, and projects with a cost-benefit ratio greater than one would not be considered, because their benefits would be less than their costs.

For example, suppose that a student was performing a cost-benefit analysis of a college education. She would compute the present value of the four- or five-year expenditure she was expecting to make, including tuition and books and the opportunity cost of her time. She does not include the cost of food and housing, because she would have to have food and housing even if she didn't decide to go to college. She then discounts those costs to the present. To make it simple, suppose her cost comes to $15,000 a year for four years and she uses a discount rate of 6 percent. If the first payment is a year away, then the present value of her costs would be

$$\$15,000/1.06 + \$15,000/(1.06)^2 + \$15,000/(1.06)^3 + \$15,000/(1.06)^4 = \$57,960.$$

What about the benefits? Suppose that she expects her earnings to increase by $12,000 a year after college for the rest of her life, or at least to a retirement that is 30 to 40 years in the future. There is a simple formula for such long periods, which is FV/r, or $200,000. From that amount, she must subtract present value of that extra income for the first five years ($55,335) when she earns nothing. The present value of the increased future income stream is $200,000 − $55,335, or $144,665. The present value of the benefits exceeds the present value of the costs by $86,705. The benefit-cost ratio is about 2.5 ($57,960/$144,665); or, put alternatively, the cost/benefit ratio is only about 0.4. That looks like an investment worth making!

Case study: is Cash for Clunkers worth the cost?

In 2009, the United States created a program known as Cash for Clunkers—a rebate for purchase of a new, more fuel-efficient car in exchange for an old car with poor fuel economy that would then be junked. The rationale for the program, which was adapted from one used in Germany, was partly a reduction in air pollution but also partly an economic stimulus for the ailing auto industry. Critics questioned whether the benefits were worth the cost.

While no cost-benefit study was done for the US program, a similar proposed program in Israel was evaluated using cost-benefit techniques (Lavee and Becker 2009). In Israel, the estimated air pollution cost of the fleet of older, more polluting cars was estimated to be $530 million. High taxes on new vehicles had discouraged replacement of older cars. Without incentives, typically 12 percent of older cars would be retired each year. The payment schedule was based on the age of the vehicle with payments ranging from 2,000 to 22,000 new Israeli shekels, or from about $500 to $5,500 per vehicle. For private cars, an estimated 98,000 cars would be retired, resulting in a 17 percent reduction in annual air pollution costs. Additional benefits considered included the value of the recycled scraps, which averaged 80 percent of the material, while additional costs included the landfill disposal of the remaining 20 percent.

Practical issues in cost-benefit analysis

Cost-benefit analysis is complicated by a number of technical issues that must be addressed. Surely, you think, there is more to college than dollars. There is football, and friendships, and postponing adult responsibility. There is culture and recreation and time to experiment. There may be missing the family or the annoyance of commuting. Where do these considerations figure in? And why an interest rate of 6 percent? Where did that number come from?

Nonmonetary costs and benefits and the discount rate are the major issues that individuals have to consider in doing cost-benefit analysis. For public projects, there are additional factors. The important issues in carrying out a public sector cost-benefit analysis are as follows:

1   Counting and assigning values to all the costs and benefits, both monetary and non-monetary.
2   Choosing an appropriate rate of discount for costs and benefits that occur in the future.
3   Taking distributional and political considerations into account.

Counting all the costs and benefits

The easiest costs to count are the explicit costs of construction and annual operation and maintenance for a capital project, or the outlays each year for the life of a program for a new service. The cost calculations may extend for the entire life of the facility or program, or just for some predetermined number of years, after which the facility or program will be reevaluated for continuation. Future costs must, of course, be discounted to determine the present value of those costs.

More difficult to incorporate in the cost-benefit analysis are the non-monetary costs and benefits of a project, for two reasons. First, some of these costs may be easy to overlook. The political process can be useful in ferreting out some of these perceived costs through public hearings where neighbors complain about noise and traffic and other drawbacks of having a public facility built in their backyard, or when users of the facilities complain that it is too far away. Second, some of those non-monetary costs are difficult to put values on so that they can be added into the analysis. Much effort has been devoted to finding creative ways to convert non-monetary costs and benefits to dollar values and incorporated into the cost-benefit analysis.

Shadow prices

One method used by economists and others to attach monetary values to nonmonetary costs and benefits is called **shadow prices**. Shadow prices are estimates of the value of an output or an input to the economy. They are measured by the marginal willingness to pay (for output) or the marginal opportunity cost (for input), that is, the value of the next best alternative sacrificed. The shadow price may be different from the market price because of externalities, because of monopoly distortions, or because the production uses resources for which no charge is made.

Three important techniques that are commonly used in cost-benefit analysis to develop shadow prices are property valuation, value of human life calculations, and estimates of the value of travel time. These three examples do not exhaust the possibilities, but they do represent some significant elements of costs and/or benefits that might otherwise fail to be counted.

Locating an elementary school, a landfill, or a recreational facility near residential property affects property values in ways that can be measured. In an area with frequent turnover in real estate, changes in selling prices will reflect increases or decreases in the value of adjacent property according to whether the new facility increased property values (as a school might do) or decreased property values (as a landfill is likely to do). Unlike many of the annual costs in a cost-benefit calculation, any changes in present property values reflect the owner's and prospective buyer's valuation of how the facility will change the total future costs and benefits of living nearby, i.e., they are capitalized in the price of the property. Thus, changes in property values are already discounted and can just be added to the present value of benefits (if positive) or costs (if negative).

The value of human life is often a factor in decisions about allocating public resources. How many lives would be saved or lost if this road were (or were not) built, if this vaccine was not tested and made available? How many people might suffer illness or death in the absence of a water-testing program? (Remember, cost-benefit analysis can also be used to terminate programs!)

Economists have developed some ingenious techniques to determine the value people place on reducing the risks to their own lives in their daily actions, especially in choosing safer or riskier occupations. Most riskier occupations carry a wage premium, and that wage premium offers at least some indication of the value the worker places on his or her life in terms of the risks assumed. An annualized value of the "price" of risk can then be incorporated numerically into a cost-benefit calculation of any project that increases or reduces risk to human life in a measurable way.

Travel expense is another way to infer a measurement of either costs of benefits. This approach was originally developed as a way of valuing recreation benefits by the travel cost people were willing to incur (including the value of time) in order to reach a recreational site. Time is usually valued at the prevailing wage, sometimes at the minimum wage. Travel expense not only offers an indirect measure of benefits but also is an important factor on the cost side in siting decisions. It may, for example, be cheaper to build a new school farther out, but the value of the travel time for students (as well as the bussing costs!) must be taken into account. Students presumably place a positive value on their time and have a measurable preference for less travel time over more travel time.

These techniques do not exhaust the highly complex subject of incorporating all the costs and benefits into the calculation, but they offer some suggestions of the more common challenges and some of the techniques used to address them.

Choosing a discount rate

There is nothing magical about 6 percent. We used that figure in our example, but we could just as easily have chosen 2, or 4, or 10, or 15 percent. The discount rate is a measure of the difference between how an asset or a benefit is valued in the present moment compared to the same asset or benefit a year hence. How much would you accept now in preference to $1,000 a year from now? How much would you be willing to postpone spending in order to have $1,000 a year from now? If your answers were $926 to both questions, your personal rate of discount is 8 percent (8%).

Different people have different time preferences just as they have different preferences in other kinds of consumption activities. The rate of discount reflects the sum of all these preferences expressed in markets where borrowing and lending takes place, adjusted for difference in risk between different borrowers. That rate changes from year to year and even month to month. Most cost-benefit analyses use some generally accepted rate of interest such as the yield on ten-year government bonds, which are relatively risk-free, for longer-term projects, and the rate of Treasury bills (short-term debt) for shorter-term projects.

The choice of a discount rate will have an important impact on the calculation of costs and benefits. If the costs come early and the benefits are delayed, a lower discount rate will make such a project look a little better relative to another project where total benefits are smaller relative to costs, but the costs and benefits are spread more evenly. If the benefits come soon and the costs come later, a high rate of discount will shrink the deferred costs and make that kind of project look more attractive.

Uncertainty

The numbers that go into the cost-benefit analysis may be contingent on both sides of the cost-benefit equation. Costs can be higher if the project runs into technical difficulties. Benefits may be less if fewer people use a new park or recreational facility than were projected. For this reason, cost-benefit analysts often develop a range of estimates rather than a single point estimate.

Distributional and political considerations

No matter how careful and "objective" a cost-benefit analysis is developed, at some point other considerations almost always come into play. Benefits to higher-income people may be weighted differently from those to lower-income people, or between single persons and married people, families with and without children, people in states with a lot of political clout and people in states with little influence. Income distributional effects are a legitimate economic and political concern, but one that is difficult to incorporate statistically into a cost-benefit analysis. Pork-barrel projects that make influential politicians look good before re-election are likely to outweigh the most impressive analysis of costs and benefits. Quick benefits and delayed payoffs may be important for the election cycle even if they force analysts to use inappropriately high rates of discount in order to make certain projects look better. Like any other technique of analysis, cost-benefit analysis is only a tool. The ultimate decisions are in the hands of voters, bureaucrats, and elected officials.

Behavioral economics: cost-benefit analysis and absolutes

Most of us perform some kinds of cost-benefit analysis in our daily lives. Consider buying a home, which involves a commitment to monthly payments that will vary depending on the location, condition, size, and amenities. Buyers must weigh the extra costs of a more desirable location, a better yard, more square footage, or other attractions against the additional monthly cost that means forgoing other pleasures, such as eating out, travel, or recreation.

But in our personal lives, and our public lives, cost-benefit analysis runs into the idea of absolutes—the musts, the nevers, the indispensibles, the unallowables. If we *must* own a home in this neighborhood, then we try to figure out a way to pay for it. Location becomes an absolute, and the cost-benefit analysis is limited to choosing among homes in this neighborhood.

In public policy, if we cannot sacrifice or even risk a single human life for some noble cause, then no cost-benefit calculation will persuade us otherwise. Saving a single snail darter or spotted owl, ruling out any chance of a substance in food causing cancer, however rarely, have shaped public policy in the environmental and health regulatory areas. On the other hand, if the cause of going to war has an absolute justification—protecting freedom or human rights, for example—then no calculation of potential losses or probability of victory will alter the decision.

Economists, by the nature of their work, tend to think in terms of tradeoffs between values or goals rather than in terms of absolutes. Absolutes are constraints that narrow the range of choices and rule certain options out right at the beginning. Both tradeoffs and absolutes play an important role in our private decisions as well as our collective ones.

Summary

- Cost-benefit analysis is a technique used in making choices in both the public and private sector based on equating marginal benefit to marginal cost, which should maximize utility. Cost-benefit analysis attempts to quantify all the benefits and costs of a proposed project, both monetary and non-monetary.
- Non-monetary costs and benefits are quantified using techniques such as changes in property values, human life valuation, and development of shadow prices. The present value of future costs and future benefits are then computed by applying an appropriate discount rate, and the costs and benefits are compared. When they are compared using a benefit-cost ratio, different projects can be ranked according to the size of the benefit-cost ratio.

Key terms

Compensation principle
Cost-benefit analysis
Cost-effectiveness analysis
Shadow prices

Questions

1 **By the numbers**. You are asked to carry out a cost-benefit analysis for a new parking lot. The cost of the parking lot is $3,000,000. Annual maintenance and operating expenses are $60,000. The revenue from users, including the estimated value of "free" parking for city employees, is $200,000 a year, and the parking lot has an estimated useful lifetime of 15 years. At a 5 percent rate of discount, what is the cost-benefit ratio for this project? What other factors might you want to take into account? How would your answer be different if the interest rate was 8 percent?

2 **Policy application**. You are the city manager of a medium-sized city, and you are asked to present to your city council a proposal for the use of certain funds that are earmarked for tourism and recreation. Council members have proposed new tennis courts at a city park, improvements to the public swimming pool, or an arts and music series to be held

outdoors from April to October. How would you go about gathering the relevant information about benefits? Whose benefits would you include?

3   **Behavioral economics**. One of the challenges in cost-benefit analysis is getting people to reveal their preferences. The rational economic person may attempt to disguise his or her preferences in order to tilt the outcome in the preferred direction. But the average person with limited information and mixed motivations has a different problem in attempting to answer a survey or express a preference for one project over another. How might these two dimensions of choice complicate the task of cost-benefit analysis?

4   **Thinking globally**. In the case of common pool resources, such as ocean fishing, how does thinking globally rather than thinking nationally alter your cost-benefit analysis of controlling the amount of fish harvested in any given year? Why might different countries discount the future at different rates?

Part 3

Funding government

Taxes, fees, and grants

The next seven chapters address the revenue side of government: the funds to pay for public programs, the distribution of the burden of paying for government, and the use of revenue instruments as means toward specific policy ends. The primary revenue source for government is taxes. Taxes are the focus of the next five chapters.

The first two chapters explore the theory and practice of tax system design. The next three discuss each of the broad categories of taxes—income, sales, and property. The final two chapters in this part examine two other important revenue sources, fees and charges and intergovernmental grants.

According to Justice Oliver Wendell Holmes, taxes are the price we pay for a civilized society. That dictum still leaves room to argue over whether the taxes are too high relative to the amount of civilization that citizens want or need or actually receive in return. It does mean that taxes are an inevitable part of living in society. Given the necessity of taxes, it is the economist's task to provide some guidance in designing a tax system that minimizes the undesired side-effects of collecting them (efficiency) and apportions the burden in some way that addresses the equity concerns raised in Chapter 5.

Although taxes are still the primary form of revenue for governments at all levels, they are not the only source. Fees and charges, discussed in Chapter 16, are a second and increasingly important way of paying for services that have some advantages in terms of both efficiency and equity. In both unitary and federal systems, intergovernmental grants represent an important supplement to own-source revenues for lower levels of government, a subject addressed in Chapter 17.

11 Principles of taxation I

Efficiency and equity issues

Introduction

Given the need to raise revenues to fund the activities of government, it is the task of economists to figure out how to design a revenue system that is both efficient (minimizing distortions in household and business decisions) and equitable (distributing the burden fairly). Figuring out how to best raise revenue has been a central concern of economists at least since Adam Smith devoted an entire book of *The Wealth of Nations* (1776) to "the revenue of the sovereign," including his famous dictum that the taxes one pays should be "proportional to the revenue enjoyed under the protection of the state." David Ricardo, an important nineteenth-century figure in the history of microeconomic theory, titled his most famous book *Principles of Political Economy and Taxation*.

Until the latter half of the twentieth century, courses in public sector economics were aptly named public finance, because they concentrated so heavily on the revenue side of the public sector to the neglect of the equally important decisions on the expenditure side. Today the balance has shifted, but an understanding of the principles of tax design, both theoretical and applied, is still a central part of the study of public sector economics.

Criteria for evaluating tax and revenue systems

Every type of tax has positive and negative attributes. Some are more stable than others, or create fewer distortions in household and business decisions. Some are more costly to collect than others. Some are hidden, others highly visible. Some have broad bases, others narrower bases. Certain kinds of taxes are useful for correcting externalities while others may lend themselves to a more equitable distribution of tax liabilities.

Ideally, economists and policy-makers would think systemically about taxes, rather than focusing on a particular tax. Public policy should be concerned with the fairness and the revenue yield of the system as a whole, rather than a particular tax. But in order to see what a particular tax might contribute to the revenue system, it's usually easier to take them one at a time.

This chapter concentrates on the two most important qualities of a tax and a tax or revenue system. One is efficiency. The other is equity. Efficiency means many things. It may mean minimizing the (negative) impact on household decisions about where to shop, where to live, how hard to work, whether to save and invest. It may mean encouraging (or discouraging) business location in the country or state or county, or encouraging investment and job creation in general. Sometimes a tax is intended to distort consumer or business decisions, such as CO_2 emissions or smoking, so its efficiency would be measured by how much it discouraged that undesirable activity. Efficiency may also mean minimizing the cost of collection and compliance, or annoyance to taxpayers. Jean Baptiste Colbert, Minister of Finance to the French king Louis XIV, is famous for observing that "The art of taxation consists in so plucking the goose as to get the most feathers with the least hissing."

Equity means fairness in distribution of the tax burden among households, and firms, including households and firms located outside the taxing jurisdiction. Efficiency lends itself to objective measurement, but equity is subjective. There is some general agreement among economists that the tax system should be at least proportional, so that it takes about the same share of everyone's income. There is less consensus about the idea that it should perhaps be even moderately progressive, taking a larger share of the income of wealthier households.

These two criteria are so important that this entire chapter is addressed to analyzing the efficiency and equity implications of taxes. Other criteria include adequacy, visibility, cost of collection and compliance, and stability. These additional criteria will be discussed in Chapter 12.

Efficiency issues in tax design

A tax is said to be efficient if it does not change any of the economic decisions that firms and households would have made in the absence of the tax. There are very few taxes that can meet that high standard of efficiency. A **poll tax**, which is a flat charge per person or per household, is one of the few taxes that do not distort economic decisions. The burden of a poll tax does not change with changes in location, work effort, consumption spending, wealth, or any of the other factors that can affect one's tax liability for income, sales, property, excise, and estate taxes. The poll tax is rarely used in modern industrial nations (it was briefly introduced in Great Britain during the 1980s and then repealed) because it is extremely regressive, i.e., it takes a much higher percentage of income from the poor than the rich. But the poll tax does provide a useful standard of non-distortion against which the effects of other taxes can be measured.

Consumer surplus and excess burden

An analytical tool that is useful in evaluating the distorting effect of taxes and their impact on consumer welfare is the concept of consumer surplus. This concept may be familiar to you from an earlier course. Recall that each point on the demand curve measures the amount consumers are willing to pay for a particular quantity of a good. But in most cases, all consumers pay the same price, the market price, even though for many consumers (or many units purchased) the price they would have been willing to pay is higher.

Figure 11.1 represents an individual consumer's demand for bread. If Q_1 is one loaf, and Q_2 is two loaves, then this consumer would be willing to pay P_1 for the first loaf and P_2 for the second loaf. When she goes to the store and finds that the actual price is P_2, she buys two loaves. The "extra utility" she receives for getting the first loaf at price P_2 when it was worth P_1 to her is called **consumer surplus**.

Consumer surplus for a quantity Q_2 is the difference between the entire area under the demand curve, $OABQ_2$, and the amount paid, which is rectangle OP_2BQ_2 (price times quantity). The consumer surplus associated with purchasing a quantity Q_2 is triangle P_2AB, the difference between the area under the demand curve up to quantity Q_2 and the amount that consumers actually pay.

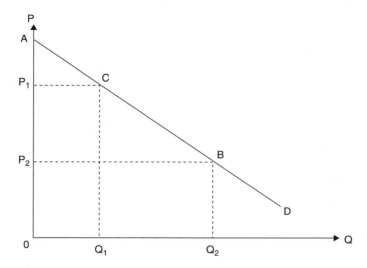

Figure 11.1 Measuring consumer surplus.

Taxes and excess burden

Anything that changes the price paid will also alter the amount of consumer surplus received. A rightward shift in supply will lower the price and increase consumer surplus, while a left-ward shift will raise the price and reduce consumer surplus. Imposing a tax will also have the effect of reducing consumer surplus.

Taxes are generally represented graphically as either **shadow demand curves** or shadow supply curves. The word shadow is intended to convey that the second demand or supply curve does not represent a shift in the original curve, but rather a wedge between the demand curve as perceived by the buyer and the demand curve as perceived by the seller.

In Figure 11.2, an excise tax is imposed on the purchase of light bulbs in the amount of AE per light bulb, the vertical distance between supply curve S_1 and supply curve S_T. To the consumer it appears as a backward shift in the supply curve, although to the producer the two supply curves represent gross and net (after-tax) price. As a result, consumers pay a higher price, buy fewer light bulbs, and experience a loss of consumer surplus measured by area P_1P_Tab.

Where does the consumer surplus go? Some of it (rectangle P_1P_Tac) is transferred to the government in tax revenue. Total tax revenue is actually the larger rectangle P_NP_1ad, with the rest of the tax revenue coming from lower net price received by the producer (see below). So this transfer is not necessarily undesirable, because the additional government services paid for with that tax revenue may compensate consumers for their loss of utility in consuming light bulbs. But there is a little piece of consumer surplus that is lost to consumers and not transferred to government, triangle abc. This loss is known as **excess burden** in a context of taxation, but is more generally labeled deadweight loss.

This excess burden or deadweight loss represents a decline in consumer surplus and consumer welfare that does not get transferred to firms or to government but is lost entirely. It represents an interaction between the higher price and the decline in quantity purchased and consumed. The rectangle of consumer surplus transferred to government only captures the effect of the higher price paid on the smaller quantity.

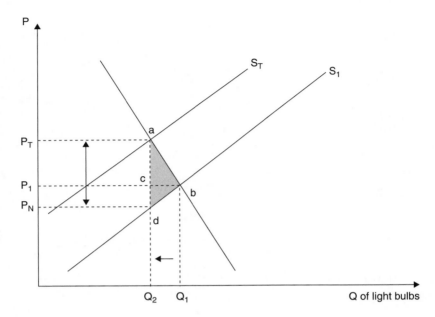

Figure 11.2 An excise tax.

Triangle abc, however, only captures part of the excess burden of taxation. There is a similar loss accruing to producers as long as supply is not perfectly elastic. In Figure 11.2, producers also suffer a loss in their surplus of revenue over marginal or variable costs (which may or may not be profit). When quantity declines from Q_1 to Q_2, producers lose revenue measured by the sum of the two quadrilaterals plus Q_2dbQ_1. The second quadrilateral is offset by a reduction in production costs as the supplier moves back down the supply curve, so the net revenue loss to the producer is P_NP_1bd. Some of that revenue loss is transferred to the government as tax, P_NP_1cd. But the triangle below the supply curve, cbd, represents a loss of producer surplus that is not transferred to the government—a second deadweight loss that is comparable to the loss of consumer surplus. Both triangles abc and cbd are also known as Harberger triangles, named for the economist who first analyzed them in detail.

These triangles in Figure 11.2 are very important both analytically and in practice. Different tax rates or levels and/or different elasticities of supply or demand will result in triangles of different size and shape that represent larger or smaller deadweight losses, or in the case of taxes, excess burden. One of the objectives of good tax and revenue system design is to minimize the excess burden represented by the Harberger triangles. The concrete, intuitive meaning behind these triangles is a forced adjustment in consumption (or sometimes production) patterns as a result of the tax. That forced adjustment generates a loss of consumer welfare over and above the transfer of resources from the consumer to the government.

Shifting, incidence, and price elasticity

If you refer back to Figure 11.2, you will notice another interesting point about the effect of taxes. In that diagram, the price paid by the buyer rose, *but it rose by less than the amount of the tax*. And if you look again, you will notice in Figure 11.2 a price P_N where S_1 crosses the supply curve. P_N is the price received by the seller, which is lower than the equilibrium market price P_1 that had prevailed prior to the tax. So part of the tax reflects a lower net price to the seller. The total revenue collected by the government from this tax is measured by rectangle $P_N P_T ad$, of which $P_1 P_T ac$ comes from the buyer in the form of higher prices paid and $P_1 P_N dc$ comes from the seller in the form of lower net price received.

It does not matter whether the law says that the tax must be paid by the seller or the buyer. Economic factors, primarily price elasticities of demand and supply, determine the division of the tax burden between the two parties. Responsibility for collecting and remitting the tax may initially fall on the seller, as it does for most sales taxes. But if the seller is able to pass part of that tax onto the buyer in the form of higher prices, then there is **shifting** of part of the tax burden. The place where the burden ultimately falls, or the division of the tax burden between the parties involved, is known as tax **incidence**.

To illustrate what determines the division of the tax burden, consider Figure 11.3, which shows a tax imposed on a commodity in completely inelastic supply—perhaps land, or tickets to a concert where seating is limited and cannot be expanded. In this case, the entire burden of the tax falls on the seller, because the seller is unable to adjust the quantity at all. Since buyers demand Q_1 at a price P_1, nothing has changed to make buyers feel any differently. The entire tax burden $P_T P_1 ab$ falls on the seller in the form of reduced net revenue. Note, too, that there is no excess burden or Harberger triangle in this case, because there is no quantity change.

Needless to say, it is very tempting for policy-makers to look for situations like that in Figure 11.3 to provide a revenue source. In the nineteenth century, economist Henry George reasoned that the most useful and appropriate tax would be a single tax on land (not improvements, such as buildings) because land was fixed in supply, and the tax would cause no distortions in behavior or deadweight loss. Henry George's ideas are again being considered in designing the property tax in some parts of the United States and Canada in

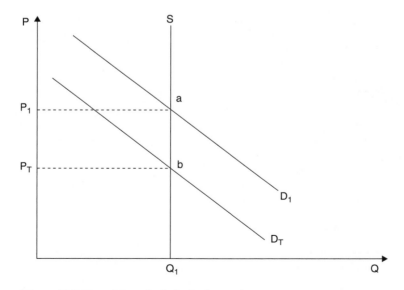

Figure 11.3 Tax with perfectly inelastic supply.

recent years. More of the value of the property is assigned to the land value and less to the buildings or other improvements, so as not to discourage improvements. More often, taxes are imposed on goods where the supply is highly if not perfectly inelastic, because the resulting excess burden triangle will be smaller than it would be for a more elastic supply curve.

Figure 11.4 illustrates the effects of imposing an excise tax on a product with relatively inelastic demand, such as cigarettes, alcohol, or gasoline. Note that in Figure 11.4, the share of the tax revenue $P_T P_1 ca$ that falls on the buyer is much larger than the share falling on the seller ($P_1 P_2 dc$). Why? Because the seller is more able to alter his behavior in response to the tax, cutting back production from Q_1 to Q_2. But because consumers are unwilling or unable to shift to substitute products, competition among buyers for the reduced quantity drives the price up to P_T. Typical items in this category are drugs (both illegal and prescription), salt, and water, all of which have very inelastic demand curves until the price gets well out of its familiar range.

Ad valorem taxes

All of the illustrations thus far show a fairly simple type of tax, called a **specific tax**, which is imposed on the basis of some quantity measure—units, volume, or weight. A tax of 50 cents on a pack of cigarettes, $1 a gallon on wine, or 20 cents a pound on imported cashew nuts would be examples of a specific tax. Much more common are **ad valorem taxes**, which (as their name suggests) are imposed as a percentage of the price or value. State retail sales taxes are ad valorem taxes imposed at rates ranging from 3 percent to 8 percent of the value of the item sold. Many excise taxes, such as those on telephone service and automobile tires, are ad valorem taxes. The property tax is also an ad valorem

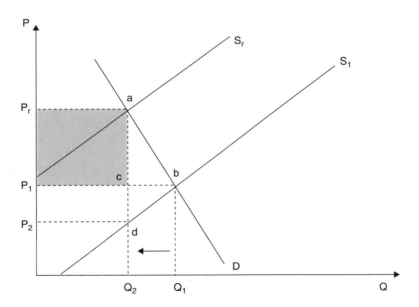

Figure 11.4 Tax with inelastic demand.

tax, because it applies a mill rate (a mill is a tenth of a cent) to the assessed value of the property.

For a specific tax, the shadow demand curve is parallel to the original demand curve. The distance between them measures the tax per unit. For an ad valorem tax, the distance between the two curves changes with the price, and the "tax wedge" gets larger and larger as the price gets higher. Figure 11.5 illustrates the effects of an ad valorem tax on price, quantity, tax revenue, and division of the tax burden between buyer and seller. As a result of the tax, price paid by the buyer rises from P_1 to P_T and price received by the seller falls from P_1 to P_2. Total government revenue, as before, is $P_2 P_T AE$, of which $P_1 P_T AC$ comes from the buyer in the form of higher prices paid and $P_1 P_2 CE$ comes from the seller in the form of lower net price received. Excess burden or deadweight loss is measured by triangle ABC for consumers and triangle BCE for producers or sellers.

Effect of taxes on income and leisure

The taxes whose effects are illustrated in Figures 11.1 to 11.5 include various kinds of sales taxes. These diagrams can also be used to analyze some kinds of income tax deductions, because an expenditure that is tax deductible has a lower effective price than one that is not deductible. A different analytical approach is needed to assess the general efficiency effects of an income tax, which is illustrated in Figure 11.6. This figure, which can be used to analyze a variety of taxes besides income taxes, shows an indifference map that describes an individual's preferences between various combinations of two desirable activities, in this case income and leisure.

Assume that this person can earn $15 an hour. Putting all waking hours (7×16, or 112) into work would result in an income of $1680 a week and zero hours of leisure. On the opposite axis, a choice of zero working hours would result in no income and 112 hours of leisure

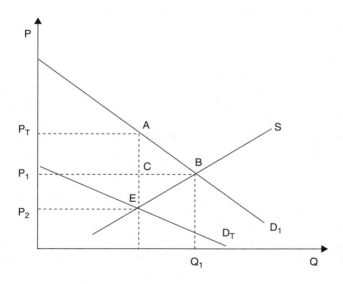

Figure 11.5 An ad valorem tax.

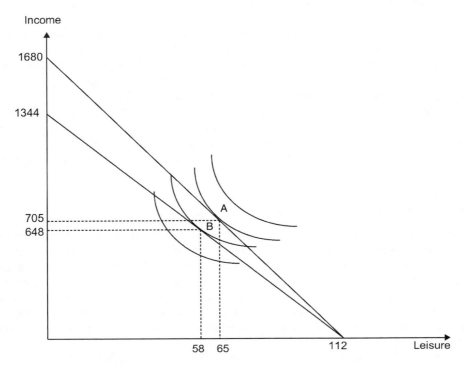

Figure 11.6 Effects of a payroll tax.

(not including sleep). Faced with the time constraint and the rate of pay, this individual chooses point A, which reflects 47 hours of work and 65 hours of leisure with an income of $705 a week. Any other choice would put this person on a lower indifference curve, implying a lower level of satisfaction or utility.

Now introduce a payroll tax as a percentage of earnings. The intercept with the horizontal axis does not change, because leisure is not taxed. But every hour of work now nets $12 instead of $15 because of the tax. The maximum weekly earnings drop to $1344, the new intercept on the vertical axis. Faced with this new "budget" constraint, this worker adjusts his/her behavior, selecting point B, which represents only 58 hours of leisure and income of only $648 after taxes. This individual experiences both an income effect (the tax reduces income) and a substitution effect (leisure is now cheaper in terms of income forgone) that impacts on his/her work behavior. Different preferences, reflected in a different shape for the indifference curve, might have actually resulted in fewer work hours and more leisure.

There is no easy way to design an income tax to avoid distorting the work/leisure choice. The same analysis can be applied to consumption and saving, where a tax on purchases makes saving less expensive than consuming, or to other choices between taxable and nontaxable options. As long as a tax is not truly universal, it will tip the balance for at least some individuals toward the decision or activity that is not subject to tax. Only a poll tax, which cannot be evaded by rearranging one's work, spending, owning, or other decisions, is neutral among consumer choices.

Who ultimately pays the tax?

Regardless of how the tax law is written, or what the incidence may be, all taxes are ultimately paid by households in one form or another. A tax such as a retail sales tax can be shifted forward to the consumer, or it can be absorbed by the seller. But even if a tax is absorbed by the seller, the impact does not end there, because the seller is merely an intermediary for workers, suppliers, and owners—often stockholders.

The share of the tax paid by the seller has to come out of the earnings of one or more of those groups. It may result in lower wages for workers, lower dividends for stockholders, lower profits in the case of a privately owned firms, or even lower payments to providers of inputs, depending on the degree of competition in each of the relevant markets. The group of households on whom the tax falls is likely to be different when more of the tax falls on the seller than when more is shifted forward to the buyers, but the burden still falls on households in one or more of their incarnations as consumers, workers, or owners.

Location effects

Another set of choices that is influenced by taxes is location decisions—where to site a new factory, open a restaurant, buy or build a home. The kinds of taxes imposed, the rates, the coverage, and other features will impact differently on homeowners than on commercial or industrial property. Even within the same category (e.g., homeowners), the impact of different taxes will be different. Younger households with children might be more sensitive to differences in the sales tax on tangible goods (the typical state retail sales tax), while older households may be hit harder by property taxes as their taxable wealth increases while their purchases of tangible goods decline. Among commercial establishments, some will generate more tax liabilities than others out of any given tax code. In any case, it is important to note that it is relative rather than absolute tax burdens and tax burdens in relation to the service package offered that influence location decisions.

Multiple tax bases and excess burden

Every tax but the poll tax causes some kind of excess burden. Because the poll tax is very unsatisfactory on equity grounds, public officials are forced to employ other tax instruments that distort people's choices. From the perspective of efficiency, is it better to employ just one distortionary tax at a fairly high rate, or several such taxes, each at a low rate? Which one will cause less loss of consumer welfare, i.e., which excess burden triangle will have the smallest area? The answer to this question is basically a proposition in geometry.

For simplicity, consider a case where supply is perfectly elastic, so that the price paid by the consumer is equal to the full amount of the tax, as shown in Figure 11.7.

Recall that the area of a right triangle is ½ the base times the height. The height of the excess burden triangle is the increase in price as a result of the tax. If the tax is ad valorem, and t is the tax rate, then the area of the excess burden triangle is measured as

$$ABC = 1/2\ t*P_1*(Q_1 - Q_T) \tag{11.1}$$

But the change in Q depends on the tax rate t, with the exact amount of the change being the result of elasticity. Elasticity, ε, is equal to the percentage change in quantity divided by the percentage change in price,

$$= \frac{t/(P_1 + P_T)}{(Q_1 - Q_T)/(Q_1 + Q_T)} \tag{11.2}$$

Solving Equation 11.2 for $Q_T - Q_1$

$$Q_T - Q_1 = \frac{t*(Q_T + Q_1)}{*P_1*(1+t)} \tag{11.3}$$

Substituting this expression into Equation 11.1 gives

$$ABC = \frac{1/2t^2 P_1 *(Q_T + Q_1)}{*(P_T + P_1)} \tag{11.4}$$

Given the initial price and quantity, Equation 11.4 conveys a very important insight. The size of the excess burden triangle, or the "waste" that takes place in transferring revenue to the government, depends on two factors. The excess burden is inversely proportional to the elasticity of demand (the greater the elasticity, the smaller the excess burden), but it increases directly in proportion to, not just the tax rate, but the *square* of the tax rate. From the same starting point and on the same demand curve, the size of the excess burden increases with the square of the tax rate. Double the tax rate, quadruple the excess burden or deadweight loss.

This bit of theory has important implications for tax policy. First, it suggests that taxes should be imposed to the extent possible on items for which demand is relatively inelastic. The instinctive response to that observation is to think of addictive substances (alcohol, tobacco, heroin), or inexpensive necessities (flour, salt). That's one possible answer.

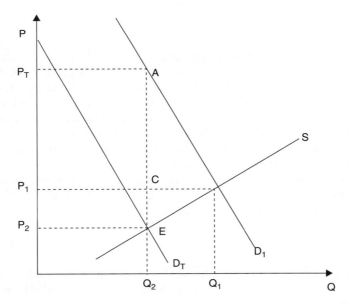

Figure 11.7 Tax rate and excess burden.

But another response is suggested by the fact that elasticity is lower when there are few substitutes.

The easiest way to design a tax where the possibility of substitution is minimal is to make the base as broad as possible. A retail sales tax has a broader base than an excise tax, because there are fewer possibilities for substitution. A retail sales tax that includes services as well as goods will be less distorting than one that only taxes tangible goods. An income tax that includes income from investments will result in less distortion in behavior than a payroll tax that only covers wages.

Second, and equally important, Equation 11.4 suggests that the distortions caused by a tax are very sensitive to changes in the rate, and that very high rates cause substantially greater distortions in people's decisions and greater excess burden over and above the revenue collected. The fact that the excess burden rises with the square of the rate is an important caution in tax design.

In order to avoid extremely high rates for a particular tax, governments usually resort to more than one broad-based tax combined with a variety of specialty taxes on particular products or services. States like Florida and Tennessee that do not have a broad-based income tax are forced to make more intensive use of sales and property taxes. High sales tax rates result in a lot of cross-border shopping in a state like Tennessee, which borders seven other states.

Tax rates, elasticity, and base erosion

A tax on any kind of spending has two effects: it raises the price and reduces the quantity. In raising the price, the tax will increase revenue, but in reducing the quantity, or eroding the tax base, it will reduce revenue. The same kind of effects can be observed in the case of taxes on income or on assets. Is there some point at which the second effect, or base erosion, dominates the first, so that an increase in the tax rate will reduce tax revenue rather than increase it? This is the question to which economist Arthur Laffer sketched out an answer on a napkin in the form of his famous diagram, the **Laffer curve**.

Laffer expressed this concern very simply. At a zero tax rate, there is no tax revenue. At a 100 percent tax rate, taxable economic activity is pointless, so there will be no tax base and there will again be no revenue. Between those extremes, the tax system will generate revenue, but there are tradeoffs between the revenue-increasing and revenue-decreasing effects of higher rates. Not all these effects are capturable in a simple algebraic or graphic model. If tax rates get high enough, people will resort to barter or tax evasion; they will go underground, reduce their work effort, leave the country, buy abroad. Under these circumstances, a reduction in tax rates (such as from 60 percent to 50 percent in Figure 11.8) might actually generate more revenue (R_2) rather than less (R_1).

Laffer's ideas were very popular in the Reagan administration in the early 1980s, although there is little empirical evidence on just how high a tax rate must be in order to cause the revenue function to turn backward. But the insight behind the Laffer curve offers a useful caution. Moving up the demand curve, eventually even the most inelastic demand curve enters an elastic range in which buyers become more and more sensitive to price increases.

The author of this textbook was asked a similar question by a state legislator, who wanted to know how high the sales tax rate would have to be in order to generate enough revenue to eliminate the property tax. The answer was that no such sales tax rate existed, because as the rate rose, people would have more and more incentive to avoid or evade the sales tax— cross-border shopping, catalog shopping, internet shopping, collusion with sellers to hide transactions, and/or just plain reductions in spending.

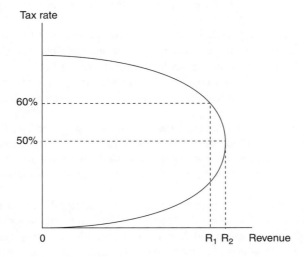

Figure 11.8 A Laffer curve.

Short-run versus long-run effects

The diagrammatic approach emphasizes immediate effects of changes in tax rates or tax structures on decisions. But remember, elasticities are always greater in the long run, once contracts expire or people have had a chance to gather information and consider alternatives. A tax that raises a substantial amount of revenue the first year or two may slack off after people have found ways to evade, avoid, or reduce the burden of the tax by a change in spending, working, investing, or locational choices.

Figure 11.9 illustrates this situation with a specific tax on soft drinks. The short-run demand curves with and without the tax are D_S and D_{ST}, and the long-run demand curves are D_L and D_{LT}. The greater elasticity reflects the opportunity to change to other kinds of beverages that are not subject to the tax, or to buy them out-of-state where the tax is not imposed. Note that in the short run the decline in quantity is very small (Q_1 to Q_2), but in the long run there is a further decline to Q_3. With the smaller base, revenue shrinks. Because the elasticity is greater and the decline in quantity larger, while the price change is the same, the deadweight loss is also greater in the long run (triangle EFG).

Behavioral economics: using taxes to alter decisions

While in general the goal of tax design is to minimize the distortions in people's decisions, taxes can also be used to deliberately alter decisions because of the positive and negative externalities associated with certain kinds of individual decisions. Taxes on alcohol, cigarettes, and gambling are intended in part to discourage consumption of those products, all of which have negative externalities of one kind or another associated with them. The tax is not only an economic incentive but also a signal about what kinds of activities are socially approved and encouraged, or socially disapproved and discouraged. So the response to economic incentives is embedded in a message about what kind of activity is socially desirable or unacceptable.

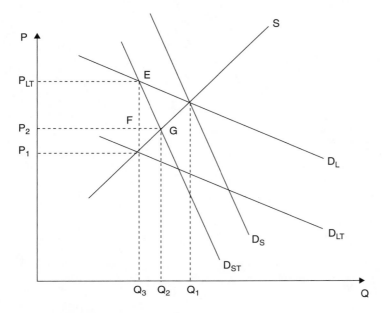

Figure 11.9 Short- and long-run tax effects.

Taxes or charges on pollution that are tied to the volume of emissions are also intended to discourage socially undesirable activities. Some tax expenditures or tax subsidies of various kinds are designed to encourage activities with social benefits, such as giving to charity, investing in one's own education, or becoming a homeowner (which presumably creates more stable communities). Finally, certain tax subsidies or tax expenditures are intended to benefit one group of taxpayers in preference to others, which is intentional redistribution of income or wealth.

Some taxes are more effective tools for altering decisions than others. For a subsidy or tax expenditure, an effective tax tool will target the population or activity fairly narrowly without losing more revenue than is needed to accomplish the objective. How much encouragement do people need to buy a house, and how many of them would do so anyway in the absence of the deductibility of mortgage interest and property taxes? Would people continue to borrow to pay for their education even if the interest on student loans were not tax deductible? How much has that borrowing increased since the deduction became available ten years ago, relative to the amount of borrowing that would have occurred without the tax break? Does the tax deductibility of charitable contributions really affect the amount people give, and does it go to causes that really fit the criterion of creating social benefits?

Figure 11.10 illustrates this dilemma. S_1 represents the annual supply of houses. With a subsidy, consumers will perceive the supply curve as S_S. The initial equilibrium is at P_1 and Q_1. Now a new tax law pays either buyers or sellers a fixed dollar subsidy for each new home purchased.

What happens? The gross price of homes falls to P_2, which is a drop that is smaller than the amount of the subsidy. There is an increase in consumer surplus of P_2P_1ac, but P_2P_1ab is

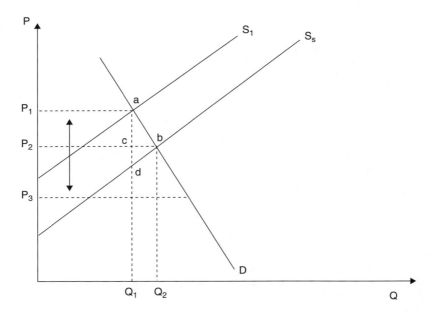

Figure 11.10 A housing subsidy.

in the form of a subsidy, leaving a net gain of triangle abc. There is likewise an increase in producer surplus of P_3P_2cd, but some of that (P_3P_2bd) is due to the subsidy, leaving bcd as the part of the gain that accrues as producers' surplus. Taxpayers lost the cost of the subsidy, P_3P_1ad, which was transferred to homeowners and builders. Subsidies such as this are one of the challenges identified by public choice, where the cost (in terms of transfers from taxpayers to new homeowners and builders) results in a very small total increase in consumer and producer surplus. Because the benefits are concentrated and the costs are diffused among all taxpayers, this kind of policy—like the rebates for first-time home buyers in 2009 and 2010 in the United States—has a great deal of political appeal.

Equity issues in tax design

Equity is at least as important as efficiency, sometimes more so to policy-makers, in designing and reforming tax systems. Every change in the tax base, the tax rate(s), or the tax rules alters the distribution of the tax burden between taxpayers. Substantial lobbying effort is expended on tax breaks for particular firms, individuals, or activities. Efforts to redistribute the burden, whether in the interests of greater equity or in response to lobbying by particular interests, are the source of much of the complexity in the tax system, especially the income tax.

Measures of ability to pay

The most widely used criterion for tax fairness is called **ability to pay**. Ability to pay as a determinant of one's tax burden implies that those who have more resources than others can and should make a larger contribution toward the cost of government and public services. (Contrast this notion with the poll tax, where everyone makes an equal contribution regardless of ability to pay.)

How is ability to pay measured? The simplest measure is income—the amount of revenue flowing through the household in a month or a year. A second measure is consumption or spending, and a third measure is assets or property owned. These three measures are the bases for the principal tax revenue sources in the US economy and most other places as well—the income tax, some form of sales or consumption tax, and the property tax. (Inheritance and estate taxes are also based on assets.) We will have more to say about the problems of measuring ability to pay for each kind of tax when we examine the various kinds of taxes in Chapters 13–15.

Some of these measures of ability to pay are more accessible to the tax collector than others. Consumption is the easiest measure to track because it involves transactions in the marketplace that can be tapped at the point of sale. Some income, particularly wage and salary income, is easy to track through payroll records, but other forms of income—self-employment earnings, interest and dividends, profits from proprietary businesses, capital gains—are much harder to uncover. Assets are the most challenging tax base of all. Few tax systems attempt to be broadly inclusive of all assets (household furnishings, stocks, bonds, jewelry, works of art, etc.) and just focus on certain kinds of property, such as real estate, automobiles and boats.

When direct information is not available, proxies are sometimes used. In Turkey, the tax collector used to assess income taxes based on "lifestyle indicators"—occupation, number of horses owned, size of house, etc. Lacking market values for real property that was rarely sold, nineteenth-century British tax collectors estimated the value of property on the basis of such easily determined factors as the number of windows. Even today, in a much more monetized economy with high turnover of real property, assessing real property (land and buildings) for tax purposes is the most challenging of all tax measurements to undertake.

The benefit principle

A second principle of taxation is the **benefit principle**. Unlike ability to pay, the benefit principle links the tax obligation to the value of the services received in exchange. Adam Smith argued that a proportional income tax is, in fact, a sort of benefit tax, because the tax payment would be "proportional to the revenue enjoyed under the protection of the state" (1776: Book V: 777). The state's social, legal and economic framework makes it possible to earn and keep one's income, and the value of those services can be assumed to be proportional to that income.

The same argument has been made for the property tax as a benefit tax. Most local services (except for education) are fairly directly related to property. Police protection, fire protection, roads, street lights, and garbage pickup are the most obvious examples. A case could be made that the value of those services to property rises with the value of the property being served or protected.

In general, however, the benefit principle is invoked for some highly specialized taxes where there is a clear relationship between the user of the taxed good or service and the user of the public service that the tax is used to finance. The best-known example of a benefit tax is the tax on gasoline, which is earmarked for highway construction and maintenance. Those who purchase more gasoline either drive more miles or drive heavier, less fuel-efficient cars, but in either case they cause more wear and tear on the roads. Those who drive little do not have to subsidize those who drive a lot, and those who drive smaller, more fuel-efficient cars do not have to subsidize those who drive gas guzzlers.

There are relatively few taxes that lend themselves to benefit principle implementation like the tax on gasoline. More recently, the benefit principle has been expressed in the increased use of fees and charges for government services ranging from marriage licenses to health clinics to libraries to public parks. The fee usually does not cover the full cost of the service, but it does shift more of the burden of paying for the service to users rather than taxpayers in general. The search for an appropriate balance between tax financing and fees for services is discussed in Chapter 16.

Horizontal and vertical equity

Earlier, we raised the question of defining equity between households with equal ability to pay (horizontal equity) and households with unequal ability to pay (vertical equity). Such equity issues are central to tax design. If taxes are perceived as unfair, there will be constant pressure to adjust the mix, and each adjustment of the mix changes the distribution of the tax burden and sparks further protests.

Both the income tax and the property tax have been subjected to such serial complaints and redistribution of the burden in recent decades. Homeowners have protested their property tax burdens in many states, persuading legislators to shift the burden to industrial, commercial, rental and personal property. Industry has also sought tax relief by threatening local governments with the loss of jobs and income if the industry moves or shuts down. In South Carolina, such relief to industry and homeowners was followed by demands for relief from property taxes on automobiles.

Regressive, proportional, and progressive taxation

While designing tax systems for equity is a highly normative issue, there are some positive ways of at least measuring the impact of alternative tax structures on different groups. The central equity issue is almost always framed as one of tax burdens relative to income. Once the distribution of the tax burden for alternative tax systems is clearly understood, a tax structure can be developed (or reformed) that represents some consensus about how the tax burden should be distributed across income classes. Within the context of that tax system, the narrower issues of equity like the one just posed can be addressed as a matter of fine-tuning the tax system.

Regardless of whether the actual base of the revenue source is expenditures (e.g., the retail sales tax), assets (e.g., the property tax), income (income or payroll taxes), some specialized economic activity (excise taxes, severance taxes, inheritance taxes), or actual use of government services (fees and charges), the measure used is to compute this burden as a percentage of income. Taxes and tax/revenue systems are then classified as regressive, proportional, or progressive according to whether that percentage decreases, remains the same, or increases as income rises.

A **regressive tax** takes a smaller percentage of income as income rises. A poll tax is the ultimate regressive tax, because it is a flat fee per person. A poll tax of $100 a year represents 2 percent of income for a person earning $5,000 a year, dropping to 1 percent at $10,000, 0.1 percent at $100,000, and continuing to decline as income rises. Retail sales taxes are regressive because they generally do not cover services, and the consumption of services becomes a larger share of total spending as income rises. Retail sales taxes are also regressive because they only tax spending; saving is exempt, and saving rises as income rises. Because the base of the retail sales tax does not increase at the same rate as the increase in income, it is regressive. Some excise taxes are regressive, while others are not, depending on how consumption patterns for cigarettes, gasoline, alcohol, and other items subject to excise taxes vary with income.

A **proportional tax** takes a constant fraction of income as income rises. It is difficult to find examples of truly proportional taxes in the US tax system. A payroll tax like Social Security taxes or many local income taxes (such as those used by cities in Ohio and counties in Maryland) appears to be proportional because they take a constant fraction of income with no exemptions or deductions. However, these kinds of taxes exclude other kinds of income such as interest and dividends, which tend to go mainly to higher-income families. Social Security taxes are collected only up to a wage and salary ceiling that is adjusted each year, and also are not collected on nonwage income. Consequently, all of these taxes that appear to be proportional are at least moderately regressive. Some states, such as Illinois, have simple, flat income taxes that take a constant percentage of all income (not just payroll or wage and salary) without any deductions or exemptions. These taxes are correctly classified as proportional.

The quotation from Adam Smith earlier in this chapter appears to support the notion of proportional taxation ("proportional to the revenue enjoyed under the protection of the state"). Much of the support for replacing the federal income tax with some variant of a flat tax in recent years was based on the perception that a proportional tax is fair in a way that a regressive or progressive tax is not. Even the proposed flat tax, however, was not purely proportional, because it exempts some base amount of income (making it progressive, as is explained below), and also because at least some versions exempted capital gains and investment income, making it more regressive.

A **progressive tax** takes an increasing percentage of income as income rises. There are two fairly simple ways of making a tax progressive. One is to tax items that are consumed much more heavily by higher-income households, such as jewelry, new cars, yachts (an experiment in the first Bush administration that was quickly abandoned), air travel, etc. A more systematic approach is to design an income tax that exempts a certain amount for each person or household (like the personal exemption and standard deduction in the US federal income tax). Consider a 10 percent income tax that exempts the first $20,000 in income for each person. Then the tax burden would look like Table 11.1.

As you can see, as incomes get very large the tax as a percentage of income gets closer and closer to 10 percent. Many state income taxes follow this mildly progressive pattern.

The progressivity of an income tax can be enhanced by the use of graduated rates. In Table 11.1, in addition to exempting the first $20,000 of income, perhaps the tax rate could be 10 percent for the next $30,000 and 20 percent for income above that level—a simple two-rate tax system. If we apply that structure to Table 11.1, we get a different pattern of progressivity as shown in Table 11.2. Note that the tax computation is a little more difficult for incomes of $50,000 and above, because income has to be segmented into parts taxed at different rates. At $100,000, for example, $20,000 is taxed at a rate of zero, $30,000 at a rate of 10 percent, and the last $50,000 at a rate of 20 percent. The degree of progressivity is the same at lower incomes but rises sharply at higher incomes.

The primary theoretical justification for a progressive rather than a proportional tax system rests on two concepts: equal sacrifice, and the diminishing marginal utility of income. If all citizens have equal access to public services (some of which they may not choose to use), then there is some equity justification for asking citizens to make equal sacrifices in order to

Table 11.1 A simple progressive income tax

Gross income ($)	Taxable income ($)	Tax ($)	Tax as % of income
10,000	0	0	0
20,000	0	0	0
30,000	10,000	1,000	3.3
40,000	20,000	2,000	5
50,000	30,000	3,000	6
100,000	80,000	8,000	8
500,000	480,000	48,000	9.6

Table 11.2 A two-rate progressive income tax

Gross income ($)	Taxable income ($)	Tax ($)	Tax as % of income
10,000	0	0	0
20,000	0	0	0
30,000	10,000	1,000	3.3
40,000	20,000	2,000	5
50,000	30,000	3,000	6
100,000	80,000	13,000	13
500,000	480,000	93,000	18.6

provide those services. But what is an equal sacrifice? A poll tax, which takes the same number of dollars from each citizen but is a much larger share of income for the poor than the rich? An equal percentage of income from all (a proportional tax)? Or is it possible that giving up a dollar is less painful to a rich person than a poor one, because of diminishing marginal utility of income?

Diminishing marginal utility of income suggests that as a person gets richer, the needs/wants being met by the additional income are less urgent or add less to total utility than those met by earlier dollars, which go to food, clothing, shelter and other basic needs. Wealthier persons may spend their dollars on culture, or gambling, or fancier homes or expensive clothes or even contributions to charity, choices that they would not have made on a lower income and which must therefore be of lower priority, value—or utility.

This concept is illustrated in Figure 11.11. The marginal utility function for income indicates that the gain in utility $(M_1 - M_2)$ from moving from income A to income B is much greater than the gain in utility $(M_3 - M_4)$ in moving from income C to income D, even though the increased number of dollars is the same in both cases. If the gain is smaller from C to D than from A to B, then the loss in utility (and particularly the deadweight loss, HIJ versus GEF) will be smaller when taxes move someone's income from D to C than when income is reduced from B to A. If individuals are similar in their capacity to enjoy income, so that their marginal utility schedules for income are similar, then the utility loss from an equal tax would be greater for a poor person than a rich one. This argument of diminishing marginal utility is often used to argue against regressive taxation, where an equal dollar sacrifice translates into a greater utility loss. It is used with somewhat less conviction to argue for progressive rather than proportional taxation.

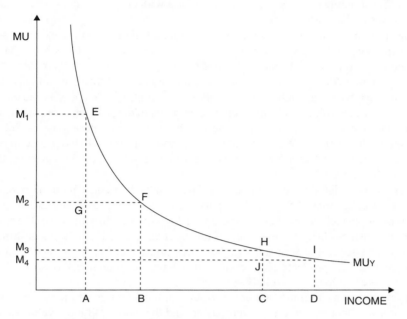

Figure 11.11 Diminishing marginal utility of income.

There are more pragmatic grounds for having at least some progressive taxes in the tax system. First, such taxes can raise substantial amounts of revenue. Second, it is inevitable that some taxes in the system will be regressive. It is very difficult to design a structure of sales taxes, for example, that is not at least moderately regressive. Having at least one progressive tax in the system may create some balance that moves the overall tax structure toward the equity measure that is easiest to defend, proportionality.

On the negative side, high marginal rates will cause greater distortion in decisions by those subject to those rates, and they may often respond by devoting more effort to tax avoidance or evasion than to productive work in order to increase their after-tax income.

Particular taxes may be inequitable along many lines, not just regressive. They may discriminate against (or for) singles versus married couples, homeowners versus renters, older people versus young families, wage earners versus self-employed. But other parts of the tax system may compensate for those weaknesses, tilting the equity back toward the center. Any tax, and any proposed tax change, needs to be viewed in the context of the overall tax system.

Business taxes and compounding

An issue that involves both efficiency and equity considerations is the taxation of business firms. Incorporated businesses in the United States typically pay federal and state corporate income taxes, sales taxes on at least some of their inputs, and property taxes on their land and buildings.[1] The rationale for taxing businesses separately from the shareholders that own them is that business firms use public services, which are a cost of doing business and should be reflected in the price of the product or service. This rationale is particularly relevant to the property tax and local public services. The problem arises with corporate income taxes and also with sales taxes on business inputs.

There has been a strong constituency for avoiding double taxation of corporate earnings—once on the corporate income tax, and again on the individual income tax where shareholders pay income tax on dividends distributed and capital gains realized on their corporate shares. (It should be noted that no equally strong constituency has mobilized on double taxation of wage earnings, which are subject to payroll taxes and also income taxes, including the income withheld as payroll taxes.) Since retained earnings of corporations are only taxed once, there is a tax-distorting incentive to reinvest earnings in the corporations instead of distributing them to shareholders. While this double taxation contributes to the progressivity of the income tax, since most shares are held by higher-income individuals, it distributes the tax burden somewhat randomly.

The more serious issue is sales taxes on business inputs, which average about 43 percent of all state sales tax collections. The share of inputs subject to tax varies from state to state and from one type of business to another. The result is a very uneven distribution of the sales tax burden among business firms. Since much of the sales tax on business inputs is shifted forward to the consumer in the form of a higher sales price, there is some distortion of consumer choice between products and services that have accumulated more sales tax burdens and therefore sell for higher relative prices.

This efficiency issue was an important consideration in the adoption of the value-added tax, first in Europe and then in some 125 countries around the world. With the value-added tax, firms pay a tax on their sales but get to subtract a credit for taxes paid on their inputs. The value-added tax is discussed in more detail in Chapter 14.

Summary

- The theoretical issues in tax design are efficiency and equity. A tax is said to be efficient if it does not alter the economic decisions of firms and households, or alters them only in intended ways, such as correcting for externalities.
- Taxes reduce consumer surplus, or the difference between what individuals pay for their purchases and their value or utility. Some of the consumer surplus is transferred to the government to finance public services, but some portion of it is just lost. That loss is the efficiency cost of collecting taxes. The size of the loss rises with the square of the tax rate.
- Elasticities of supply and demand determine how the burden of a tax on consumption or spending is apportioned between the buyer and seller. If demand is relatively inelastic, more of the burden falls on the buyer in the form of higher prices paid, while if supply is relatively inelastic, more of the burden falls on the seller in the form of lower net price received.
- The allocation of the burden is referred to as incidence. Shifting means the change in incidence from the party originally responsible for collecting and remitting the tax to the other party.
- Tax shifting and incidence and measurement of excess burden can be represented with shadow demand curves. The shadow demand curve for a specific tax (one based on volume, weight, or quantity) is parallel to the regular demand curve, while the shadow demand curve for an ad valorem tax (percentage of price) will be flatter than the regular demand curve because the difference widens as the price gets higher.
- Excess burden increases in proportion to the square of the tax rate and is inversely related to the elasticities of demand and supply. The net effect of a tax increase on

revenue is the outcome of the higher rate itself (positive) and the resulting erosion of the tax base (negative). If the rate is high enough, further increases could reduce rather than increase revenue.

- Income and payroll taxes distort the income–leisure tradeoff. In some cases work effort may increase to maintain income, in other cases work effort may decrease as the opportunity cost of leisure declines.
- Tax subsidies and tax expenditures are intended to alter people's decisions in order to correct externalities, encourage desirable activities, and in some cases, to redistribute income. Short-term effects of tax changes are often different (more revenue, less base erosion) than long-run effects because long-run elasticities of demand are greater.
- Tax equity is based on two principles, ability to pay and the benefit principle. Ability to pay favors a proportional tax over either regressive or progressive taxes, which take (respectively) smaller and smaller or larger and larger shares of one's income as income rises. However, a system with multiple revenue sources can and probably will include a mixture of regressive, proportional, and progressive taxes.
- The arguments for progressive taxation are: (1) diminishing marginal utility of income and the principle of equal sacrifice; and/or (2) as a balancing component of a revenue system that also includes regressive elements.
- The benefit principle assigns tax/fee burdens in proportion to the intensity of use of the public service that is being financed from that revenue source.
- Taxes on business firms can lead to some distortions in consumer and investor decisions. Taxing business net earnings discourages investors from investing in corporate shares compared to other types of investments. Sales taxes on business inputs are distributed unevenly across the range of consumer products and services and may distort consumer choices.

Key terms

Ability to pay
Ad valorem tax
Benefit principle
Consumer surplus
Excess burden/deadweight loss
Incidence
Laffer curve
Poll tax
Progressive tax
Proportional tax
Regressive tax
Shadow demand (supply) curve
Shifting
Specific tax

Questions

1 Tax incidence can be measured with shadow supply curves instead of shadow demand curves. When a tax is imposed, it can be visualized with a shadow supply curve S_T, which lies above and to the left of the original supply curve. Using that information,

analyze both a specific tax on gasoline and an ad valorem tax on gasoline and determine the new price and quantity and the division of the tax burden between buyer and seller. Do you think your conclusions would be any different if you used a shadow demand curve instead of a shadow supply curve? Why or why not?

2   Suppose that you work for the legislature's Ways and Means Committee. They are searching for a way to pay for beachfront improvements along the coast, which is visited by both residents and nonresidents in large numbers. Taking into account equity as well as efficiency considerations, come up with a mixture of at least three revenue sources to finance these improvements. Justify your choices.

3   Supply and demand analysis can also be used to think about other kinds of taxes, such as the payroll tax. The payroll tax in the United States is legally shared equally between the employer and the employee, each paying 7.6 percent of wages. Using graphs, analyze the incidence and excess burden of this tax if:

(a) labor supply is perfectly elastic;
(b) both labor supply and demand are highly elastic;
(c) labor supply is relatively inelastic, labor demand is relatively elastic;
(d) labor supply is relatively elastic, labor demand is relatively inelastic.

4   Which of the following taxes do you think would cause the larger deadweight loss? Why?

(a) a poll tax or a sales tax;
(b) a sales tax on both services and goods or a sales tax only on goods;
(c) an income tax only on interest and dividends or an income tax on income from all sources;
(d) a tax on soft drinks or a tax on all beverages.

5   **By the numbers**. Using the following rate schedule for a progressive income tax, determine the percentage of gross income paid in tax for a household with incomes of $25,000, $50,000, $75,000, $100,000, $200,000, and $500,000. Plot a graph of income on the horizontal axis and percentage paid in tax on the vertical axis.

| Income ($) | | Tax rate |
From	to	(%)
0	20,000	0
20,001	40,000	5
40,001	60,000	10
60,001	80,000	15
80,001	100,000	20
100,001	150,000	25
150,001	200,000	30
Over 200,000		35

6   **Policy application**. A legislator asks you to figure out how to eliminate the property tax and replace the lost revenue with a higher sales tax. Both the sales tax and the property tax each currently provide about 25 percent of total state and local revenue. She wants to know how high the rate would be. Marshal your arguments to persuade her that this is not such a good idea, using the concept of elasticity. Figure 11.10 and Equation 11.4 should be used in developing your answer.

7   **Behavioral economics**. The effects of taxes on earnings on the choice between work and leisure assume that earnings are the sole motivation for working, so that reduced net earnings will reduce work effort. How might the motivation for working be expanded to include other reasons? What are some of those other reasons?

8   **Thinking globally**. One of the choices that may be distorted by taxes is the choice of a business location. What kinds of taxes would be most important to you if you were considering a location for a corporate headquarters? How might your answer be different for locating a factory that was very labor-intensive?

12 Principles of taxation II
Applied issues

Introduction

Along with the theoretical considerations in tax system design from Chapter 11, what other factors do policy-makers need to consider? This chapter addresses some of the more pragmatic considerations that enter into the design of a revenue system as well as some of the implementation issues in making changes in that system.

The criteria developed here and in the previous chapter should be applied in subsequent chapters to the four broad groups of revenue sources: income taxes, consumption/sales taxes, wealth/property taxes, and fees and charges. Within each group there are broad-based taxes, like the individual income tax and the retail sales tax, as well as narrow taxes with limited bases, like some state taxes on interest and dividend income or excise taxes on tobacco and alcohol.

Additional criteria for designing tax systems

Taxes and nontax revenue sources have a number of different attributes. Chapter 11 made it clear that different revenue sources have different impacts on taxpayers' economic decisions (efficiency effects) and on the distribution of income and wealth (equity effects). Some taxes generate more revenue than others. Some are sensitive to economic growth and/or inflation, while others are not. Some revenue sources are stable, others volatile. Some are readily apparent to taxpayers while others are hidden. Some taxes are complicated or expensive to collect or to pay, while others are not.

Finally, taxes are used as a competitive tool by nations, states, and local governments, with different taxes having different competitive effects. Different taxes or revenue sources will score higher on some of these criteria and lower on others. A good revenue system will use a mix of sources with different desired characteristics.

Chapter 11 was largely devoted to an analysis of taxation from both an efficiency and an equity perspective. Taxes that minimize unintended distortions of economic decisions in the private sector while steering taxpayers toward desired choices involving externalities are the foundation of a good revenue system. Designing taxes that achieve both equity (ability to pay and benefit principle) and revenue objectives is also important to creating a good revenue system.

Recognizing that all revenue sources have weaknesses in terms of both equity and efficiency, the logical conclusion is that a good revenue system relies on a diversity of sources. As additional criteria are developed, however, bear in mind that the criteria of efficiency and equity remain at the top of the list in selecting and designing both taxes and non-tax revenue sources.

Adequacy

A revenue system has to generate adequate funds to pay for the desired level of public services. **Adequacy** is a tricky concept, because there is a weak connection between revenue and services. Unlike private markets, public revenues and expenditures do not have a one-to-one correspondence in the form of payment for goods sold or services rendered. Some kinds of revenue systems could generate too much revenue relative to the optimal level and mix of public services to be funded. Legislators awash in funds are rarely without pet projects to fund, and will respond to a revenue windfall with additional spending, although sometimes they do respond to rapid revenue growth with tax cuts. It is the fear that the revenue system will prove "too adequate" that drove many of the tax and expenditure limitations enacted in the 1970s and 1980s, and that was the foundation for federal income tax cuts in the past decade. At other times, revenue can fall short of the amount needed to fund basic services at the desired level, as happened in many countries during the financial crisis that began in 2008.

In general, revenue needs to grow at least as fast as the increase in population and in the costs of inputs into providing public goods as well as public services (administration, regulation, etc.).[1] It may also need to keep pace with real income growth, because demand for public services as a complement to private consumption can be expected to increase as the standard of living rises.

Unlike other attributes, adequacy is more a property of a revenue system as a whole than of a particular tax or revenue source. But some taxes (or revenue sources) contribute more to adequacy than others. At least one tax with a broad base—income, consumption, or wealth— is an essential part of the revenue system for each level of government in order to ensure adequacy. In most cases, states and their local governments use all three.

Those states that attempt to rely on only two of those three broad-based taxes (or in the case of New Hampshire, only one) find it difficult to fund public services and are forced to use fairly high rates for the broad-based taxes they do collect. (Alaska is an exception because of unusual other revenue sources.) Five states have no retail sales tax—Delaware, New Hampshire, Montana, Oregon and Alaska. Nine states, including New Hampshire, do not have a full-scale personal income tax. In the absence of a broad-based income tax, Tennessee has leaned heavily on the sales tax with very high rates. Florida attempted to compensate for its lack of an income tax in the 1990s with an unsuccessful attempt to broaden the base of the retail sales tax to include many services. Texas, also with no state income tax, has found it very difficult to equalize per pupil education funds among school districts because schools in that state rely primarily on local property tax funding, and the property tax base is distributed very unevenly among districts.

Specialty taxes—accommodations, admissions, severance, alcohol, gasoline—make a contribution to adequacy. But with a few exceptions (accommodations taxes for major tourism destination cities, royalties and severance taxes in mineral-rich states) these more narrowly based taxes score low on the adequacy criterion.

Ensuring and defending adequacy means that legislators must be sensitive to the dangers of base erosion. Adding exemptions to the sales tax, increasing deductions on the income tax, using corporate income tax breaks to lure industry all exact a cost in terms of not just current revenue adequacy but also future revenue flows.

Collection and compliance costs

In addition to the excess burden discussed in Chapter 11, there is an even more direct cost of transferring revenue from taxpayers to governments that does not get translated into increased government services. In order to collect taxes, bureaucracies must be created to interpret the tax laws and ensure that taxes are collected. The cost of printing forms, processing and auditing returns, and assessing tax liabilities is the **collection cost**.

Taxpayers also incur costs in addition to the excess burden. They have to keep records, fill out forms, go through audits, and pay tax accountants to make sure that they are in compliance. These costs that fall on the taxpayers are called **compliance costs**. Some taxes are costly to administer but not to comply with, like the property tax, while others are burdensome on both the tax collector and the taxpayer, like the individual income tax. In some cases, compliance costs fall on third parties—employers who must keep the records and file the returns for Social Security taxes or retailers who must collect and remit the retail sales tax.

The remaining tariffs imposed by the US government probably win the "prize" in terms of collection costs, because they cost more to administer than they generate in revenue. However, these residual tariffs are not designed to raise revenue, but to protect certain industries from foreign competition. In the early days of the nation, the tariff was a primary source of federal government revenue. Today's collection costs are only high relative to the small amount of revenue generated. If politicians chose to impose more and higher tariffs, as the United States did prior to 1934, then the collection costs would be a relatively small percentage of the amount of revenue generated.

While compliance costs for property taxes are low, these taxes are quite expensive to administer because of the need to assess the market value of a variety of assets, and to handle disputes and appeals over the values assigned. Being the property tax assessor is one of the most frustrating tasks in local government!

There are a few rules of thumb that provide some guidance in reducing these costs. As a general rule, it is cheaper in terms of collection costs to administer a tax centrally than locally, because each local government will need its own staff. There are substantial economies of scale in tax administration. That's the reason why counties often collect property taxes on behalf of municipalities and states collect and distribute local sales taxes on behalf of their cities and counties. It is also less expensive to administer a broad-based income tax than one with many exemptions, exclusions, adjustments and deductions. For retail sales taxes, it is less costly to administer and to comply with a tax that is broad-based in terms of tangible goods, because neither the tax collector nor the retailer has to worry much about separating taxable from nontaxable sales. On the other hand, expanding the retail sales tax to include most services (as is the case in five US states and most countries with a value-added tax) will increase the costs of both collection and compliance, because of the large number of small service-producing firms.

Stability

Some of the revenue sources in the overall system need to offer a cushion of **stability**, particularly for state and local governments that must balance their budgets annually through recessions as well as periods of prosperity. Stability means that the revenue flow is not unduly sensitive to fluctuations in economic activity.

Stability is not as important a criterion for the central government, which can run deficits during recessions and surpluses during prosperous years—although many governments, including the United States, run bigger and more frequent deficits than surpluses. But most state governments are required to balance their budgets by statute or constitutional law, and local governments have little leeway in running deficits. For local governments, an important positive attribute of the property tax is its stability.

For the two major state taxes, the appropriate measure of stability is the short-run income elasticity of tax revenue relative to personal income. That elasticity depends on whether the income tax base (taxable income) or the sales tax base (taxable retail sales) fluctuates more than, less than, or about the same as fluctuations in state personal income. For the state income tax, the short-run elasticity for the United States is estimated at 2.58, with variations depending on the state's tax structure and the composition of personal income. That elasticity means that income tax revenues fluctuate more than twice as much as personal income over the course of the business cycle. Revenue from an income tax that is indexed, like the US federal income tax and many state income taxes, will fluctuate less in proportion to changes in personal income than one that is not (Felix 2008).

If the income tax rate structure has any progressivity to it, the revenue from the income tax will fluctuate more than the tax base even with indexing for two reasons. First, as real incomes rise, people will find themselves in higher tax brackets during expansions; when real incomes decline, they will be in lower tax brackets during recessions. Second, the exempt amount (personal exemptions and standard deductions), even after indexing, becomes a smaller proportion of total personal or adjusted gross income during expansions and a larger proportion during recessions.

For the retail sales tax, the US average estimated short-run elasticity is 1.24, which makes sales taxes more stable than income taxes in the short run but still relatively volatile. Elasticities are higher in states that do not tax food, because food purchases are more stable than other spending. Some purchases of consumer durables (appliances, cars, furniture) and nondurables (housewares, clothing) are postponable during times of unemployment or economic uncertainty. These items are some of the major sources of sales tax revenue.

The corporate income tax, which is a substantial revenue source in some states, is extremely sensitive to fluctuations in income because profit or net corporate income is very sensitive to recessions and expansions. The short-run elasticity of corporate taxable income is estimated at 2.61, meaning that a 1 percent change in personal income results in more than a 2 percent change in corporate net income.

Stability has a price. A tax or revenue source that is stable over the business cycle tends to be unresponsive to growth in population, income, and/or the price level (inflation). For this reason, a stable tax is an important component of the revenue mix, but it needs to be balanced with other taxes that are more responsive. Some taxes, like the retail sales tax, lie toward the middle of the spectrum of these two opposing attributes. The retail sales tax is more stable than the individual income tax at both the state and national level but is moderately sensitive to income growth and somewhat more sensitive to population growth and inflation.

The mirror image of stability is sensitivity to growth and inflation, which allow government revenues and expenditures to keep pace with changing costs and needs. Growth has three different components. One is population growth. The second is inflation. The third is real income growth. To understand the interaction between these three, imagine a community of 1,000 people with a total personal income of $12 million, which comes to $12,000 per capita. Suppose that in this year personal income has risen to $15 million, a 25 percent increase. Population has increased to 1,100, and the price level has risen by 8 percent. What are the components of that growth?

There is a temptation to think that the answer to this question is one of simple addition. If population has risen by 10 percent, and prices by 8 percent, the other 7 percent of personal income growth is real growth in per capita income. That answer is sometimes approximately correct if all the numbers are small, but not in this case. The first step is to deflate the personal income growth, which means dividing $15 million by 1.08 to convert it to real income of $13,888,888 in base year prices. The second step is to convert that figure to per capita income by dividing by the new population of 1,100, which gives a per capita income of $12,626. Finally, divide the new per capita income by the old one, which gives a result of 1.052. Real per capita income growth was 5.2 percent, not 7 percent.

It is important to separate growth into these three components before evaluating the sensitivity of revenue sources to growth, for two reasons. First, some revenue sources are sensitive (or not) only to inflation, or only to population, or (more rarely), only to real income growth. Second, demands for public expenditures react differently to each of these three components of nominal income growth.

As the population grows, revenue needs to grow in order to finance the additional services required by a growing population, although there is not necessarily a one-to-one correspondence. Population growth may make it possible to achieve scale economies in the provision of some services, so that revenue does not need to grow quite as fast as population. The additional revenue required to serve a growing population also depends on where the new residents are located (infill versus new development, rural versus urban, isolated versus clustered in subdivisions), what the age distribution of the new residents is, and whether there is a concentration of special needs populations, such as immigrants in states like California, Texas, and Florida. Population growth in young families will create demand for more spending on the largest component of local government expense, public education. Older citizens typically have lower service demands.

It is more difficult to find clear links between growth of population and growth on the revenue side of the ledger. Retail sales tend to be tied to population growth, particularly at younger ages, i.e., a high birth rate rather than an influx of retirees. The residential and commercial components of the property tax base reflect population growth, but in some cases the quality (and therefore taxable value) of the property will grow faster than population if new developments are upscale. In other cases those values will grow more slowly, e.g., mushrooming mobile home parks and low-income housing developments. In this case, the income of the new residents will be the deciding factor as to whether property tax revenue grows faster than, more slowly than, or at about the same pace as population. The same is true, obviously, of income tax revenue.

Inflation also impacts both the expenditure and revenue sides of government budgets. Inflation drives up the cost of providing public services. The revenue side is more complicated. Prolonged periods of inflation result in increased demand for real property, especially houses and undeveloped land, as an inflation hedge. Property values tend to rise more rapidly than the overall inflation rate, increasing property tax revenues faster than the rate of inflation, as they did most notably in California in the 1970s, resulting in the property tax revolt. Until the federal income tax code and most state income taxes were indexed for inflation (mostly in the mid-1980s), revenue from income taxes also tended to grow very rapidly during periods of inflation. With indexing, inflation has little or no effect on individual income tax revenue, although growth in real income does increase revenue. Retail sales tax revenue tracks the inflation rate fairly closely if the inflation is spread broadly over the full range of goods and services. When inflation is largely concentrated in such items as health care and housing, both of which are not subject to retail sales taxes, then sales tax revenue is more likely to lag behind the rate of inflation.

Real income (income adjusted for inflation) grows with population but also independently. Over the past four decades the average rate of real growth of personal income has been about 2.5 percent a year, and the average rate of growth of real per capita income has been about 1.4 percent a year. If real per capita income grows, there will be increases in revenue from all major and most minor sources as spending, income, and property values all increase. There will also be some increase in demand for government services.

The long-run elasticities of the major state taxes are lower than the short-run elasticities. Individual income taxes have a long run elasticity of 2.03, which is still quite high. Retail sales tax elasticity is .92 for the average US state, and is even less elastic corporate taxable income (.53) (Felix 2008). States that rely primarily on sales taxes and do not have an income tax are at a disadvantage in trying to generate the revenue to keep pace with long-term growth of population, inflation, and demand for public services associated with real income growth.

Visibility

One of the more controversial attributes of a tax or tax system is **visibility**, or how obvious the amount of tax is to taxpayers and others. Value-added taxes are typically low visibility because they are reflected in the quoted prices of goods, while retail sales taxes are much more visible because they are added to the quoted price at the time of purchase. However, people are not very aware of how much they pay annually in retail sales taxes because they are collected frequently and in small amounts. The painful visibility of income taxes, likewise, is reduced by weekly or monthly withholding. Property taxes, in contrast, are extremely visible because they are usually collected in a lump sum once a year.

In a progressive income tax, often the **marginal tax rate** is more visible to the taxpayer than the **average tax rate**. In US parlance, the marginal rate is one's tax bracket—the rate paid on the last dollar of taxable income. So, for example, a married taxpayer in 2009 with an income of $100,000 would be in the 25 percent tax bracket. The last dollar and the next dollar of her income are taxed at 25 percent. But that doesn't mean that the taxpayer is paying 25 percent of her income in taxes. Her actual tax bill is only $10,563, or 10.6 percent of income. Some income is not taxed at all, and other parts of income are taxed at 10 percent and 15 percent.

Confusing the marginal rate with the average rate may lead to a false impression of overtaxation. On the other hand, the marginal rate is important to decision-making about earning and investing. As we noted in Chapter 11, a higher marginal rate may encourage workers to substitute leisure for income, and particularly discourage a second worker in a household from entering the labor force. Different tax treatment of different kinds of investment income may lead those subject to high marginal rates to restructure their investment portfolios away from interest-earning investments toward riskier investment that yield dividends and/or capital gains.

Is visibility desirable? It depends on one's perspective. Those who think that government is too large prefer that taxes be highly visible so that the pain of paying taxes will be weighed carefully against the benefits from government services, especially at the margin. Others argue that, because many government services are low visibility, taxes should be equally low in visibility in order to avoid limiting the size and scope of government activity to a level that is less than optimal.

In practice, there is a mix of taxes and revenue sources in the system that range from highly visible (property taxes) to moderately visible (sales taxes, payroll taxes) to low visibility (excise taxes included in the price). Likewise, government services range from high visibility (road repairs, trash pickup, schools) to moderately visible (national defense, parks, prisons) to low visibility (building inspection, financial administration).

Taxes can be made more visible in a variety of ways. Referenda, usually on bond issues for schools and other capital expenses, give taxpayers a chance to directly weigh an increase in taxes against an increase in services. Stating the retail sales tax separately from the price, a practice in most states with retail sales taxes, makes it more visible. Posting the excise tax on the pump at gas stations is another way to try to make consumers more aware of how much of what they pay is for the product itself and how much is tax.

Tax targeting and tax expenditures

There are taxes in the system, and features within those taxes, that score poorly on several, most, or sometimes all of these criteria. For example, consider the exemption of food from the state retail sales tax, which is the case in about two-thirds of the states with retail sales taxes. Eliminating food from the base makes the retail sales tax less productive of revenue (reducing adequacy) and less stable over the course of the business cycle. A retail sales tax without food in the base is also more costly to comply with and to collect, because the retailer (and the tax collector) must carefully distinguish between taxable and exempt items. While the food exemption is touted as a way to help the poor, and it does appear to make the sales tax less regressive, it is a relatively inefficient equity tool, because the tax savings go to all income levels, not just the poor.

So why is there a food exemption? In part this exemption is used because of the tax on food (or its exemption) is highly visible, which makes its small contribution to equity more visible and hence more politically popular. This exemption is also in part a response to the idea of a basic right to food regardless of ability to pay, an important cultural norm that may override the rather abstract principles of good tax design. Almost every tax has some exceptions of this sort that transcend economic considerations in the name of some other purpose, value, or interest group.

Tax targeting is a catchall term for provisions of tax law that single out particular income groups, age groups, products or services, or other subgroups for special treatment. Most tax targeting reduces the tax burden on the targeted group, product or service. Homestead exemptions reduce property taxes for homeowners (or sometimes the elderly) relative to other groups. Prescription drugs are generally exempt from retail sales taxes, singling out those who have higher than average medical expenses. Food purchased with SNAP (formerly food stamps) is exempt from state retail sales taxes even in those states that tax food. The advantage of targeting as opposed to a blanket reduction or exemption is that the revenue loss is smaller, which helps the adequacy goal. The drawback to targeting is that it is an open invitation to lobbyists for special interests to plead the case of their "deserving" clients.

Some provisions in the tax law are intentionally designed to encourage or discourage specific kinds of consumption or production activities. Taxes on alcohol and tobacco, also known as sumptuary taxes, are intended to discourage the consumption of harmful substances (and there is still a strong constituency to add marijuana to the list as a legal but taxed-and-discouraged substance). Taxes on emissions of various kinds that reduce the quality of air or water are intended to correct negative externalities. Income tax breaks for energy-efficiency retrofitting are increasingly popular at both the federal and state levels in the United States.

Tax expenditures focus on the loss of revenue from provisions inserted into the tax law to exempt certain taxpayers, organizations, or activities from taxation, or to reduce their tax burden relative to others. The loss of revenue depends on the tax rate, the amount of the activity prior to the exemption, and the responsiveness of the activity to the stimulus of the tax break.

Many tax expenditures favor charitable organizations. These nonprofit firms that meet certain tests (mainly not using their funds for lobbying purposes) are often exempt from paying state sales taxes and local property taxes, and contributions to such organizations are deductible for federal and many state income tax purposes. Their net income is considered "surplus" rather than a taxable "profit" and is not subject to income taxes at any level. The revenue lost from the federal income tax deduction for charitable contributions alone is estimated at $26 billion in 2000.

At the federal level, a list of tax expenditures associated with each budget has been published each year beginning with the Congressional Budget Act of 1974. These tax expenditures run to hundreds of billions of dollars, with the largest share coming from the federal income tax. Both of the top ranked categories in 2008 were employee fringe benefits, employer contributions to medical insurance and medical care ($131 billion) and exclusion of pension contributions and earnings in employer plans ($118 billion). The 12 largest tax expenditures in the income tax accounted for revenue loss of over $600 billion in the 2008 budget forecast. In addition to the two fringe benefit items, the top 12 included deductions for mortgage interest, state and local taxes, and charitable contributions, and favorable treatment of capital gains and depreciation.

Tax expenditures have both advantages and drawbacks in comparison to direct expenditures as a means of furthering a particular social goal. Tax expenditures are less visible and thus easier to enact, which is both an advantage and a drawback. They are less likely to come up for annual review. Because they create demand in the private sector for delivery of services, they develop strong lobbying constituencies, e.g., banks, home builders and realtors defending the mortgage interest deduction.[2] Tax expenditures can be put into effect more quickly than direct expenditures and do not create an administrative bureaucracy, although they do increase the cost of tax administration.

Finally, they create tax relief for activities that were already ongoing or would have been undertaken anyway, so that their marginal impact in offering incentives requires a fairly high expenditure over the total range of the target activity to achieve an often modest increase or decrease. For example, how much additional home ownership is there as a result of the mortgage interest deduction, and how much tax revenue did it cost to provide that relief both to those who required an incentive and those who did not? Rather than encourage home ownership, did the tax incentive merely make it possible for many home buyers to buy larger and more expensive homes than they would otherwise have chosen? Perhaps it would be more efficient to target particular populations through a direct subsidy, such as a voucher or a mortgage guarantee. Tax expenditures remain a very popular policy tool, but they are not always the best way to attain a particular goal at the lowest possible cost.

Taxing across borders: interstate and international tax issues

State and local governments have to consider equity and efficiency in a competitive context. Will this change in the tax law affect decisions about locating a business, shopping out of state, choosing where to retire? Those are efficiency aspects of interstate taxation. How should the burden of taxation be apportioned equitably among business firms and individuals, in-state and out-of-state buyers and sellers? How will those equity decisions affect the competitive status of this state?

State and local governments are not the only ones that are constrained by competition in designing revenue structures. Even national governments have to take into consideration the effects of their tax structures on decisions by firms and individuals about where they live and work, where they locate their businesses and invest their financial assets, and where they make their purchases and sales. Firms, resources, and individuals are increasingly mobile, particularly in an electronic age.

The taxation of corporate net income has been a hotly contested issue; firms tend to locate their headquarters where the terms of taxation are most favorable. Ships register in Liberia because of favorable tax considerations. Wealthy jet-setters choose their citizenship according to where their income tax burdens will be lowest. Some kinds of taxes on goods are rebated on export (value-added taxes in particular), which may give an advantage to exporters from nations that rely more heavily on value-added than on income taxation.

Different tax structures will be more attractive to some firms, some citizens, or some investors. Nations that are interested in attracting multinational firms and financial investors will structure their tax packages with the goal of offering an attractive fiscal surplus, sometimes at the expense of some fraction of their own citizens. The same kinds of positive and negative effects of fiscal competition that states experience also apply to nations, particularly small nations but increasingly even large countries like Canada and the United States.

Efficiency and cross-border competition

Competition for industrial and residential location can both enhance and reduce economic efficiency. Some of the benefits of competition apply to nations and states as well as to private firms. If states are forced to be more efficient in the provision of services in order to hold down taxes while satisfying residents' demands, then interstate competition is efficiency-enhancing. Interstate competition places some important constraints on the actions of legislators and city councils to reinforce the voters' efforts to make them responsive in terms of both taxes and services.

However, competition can also push governments from beyond optimal to below optimal levels of taxes and spending in attempting to make government lean, and fiscal surpluses attractive to newcomers. Given the rational ignorance of most voters, and the short-term time horizon of most elected officials, success in holding down taxes and attracting industry and jobs may be more visible and more influential in voting decisions than longer-term decisions about maintaining infrastructure and providing quality public services. This argument is particularly relevant in evaluating economic development incentives.[3]

Equity and cross-border competition

How does competition to lure high-income residents and attractive industries affect the equity of the revenue structure? Tax incentives, whether for retirees (usually income and property tax relief) or industry (most often corporate income and property tax breaks), shift the burden of taxation to other groups. Some of that increased burden may fall on existing industry, including commercial and service firms. Often the tax burden falls more heavily on the state's least mobile residents, who are likely to be lower- to middle-income groups.

Alternatively, the quality of public services may be allowed to decline as the increase in residents and firms to be served is not matched with an increase in resources to provide the additional services. In that case, the burden of providing such tax incentives falls on the existing population as a whole, both individual and industrial/commercial.

Comparing taxes

While it's true that the particular mix of taxes used by a state and its local governments will affect families in different ways, depending on age, family size, income, spending patterns, and other factors, the most honest and accurate way to compare taxes from one state to another is to look at the total tax burden. Property, sales, excise, income—add them up. It's important to include local taxes, because states with relatively low state taxes usually depend heavily on the property tax to fund education.

The two most widely used comparisons are taxes as a percentage of income and taxes per capita.[4] If you are trying to measure the "burden" of taxation—how much of their income individuals and households have to sacrifice to the state in order to pay for public services—then this is the correct measure to choose. But often people make their comparisons based on taxes per capita. How much tax was collected for each person living in the state?

Per capita taxes do *not* measure tax burdens. Instead, per capita taxes offer a measure of tax *resources*—how much state and local governments have to work with in trying to fund public services. The cost of public services is largely driven by the number of people to be served. Other factors such as the age distribution (lots of elderly citizens or school children), poverty, population density and climate may figure into the cost of public services, but population is the primary driver of the cost of those services we expect in every state—highways, public safety, public education, parks and recreation, environmental protection, libraries, public health. So it makes sense to compare resources by adjusting for differences in population from state to state. Low per capita taxes, unless they are supplemented by nontax revenue sources such as fees, charges, and revenue from natural resources, are likely to mean low levels of services.

A third, more complex measure is the Representative Revenue System, which is described in an appendix to this chapter. This measure compares how much revenue states could raise if they used the typical array of taxes at national average rates, and then compares what they could raise to what they actually raised. Unfortunately, this measure is much more difficult to compute, so it is usually only available with a time lag. For more timely measures, per capita and percentage of income remain the most widely used methods of making comparisons.

Tax exporting

State and local governments (and sometimes national governments as well) are always alert to opportunities to shift the burden of paying for government to nonresidents, also known as **tax exporting**. The theoretical justification for such shifting is that nonresidents benefit from services that the state provides but make little if any contribution toward the cost. States that attract large numbers of tourists, for example, incur high costs for extra infrastructure, police and fire protection, solid waste disposal and public recreational facilities for a transient and seasonal population. These states can use accommodations taxes, admissions taxes, and special fees of various kinds to recoup some of that cost.

The pragmatic justification for tax exporting is that residents are more likely to vote than nonresidents. If some of the pain of paying for public services can be shifted from likely voters to those who have no voice or vote, politicians will have a more contented citizenry and will be more likely to be re-elected. Public choice theory plays an important role in explaining the preference for tax exporting!

The opportunities for tax exporting are usually fairly limited. For most goods and services, a single state is in a highly competitive situation and is a price taker. The exceptions occur where a state (or a city or county) has some limited degree of monopoly power. There are two sources of monopoly power. One is access to unique or exceptionally attractive tourist/ business destinations—large cities, beaches, national parks, ski areas. The other is natural resources such as oil, natural gas, coal, or various minerals. Taxes aimed at tourists and business travelers are very popular in states such as Florida and Hawaii. Natural resource extraction is usually subject to a severance tax which is successfully shifted forward to the buyer because there are few good alternatives. Wyoming, Texas and Louisiana are among the states that make good use of severance taxes as a revenue source.

The origin and destination principles

Many individuals and firms engage in economic activities that cross state or national lines. Firms have multiple plants and buy inputs and sell their products throughout the country and beyond. Individuals may live in one state and work in another, and almost always will make some of their purchases out-of-state, either directly when they travel or indirectly through catalogs or the internet. Since states have different tax bases and rates, these transactions across state lines create problems for the taxpayer and the tax collector.

For most state income taxes, the preferred solution is to apportion income according to the state(s) in which it was earned. The challenging questions occur most often in the case of retail sales taxes. Most states consider the retail sales tax to be an obligation of the buyer, but it is collected as a matter of convenience by the seller, who may be located in another state.

The same issue arose in the formation of the European Union as all six of the original member countries agreed to reform their various kinds of sales taxes into a value-added tax, eventually at a uniform rate. If both buyer and seller are in the same state or country, there is no problem. But what if the seller is in one place and the buyer is in another? Which state or nation gets the revenue, and whose rate and structure applies—that of the seller (the **origin principle**) or that of the buyer (the **destination principle**)?

There are two economic questions involved in a choice between the origin and destination principle. The first economic question is where the actual economic incidence of the tax falls, i.e., whether the primary effect is to raise the price paid by the buyer or to reduce the price paid by the seller. If the incidence is primarily on the buyer, then it seems appropriate that the revenues accrue to the state or nation where the buyer resides. The buyer will then benefit from the services that those taxes finance. If the seller bears more of the burden, perhaps the state or nation of the seller is entitled to the revenue. In the case of a broad-based retail sales tax or value-added tax, demand is quite inelastic (because there is limited opportunity for substitution), so most of the incidence falls on the buyer, which tilts the balance toward the destination principle.

The second question is more subtle. If the nation or state of origin is also the place of production, then one might consider state and local services—roads, police and fire protection, etc.—as inputs to the production process. In that case, one could argue that the state in which the product is produced is entitled to at least some share of the revenue. In general, however, the incidence consideration has dominated the discussion of where to impose and collect the tax. Both the value-added tax in the European Union and retail sales taxes in the United States are imposed and collected on a destination basis.

The choice of an origin or destination principle is not merely a theoretical issue. A number of US Supreme Court cases have wrestled with this question from a legal as well as an economic standpoint. States have created a complement to the retail sales tax called a use tax, in order to ensure that their states' residents have a legal obligation to pay tax on out-of-state purchases that they bring into the state by car, truck, mail, or other delivery systems that bypass the local tax-collecting retail merchant.

Case study: taxation of interstate mail order sales

With the rapid growth of internet sales, the revenue loss from being unable to require vendors to collect retail sales taxes of destination states has become an important national issue in the United States. The revenue losses that result from collecting sales taxes on the destination rather than the origin principle are substantial and growing.

No single issue captures as many of the applied issues in tax design in the modern post-industrial economy better than the tax treatment of interstate mail order sales. The retail sales tax is a destination principle tax. The use tax, a companion to the sales tax for out-of-state purchases, is owed by the buyer to the buyer's state. It is normally, but not always, collected from the seller. However, a series of Supreme Court cases, most notably *National Bellas Hess vs. State of Illinois (1967)* ruled that a state cannot compel an out-of-state firm to collect and remit sales taxes on purchases by its residents unless the firm has some tangible link to that state.

Known in legal terms as nexus, that connection may be a warehouse, a resident sales office, a retail outlet, a catalog store, or other kinds of physical presence. The nexus requirement was originally based on the due process and interstate commerce clauses of the Constitution. A 1994 decision in the case of *Quill*, however, determined that only the interstate commerce issue was valid, opening the door for remedial legislation by Congress, which has authority over interstate commerce. Thus far, Congress has not acted, primarily because the pressure from organized mail order retailers has been more effective and better funded than the less organized efforts of state revenue officers and competing Main Street merchants—an object lesson in the public choice principles set forth earlier.

National firms with extensive catalog sales like Sears and J.C. Penney have nexus in most states. Some major catalog firms have gone to great lengths to avoid creating nexus in any state except the one from which they operate, even avoiding 800 phone numbers as a possible indicator of intent to sell in the destination state that could be construed as nexus. States have therefore had either to attempt to establish nexus, develop voluntary agreements, try to collect from the buyer, or to forgo substantial amounts of revenue. The General Accountability Office estimated that state sales tax revenue losses from all remote sales (catalog, internet, and other) in 2003 lay in the range of $2.5 to $20.4 billion, or 2–5 percent of state sales tax revenue (General Accountability Office 2000).

From an efficiency standpoint, this tax advantage for the mail order firm distorts consumer decisions in favor of catalog shopping rather than in-state malls or Main Street merchants. From an equity standpoint, the nexus rule discriminates arbitrarily between classes of consumers by how they choose to shop. Additionally, as shoppers shift to tax-free catalog shopping in the long run, there will be more base erosion and revenue loss.

Based on the criteria developed in these two chapters, it would be desirable for states to be allowed to collect retail sales taxes on all mail-order and internet purchases. From a practical standpoint, higher collection and compliance costs might justify exempting smaller mail order/internet firms from collecting the tax. Proposed legislation, stalled for more than 15 years in Congress, offered a sales threshold below which firms would not be required to collect the tax.

In the past few years, the arguments over catalog sales have paled in comparison to the phenomenal growth of internet retailing. Congress created a national commission to study the taxation of internet sales, which at present is under a moratorium that prevents states from collecting from internet firms without nexus. There is political pressure from the electronic commerce lobby to extend the moratorium indefinitely.

Representatives of state and local governments, recognizing the threat not only to sales tax revenue but to their state retail establishments, have attempted to offer some compromises to simplify compliance costs. The most likely proposal will result in a uniform state sales tax base and a single rate for each state, combining the multiple local rates in some way, in order to greatly reduce compliance costs for vendors.

Taxation of mail order and internet sales is a useful case study in policy analysis. It blends legal (nexus, due process, interstate commerce), political (the power of organized lobbyists, federal–state relations), and economic (efficiency, equity, and collection and compliance costs) dimensions. From the standpoint of state revenue officers, however, it represents more than 30 years of frustrated efforts to protect their retail sales tax bases and provide a level playing field between their own in-state retailers and their out-of-state competitors. With internet shopping growing rapidly, the biggest challenges may still be ahead.

Behavioral economics: implementing and resisting change

In any area of public policy there is always a debate over the appropriate pace and amount of change. There are always plenty of sound bites to avoid change ("If it ain't broke, don't fix it," "The best is the enemy of the good," "Better the devil that you know than the one you haven't met," etc.). But there are also some important economic principles related to the stability of the tax code and the pace at which changes are implemented.

Stability of the tax law as well as the revenue it generates can be considered an important economic and political value. Gradualism can be an issue on the expenditure side as well. Changes in Social Security are often phased in so that people currently retired or about to retire do not feel the full impact, while younger people have more time to adjust their financial planning. The notion of Pareto optimality, or at least the compensation principle, may well be better served by gradual than immediate implementation.

The tax code represents a part of the operating rules or social norms and expectations of a city, county, state, or nation, along with other structures and institutions like contract law and penalties for misdemeanors and the right to attend public schools. People make decisions and commitments based on the current tax code and the expectation that those tax rules will continue into the future. They buy houses with 30-year mortgages, expecting to be able to deduct the mortgage interest and property taxes on their federal and state income tax returns, and they calculate how much house they can afford based on that expectation. They choose to invest in municipal bonds (which pay lower interest, but the interest is tax exempt), or in stocks that offer more hope of capital gains than dividends, based on current tax treatment of municipal bond interest, dividends, and capital gains.

Firms build plants in particular locations based on certain assumptions about local property and state corporate income taxes. Some of those tax rules are contractual arrangements between the government and the firm, others are subject to change without notice. Both households and firms prefer certainty in making long-term plans.

When the rules change, there are windfall gains and losses. Eliminating the deduction for local property taxes would result in a decline in the price of houses. The decline would vary from one section of the country to another and be greater for more expensive houses (both because their property taxes are higher and because, in a higher tax bracket, the value of the lost exemption was greater). A rate increase. The loss of a deduction, a broadening of the tax base all change the rules to which taxpayers have become accustomed and that were factored into their planning.

For this reason, the federal income tax code only undergoes major revisions about every ten years, although there are smaller changes almost every year. Even if the tax code is imperfect, or inequitable, it is not clear that the gains from frequent alteration outweigh the cost of adjustment falling on taxpayers, who made decisions on the basis of existing tax rules.

There are other costs to frequent changes as well. Frequent changes in the tax law make it more difficult and expensive to administer the tax code and for taxpayers to understand the rules. More than half of US taxpayers now pay someone else to compute their individual income tax returns for them, a sign of both increased complexity and frequent change.

The impact of a change in the tax rules can be mitigated by phasing it in, or delaying its implementation. There are advantages and disadvantages to gradualism in changing tax policy or indeed in changing any policy, as noted above, but there are also good arguments for making changes quickly and decisively.

First, if the change in the tax rules was undertaken in order to raise more revenue, the revenue will come in more slowly. The total amount of revenue increase will be smaller by missing the immediate/short-run effect when elasticities are very low.

Second, if the tax change was proposed in order to mitigate an inequity or provide desired incentives or disincentives, the gradual or delayed implementation will mean that citizens have to live with a less optimal situation in terms of either efficiency or equity for a longer period of time.

Finally, tax changes should be no different from changes that take place suddenly in the market. The signals of impending change are always there well in advance, whether the change is in market interest rates or federal income tax indexing. Quick changes induce faster responses, and dynamic change is both a benefit and a cost of a market system.

What are the advantages of gradual or phased implementation of tax changes? The main advantage is an offshoot of the value of stability itself, discussed above. If taxpayers cannot have stability in the tax rules that affect their economic and financial decisions, the next best thing is to have enough time to prepare for and adapt to changes in those rules. In that way they can better shield themselves from potential negative impact or position themselves better to experience a positive impact from a change in the tax treatment of out-of-state purchases, sales tax exemptions, income tax treatment of capital gains, or changes in allowable income tax deductions. By giving taxpayers advance notice, they can act to mitigate some of the windfall redistribution of income, wealth, and tax burdens resulting from a change in the tax rules.

Summary

- In addition to equity and efficiency, other criteria for tax design include adequacy, stability, visibility, and collection and compliance costs.
- Adequacy means generating enough revenue in order to fund the desired level of public services. At least some major components of the revenue system should also offer stability, so that revenue will not be unduly sensitive to fluctuations in economic activity. Some major components also need to be responsive to economic growth, which reflects increases in population, the price level (inflation), and real income growth.
- Collection costs are administrative expenses that governments incur in collecting taxes. Compliance costs fall on the taxpayer—record keeping, filling out forms, and related costs. Taxes can be high or low in either or both types of costs.
- A tax is visible if taxpayers are highly aware of its existence and size. Increased visibility can lead to increased tax resistance. Visibility is a positive attribute if it

contributes to restraining excess growth of government, a negative attribute if it restrains government spending to below the optimal level.

- Stability is measured by short-term income elasticities of the tax bases. Responsiveness to growth is measured by long-term income elasticities.
- Tax targeting favors particular groups, institutions, or goods and services. Some tax targeting is intended to change the distribution of after-tax income, while others favor particular politically powerful groups.
- Some taxes are part of the system not because of their high score on the various criteria but because they serve to promote or discourage certain kinds of economic activity that is deemed desirable. One technique for targeting desired activities is tax expenditures, which exempt or exclude certain kinds of activities, income, or wealth from taxation.
- Both national and state tax systems operate in a competitive environment. Governments compete for export markets, high-income residents, industry and jobs, and investment dollars. Competition may force taxes and/or services below the socially optimal level, or it may provide a useful constraint on the growth of government. It may also redistribute the tax burden toward existing firms and residents or to nonresidents. or toward those that are least mobile. States also attempt to shift part of their tax burden to non-residents.
- The origin and destination principles determine which government is entitled to the tax revenue. The destination principle claims the tax revenue for the state or nation of the consumer, the origin principle for the state or nation of the producer.
- There are costs associated with frequent or rapid changes in tax rules. People make decisions based on existing tax rules and experience windfall gains and losses resulting from sudden or unexpected changes in tax laws. Making changes less frequent, or phasing in changes gradually in some cases, can reduce these windfall losses and gains and make it easier for individuals to plan.

Key terms

Adequacy
Average tax rate
Collection cost(s)
Compliance cost(s)
Destination principle
Marginal tax rate
Origin principle
Stability
Tax expenditure
Tax exporting
Tax targeting
Visibility

Questions

1   Take a look at the tax structure of your state in comparison to neighboring states and the US average. In what ways is it similar? In what ways is it different?
2   Why do you think Alaska and New Hampshire chose to consider adopting an income tax rather than a sales tax as a way to increase state revenue? What strengths and weakness does each tax have for those states in terms of the criteria developed in this chapter?

3   Some economists have argued for a balanced state–local revenue structure in which the "big three" (sales, property, and income taxes) account for the bulk of the revenue, with a relatively minor role for excise taxes and fees and charges. How would you defend (or criticize) that model in terms of the criteria in this chapter?

4   **By the numbers**. Refer to Table 12A.1 on p. 203 to find the indexes for tax capacity, tax effort, fiscal need and fiscal comfort for your state and three neighboring states. How does your state compare? What factors do you think influence your state's tax capacity and fiscal need? Based on this information, would you argue that your state is a high, low, or average tax state? Explain your answer.

5   **Policy application**. A legislator would like to introduce a new tax on automobile repair services that would be used to pay for accident prevention and emergency services. This proposal is appealing in terms of the benefit principle, but automobile repair services are carried out by many small service providers and funded largely through insurance payments. Armed with these considerations, evaluate this proposal in terms of the criteria in both this chapter and Chapter 11.

6   **Behavioral economics**. The rational economic person is in possession of full information about potential policy changes and their consequences for his/her choices, so that gradual implementation of changes or stability of tax policy is not important. How does what we know about actual people and their limitations alter the importance of stability and gradual change?

7   **Thinking globally**. The advantages and disadvantages of harmonizing tax systems across countries, i.e., using similar taxes with similar rates and coverage, are largely related to competition and to intended or unintended distortion of household and business decisions. Explain.

Appendix: interstate comparisons: revenue capacity, effort, and need

Suppose that you, as an interested citizen, are attending a political debate in which one candidate claims that your state's taxes are much higher than its neighboring states and he plans to reduce them substantially if elected. The opponent cites figures to prove that your state is in fact a low tax state and that tax cuts would further reduce the ability of the state to fund needed public services, especially education. This scenario is far from hypothetical; it happens on a regular basis. As a student of public finance, how do you sort out these claims?

First, make sure that both candidates are talking about the overall level of taxation (or even revenue, which includes fees and charges as well as taxes), rather than just zeroing on one particular tax. Sales taxes may be high in your state because property taxes are low and the sales tax funds the schools, or perhaps because you live in one of the nine states without a broad-based income tax. If a particular tax is high, then perhaps its role in the revenue system needs to be reconsidered, but that's a different matter from the level of the overall tax burden.

Second, any such comparisons need to be made with combined state and local taxes or revenue, because different states divide up responsibilities and revenue sources in various ways. Connecticut has traditionally had low state taxes but high property taxes because the property tax pays a larger share of the public education bill. Other states may fund more of education, highways, or law enforcement at the state level and thus have lower local (mostly property) taxes.

After resolving these two problems, what is the best way to compare taxes, and specifically the tax burden on citizens, between states? As was already noted, per capita taxes are misleading because the same tax will raise less per capita in a low-income state than a high-income state.

Taxes as a share of personal income offer a somewhat more meaningful comparison. However, there is one important difference between states that is not captured by this measure. You may notice that Alaska has exceptionally high revenue both per capita and as a percentage of income, but a careful look at the specific familiar taxes (sales, income, property) shows no sales tax (except for some local sales taxes), no state income tax, and no property tax. Where does the money come from? Oil! Some states, especially Alaska and Texas, have much greater ability to extract tax revenues from nonresidents than others.

The process of shifting the tax burden to nonresidents is called tax exporting. Two of the major opportunities for tax exporting are natural resources (gas, oil, minerals) and tourism. States capture revenues from out-of-state buyers of depletable mineral resources mainly through severance taxes, and from tourists through accommodations taxes, amusement taxes, gambling taxes, and sales taxes.

In order to account for these differences, the US Advisory Commission on Intergovernmental Relations developed a standardized measure based on the Representative Tax System (RTS), later expanded to the Representative Revenue System (RRS). RTS and RRS created a hypothetical "average" tax and revenue system using 27 commonly used state and local revenue sources at national average rates and "typical" structures (food exemption from the sales tax, typical deductions/exemptions on income tax, etc.). The large number of taxes reflects many specific excise taxes on items such as gasoline, tobacco, and alcohol.

Once this hypothetical structure was created, it was applied to the tax base in each state: retail sales for the sales tax, cigarette sales for cigarette taxes, personal income for the income tax, and so forth. That calculation determined the amount of revenue a state could raise per capita if it used all possible revenue sources at national average rates and with typical exclusions and exemptions. This measure, expressed as a percentage of the national average, is fiscal capacity. For example, a state with a fiscal capacity of 85 would be able to raise per capita revenue of 85 percent of the national average if it used that standardized revenue system.

A second measure then compared that per capita potential revenue figure to actual per capita collections, again expressed as a percentage. This second measure was called fiscal effort, because it measured how hard the state was trying to raise revenue—the percentage of what it could collect against what it was actually collecting. A state like Mississippi might score very low on fiscal capacity because of low personal income, yet high on fiscal effort because it was collecting a high share of its potential relative to other states.

These two measures provide a different and useful perspective on the concept of high and low tax/revenue states. Table 12A.1 gives the revenue capacity and revenue effort measures for the 50 states in 2002. As you can see, some states are high in both capacity and effort, particularly in the Northeast (New York, Connecticut, Massachusetts, Delaware, New Jersey, and the District of Columbia). Other states, especially in the South, are low in both capacity and effort—Alabama, Arkansas, Louisiana, and South Carolina, among others. A few states, like Alaska, Colorado, and Hawaii, enjoy the luxury of high capacity and low effort, because relatively low tax rates yield more than adequate revenue—a result of tax revenues from tourism and/or mineral extraction. And finally, there are some states with below-average capacity that attempt to maintain a high level of services by taxing that capacity more heavily than average, like Rhode Island and Wisconsin.

Table 12A.1 Revenue capacity, revenue effort, and expenditure need

State	(1) Revenue capacity	(2) Revenue effort	(3) Expenditure need
Alabama	82	103	108
Alaska	118	155	100
Arizona	76	101	102
Arkansas	81	92	109
California	109	102	103
Colorado	113	93	93
Connecticut	135	87	90
Delaware	122	105	93
Florida	102	93	94
Georgia	93	95	105
Hawaii	104	99	87
Idaho	84	91	88
Illinois	104	94	102
Indiana	92	99	98
Iowa	94	104	91
Kansas	91	102	97
Kentucky	91	92	102
Louisiana	83	112	93
Maine	93	112	93
Maryland	107	98	95
Massachusetts	129	86	95
Michigan	97	101	104
Minnesota	109	108	92
Mississippi	72	112	113
Missouri	93	89	97
Montana	90	94	97
Nebraska	95	104	94
Nevada	112	89	91
New Hampshire	118	76	88
New Jersey	121	98	97
New Mexico	85	107	108
New York	112	122	101
North Carolina	92	99	102
North Dakota	94	103	104
Ohio	94	105	107
Oklahoma	82	104	101
Oregon	99	95	93
Pennsylvania	95	104	93
Rhode Island	101	98	93
South Carolina	83	101	105
South Dakota	93	85	96
Tennessee	89	93	104
Texas	92	94	107
Utah	86	108	103
Vermont	100	97	91
Virginia	102	96	96
Washington	105	101	96
West Virginia	76	113	104
Wisconsin	96	108	93
Wyoming	115	115	98

Source: Yilmaz *et al.* (2007).

The third column in Table 12A.1 presents yet another useful comparative measure on the expenditure side, the need index. Developed by Robert Rafuse of the US Treasury in the late 1980s, this measure has been refined and updated by Robert Tannewald at the Boston Federal Reserve. This index attempts to compare states on the basis of the service demands facing governments.

While some spending is proportional to population, the Rafuse study identified six functions for which the level of spending is influenced by state-specific factors other than income or demand and population. These six are elementary and secondary education, higher education, public welfare, health and hospitals, highways, and police and corrections, which account for more than two-thirds of total state and local spending. Such factors as vehicle miles traveled, the poverty rate, and age distribution of the population (particularly the percentage of school age, for education needs, and elderly, for Medicaid expenses) are important components of the revenue need calculation.

The expenditure need index is also expressed as a percentage of the US average. The variation in this index is much smaller than the variation in the tax capacity index. While revenue capacity ranges from 135 in Connecticut to 72 in Mississippi, the revenue need index ranges only from 113 in the Mississippi to 87 in Hawaii.

13 Taxes on income

Introduction

Every April 15th there are gatherings at US post offices across the country to observe one of the rites of spring, the last minute filing of federal income tax returns. Many post offices stay open till midnight so that procrastinating taxpayers can get that crucial April 15th postmark on their tax returns and avoid penalties for late filing. Other taxpayers are mailing a much thinner packet that contains a request for an extension, some because of special circumstances, others because they want to delay incurring the costs in time and irritation to pull together the necessary records, make the calculations, and fill out the forms.

An increasing number of Americans, baffled and intimidated by the complexity of the federal income tax, have turned the whole problem over to their accountants or professional tax preparers, while others rely on annually updated tax preparation software to guide them through the process. Having filed, some taxpayers wait for a refund, others for questions or revisions from the Internal Revenue Service (IRS), or in less than 2 percent of returns, the dreaded audit.

The income tax is the largest but one of the newest sources of federal revenue. In the early years, the new nation funded its federal government largely with land sales and tariff revenue. The two largest sources of federal revenue today, the individual income tax and the Social Security payroll tax, are twentieth-century innovations. The income tax actually required a Constitutional Amendment, the 16th, passed in 1913, because the Constitution forbade direct taxation.

The term income tax registers in most people's minds as the federal **individual income tax**. But there are several other kinds of taxes that are also based directly on income. The **Social Security tax** and other **payroll taxes** are also income taxes, as is the **corporate income tax**. Many local business license taxes are income taxes because they are based on the firm's gross receipts, or income.

Unlike most other countries, the United States relies almost exclusively on income taxes to fund its central government. In addition, 41 states and more than 4,000 local governments also depend on individual income taxes as a source of revenue. Table 13.1 summarizes the role of individual and corporate income taxes and Social Security taxes as revenue sources at the federal, state and local levels. The United States is exceptional among Western industrial nations in the degree of reliance on income taxes of various kinds as the primary federal revenue source.

Table 13.1 Share of income and payroll taxes in US public finance

	Percentage of revenue (unified budget)	Percentage of own source revenue
Federal (2009)		State and local (2006–07)
Individual income tax	43.5	15.5
Corporate income tax	6.6	3.3
Social Security payroll tax	42.3	
All Federal income taxes	**92.4**	

Sources: Economic Report of the President 2010 (federal); US Bureau of the Census (state and local).

Why tax income?

To those people who have lived with the income tax for most of the twentieth century, this question may sound strange. But income is notoriously tricky to discover, track, and/or define. It is easier to hide from the tax collector than many other kinds of tax bases. For most of human history, taxes have been collected where "tax handles" can be found—a visible asset, a transaction, a border crossing. Property taxes, poll taxes, sales and excise taxes, and tariffs or tolls have a much longer history than income taxes. Even today, the United States is unique among modern industrial nations in its high dependence on income and payroll taxes as a source of both central government and regional government revenues.

In many countries, sales taxes (particularly value-added taxes, described in Chapter 14) play a much bigger revenue role. Often the choice of sales rather than income tax as the primary revenue source reflected an actual or expected high degree of noncompliance with the income tax. Income taxes depend heavily on the voluntary cooperation of taxpayers and employers, backed by threats of audit and penalties for at least some tax cheaters.

If it is possible for the government to generate the paper trail necessary to administer an income tax, however, this tax has certain significant advantages. It can be a highly productive revenue source. Progressive income taxes are the only major federal or state revenue source with an elasticity greater than one, meaning that a 1 percent increase in income leads to more than a 1 percent increase in tax revenue. This tax lends itself to fine-tuning both in terms of equity and in terms of achieving social goals of encouraging desirable activities. It generates a regular flow of revenue to the government through withholding, unlike the property tax which comes in all at once for most local governments. And it even provides information that enables tax collectors to do a better job of enforcement on other taxes.

Although there are a number of taxes that fall under the heading of income tax, most of this chapter is devoted to the US federal income tax and its counterparts at the state and local level. Corporate income taxes also get some attention here, although they are a much more modest and declining source of public revenue, especially at the state level. Payroll taxes for Social Security are addressed briefly here and again in Chapter 19 in connection with other Social Security issues.

Measuring income for tax purposes

You may have an intuitive sense of what income is—that flow of money into your checkbook and your wallet that enables you to pay the bills and make purchases. That's a start, but it's not good enough. Some of that flow may consist of scholarships and/or gifts from parents or others, which is not considered income for tax purposes. Some of the flow may come from the sale of assets—shares of stock, a used car, or a home. To the extent that you sold that asset for more than you paid for it, the difference may be considered income (capital gains), but the recovery of the purchase price is not income—even though it does generate funds to pay bills and make purchases.

Recall from your principles course the distinction between stocks and flows. Wealth is a stock of assets; income is a flow. But there are several important relationships between the stock of wealth in a household and the flow of income. First, wealth or assets generate income. Second, any flow of income into the household must by definition either be consumed or saved, and any consumption or saving must be financed by an inflow of revenue from earnings, income from capital (interest, dividends, rents and royalties), gifts, asset sales, or increased debt.[1] So one possible definition of a household's income is the change in a household's net wealth over the course of a year plus consumption spending. This definition would incorporate all flows into the household less any debt incurred, because any increase in debt reduces the household's net wealth.

Income taxes are based on the flow of money into a household or firm.[2] This definition of income is broader than most governments would choose to use as a base for an income tax, but it does provide a starting point from which adjustments can be made. Adjustments are made (and criticized) primarily for three reasons: efficiency, equity, and costs of collection and/or compliance. Policy-makers have to bear in mind that any exclusion of categories of income from the base will reduce the base and either reduce potential revenue or require a higher tax rate to achieve the same revenue.

Efficiency issues in income taxation

Chapter 11 demonstrated that taxing income but not leisure is likely to distort work–leisure decisions by individuals. The substitution effect of an income tax is to encourage replacing taxed working hours with untaxed leisure time. It also has an income effect because it now takes more working hours to earn the same take-home pay. Different taxpayers will react differently to the imposition of income taxes, but all of them will see some distortion of their choices relative to what they would have done in the absence of an income tax.

Creating exclusions or favoring certain sources of income over others provides an incentive to arrange one's sources of income so as to minimize the tax liability. If dividends are taxable and capital gains are not, there is an incentive for taxpayers to encourage firms in which they hold stock to focus on creating capital gains in the form of higher stock prices instead of distributing net earnings of the corporation in the form of (taxable) dividends. If earnings from student jobs are taxable but scholarships are not, then colleges and students will favor a student aid mix higher in scholarship money than in paid on-campus jobs, even though the latter may be more desirable in terms of valuable student learning experiences. If some financial assets receive highly favorable tax treatment (such as municipal bonds or tax-deferred annuities), funds will shift toward those assets, reducing the interest rate and saving the issuers debt service costs while driving up interest rates on competing non-favored financial instruments.

These distortions of household decisions in response to tax rules are among the most important efficiency effects of income taxation. If efficiency were the only goal, the tax code would use the broadest possible base for the income tax in order to minimize such changes in behavior. Such a broad base would also make it possible to collect the same revenue with lower rates, reducing those distortions in income–leisure choices that rise with the square of the tax rate.

The broadest possible base, however, is a difficult standard to maintain when the tax collector must deal with actual flows of revenue through households. Some kinds of income create greater challenges in tracking and collecting than others. Consider, for example, increases in the market value of assets owned by households, better known as capital gains. Should those gains be considered taxable income each year because they increase household wealth, even if the asset is not sold and no actual cash flow is generated with which to pay taxes? If such unrealized capital gains were taxed, then the income tax collector would be forced to get into the business of assessing the value of household assets (including real estate), and the cost of administering the income tax would rise astronomically.

But if capital gains on assets are excluded from **taxable income** until the assets are sold (thus dodging the assessment problem), then there is a "lumping" of income in a single year when an asset is sold, often pushing the taxpayer into a higher tax bracket. The result is a greater tax burden than would occur if capital gains were taxed as they accrued. The tax treatment of capital gains is but one of many difficult issues involved in designing an efficient income tax.

An important conflict in designing any tax policy is the desire to avoid certain tax-induced changes in behavior while encouraging others. Many of the exemptions, deductions and credits on the income tax are designed specifically to encourage certain actions, such as making homes more energy efficient or contributing to charity. In this context, efficiency has an entirely different meaning. The efficiency question becomes how much additional energy conservation or charitable contributions results from a dollar of revenue loss.

Equity issues in income taxation

All taxes raise issues of equity, but equity is particularly important in income taxation because it is possible to fine-tune the distribution of the burden of the income tax more closely than most other taxes. The income tax is also one of the few taxes that lends itself to a progressive structure.

Both horizontal and vertical equity are important issues in income tax design. Recall from earlier chapters that horizontal equity means treating people equally when they are in equal economic situations. The definition of equal economic situations is closely linked to equal annual income flow. However, the income flow is only a starting point in defining equal situations, because other factors affect the relative taxpaying ability of two households with the same income flows. There may be a difference in wealth, or household size, or other obligations (medical expenses, caring for aging parents, child care expenses, etc.) that should be taken into account. Such equity concerns account for a significant amount of the volume and complexity of the current federal income tax code.

Vertical equity means treating people with an appropriate degree of difference based on differences in their economic situation or ability to pay. In the case of the income tax, some would argue that proportional taxation constitutes vertical equity, part of the argument for the flat tax discussed later in this chapter. Others argue that progressivity can create an appropriate degree of difference because, based on the diminishing marginal utility of income, the loss of an additional dollar to taxation represents a smaller sacrifice to a rich person than a poor person.

As a middle ground position, vertical equity can be viewed as a function of the tax system as a whole, not just one particular tax. Since many other taxes in the system are regressive, a progressive income tax functions as a counterweight in the overall system, moving it toward proportionality.

Progressivity can be built into an income tax in two different ways. One way is to exclude a certain base amount of income from tax through exemptions, exclusions, and/or deductions. The second way is to have a graduated series of tax rates that apply to increments of income. The first method increases equity at the expense of creating more complexity, which means higher collection and/or compliance costs.

The second method, progressive rates, may improve equity at the expense of efficiency. Progressive rate structures increase the distortions in people's decisions and also cause them to accelerate or postpone some of those actions on the basis of the tax bracket they would find themselves in in one year versus another. End-of-year charitable contributions, bunching of medical expenses in a single year, and postponing or accelerating receipt of certain kinds of income are all "inspired" by the tax consequences under a system with progressive rates.

Collection and compliance costs for income taxes

The area of compliance and collection cost is the most contentious one in income taxation. Creating a broad tax base for efficiency reasons requires more effort by both tax collectors and taxpayers to keep track of a variety of income flows, increasing both collection and compliance costs. On the other hand, making adjustments in the tax base to accommodate horizontal equity concerns makes the tax law more difficult to administer and more confusing for the taxpayer to comply with. A progressive rate structure, which was put in place in the interest of vertical equity, makes the tax liability somewhat harder to compute, although the use of tax tables and tax software has largely resolved that problem.

The expense of administering the federal income tax is fairly low as a percentage of revenue collected. However, the low collection cost is somewhat offset by shifting much of the cost to the taxpayer and the taxpayer's employer, who must maintain records and fill out various forms in order to comply with the tax.

Other forms of income taxes, such as payroll taxes and many state and local income taxes, are simpler to administer and to comply with for a variety of reasons. In some cases, particularly local income taxes and Social Security taxes, there is a single flat rate and most of the collection is through payroll withholding, often without a need to file a return. In the case of many (but not all) state income taxes, once the federal return is complete, the additional effort required to file a state return is very small.

The US federal income tax

The United States has had a federal income tax since the 16th Amendment to the Constitution in 1913. Initially the tax was at very low rates with large exclusions, so that only the wealthiest households paid the tax. By the end of World War II, however, the pressing demands of war finance had driven the top bracket rate to 98 percent, and a much larger proportion of households paid income taxes. A series of major tax reforms in 1954, 1964, 1981, and 1986 reduced those top rates. Currently the lowest bracket is 10 percent, and the top bracket is 35 percent.

Defining taxable income

The process of determining federal income tax liability is conceptually simple, even though the actual process may be very time-consuming. The first step is to determine gross income—

income from all sources, wages, salary, rents, royalties, pensions, interest, dividends, self-employment earnings, gifts, scholarships, etc. (The largest single source of income is wages and salaries; in 2008, they accounted for 81.4 percent of personal income.) The taxpayer must then determine which of these income sources need to be reported as income and which do not. Those kinds of income that are not included in gross income are referred to as **exclusions**.

Exclusions can be total or partial. Among the income sources that typically do not have to be reported at all are insurance claims income, most employee fringe benefits, scholarships, gifts received, and interest on state and local bonds. Partial exclusions include a portion of Social Security benefits for higher-income households (lower-income households get to exclude all Social Security benefits).

From gross income to taxable income there is a series of steps called adjustments, exemptions, and deductions (see Table 13.2). Adjustments are those additions or subtractions that are made to get from gross income to **adjusted gross income**. Adjusted gross income is not yet the basis for tax computations, but this figure is important, because it is used to determine various limitations on exclusions and tax credits and ceilings on certain deductions. Among the adjustments made at this point are subtractions from gross income of contributions to various kinds of retirement saving plans, part of health insurance premiums, moving expenses (job-related), rent and royalty expenses, self-employment health insurance and half of self-employment tax, and alimony payments.

For some people, whose income is modest and comes almost entirely from wages or salary, and who have no self-employment income or other complications, the determination of adjusted gross income is very easy. They can use one of two short, simple tax forms, 1040A or 1040EZ. For others, particularly those with higher incomes, or with self-employment income (and expenses related to earning that income), extensive investments, job changes, or multiple income sources, determining adjusted gross income is the most difficult and demanding part of the whole process.

Filing status, exemptions, and the standard deduction

At this point the **filing status** of the taxpayer becomes a factor in determining how much to subtract. Filing status options are joint (a married couple filing a combined return, whether both or just one had income), head of household (a person who has at least one dependent

Table 13.2 A flow chart for federal income tax

Start with all sources of income
Less exclusions
= Gross income
Less (or plus) adjustments
= Adjusted gross income
Less exemptions and deductions
= Taxable income
STOP! COMPUTE TAX LIABILITY HERE!
Tax liability
Less withholding
Less other credits
Plus other taxes due
= Tax due or refund due

child living with him/her), single, or married filing separately. Filing status affects the standard deduction, the adjusted gross income used to calculate phaseout of exemptions and deductions, and the tax rates or table used to compute tax liability.

The two components of the difference between adjusted gross income and taxable income are personal **exemptions** and either **standard or itemized deductions**. These two components, which are available to every taxpayer, exclude a base amount of income from taxation. Exemptions and deductions would make the income tax progressive even without a series of graduated tax rates. Taxpayers are entitled to one personal exemption (currently $3,650) for each member of the household. There are special rules governing children with earnings of their own, college students, dependent parents, children of divorced parents, and unrelated dependents. For most households, it is pretty easy to figure out how many exemptions to claim, multiply by $3,650, and subtract.

Standard and itemized deductions serve several important public policy purposes. Itemized deductions consist of various taxpayer expenditures that Congress has favored with special tax treatment. The major categories are medical expenses over a certain percentage of income, state and local taxes paid (mostly income and property taxes, but not sales taxes), interest on mortgages and student loans, charitable contributions, and unreimbursed employee business expenses over a certain percentage of income. The deduction for state and local taxes amounts to a limited indirect subsidy of state and local government. The home mortgage and student loan interest deductions are intended to encourage home ownership and investment in education. The deduction for charitable contributions is justified by the expectation that private charities will create substantial positive externalities and sometimes even local public goods, and that it may be cheaper or more efficient to subsidize such activities indirectly through the deduction than to provide them directly through government. The unreimbursed business expenses are a cost of earning income, and are somewhat out of place in itemized deductions; they would more logically belong in adjustments to gross income.

Taxpayers may choose to itemize, i.e., to list all the deductible expenditures that they made during the tax year and subtract them from adjusted gross income, or they may elect to take the standard deduction, which was $11,400 for married taxpayers filing jointly in 2010. The standard deduction is often more than the taxpayer could claim by listing deductions separately, and also saves considerable headaches in record-keeping for taxpayers. Only one taxpayer in four itemizes their deductions. Mortgage interest, charitable contributions, and state and local taxes are the most important itemized deductions for most households that itemize.

Computing tax liability

Having arrived at taxable income, the next step is to determine taxes owed. Here filing status becomes very important, because there are different tax rates and schedules for married filing separately, single, married filing jointly, and heads of households, again reflecting some difficult equity decisions in designing the tax structure. For taxable incomes up to $100,000, taxpayers can use a table to determine their tax liability. For taxable incomes above that level, there is a tax rate schedule. In 2010, rates ranged from 10 percent of the first $16,700 to 35 percent of taxable income above $208,850 for married couples filing jointly.

One of the most common sources of confusion in the federal income tax is the difference between the **average tax rate** and the **marginal tax rate**. The marginal rate is the tax rate applied to the last dollar of taxable income, while the average rate is simply the tax due as a fraction or percentage of taxable income. Table 13.3 illustrates the difference. This table

Table 13.3 Federal income taxes as a percentage of adjusted gross income, 2010 family of 4, standard deduction

Income range ($)	Taxes as percentage of income	Marginal tax rate as % of income
10,000	0	0
25,000	0	10*
50,000	14.4	15
75,000	18.2	25
100,000	18.8	25
200,000	24.5	33
500,000	30.8	35

Note: *10% rate starts at $25,001.

shows the progressivity of the US federal income tax, measuring taxes as a percentage of adjusted gross income.

For example, a married couple filing jointly in 2010 with a taxable income of $200,000 would have a marginal rate of 33 percent that applied to that portion of their income that fell between $137,050 and $200,000. But the first $137,050 would have been taxed at the lower rates of 10 percent, 15 percent and 25 percent. Their total tax liability of $49,000 is the result of applying four different marginal rates to four different parts of their income; it comes to 24.5 percent of their taxable income.

For some taxpayers, a second computation is necessary, called the alternative minimum tax. These are the taxpayers, generally high income, who have managed to reduce their taxable income through extensive use of itemized deductions and/or other tax preferences such as tax exempt-interest income, tax-sheltered business losses, and accelerated depreciation. The alternative minimum tax was designed to increase equity by ensuring a fair contribution from higher-income taxpayers, but it also increased the complexity of the tax system considerably from the standpoint of both collection and compliance costs.

The last step: who owes whom?

Finally, the tax form asks the filer to figure out how much has already been paid, what other kinds of taxes need to be figured in, and what credits might apply. The difference will be either the amount owed (write a check and attach it to the return) or a refund, which will probably take 6–8 weeks to arrive if everything was done correctly. Electronic filing, which is becoming increasingly popular, speeds that process up a little.

Most taxpayers who have any tax liability have already paid a part of their taxes either through payroll withholding (the most common method), or through quarterly filings of estimated tax, or both. Payroll withholding not only guarantees the government a steady flow of revenue but also reduces the visibility and the pain of the annual ritual of settling accounts with the federal government.

Taxpayers who are self-employed or who have other kinds of income not subject to payroll withholding (interest, dividends, rents, royalties, consulting, taxable pensions, etc.) usually find it necessary to file an estimated tax form each quarter and send in a payment.

Taxpayers whose withholding and estimated tax payments are less than 90 percent of their tax liability may face a penalty for underpayment. That penalty is a strong incentive to make sure that advance payments cover most of the bill.

Taxpayers may also owe other kinds of taxes that are collected through the Internal Revenue Service and which have their own lines on Form 1040. Self-employment taxes for Social Security are the biggest item, along with a few specialty taxes such as environmental excise taxes related to oil spills and oil-depleting chemicals. These additional taxes are added to the tax liability computed on the basis of taxable income and filing status.

Finally, there are credits. **Tax credits** are different from deductions because the value of a tax credit is closer to being equal for all taxpayers, whereas the value of an itemized deduction is greater to a person in a 35 percent tax bracket than one in a 15 percent tax bracket. $100 spent on child care would save $35 in taxes owed for the first person and only $15 for the second person as an itemized deduction. Originally the child care credit was a flat 20 percent of allowable expenses for children under age 15. Now it ranges from 20–30 percent of expenses, with a ceiling of $3,000 for one child and $6,000 for two or more. The higher credit rates are provided for lower-income households, adding a bit of progressivity to the credit in order to encourage lower-income families to seek out and use quality child care services.

The child care credit is one of the larger individual income tax credits, amounting to a $28.4 billion tax expenditure in 2008. The child care credit, which was expanded in the 2001 tax cut legislation, covers children with two working parents, for whom child care is a cost of earning income. The most significant credit for low-income working households, however, is the Earned Income Tax Credit or EITC, which was estimated to be about $50 billion in 2010. Canada, Ireland, New Zealand, Austria, Belgium, Denmark, Finland, Sweden, France, the United Kingdom, and the Netherlands have similar programs.

Other tax credits that have gained in popularity in recent years are offered for energy efficiency in various forms, including retrofitting houses and purchase of energy-efficient vehicles and appliances. Some of these credits are temporary, such as the Cash for Clunkers program in 2009, while others are more permanent. A temporary large tax credit for first-time homebuyers was used as part of a stimulus program in 2009 and 2010 to help the beleaguered housing industry in the wake of the mortgage crisis.

Finally, the bottom line: tax liability, plus other taxes owed, less withholding, less estimated taxes paid, less credits equals balance due or refund. Sign it, add a check if needed, mail it, and the taxpayer's work is done for another year.

Evasion, avoidance, and the likelihood of audit

Tax evasion is illegal. Tax evasion means falsifying information on your tax return in order to reduce your tax liability, or even not filing at all. Tax evasion can result in financial penalties or even prison sentences. **Tax avoidance** is legal. Tax avoidance means arranging your affairs so as to minimize your tax burden by incurring deductible expenses, investing in tax-exempt bonds, putting money in tax-deferred retirement savings, or other legal techniques. There are also activities that fall into the gray area, sometimes called "tax avoision." Many of the tax shelters that were set up in the 1980s to create large deductible losses have since been disallowed by the IRS.

Audit (examination is the preferred IRS term) is low probability, particularly for taxpayers with moderate income and few deductions, credits, or exclusions. The IRS will review your return, check your arithmetic, compare it with reports received from others on your income sources and some deductible items, and notify you by mail if there are discrepancies. Sometimes they may send an unexpected refund! Some returns, however, are selected randomly for a fuller review and verification. Others are selected because of certain "flags" that call your return to the attention of the IRS. Among the most common flags are exceptionally high itemized deductions (especially for charitable contributions) relative to your income, tax-shelter losses, occupations that lend themselves to significant cash payments, large business expenses relative to income, or having been called in for a prior audit.

Directions for reform

The US federal income tax undergoes frequent changes and occasional major reforms. The last truly major overhaul of the income tax took place in 1986, with a tradeoff of base broadening (also known as eliminating loopholes or tax preferences) for a reduction in marginal rates.

Piecemeal changes

The gradualist school of tax reformers always has a laundry list of improvements in the income tax code to increase efficiency, improve equity, and reduce collection or compliance costs while maintaining adequate revenue. High on the list are eliminating the marriage tax penalty, more tax relief for parents of small children and/or college students, and stronger incentives for saving, especially for retirement. Reformers are also critical of exempting labor income in the form of employee fringe benefits such as health insurance, health services, employer contributions to pension plans, company recreation programs, and subsidized cafeteria meals, which together constitute the biggest source of tax expenditures.

Taxation of capital gains is a perennial issue. Capital gains are taxed at a lower effective rate than income from other sources. Some tax reformers would like to eliminate the tax on capital gains altogether. Proponents of both special treatment and elimination argue that capital gains consist largely of inflation rather than real increases in income. While the same can be said for other sources of income (your salary increase each year is at least partly a compensation for inflation), the bunching of capital gains at the time of an asset sale can kick the taxpayer into a higher tax bracket. This bunching effect is part of the rationale for a lower marginal tax rate on capital gains.

Proponents of special treatment for capital gains income also argue that encouraging investment in assets that are likely to create capital gains constitutes an incentive to invest, which encourages economic growth. There may be some validity in this argument, but the current special treatment also applies to antique cars, works of art, and other financial assets that do not relate to economic growth.

Major reforms

The alternative approach to gradualism or piecemeal tax reform is a truly major overhaul of the tax code, some going so far as to replace the existing system with either a flat tax (described below) or a national value-added tax, discussed in Chapter 14. Some advocates of a major overhaul would like to shift to a tax on consumption, modeled on the one developed by British economist Nicholas Kaldor in the 1950s and tried briefly in India and Sri Lanka. The household's assets at the beginning of the year, plus borrowing, less investment, less the end of the year value of assets, would be the amount consumed. Saving and (financial) investment would not be taxed. Unlike most kinds of taxes on consumption or sales, an expenditure tax could be designed to be progressive.

The reality of public choice, however, suggests that there are too many interests that are invested in the present system and that the adjustment costs of major change may be too high relative to the benefits. The United States is likely to continue its uneasy relationship with the Internal Revenue System and the federal income tax code with periodic tinkering to respond to complaints about efficiency, equity, and compliance costs.

Behavioral public finance: voluntary compliance

Strictly speaking, complying with the income tax is not voluntary. There are penalties for failing to file or for falsifying information on your tax return. However, the IRS has very limited resources, so they depend heavily on the honesty and integrity of taxpayers. The simple model of *Homo economicus* would suggest that individuals would take advantage of this situation to reduce their tax burdens by deliberately understating income or overstating deductions. And indeed, many do. Payments in cash to avoid reporting income to the IRS, overstating expenses in a non-corporate business, and overstating charitable contributions are three fairly common practices.

Income tax compliance is a much bigger problem in many parts of the world, including Italy and many countries in Central and South America. As income tax compliance begins to decline, it can create a downward spiral as the burden is shifted to fewer honest taxpayers and those honest taxpayers resent the lower tax burden on their noncompliant friends, neighbors, and relatives. So there is a strong cultural factor in tax compliance.

While the risk of audit, fines, and even potential jail time is certainly a consideration, most Americans pay their income taxes out of habit and in response to cultural norms as much as out of fear of penalties. *Homo economicus* is an isolated, self-interested individual, but the taxpayer in behavioral economics is more of a social animal and a creature of habit. That makes the job of the IRS much less complicated!

The flat tax

Since the early 1990s there have been persistent proposals to replace the present income tax with a **flat tax**. Developed in the 1980s by economist Robert Hall and political scientist Alvin Rabushka, the notion of a flat (and simple) federal income tax has caught the public imagination.

There are many variants of the proposal, but the common features of most of them would be elimination of itemized deductions, a single combined large exclusion of some base amount of income, and a single (non-progressive) tax rate. Proposed rates range from 17–21 percent, which are significantly higher than the lowest bracket rate for the current income tax but lower than the current average rate for many taxpayers.

The business tax would be imposed on all businesses, not just corporations, so taxes on self-employment earnings would be separated from the individual income tax and grouped with income of partnerships and corporations.

The elimination of personal exemptions, itemized or standard deductions, tax credits, and many current adjustments to gross income would broaden the tax base. This broader base, together with an expected stimulus to private sector economic activity from the lower (and single) tax rate, is expected to offset any revenue loss from the large flat exemption and the lower flat rate.

The flat tax proposal, which has many variations, has generated heated debate and numerous studies about its revenue potential, its impact on horizontal and vertical equity and on compliance and collection costs. Proponents argue that the current system wastes too many resources in compliance costs, a problem that could be resolved by a simple flat tax. Critics have noted that it is possible to get the simplification effects of the flat tax while retaining progressive rates, since it is not the actual calculation of tax liability that causes taxpayers so much time and effort in compliance cost. Tax rate schedules, tax tables, and tax software have made that task easier.

On the equity front, one study of a fairly typical variant of a flat tax proposal finds that senior citizens, one-income families, and single parents gain at the expense of non-seniors and two-income households. There is also a decided shift of the tax burden away from higher-income households to lower-income households, a conclusion affirmed in other research as well (Fougere and Ruggeri 1998).

In addition to the equity issue, the biggest challenge to a flat tax is the entrenched interests in certain provisions of the federal tax code, ranging from deductions for mortgage interest and charitable deductions to the special treatment of employee fringe benefits and various kinds of retirement savings plans. Elimination of those provisions would be costly to people who made long-term financial decisions on the basis of those tax rules, and might have a significant negative impact on related industries—home building, nonprofits, and financial services, for example.

Income taxes in other countries

Many other countries use income taxes, although most do not depend as heavily on them as the United States does. Among other major English-speaking countries, India, Australia, Canada and the United Kingdom all use individual income taxes with progressive rates and features similar to those of the US federal income tax. Rates range up to 29 percent in Canada, 30 percent in India, 35 percent in Australia, and 50 percent in the United Kingdom. These rates, except for the United Kingdom, seem comparable to those of the US income tax, but unlike the United States, these countries also have national value-added taxes as a major revenue source.

The United States has had difficulty in defining the taxpayer. Is it the individual, or the household? The question is complicated by the mixed heritage of English, Spanish and French law in different parts of the country that resulted in community property states where all income belongs to both partners in a marriage, regardless of who earned it. India also uses a mix of individual and household definitions, but Canada, Australia and the United Kingdom tax the individual, not the household.

One peculiarity of the US income tax that is not generally replicated in these other countries is the preferential treatment of owner-occupied housing. In the United Kingdom, owners may take deductions for property taxes and interest on mortgages, but there is a tax on the implicit rental income earned by the owner in his capacity as his own landlord. In India, there is no tax on implicit rental income but also no deduction for property taxes or mortgage interest.

State and local income taxes

Forty-one US states, the District of Columbia, and more than 4,000 local governments impose broad-based individual income taxes. Among the remaining nine states, two imposed limited income taxes on interest and dividend income. Income taxes have a longer history than sales taxes as a state revenue source, beginning with Hawaii, which adopted its income tax in 1901. Nineteen states had individual income taxes in place before the first state retail sales taxes appeared on the scene in 1933. Part of the appeal of the income tax to states is its sensitivity to growth.

Except for school districts in Louisiana, counties in Maryland, and multiple local governments in Pennsylvania, most local income taxes are levied by large cities. Some cities levy their income taxes on residents, but the most common form of municipal income tax is a payroll tax at a single rate on employees, some of whom reside in the city while others commute into the city from the suburbs. This kind of tax is somewhat regressive, since the base is limited to wages and salaries, but it is very easy to administer.

Structure of state income taxes

State income taxes are somewhat more diverse than local income taxes. To simplify compliance by taxpayers, and provide an opportunity for cross-verification between federal and state governments, most state income taxes are connected to the federal income tax in some way. A state may choose as a starting point either federal adjusted gross income, federal taxable income, or federal tax liability. The approach with the lowest compliance and collection cost, used in just three states, is to direct the taxpayer to send in some percentage of federal tax liability.

Most states like to differentiate their individual income tax codes to a greater degree than this method provides. Thus, a second approach is to start with federal taxable income and make certain additions and subtractions. Here are some common adjustments:

- add back any itemized deduction for state income taxes paid;
- make an adjustment for interest earned on federal government bonds;
- different treatment of retirement income, including Social Security;
- different treatment of two-earner households.

The third and most popular approach is to start with federal adjusted gross income and then approach personal exemptions and itemized or standard deductions differently. One advantage of this approach is that it makes it possible for those states that do not have community property laws to treat husbands and wives as separate taxpaying entities and thus eliminate any marriage penalty. It does, however, increase the compliance cost for the taxpayer and the collection cost for the state.

The fourth method is to completely separate the state income tax from the federal income tax. Taxpayers must start over to compute their state tax liability.

Competitive issues in state income taxation

Interstate competition for higher-income residents and business location is a factor in all major state tax decisions, including the issue of whether or not to have an income tax. There are advocates in several of the nine states without a broad-based income tax to adopt one in order to reduce dependence on sales and property taxes. But for several of those states— particularly Texas, Florida, and New Hampshire—the absence of a state income tax has been a "draw" to attract certain kinds of residents and firms.

Non-corporate business firms (partnerships and proprietorships) may find a state without an income tax an attractive place to matter if other location factors are not significant. Higher-income retirees have moved to states like Florida and Texas at least in part because of the absence of an income tax. In response, other states have fine-tuned their income tax systems in order to compete for wealthy retirees by offering special exemptions either based on age or targeted at retirement income (pensions and/or Social Security).

Competition among states also tends to put downward pressure on income tax rates and particularly on the degree of progressivity. Many states have a flat rate, while even those that are progressive have top bracket rates that are no more than 11 percent. At the local level, except for those states that impose a uniform rate for all counties or school districts, individual income tax rates are almost always flat and generally very low. Local governments are even more sensitive to the pressures of competition for location of commercial facilities and residents.

Another competitive dimension of any state or local tax is deductibility. Unlike retail sales taxes, state and local individual income taxes qualify as an itemized deduction for taxpayers who do not take the standard deduction. Deductibility reduces the effective state income tax rate for those taxpayers, who tend to be in higher tax brackets at both the state and federal levels. For example, a taxpayer whose average state tax rate was 7 percent and whose marginal federal tax rate was 33 percent would be able to claim a deduction that reduced his or her effective state tax burden from 7 percent to 7 percent*(1−.33), or 4.62 percent.

Because the federal tax is progressive and because itemizing is more common among higher-earning households, deductibility of state and local income taxes tends to reduce the progressivity of the total income tax system. On the plus side, deductibility of state income taxes reduces some of the competitive pressures on states to hold their top bracket rates down.

Corporate income taxes

The federal government and 45 states (and the District of Columbia) impose a **corporate income tax**, corporate profits tax, or franchise tax on incorporated business enterprises. Unincorporated enterprises, whether partnerships or proprietorships, are usually taxed as part of the individual income tax. Many of these enterprises are also subject to a franchise fee or other form of business tax at the state level. Canada and Australia also have a separate corporate income tax.

The federal corporate income tax is levied on income after expenses (the bottom line on the income statement) at rates ranging from 15 percent up to 39 percent. Most state corporate income tax rates are in the 4–7 percent range, with 33 states using a single flat rate and 12 states using progressive rates. The base of the corporate income tax (corporate net income) is the most cyclically sensitive of all the major tax bases, so corporate income taxes are a very volatile revenue source.

The federal corporate income tax is very complicated to administer because of the problems in defining allowable expenses that can be deducted. These definitional issues also have the potential to distort firms' decisions. There is relatively little difficulty in identifying and deducting firms' expenditures for labor, utilities, supplies of raw materials, capital equipment, land, buildings or rented property, and interest on borrowed money. However, some other expenses fall into a gray area that looks like tax avoidance or even tax evasion. Some provisions in the tax code inflate deductible expenses beyond what normal cost accounting would suggest is appropriate.

There are three particular areas of controversy in relation to these allowable expenses: depreciation of capital equipment, consumption-type expenditures, and the incentive to borrow rather than to finance new or expanding firms with equity (stock).

Depreciation

Capital equipment that has a useful lifetime of more than one year must be depreciated over several years. The rules on the timing of depreciation can affect the amount of tax owed and favor some kinds of capital over others, or capital over other inputs. Allowing a firm to write off the cost of capital equipment much more rapidly than the actual decline in its economic value (**accelerated depreciation**) is regarded as an incentive to invest in new equipment.

Accelerated depreciation was introduced in the federal tax code in 1981 and modified in the 1986 tax reforms. This tax expenditure, which is one of the more costly tax breaks in revenue terms, also distorts the firm's choice between new equipment and repairing old equipment, and discriminates in favor of capital-intensive firms compared to other kinds of corporations.

Disguised consumption

A second area of long-standing controversy is distinguishing between expenditures made in order to produce the firm's product or service and those that are disguised consumption for the owners of privately held corporations or the stockholders in closely-held corporations. Where stockholders are ineffective at making management accountable, management may enjoy a variety of "perks" that are actually consumption disguised as allowable business expenses. From the three-martini lunch and the corporate management retreat in the Caribbean to the on-site health club, fancy furnishings, and subsidized executive cafeteria, the possibilities for providing tax-free in-kind income to owners and managers are almost endless. Some efforts have been made to crack down on the most flagrant abuses, but it is virtually impossible to monitor and require justification for all of a firm's outlays.

Debt versus equity financing

The third distortion that arises from the treatment of allowable expenses is the deduction for interest paid on borrowed funds. When firms need additional capital, they have three possible sources: borrowing (debt), issuing stock (equity), or using retained earnings. If there were no tax distortions, market forces would establish an appropriate balance between these three methods based on their relative cost and other considerations.

Using retained earnings means forgoing what those funds could earn in a competitive marketplace, so the opportunity cost of using internal capital for investment should be the same as external borrowing. If additional shares of stock are issued, those added shares dilute the value of existing equity (stock), reducing the value of each outstanding share. Pressure from stockholders to maintain the value of their holdings will discourage management from overusing equity rather than debt financing.

The effect of the deductibility of interest payments is to tilt the balance in favor of issuing bonds (borrowing or debt financing) rather than stock (equity financing). Corporations put themselves in a riskier financial position with a high debt/equity ratio, because stockholders have no choice during bad times but to wait it out, while bondholders have a guaranteed and enforceable claim to payment that could force a firm into bankruptcy.

Who pays the corporate income tax?

The incidence of the corporate income tax has been a source of debate among economists for years. The burden must fall in some combination on owners (stockholders), workers, and/or consumers of the firm's product, because those constitute all the possible parties to any activities in which the burden can be shifted. If (1) all firms were corporations, (2) all owners were individual taxpayers, and (3) all relevant markets were highly competitive, then the corporate income tax would become a tax on capital which, like a tax on raw land, could not be shifted. In the short run, all of the burden of the tax would fall on the owners of the fixed supply of capital, or the shareholders, who would receive a reduced return on their investment, much like owners of land who are faced with a property tax.

In the long run, however, the supply of financial capital is highly elastic and also flows freely between countries and between business firms and other borrowers, such as government and consumers. In order to offer the same rate of return as other borrowers (non-corporate borrowers in the same country, or corporations in other countries) who are competing for funds, corporations would require a higher pre-tax return in order to generate the same after-tax return. They would move up their demand curve for capital, acquiring less capital by only choosing those investment projects with much higher rates of return. Corporations may invest less in capital per worker than they would otherwise. Capital is both a substitute and a complement to workers. Less capital investment may mean more workers, but less productive ones (since each worker has less capital to work with), and hence lower wages. In this way some of the burden of the corporate income tax may fall on workers in the long run.

This theoretical analysis is complicated by the fact that corporations compete for funds, for workers, and for customers with other types of firms that are not corporations. While corporations produce most of the output in the US economy, most of the firms in sheer numbers are organized as partnerships or proprietorships. Partnerships and proprietorships lack some of the special advantages of corporations, like limited liability and unlimited life-times, but they are generally more attractive from a tax perspective, because their net income is taxed to the owner or partners as individual income.

Consequently, one effect of the corporate income tax may be to encourage firms to be organized as partnerships or proprietorships (or one of the special forms of corporations provided for in the tax law) in order to reduce their tax burdens. The result is a less efficient mix of kinds of business organizations than would otherwise occur. A second effect may be that the higher cost of capital to corporations translates into higher prices for their products relative to those of non-corporate firms, shifting some of the burden of the corporate income tax to buyers of products produced by the corporate sector.

A third effect is the movement of corporate headquarters elsewhere in the world. Corporations increasingly compete not just with non-corporate firms but also with corporations in other parts of the world that do not pay their governments corporate income tax.

In the majority of countries, the primary source of government revenue is taxes imposed on sales, most commonly a value-added tax. Many countries also rely heavily on individual income taxes, but less on corporate income taxes. Firms located in these countries will find it easier to attract investors, so they can issue more equity and less debt. As a result they will have a lower cost of capital, and may be able to pass on some of those savings to consumers in the form of lower prices.

Those US corporations that compete heavily in global markets will be at a disadvantage. If they also hire labor in highly competitive markets, the ability to shift some of the tax burden to their workers will also be limited, so that shareholders will bear the burden of the corporate income tax.

As you can see, the analysis of the incidence of the corporate income tax is quite complex, particularly when it is considered in a context of the US individual income tax. Nevertheless, as long as markets are competitive on both a national and international scale, the main burden of the tax falls on shareholders.

The case against the corporate income tax

The analysis of incidence leads directly into the major criticism of the corporate income tax. Corporations are owned by their shareholders. Their net income, or profit, belongs to their shareholders. When the shareholders receive part of that income as dividends, it becomes part of their personal income and is subject to individual income tax. When the corporation retains (and reinvests) part or all of its profit or net income, that reinvestment should increase the value of the shares of stock. When the shareholder sells the stock, the capital gain (increase in the value of the stock) is taxable income.

The primary issue for many people, then, is both an efficiency and equity issue. When dividends and capital gains are both taxed as ordinary income to stockholders, an additional tax on corporate net income amounts to double taxation. It is for this reason that there has been at times (but not currently) a limited dividend exclusion on the individual income tax, and favorable treatment of capital gains.

The alternative proposal is called full integration of the individual and corporate income tax so that corporate profits are taxed only once. If they are taxed at the source, then any distribution or capital gain from sale of stock should be exempt from individual income taxes, or should only be taxed to the extent that the taxpayer is in a higher tax bracket than the corporation. There are a variety of ways of achieving integration. One of them is the proposed flat tax, which separates individual income tax from all kinds of business income, including proprietorships, partnerships, and corporations, which are taxed separately with a parallel business tax.

Full integration assumes that all stockholders are individual taxpayers. A significant amount of corporate stock is held by entities that either pay no taxes or can defer taxes for very long periods of time. The former group includes schools and colleges with endowments, foundations, and charitable organizations of various kinds. The latter includes pension funds, tax-deferred annuities, and Individual Retirement Accounts. For these stockholders, there is no issue of double taxation of either dividends or capital gains, because they do not pay any individual income tax.

The case for the corporate income tax

There are some valid arguments for taxing corporate net income. One is a matter of convenience. Tax collectors need "tax handles"—visible flows of funds, assets, transactions as something to latch onto that provides a measure of ability to pay. Corporate net income, which must be disclosed to stockholders each year, is a good tax handle.

A second reason is that corporations benefit from government services ranging from fire and police protection to transportation systems, educational services, and various kinds of infrastructure. The corporate income tax can be regarded as a way to make corporations pay some or all of the cost of these inputs into production.

The problem with this second argument is that there is a weak link between the value of services received and the corporation's net income or profit. Firms that use substantial amounts of public services but generate no profit contribute nothing toward the cost of these services, while highly profitable firms contribute heavily even if they use very few services. Fees for services are often a more equitable and effective way of "billing" firms of all kinds for the services that they consume.

A third argument is that taxation of corporate income or profit adds a degree of progressivity to the overall tax system, because shareholders come from the upper end of the income spectrum. Closely related is the argument that if this tax is indeed a tax on capital, it helps to counterbalance any burden of the Social Security payroll tax (see below) that falls on the employer rather than the employee. Absent a tax on capital, the firm may have an inefficiently strong incentive to substitute capital for labor.

Fourth, opposition to the corporate income tax is based on an unrealistic assumption of highly competitive markets. Many corporations enjoy some degree of market power. Some of their net income may be monopoly profit. Unlike normal profit, which is just enough to keep the owners' capital invested in the business, or temporary profit, which serves as a signal to expand output and a reward for a fast response, monopoly profit serves no socially useful function. Taxing monopoly profit is attractive from the efficiency standpoint (no undesirable changes in economic behavior) as well as equity (since firms with monopoly power are generally owned by higher-income individuals).

Finally, while dividends are taxed in the year that they are distributed, capital gains are another matter. If there were no corporate income tax, then, under the present system, capital gains that result from reinvesting retained earnings would not be taxed under the individual income tax until they were distributed as dividends (which might never happen) or the shareholder realized the gains by selling the stock. There are unlimited possibilities for deferring this income, perhaps until death, when it might never be taxed unless the estate is very large. The corporate income tax makes sure that a substantial annual flow of income is taxed in the year when it is earned, rather than after long delays, or in some cases, not at all.

Social Security taxes

Social Security taxes are simple (but not uncontroversial). They are part of a broader category called payroll taxes that involve only wages and salaries (including self-employment income). This category also includes many local income taxes that are levied only on payroll. Employer and employee each pay 7.65 percent of wages and salaries up to a maximum ($106,800 in 2010). Self-employed persons pay both parts, but with an income tax adjustment to cover the employer part. Of this amount, 1.45 percent for both employer and employee goes to the Medicare trust fund, and the remaining 6.2 percent goes to the OASDI (Old Age, Survivors', and Disability Insurance) trust funds. The Medicare tax also applies to income above the maximum. Again, self-employed persons pay the combined employer/employee rates but receive certain adjustments on their individual income tax returns.

Because the tax is only on wages and cuts off at an income ceiling, the Social Security tax is moderately regressive. (Other payroll taxes at flat rates are also regressive because they exclude income from investments, which tends to accrue mostly to higher income households.) It is not a pure tax, nor is it a pure insurance premium, although it does take payments for a specified number of quarters to be eligible for benefits and the value of the benefits is somewhat related to the level of contributions.

The trust funds have been a source of great controversy in the past two decades. These trust funds have been running large surpluses, with taxes and interest earnings greatly outdistancing payments to retirees, disabled workers and survivors. The surplus is invested in Treasury bonds, which finance part of the deficit in the regular budget. At some point in the distant future the balance in the trust funds will be exhausted, and the Social Security system will not be able to continue paying benefits at current (inflation-adjusted) levels. These issues are discussed in more detail in Chapter 19.

Summary

- Income taxes. including individual and corporate income taxes and Social Security payroll taxes, account for almost all US federal government revenues and a substantial share of state and local government revenues. Income taxes can be customized to improve equity in income distribution and to address other social goals.
- Income tax design must define what constitutes income and which kinds of income should be subject to the tax. Defining income involves not only equity issues but also tradeoffs between a broad base and low rates on the one hand and costs of collection and compliance on the other.
- The primary efficiency issue with a broad-based income tax is distorting the income–leisure choice. Most efficiency issues result from adjustments, exemptions and deductions that encourage taxpayers to rearrange their economic choices so as to minimize their tax burdens. The US federal income tax has low collection costs but high compliance costs for taxpayers.
- The flat tax movement advocates radical simplification of the income tax in order to reduce compliance cost and reduce distortion, but would also make the tax much less progressive.
- Attempting to create horizontal equity with equal tax burdens for people in equal economic situations makes the income tax more complex. Vertical equity is addressed by exempting a base amount and a progressive rate structure.
- Income tax liability starts with gross income for tax purposes, which excludes certain categories of income and costs of earning income to arrive at adjusted gross. Subtracting exemptions and itemized or standard deduction gives taxable income, the basis on which tax liability is computed. This tax liability is then adjusted for tax credits and additional taxes due (e.g., self-employment tax). The difference between this figure and tax already paid through withholding or estimated tax is tax or refund due.
- The federal income tax system relies heavily on voluntary compliance, with the "incentive" of being audited if a return shows evidence of misrepresentation. The audit rate is low, but the penalties can be substantial.
- The gradualist school of tax reform recommends adjusting problem areas such as the treatment of capital gains and employee fringe benefits. The alternative is a major structural change, moving toward the flat tax or some kind of consumption tax.
- Forty-one state governments and more than 4,000 local governments also levy income taxes. Most state income taxes are tied to either federal adjusted gross income or federal taxable income as a starting point. Some calculate state income tax due as a percentage of federal income tax liability. A few states operate completely independent systems. Deductibility of state income taxes on the federal income tax reduces the progressivity of the tax system.
- Corporations pay a separate tax on corporate net income or corporate profits. One major problem with the corporate income tax is defining allowable expenses. Contentious areas include treatment of depreciation and consumption spending for managers and/or employees. A second problem is double taxation and integration of the individual and corporate income tax. A third challenge is the incentive to rely more heavily on debt than equity financing because interest expenditures are tax-deductible. A fourth challenge is the international competitive effects on location of business activity and corporate headquarters.

- In the short run the incidence of the corporate income tax is on capital or shareholders, but in the long run part of the burden may fall on workers or consumers of products of the corporate sector.
- Arguments for the corporate income tax include convenience of collection, progressivity, use of government services by firms, monopoly power, and the use of corporations to avoid or defer paying taxes on unrealized capital gains.
- Social Security payroll taxes are mildly regressive and a significant revenue source for the federal government.

Key terms

Accelerated depreciation
Adjusted gross income
Average tax rate (income)
Corporate income tax
Exclusions
Exemptions
Flat tax
Individual income tax
Marginal tax rate (income)
Payroll tax
Social Security tax
Standard/itemized deductions
Tax avoidance
Tax credit
Tax evasion
Taxable income

Questions

1   What steps could be taken to make the federal individual income tax more progressive? Less progressive? What advantages does the income tax have over other taxes in terms of attaining a desired degree of progressivity?

2   Evaluate the flat tax in terms of efficiency, equity, and compliance/collection costs.

3   Taxes affect not only primary markets but also related markets. If the corporate income tax is a tax on capital in the corporate sector, use a diagram to describe the effects on (a) demand for labor in the corporate sector, and (b) the cost of capital in the non-corporate sector.

4   Use the standard microeconomic model of monopoly (cost curves, demand, and marginal revenue) to analyze the effect of a percentage tax on corporate profits on the monopolistic firm's output level and the price of the product.

5   **By the numbers**. For an average four-person household in the United States, the 2010 combined standard deduction and personal exemptions came to $26,000. Assume that there are no progressive rates, just a flat tax of 20 percent of income. (This tax is similar to the flat tax proposal described in the chapter.) To show the progressivity, create a table that shows the tax liability in dollars and as a percentage of income for gross incomes of:

$25,000
$50,000
$75,000
$100,000
$150,000
$200,000
$400,000
$1,000,000

Graph your results.

6   **Policy application**. Suppose that you as an economist are asked to evaluate a proposed state tax provision to exempt the first $20,000 of retirement income for anyone over age 65 from the state income tax. The estimated revenue loss from this provision is $85 million in the first year. In the future, the revenue loss will rise only with the growth in the elderly population since the $20,000 exemption is not indexed for inflation. Evaluate this proposal in terms of equity, efficiency, and other criteria set forth in Chapters 11 and 12.

7   **Behavioral economics**. Firms are more likely to behave like *Homo economicus* than individuals in response to taxes. Consider the differences you might expect to see in tax-responsive behavior between firms and individuals in location decisions, borrowing, and concealing income from the IRS. What role do motivation and limitations on information acquisition and processing (cognition) play in each case?

8   **Thinking globally**. Most other countries that are similar to the United States in size and development rely on a more balanced range of central government revenues that include taxes on sales or consumption as well as income taxes. What are the advantages and drawbacks of the United States relying so heavily on income taxes?

14 Taxes on sales and consumption

Introduction

Sales taxes lack the drama of the annual income tax return or the shock effect of the annual property tax bill. Every trip to the store, every impulse purchase, every stop at the pump to tank up the car generates a few cents of federal or state excise taxes or state and local retail sales taxes. The sales tax always is ranked number one in popularity (or more accurately, least unpopular) when compared in polls with the income and property tax. Why? Perhaps it's the fact that sales taxes are relatively painless; they are extracted on a daily basis in very small sums. Economists may prefer that taxes be visible, but taxpayers seem to prefer those taxes that are less obvious.

While income taxes are the mainstay of the federal government in the United States, sales taxes are the top-ranking source of state revenue. Federal excise taxes and some limited tariffs on imports (both sales taxes) contribute less than 10 percent of federal tax revenue. These taxes (including gasoline, alcoholic beverage, tobacco, air transportation and telephone taxes) are the remnants of a federal revenue system in the eighteenth and nineteenth centuries that relied almost exclusively on excise taxes, tariffs on imports, and public land sales to finance the central government.

In the last half of the twentieth century, a large number of other countries adopted some form of the value-added tax (discussed later in this chapter), as the primary form of central government revenue, including most of Europe, South America, Africa, Canada and Mexico. So the US system in which sales taxes are used heavily at the state and local level but very little at the national level is very different from most of the rest of the world.

State sales taxes of various kinds, mostly retail sales, accounted for 34 percent of state own-source general revenue in 2007. (The share is higher in those states with no broad-based income taxes.) At the local level, retail sales taxes and/or excise taxes are used by more than 7,500 cities and towns, counties, townships and parishes, school districts, and special districts. For these governments, most of which rely heavily on property taxes, sales taxes generated 22 percent of own source revenue in 2007.

Why tax sales?

Sales or transactions are taxed for both theoretical and practical reasons. The most important practical reason is that transactions provide a "tax handle," consisting of an activity (buying and selling) in which a value is established on which to base the tax, as well as two parties (buyer and seller) who each provide a cross-check on the reporting of the other. The oldest form of sales tax is probably the tariff, a tax on goods entering the port or the city from abroad. Where there were limited points of entry—airports, docks, city gates—that narrow funnel through which goods must pass created an opportunity for tax collectors to gather and levy the tax with relative ease.

As the number of buyers, sellers, and locations grows, however, the sales tax becomes more difficult to administer. The growth of first mail-order and later internet commerce has posed some serious challenges to the state and local retail sales tax in this country. Most states do not attempt to include all retail transactions in their base because of the compliance and collections costs of extracting revenue from sporadic sellers or very small retailers. However, sales and transactions, with all their limitations, still offer one of the most visible and accessible tax handles.

A second reason for taxing sales is that consumption spending, along with ownership of assets and income, is a measure of ability to pay taxes. The more one spends, presumably, the more taxpaying capacity one has. It is easier to conceal income from the tax collector than it is to conceal purchases. So a sales tax is a way of extracting a contribution to the public treasury from those who are engaging in either legal tax avoidance (by the form in which they get their income) or illegal but undetected tax evasion.

A third reason for taxing sales is particularly important at the state and local level. This tax offers a way of capturing revenue from commuters, tourists, and business travelers who use the public services provided by state and local governments. The sales tax is highly exportable for states that are major travel destinations and for cities that attract large numbers of nonresident commuters and shoppers during the day.

Retail sales taxes, the most common form of sales tax in the United States, are relatively responsive to short-run cyclical changes in income, less so to longer-term growth. Thus, states that rely heavily on sales taxes need to complement them with other revenue sources that have higher long-run income elasticities.

Behavioral economics: the preference for sales taxation

According to a series of Gallup polls in the United States, the sales tax consistently beats the local property tax and the federal income tax in perceived fairness. Those responding that the sales tax was the least fair ranged from 12–17 percent of those polled over a period of 16 years, while the property tax was rated least fair by 24–42 percent of respondents, and the federal income tax was considered least fair by 20–27 percent of respondents.

One reason for this ranking is that the sales tax is lower in visibility than the other two. Property tax bills come once a year. Income tax is a major headache to file every spring. But sales taxes are just quietly added to the bill in small daily amounts. People also feel that they have more of a choice about paying the sales tax than the property tax or the income tax. Once they own a home, they are at the mercy of local governments when the property tax rate or the assessed value of the property goes up. The average family doesn't have a lot of options to reduce its income tax burden. But the sales tax burden can be controlled by buying less, shopping on the internet or across state lines, or shifting consumption to those items that are not taxed. So when state and local governments got into fiscal difficulties in the first few years of this century, many of them turned to sales taxes to help fill the budget gap.

Sales taxes have their drawbacks. They are expensive to collect, and compliance costs are high, especially for small sellers. They are regressive. Revenue tends to lag behind growth of personal income, so they are not dependable, especially in the short run. But these drawbacks don't impact directly on the individual consumer. The combination of low visibility and a sense of control or choice frames the sales tax in a way that makes it very appealing, or at least a lot less unappealing, to the average citizen.

Sales taxes, value-added taxes, and excise taxes

The variety of taxes on consumption or transactions is almost endless, but there are only three basic types in widespread use today; the **retail sales tax** (or sometimes the wholesale tax), the **value-added tax**, and selective sales taxes on specific items, such as gasoline, automobile tires, or cigarettes, known as **excise taxes**. Tariffs are a special form of excise tax that apply only to imported goods.

There are several ways of sorting the various kinds of sales taxes. One grouping is to sort into multistage or single stage. Tariffs, excise taxes, some kinds of wholesale taxes, and retail sales taxes are single stage. The value-added tax and its predecessor, the cascade tax (*Umsatzsteuer* in German) are multi-stage taxes.

A second way to classify the tax is by the breadth of the base. A universal base of all sales or purchases (value-added taxes come close) would represent one extreme, while excise taxes or tariffs on specific items would represent the opposite end of the spectrum. Retail sales taxes are closer to the universal end of the spectrum, but the breadth of coverage varies greatly from one jurisdiction to another.

A third classification would be on the basis of who is legally liable to pay the tax, which often bears little relationship to actual economic incidence. Retail sales taxes and their companion use taxes (for goods and services purchased by residents outside the state) in the United States are an obligation of the buyer, although in practice they are collected mostly by the seller. Value-added taxes in most countries are an obligation of the seller.

When goods are sold to nonresidents, the value-added tax of the sending jurisdiction is rebated at export and the value-added tax of the receiving jurisdiction is imposed at import. This practice not only implements the destination principle but also ensures a level playing field (nondistortion of choice) between domestic and imported goods.

Tariffs are generally levied on the importer, excise taxes on the seller in most cases. The distinction is particularly important to tax collectors when there are multiple competing jurisdictions with different rates and coverage, because someone must decide which jurisdiction gets to collect the revenue and impose its tax rules.

Efficiency issues in sales taxation

A primary objection to sales taxation is that this sales tax tends to erode its own base over time, particularly if the base of the tax is anything less than total consumption or the tax rates are very different in adjacent jurisdictions. There are a variety of ways in which to legally avoid the sales tax or reduce the amount paid, particularly in the long run. One is to shop in markets where the tax is lower or nonexistent. In the United States, there are five states with no sales taxes and other states where certain items are exempt that are not widely exempt elsewhere, like clothing in Pennsylvania. There are stores that will (legally) waive the state and local sales tax on items being shipped out of state. And, of course, there is a large volume of mail order and cross-border transactions that escape the tax because Congress has not yet addressed the issue of letting states compel out-of-state firms to collect tax on their behalf.

Yet another way to avoid the sales tax is to shift purchases from taxed to exempt items—buy more food and less clothing in states where food is exempt and clothing is not, more services and fewer tangible goods in almost every state. Adding to the erosion of the base by the action of buyers is the tendency of state legislatures to add exemptions and exclusions. Among the more popular exclusions for equity reasons are prescription drugs, food, and purchases by charitable organizations. All these exemptions and others may have strong equity justifications, but they must also be evaluated as tax expenditures that reduce revenue and further distort consumer choices.

Shifting between markets

Figure 14.1 illustrates a simple case of shifting purchases between taxed and untaxed markets as a result of a tax in one market (which might be a state or a city). Remember, another geographic location is a form of substitute just as another local seller or another product can be a substitute.

To minimize complications, assume perfectly elastic supply and a tax that is fixed in terms of physical units (e.g., 2 cents a gallon for gasoline). The price, P_0, is initially the same in both markets in equilibrium. It is also assumed that some buyers are willing and able to shift to other markets relatively costlessly by mail order, internet, or travel, while others lack the information or flexibility to shop outside the local market even with enough time to adjust. Consequently demand declines in the taxed market but does not shift entirely to the untaxed market.

What is the effect of the tax in the two markets? Initial revenue in the first market from a tax per unit of $P_T–P_0$ is rectangle $P_T P_0 ab$. However, once consumers have had the opportunity to adjust, the base of the tax declines from Q_1 to Q_2 and revenue drops to rectangle $P_T P_0 dc$.[1] In the untaxed market, of course, sales increase, although no tax revenue is generated.

This ability to shift purchases between taxed and untaxed markets, or between taxed and untaxed consumption, is the primary source of base erosion. The broader the coverage of the tax in terms of both geographic extent and variety of purchases subject to the tax, the less base erosion there will be.

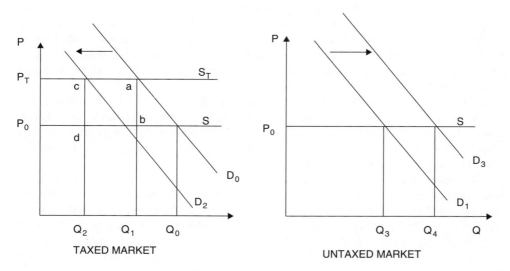

TAXED MARKET   UNTAXED MARKET

Figure 14.1 Tax base erosion with an excise tax.

Avoiding cascading

Another efficiency issue in sales or consumption taxes is to ensure that that taxes do not accumulate so that some items are taxed only once and others two or more times, resulting in different tax burdens on different purchases and an unintended distortion of consumer choice. Some earlier forms of sales taxes, still in use in a few less developed countries, collected sales taxes at multiple points during the processing of a good (or service) from one stage of production to another. Wheat sold by the farmer would be taxed, again as flour when sold by the miller, again as bread when sold by the baker to the retailer, again when the final customer bought the bread at the grocery store. The tax burden on each good depended less on the tax rate than the number of times it changed hands and caught the attention of the tax collector!

For example, assume that in the absence of the tax, the wheat sold for $1, the flour for $2, and the bread for $3 wholesale and $4 retail. Ignoring any reduction in sales that might result from the tax and assuming that all taxes are shifted forward to the buyer, what would be the effect of a 10 percent tax? The wheat would sell for $1.10, and the flour for $2.21. The wholesale price of bread would rise to $3.53, and the retail price to $4.98. With no change in the net revenue to sellers, and a 10 percent tax rate, the price of bread will have risen by almost 25 percent!

An integrated operation, however, that owned its own wheat farm and flour mill and sold directly to consumers would be taxed only once, so that its bread would sell for $4.40, a true 10 percent tax. Clearly such a tax has the potential to create large and unintended changes in consumer decisions in response to very uneven tax burdens on different goods or different producers/sellers.

Germany and the Netherlands had such **cascade-type taxes** when they joined the European Community (now the European Union) in the late 1950s, but by 1968 they had replaced these taxes with a value-added tax (see below). With the support and encouragement of the World Bank, and the example of the European Union's success with the value-added tax (VAT), most of the nations using cascade taxes have replaced them with VATs or some other, less distorting form of sales tax.

The retail sales tax is collected at the point of final sale from retailer or distributor to the final consumer. Ideally, each item would be taxed once and only once. One reason for using a single stage tax (either wholesale or retail) is to avoid cascading or accumulation of tax on tax. However, cascading can occur in a nominally single-stage tax like the retail sales tax if some business purchases at the taxable stage are incorporated into products or services also subject to the tax.

One source of cascading in a single stage tax is the fact that many items are purchased both by business firms and individuals. When a bakery buys flour, flour should not be taxed, because there will be a tax at retail on the consumer's purchase of the loaf of bread. When a household buys flour with which to bake its own bread, it is truly a final sale and should be subject to tax (unless, of course, food is exempt).

Office equipment, tools, office supplies, packaging materials, and software are just a few of the many items that are sold to both business firms and households. If the business firm must pay retail sales tax on its inputs, that tax is reflected in the selling price, and the retail sales tax on the final purchase is compounded by the tax at this earlier stage of processing. If the final product is tax exempt (e.g., a lawyer buys software and office supplies, but her services are typically not subject to retail sales tax), then the intent of the tax code to exempt legal services from the retail sales tax is not being fully realized.

How substantial is this problem of cascading with the US retail sales tax? According to economist Raymond Ring, the share of the sales tax falling on business purchases varies greatly from state to state, with an average of 41 percent and a range from only 11 percent in West Virginia to 72 percent in Hawaii where most services (including business services) are subject to sales tax (Ring 1999: 79ff.). In states where business purchases are heavily subject to sales tax, cascading can be a significant problem.

On the other hand, a case can be made on both efficiency and equity grounds for some amount of the sales tax in the state of origin being reflected in the price of the good and passed forward to consumers wherever they live. To the extent that such sales taxes are used to pay for public services that benefit producers, these firms are purchasing inputs into the production process that might properly be considered a cost of production—for example, paying for the fire and police service that protects the plant or the roads on which raw materials and final products are transported. Unfortunately, there is rarely any close connection between the amount of sales tax paid on inputs and the amount of public services consumed by the firm.

Making sales taxes more equitable

The primary objection to sales taxes is that they tend to be regressive, except for certain excise taxes on luxury goods. A broad-based tax on sales or consumption, whether a value-added tax, a wholesale tax, or a retail tax, excludes saving by definition. Since saving rises with income (higher-income households save a substantially greater fraction of their incomes) consumption and sales tax burden on that consumption become a smaller fraction of income as income rises.

Given the popularity of sales taxes (at least in comparison to income and property taxes), what can be done to make them less regressive? There are four strategies, described here in the context of US state retail sales taxes but also applicable to other kinds of broad-based sales taxes:

1   Broadening the base, primarily by including some services, to keep the rate low and include more of the consumption spending of higher-income households.
2   Narrowing the base by eliminating consumption that represents a large fraction of income for lower-income households (especially food).
3   Fine-tuning the retail, wholesale, or value-added sales tax with excise taxes or differential rates on certain items that are consumed more heavily by upper-income classes (e.g., luxury taxes, admissions and amusements taxes, travel and tourism taxes).
4   Rebating some of the sales tax through means-tested income tax relief.

Broaden the base

A few states have sales taxes that cover a substantial number of services, most notably Hawaii, New Mexico, and South Dakota. In recent years, a number of other states have explored the expansion of their retail sales tax base to include more services. Including services makes a retail sales tax or VAT less regressive, because the consumption of services tends to rise with increases in income. Broadening the base also makes it possible to raise the same amount of revenue with a lower tax rate.

Services most commonly covered by state retail sales taxes include transient housing (motels, hotels, resort villas, etc.), personal services such as massages and hair care, transport services such as auto rentals, and miscellaneous household services such as auto repair, dry cleaning, and lawn care. However, broad coverage of services has been difficult to achieve in most states.

In 1995, Florida approved a major expansion of its sales tax base that included legal services, advertising services, and a variety of other personal and business services. Within six months, the governor and the legislature were forced by political pressure to rescind these changes.

Part of the problem in Florida was the power of an organized lobby, led by lawyers and fueled by the power of advertising when both legal services and advertising were targets for taxation. But there are more fundamental challenges to taxing services. Services are more likely to be produced and sold by very small firms, greatly increasing the collection costs for the state and compliance costs for firms. While many states have some services in their retail sales tax bases, the tax still falls primarily on tangible goods.

Narrow the base

The alternative strategy to make a sales tax less regressive is to exempt certain items. For most low-income families, the biggest item in the budget is housing (rent), which as a service is exempt in most states. Among tangible goods, the most common exemption is food.

The food exemption is appealing, but difficult to administer because of the challenge of defining food. Does cat or dog food qualify? Do the tax writers mean to exempt caviar? What about alcoholic beverages? Does it cover everything purchased in the grocery store, which is likely to include toilet paper, toothpaste, and the *National Enquirer*? Cash registers must be programmed to distinguish between taxable and nontaxable items, which increases both collection and compliance costs. (Some states have resolved this problem by defining food as anything eligible to be purchased with food stamps, for which most cash registers are already programmed.)

The food exemption significantly reduces the base of the tax and makes the revenue less stable. In addition, the food tax exemption suffers the usual problem of tax expenditures in terms of not targeting a particular group very efficiently. Exempting food is a rather inefficient mechanism if the intent is to reach only the poor. Remember that 85 percent of the population is not poor, yet their food purchases are also exempt!

Despite these drawbacks, two-thirds of the states with sales taxes now exempt food, and there is pressure in the remaining states to follow their example. Louisiana, Georgia, and North and South Carolina are the most recent states to adopt a partial or total exemption of food. Food is also commonly exempt (zero-rated is the preferred term) in many value-added taxes in other countries for the same reasons.

Other widely-used exemptions that are intended to reduce regressivity are utilities (electricity, gas, water), prescription drugs, and in a few states, clothing. The clothing exemption (almost always restricted by price or to children's clothing) is somewhat questionable as a technique to make the tax less regressive.

Impose excise taxes on luxuries

A third tactic for improving the equity of the retail, wholesale, or value-added sales tax is to impose an excise tax or differential tax rates on certain items that are consumed more heavily by upper-income households. In the past, these taxes have been used for that purpose at the federal level in the United States, with excise taxes on jewelry and leather goods as well as airline tickets.

Most states have admissions and amusements taxes, sometimes at the same rate as the sales tax, sometimes higher, but in either case marking a relatively rare expansion into taxing services. The reasonable presumption is that attending concerts, plays, and sporting events is an expenditure of discretionary income more likely to be found in middle to upper-income households. Likewise, travel taxes (on airline departures, motel accommodations, and restaurant meals) at rates usually higher than the retail sales tax offer both a way to impose taxes on nonresidents (tax exporting) and an extension of sales taxes into services consumed primarily by higher income households.

Rebates

Seven states operate a rebate program for part of the sales tax, usually subject to an income limit, as a way to provide relief for lower-income households. Four states—Hawaii, Idaho, New Mexico, and Vermont—offer a rebate through the personal income tax, while three others (Kansas, South Dakota, and Wyoming) operate the refund separately. In some cases the rebate is only to reimburse for sales taxes on food.

This approach has the advantage of targeting low-income households and thus sacrifices less revenue than the tax expenditure approach of exempting food or other items heavily consumed by lower-income households. It can be used in combination with the other three strategies to significantly reduce the regressivity of a broad-based retail sales tax, such as most states use in the United States.

State retail sales taxes in the United States

The most important sales tax in the United States in terms of revenue is the state retail sales tax. This tax is a single-stage tax on final sales, primarily to consumers. While states vary greatly in how they design and administer the tax, the similarities outweigh the differences, so for practical purposes they can be grouped together in terms of structure, history, and evaluations.

Efficiency issues

In addition to the general efficiency issues associated with all types of sales taxes, retail sales taxes have their own particular challenges. The retail sales tax can be administered as either an origin principle tax or a destination principle tax, as discussed in Chapter 12. Arguments can be offered for either approach, but the fact that the incidence of a broad-based retail sales tax falls mainly on the consumer supports the choice of a destination principle, so that the person actually paying the tax will be consuming the public services that those taxes support.

The US retail sales tax is primarily a destination principle tax with some notable exceptions. Tourists and business travelers pay state and local taxes in the places where they travel, not those of their home states. Many purchasers by mail order and internet have been able to avoid sales and use taxes altogether because of the difficulty of collecting from the final consumer rather than the retail seller. The gap between taxable sales and actual revenue generated represents not only a revenue loss but an efficiency challenge distorting consumer choice in the direction of those sellers who are able to avoid collecting the tax. This gap, and its growth with the development of e-commerce, represent a serious threat to the revenue base of the retail sales tax in the future. A report by the General Accountability Office estimated the revenue loss from these two sources in a range from $2.5–$20.4 billion for 2003 (U.S. General Accountability Office 2000: 36).

The fact that the base of the retail sales tax is less than 100 percent of consumption is also a source of distortion in consumer decisions. The incomplete coverage raises the after-tax price of some items relative to others, encouraging consumers to shift their consumption over time to untaxed items such as food (in about 70 percent of states) and many services as well as to out-of-state retailers through mail order and internet purchases.

Retail sales taxes can also distort locational decisions for not only commercial facilities (often located near state lines to attract buyers from higher-tax nearby states) but also industrial firms, because some states tax a wider range of business purchases than others. For firms that buy a large quantity of materials and supplies that are taxable in some states and not in others, there is an incentive to locate their facilities—or at least their purchasing departments!—to states that offer the most attractive tax situation.

Equity issues

Regressivity is the primary equity issue for most kinds of broad-based sales or consumption taxes, but the retail sales tax has some specific equity challenges as it operates in the United States. The failure to tax most services in most states is an equity as well as an efficiency issue inasmuch as inclusion of services makes the tax less regressive.

The destination principle creates serious challenges for tax administrators in collecting sales or use tax on a large share of sales by mail order and/or internet, which often escape taxation in either the state of origin or the state of destination. This loophole discriminates among consumers on the basis of the way they choose to shop. Since the internet and mail-order methods tend to appeal to more sophisticated buyers, it is likely that failure to tax a large share of mail order and internet sales makes the sales tax more regressive.

Excise taxes

Excise taxes are imposed at all levels of government. The drawback of a specific tax is that revenue only grows with population and sometimes income, but not with inflation.

An excise or selective sales tax is imposed on named goods, such as the tax per gallon of gasoline or pack of cigarettes. Many excise taxes are specific, i.e., stated in terms of the physical units (so many cents per gallon or pack), while others are ad valorem, expressed as a percentage of the price.

Ad valorem taxes increase not only as more units are sold but also as the price per unit goes up. A specific tax can be represented with a parallel demand or supply curve, while an ad valorem tax results in a steeper slope on the shadow demand or supply curve. The most common excise taxes in the United States are levied on gasoline, cigarettes, and distilled liquor by both federal and state governments.

The rate and the base

Figure 14.2 shows an excise tax on gasoline that is expressed as a percentage of the price. Demand for gasoline is relatively price-inelastic in the short run, since it has few good substitutes for most of its uses (driving cars and trucks and running lawn mowers and motorboats). Supply is moderately elastic since petroleum can be converted between its multiple uses depending on the price that can be obtained for each end product (gasoline, heating oil, plastics, fertilizer, etc.).

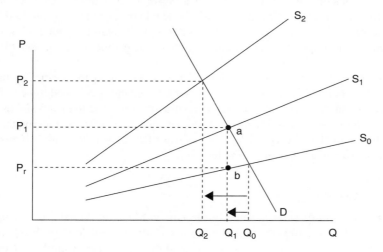

Figure 14.2 An excise tax on gasoline.

In this situation, the tax (the vertical distance between S_0 and S_1) will be shown up primarily as an increase in the price paid by the buyer, and there will be only a modest reduction in the tax base from Q_0 to Q_1. Tax revenue will be equal to P_rP_1ab. However, further increases in the tax (such as that represented by shadow supply curve S_2) will push buyers into the more elastic range of the demand curve.

As the tax rate escalates, both the absolute and percentage decline in Q accelerates also (and so does the excess burden or deadweight loss). That is, an increasingly larger increase in the tax rate is required to generate the same increase in revenue (or the same increase in the rate will generate less revenue) because of **base erosion**. Rate and base relationships always offer a challenging tradeoff for tax policy of any kind, but particularly so for excise taxes, because the base is already narrowly defined.

Goals of excise taxation

Excise taxes serve multiple purposes. One is revenue. A second purpose is to tax items consumed more heavily by upper-income groups, in order to offset the regressivity of a general sales tax at the wholesale or retail level. A third goal is to discourage consumption of goods or services as a way of reducing negative externalities (**sumptuary taxes**). In fact, many excise taxes are known as "sin" taxes because they are levied on alcohol, cigarettes, and casino games at least in part to discourage drinking, smoking, and gambling. In addition to the effect on price, the tax or tax increase sends a signal of social disapproval for those activities.

These goals are not always consistent. Revenue and equity goals call for collecting more tax, while sumptuary goals are aimed at shrinking the base. However, governments can regard excise taxes on activities that are socially undesirable as a win–win situation. If people cut back on smoking, drinking, or gambling, they reduce the associated health and social problems related to those activities. If they continue their "bad habits," the government receives more revenue.

However, there are limits on the usefulness of taxes as a way to discourage consumption. If the tax rate gets too high, it may be worth it to risk the legal consequences to supply this demand through the black (illegal) market. From bathtub gin to cigarette bootlegging to illegal numbers games, citizens have always found ways to evade excise taxes imposed "for their own good."

Some excise taxes, like the tax on airline tickets, are not intended to discourage the activity. Instead, the tax is levied on a luxury good for which demand is believed to be relatively price-inelastic, so that the base will not shrink too much in response to the tax. Recall, however, that demand for most commodities and services is more elastic in the long run than in the short run, so that a tax that is very productive in terms of revenue in the short run may erode the tax base and reduce tax revenue in the long run.

Case study: taxes on gambling

An increasingly popular form of state revenue in the United States in the last part of the twentieth century was to legalize and tax gambling in various forms. State lotteries had been banished after scandals in the late nineteenth century and did not reappear until the New Hampshire lottery in 1964, with a slow spread that picked up speed in the 1980s and 1990s. Thirty-seven states operate lotteries, with the state retaining from 25–50 percent of gross lottery revenues. However, lotteries are a relatively modest source of state revenue, typically producing 1–4 percent of own-source revenues.

Most gambling was privately run with state regulation and taxation. Atlantic City and Mississippi, along with a number of Indian tribes, found a gold mine in casino gambling. Indian gambling, authorized under certain rules by 1988 Federal legislation, is not a substantial source of state revenue, although some states (notably Connecticut) have negotiated mutually beneficial agreements with their recognized Native American tribes for sharing some of the revenue. More often, Indian-sponsored gambling has been in competition with other gambling-based sources of state revenue, such as state lotteries, taxes on bingo, casinos, or free-standing video machines in six states.

States along the Mississippi River have turned to riverboat gambling. Betting on horse and dog racing is a long-standing source of revenue for some states, including Florida and Connecticut. Almost every state that has some kind of legal gambling other than a state lottery also has a regulatory authority (typically a Gaming Commission) responsible for regulating the industry in order to protect consumers, limit access by minors, and generate revenue for the state.

Like other activities with negative externalities that are subject to excise taxes, gambling challenges governments to order their priorities. Is the goal of gambling regulation consumer protection? Or is it to discourage people from gambling, especially minors, because a minority of gamblers become habitual or compulsive or even addicted gamblers? Or is it an easy and somewhat painless source of revenue that makes it possible to fund better services without higher taxes? If it is all three, how are those conflicting goals balanced? Taxes on alcohol and cigarettes may suggest a win–win situation for states—either people continue to use these products and generate revenue or they reduce their consumption and live healthier lives. But gambling is a little different, because it poses no direct risk to physical well-being.

Governments that sponsor lotteries are torn between the pressure to restrict an activity that is potentially addictive and socially destructive and the attraction of the revenue that lotteries can provide. Often the focal point of that conflict of goals comes down to the amount of effort that should be made in marketing, advertising and promotion of the lottery, crossing the line from permitting gambling to encouraging it. Governments that allow casinos have used revenues to provide valued public services and relieve pressure on taxes but also recognize that they are not only encouraging undesirable behavior but also attracting an industry with a high proportion of low-wage, dead-end jobs.

There are no easy answers to these questions. The gambling phenomenon is not just American, but world-wide, both in lotteries, in traditional forms of gambling (casinos, sports betting, card rooms, slot machines) and in newer electronic forms, including video gambling and internet casinos. Gambling revenue has a strong appeal to politicians looking to ease the pain of paying for public services, but the social and economic price tag may be higher than they were betting on in the longer term.

Case study: taxing the tourist

In general, tax exporting to residents of other states or countries as a way of easing the burden of taxation has limited potential for providing one's own citizens with tax relief. One exception is taxing tourists, a practice at which states and nations have become increasingly creative. Local sales taxes in tourist destinations are one technique, but it is more effective to target those activities and services used primarily by travelers in order to shift a share of the burden to out-of-staters or foreigners. Of course, it is impossible to totally exempt a state's or nation's own residents, who do travel within as well as beyond the borders!

Taxing transient accommodations (hotels and motels) and rentals, rental cars, airport parking, airport and cruise ship departures, admissions, amusements, downtown parking, restaurant meals, and gambling are all ways to target visitors. Since most of these items (excepting gambling outside casinos) are consumed largely by upper-income groups, the part of the tax that does fall on in-state residents contributes to reducing the regressivity of sales taxes within the state.

There is a risk in pushing tourism taxes too hard. Like most services, tourist services are in a highly competitive and price-sensitive industry. Taxes can make prices too high relative to other almost equally attractive destinations at home or abroad, so tax officials have to keep an eye on the competition and set their rates accordingly. Over time, travelers may respond to the higher total cost including tax by shifting to cheaper ways of getting around. They may drive their own cars instead of flying and renting, stay with friends and relatives, camp or stay in places with cooking facilities to avoid eating out, or find other economy methods that reduce the yield of the tax.

But some localities provide access to unique desirable features, such as breathtaking scenery, long stretches of unspoiled ocean beaches, tropical forests, or whitewater rivers for rafters. These communities may enjoy enough monopoly power in the possession of their unique tourism assets to make demand relatively price-inelastic. In that case, tourism taxes could be somewhat higher than those of the nearest substitute destination without substantially eroding the tax base.

While tourism taxes get fairly high marks for equity and moderate to low ratings on efficiency, they have other drawbacks. Tourism is a very cyclically sensitive industry, so tourism taxes fluctuate much more than total economic activity, which makes them a rather undependable revenue source. As a local tax (a fairly common assignment), the revenue potential is distributed very unevenly among counties and municipalities within a given state, and often it is the wealthier communities in resort areas that have the most revenue potential even though the revenue needs are greater in other parts of the state.

The tourism industry (owners of tourist accommodations and facilities and providers of travel services) has lobbied heavily to either limit tourism taxes or earmark the revenue for tourism promotion and tourism-related services. While economists are generally skeptical about earmarking revenues, often it is the only way to appease the affected business interests.

Beyond the public choice aspects of earmarking, however, are some equity and efficiency considerations that might make earmarking less harmful. First, the use of the revenue to provide the additional local services (garbage pickup, police and fire protection, park facilities, parking, local transportation, etc.) can convert tourism taxes into benefit taxes and thus avoid distributing some of the additional cost of accommodating tourists to the local permanent population, especially those not employed in the tourism industry. Second, the use of some of the revenue for tourism promotion may help to offset base erosion and maintain revenue in the face of competition for visitors.

Value-added taxes

The **value-added tax** emerged from France to become the dominant form of sales tax in the European Community (now the European Union) in the late 1960s. As the EU grew from 6 members to 27, new entrants adopted the value-added tax. With the aid and encouragement of the World Bank in many cases, this complex tax was a surprisingly popular revenue tool in South America, Asia, and Africa as well. Most of these countries used the new tax to replace (or integrate with) tariffs, excise taxes, cascade-type sales taxes, single-stage taxes at the manufacturer's or wholesaler's level, or other less satisfactory revenue sources in the sales tax category.

Because income taxes are used in much more limited fashion in most other countries, the VAT is not only the predominant form of sales tax but also a major source of central government revenue. In most cases it is administered on the destination principle, although some of the formerly Communist nations of Eastern Europe apply the origin principle.

The United States' two partners in the North American Free Trade Area, Mexico and Canada, both use the value-added tax as an important revenue source. The VAT has been actively promoted as a possible replacement for the US federal income tax, which would make the US tax system more similar to those of its trading partners and follow recommendations from the World Bank and the International Monetary Fund.

The primary obstacle to such a move is that a VAT would compete on the same tax turf as long-established state and local retail sales taxes and would therefore meet considerable political resistance. In a sense, state and local tax authorities have "pre-empted" the sales tax field and made it less available to the central government.

Basic features

The tax on value added (VAT) is imposed on the value that a producer adds to his raw materials or purchases (other than labor) before selling the product or service. The value added, therefore, consists of labor costs (L) and profit (Π). The VAT can be computed in two different ways:

1   As a tax on labor plus profit, calculated separately or together:

$$tL + t\Pi \qquad \text{or} \qquad t(L + \Pi)$$

If the tax rates are the same on both wages and profits, the choice of a method is based only on relative ease of calculation.

2   As a tax on the difference in the value of output (Q) and the value of purchased inputs (I), which can be calculated separately or together:

$$tQ - tI \qquad \text{or} \qquad t(Q - I)$$

The most popular method is $tQ - tI$ because it is the easiest one to compute. The tax rate is simply applied to the value of sales, with a credit for taxes paid on any taxable inputs purchased. Because taxes paid on earlier stages of the production process are always credited against tax due, there is no accumulation or cascading of taxes, and the tax burden on the final product is the same percentage of the price as it was on raw materials and intermediate goods. Some VATs extend to the retail stage, while others end at wholesale.

The multi-stage feature of the VAT is attractive from the standpoint of international trade, and particularly trade within a free trade area, customs union, or common market. The VAT can be integrated with customs to ensure that any product arriving in a country with a VAT is subject to the tax of the destination country. Accumulated VAT at export (which is often at the wholesale stage) is rebated at export, and compensating VAT in the importing country is collected when the product is imported. Thus, a skillet or a VCR will have the same amount of VAT accumulated at final sale in Mexico regardless of where it was produced or at what stage of production or distribution it was imported.

Some countries use a single rate, others multiple rates (Belgium has six rates, France and Mexico five each), but the central or basic rates range from 6–23 percent with many clustered in the 15–20 percent range. Exemptions are often handled by zero-rating: charging a tax rate of zero on the final taxable sale, which allows the final seller to receive a rebate for taxes accumulated to that point. Multiple rates are a way of integrating excise taxes into a single system, but they also greatly add to the collection and compliance cost of the system.

Efficiency and equity issues

Value-added taxes share the same efficiency and equity attributes as other broad-based sales taxes. In many cases, they are an improvement in efficiency over the kinds of taxes they replaced. Excises and tariffs are more distorting of decisions than broad-based taxes because they single out a few products on which to levy the tax, and usually involve higher rates, increasing the deadweight loss.

Cascade taxes, which VATs have also replaced, create a variety of effective tax rates on different products depending on how many times the inputs, intermediate products, and finished products pass through the market and are taxed. While it is often appropriate on both equity and efficiency grounds to tax different products and services at different rates, a cascade or cumulative tax means the level of tax on any given product is somewhat random rather than reflecting intentional distribution of the tax burden.

Because the VAT is a sales tax at fairly high rates (compared to the rates for retail sales tax in the United States), it comes under criticism on both equity and efficiency grounds. Like all sales taxes, it is regressive, although there are various ways to reduce the regressivity, such as zero-rating food.[2] The high rates increase the deadweight loss or excess burden. It is also criticized in terms of its high collection and compliance costs. VAT both requires and creates an extensive paperwork burden on both tax collectors and taxpayers. However, some countries have found the paper trail useful in attempting to enforce other taxes and regulations, so there may be some benefits as well.

The Fair Tax: a national sales tax for the United States?

In the past 15 years, a movement has developed and spread in the United States to replace the federal income tax (both individual and corporate) and the Social Security payroll tax with a very broad-based national sales tax at a 23 percent rate. That rate is higher than most VAT rates in other countries, especially since the VAT in most countries does not extend to the retail level.

The proposal does provide a rebate for all households based on the poverty income level. For example, a poverty income level of $25,000 for a family of four would generate a rebate of $5,750 for all four person households, with correspondingly lower or higher rebates for other family sizes. The rebate, like the standard deduction and personal exemption on the present income tax, introduces some progressivity into the system even with a single flat rate.

The tax base would be very inclusive. Households would pay taxes on rent, now one of the biggest exemptions. Other additions to the tax base would include gasoline (in addition to the excise tax), medical bills, purchase of new homes, utilities, most services, and interest on all kinds of loans.

Supporters claim that the revenue from this tax would be sufficient to replace those three taxes at current levels. Critics argue that the 23 percent rate is actually a 30 percent rate, since it is 23 percent of the price *including the tax*. They further argue that the required rate would be higher, perhaps as much as 34 percent, in order to generate the same revenue as the tax it replaces.

There would be some redistribution of the tax burden, with low-income and high-income households paying less and middle-income households paying more. The low-income households gain from the rebate and from not paying Social Security taxes, while the high-income households gain because they save more of their income and because they are no longer paying the top bracket rate on a progressive income tax.

State and local retail sales taxes would be added to the 23 percent (or 30 percent, or 34 percent), pushing the combined rate even higher. States might have to adjust their bases to conform to the national tax in the interest of reducing collection and compliance costs.

A radical change such as the **Fair Tax**, or the Flat Tax described in the preceding chapter, creates some transition and evasion issues. Does the government phase one tax out and another in? What about windfall losses to those who made decisions and commitments based on one tax regime only to see it change radically? Without the extensive paper trail that is built into a VAT, will there be a substantial increase in underground economic activity in order to avoid paying such a large tax?

Finally, recall from Chapter 11 that a fundamental design principle in tax systems is to use several broad bases at low rates rather than fewer bases at high rates in order to minimize distortions in people's decisions and also to minimize deadweight loss. The three broad bases of income, consumption or sales, and property or wealth represent three different measures of ability to pay and ensure that everyone makes an appropriate contribution to the cost of public services. The Fair Tax would essentially eliminate income from that list, reducing the number of broad bases to two. With the reduction in the estate tax and the limited property base (mostly real estate) of the property tax, there is a significant loss of breadth and diversity in the tax base.

Summary

- Taxes on sales are primarily a state and local revenue source in the United States. Sales taxes are appealing because transactions offer a convenient tax handle. They also permit tax collectors to tap one of the three measures of ability to pay (consumption) and provide a way of exporting some taxes to nonresidents.

- The types of sales taxes that are in widespread current use around the globe are retail sales taxes, selective sales or excise taxes (including tariffs), and value-added taxes. Sales taxes can be single- or multi-stage, broad-based or narrowly focused, or levied on either the buyer or the seller.

- The retail sales tax is more elastic in the short run than the long run, making revenue vulnerable to economic downturns but relatively insensitive to long-term growth.

- Sales taxes, particularly selective ones, tend to erode their bases over time as consumers shift their purchases to untaxed goods and services or untaxed markets. Distortions of decision making are increased by any compounding or cascading, including retail sales taxes on business purchases.

- Sales taxes are regressive. The regressivity can be reduced by broadening the base; narrowing the base by eliminating certain consumption items; using excise taxes on items consumed more by higher-income individuals; and/or rebating some of the sales tax through means-tested income tax relief.

- Efficiency issues specific to the retail sales tax include the taxation of business inputs and the incomplete coverage of consumption, both of which distort location decisions and allocation of consumer spending among various goods and services.

- Excise taxes are used for revenue, to reduce the regressivity of the retail sales tax by imposing higher taxes on luxuries, and to discourage undesirable activities. Excise tax rates tend to be higher than typical retail sales tax rates and cause more deadweight loss.

- Value-added taxes have come into use in a large number of countries since the 1960s. This tax is levied on the difference between the value of inputs (other than labor) and the value of output or sales. Rates for most VATs are quite high, as are both collection costs and compliance costs.

- The Fair Tax is a proposed national sales tax for the United States, intended to replace the income tax and Social Security taxes. A per-household rebate based on the poverty level of income would make it progressive, and its broad consumption base would reduce distortions. However, the high rate would encourage evasion and there is a challenge of how to integrate this tax with the present widespread use of state and local sales taxes.

Key terms

Base erosion
Cascade-type tax
Excise tax
Fair Tax
Retail sales tax
Sumptuary tax
Value-added tax

Questions

1   Referring to Figure 14.1, how might the outcome of imposing a tax in the first market be different if supply were less than perfectly elastic (i.e., upward sloping) in both markets? Will there be more or less deadweight loss and/or base erosion? Why?

2   Excise taxes are sometimes used for pollution control. Referring back to Chapter 5 and the analysis of taxes to control negative externalities, draw a diagram that involves a tax on textiles in order to incorporate the social costs of water pollution resulting from the chemicals used in the production process. Assume that supply is highly but not perfectly elastic and that demand is moderately elastic. Using the diagram as a starting point, analyze the short-run and possible long-run effects of this tax on:

(a) price of textiles
(b) quantity of textiles purchased/sold and tax base
(c) tax revenue from this particular tax
(d) the amount of water pollution
(e) deadweight loss
(f) distribution of the tax burden between customer and supplier
(g) other possible effects (e.g., shift to alternative production processes)

3   Consider again the issue of base erosion posed in Figure 14.1. Instead of looking at two markets, try analyzing the difference between short-run and long-run base erosion. Draw two demand curves through the initial, pre-tax price and quantity combination Q_0, P_0. The original demand curve is the short-run demand curve. The second demand curve should be a long-run demand curve that is more price-elastic (flatter) than the short-run demand curve. Determine the difference in the amount of tax revenue raised in the short run versus long run. What are the policy implications for tax design?

4   Identify the deadweight loss or excess burden triangles for consumers and producers when the first tax is imposed in Figure 14.2. By how much do these triangles grow when the tax increases so that the shadow supply curve is S_2? What can you infer about the effects of steadily escalating tax rates on excess burden?

5   **By the numbers**. Suppose that the legislature was considering an increase in the tax on cigarettes of 50 cents a pack. The current price of a pack of cigarettes is about $3.00, and sales in your state are two million packs a year. The estimated short run elasticity of demand for cigarettes at the current price and quantity is .4. The long-run elasticity of demand (a year or longer) is .75. How much additional revenue can you expect in the first year, ignoring any growth in population of smokers? By how much will smoking be reduced? What about the second and subsequent years?

6   **Policy application**. What would be the advantages and drawbacks of replacing the US individual income tax with a value-added tax? What if the VAT instead replaced the state retail sales tax? Who would be the gainers and losers in each case?

7   **Behavioral economics**. How would *Homo economicus* (the fully informed, rational, calculating individual) react to an increase in the excise tax on a product or service such as gambling, alcohol, or tobacco? How might the response differ for a person with more complex motivation (concern for others, sensitivity to social pressures, etc.), less perfect information, and/or more inclination to make decisions by habit? What role might tastes and preferences, or addiction, play in each case?

8   **Thinking globally**. Tax structures can influence the location of firms and mobile individuals. Based on the kinds of products or services they produce, what kinds of firms or individuals might be attracted to a country, or state, that relies primarily on sales taxes as opposed to income and payroll taxes?

15 Taxes on property and wealth

Introduction

The tax everybody loves to hate. The most unfair tax of all. A violation of one's right to be safe from unwarranted intrusions into private property. An attack on the private property foundation of the market economy. These are just a few of the rhetorical attacks on the basic funding source of local governments in the United States and elsewhere: the property tax.

Property taxes are among the oldest taxes in the United States. They are widely used in other countries as well, not only developed industrial countries but at least in the urban areas of less developed countries. Even in the formerly Communist nations of Eastern Europe prior to the revolutions of the late 1980s and early 1990s, where private property had supposedly been abolished, there was a vestigial property tax on some privately owned shops, homes, land, and other tangible assets. Property, especially "real" property (i.e., land and improvements thereon) is one of the most visible and stationary of tax handles to attract the eye of the tax collector.

Until the Great Depression in the 1930s, both state and local governments relied heavily on the property tax. Beginning in the 1930s, most states shifted to income and/or sales taxes, leaving the property tax largely to local governments as a revenue source, although there are still state property taxes in some places. Just because the revenue and the power to set the tax rate were handed over to local government, however, did not mean that state governments were out of the property tax business. States continue to set the rules and oversee the administration of local property taxes.

Property taxes are a significant source of funding for schools as well as for general purpose local governments (cities, counties, and townships). In fiscal year 2007–08, property tax collections amounted to $410 billion. Property taxes provided 72 percent of local government tax revenues, 45 percent of local own-source revenues, and 28 percent of all general revenue.[1]

The property tax is the primary but not the only form of tax on wealth. The poll tax is a very old tax on wealth in the form of human beings, assessed at a flat rate per person or per household. While the poll tax is largely a historical footnote in the United States, it is still in use in other nations, particularly in Africa. Estate and inheritance taxes are also taxes on wealth, collected at the time of transfer to heirs. Gift taxes cover transfers of assets among the living. These other taxes on wealth are also considered in this chapter.

Why tax property?

There are several reasons for singling out property as an object of taxation. These rationales are ability to pay, the benefit principle, and the relative immobility of the tax base.

Like purchases (or consumption) and income, property broadly defined to include all assets is a measure of ability to pay taxes. Assets produce income, sometimes explicitly (interest, dividends, rent) and sometimes implicitly, in the form of services rendered. Owning a car means that you can consume transportation services without additional payment, rather than renting a car or using public transportation. That reduced expense means that you have more income available for other purposes, including paying taxes, compared to a non-car owner. The same is true of homeowners, who enjoy housing services that have a market value and who would otherwise have to pay explicit rent. The present system of making mortgage payments makes owning and renting seem more similar, so that one might question whether homeowners still can be assumed, on average, to have greater capacity to pay taxes than renters.

Another aspect of the ability to pay argument is that the property tax is a way of ensuring that everyone pays at least some tax. Those who can hide their income and make their purchases largely outside the realm of the tax collector can be compelled to make some contribution to the public treasury with property taxes.

The property tax narrowly defined (on land and improvements) has some elements of a benefit tax. Many local services funded with property taxes are services to property, such as roads, fire and police protection, street lights, and garbage pickup. These services enhance or protect property values, so the value of the services could be considered to be roughly proportional to the value of the property being served.

Finally, real property is a much less mobile tax base than income or sales. It may decline in value, but real property is stuck inside the taxing jurisdiction. Since local governments are in a highly competitive situation for attracting higher-income residents and business firms, they will be sensitive to keeping their property tax rates somewhat in line with competing jurisdictions, but at least they can count on real property (land and improvements) staying put even if it is subjected to tax.

Drawbacks to taxing property

There are four major practical problems involved in taxing property: high visibility, the limited base, the problem of valuation, and base erosion. We will consider each of these problems in turn.

Visibility

While visibility may be considered a good quality in a tax, the property tax is distinctly more visible than other kinds of taxes such at taxes on income and sales. It is often paid once a year in a large lump sum, while income taxes are withheld weekly or monthly and sales taxes are paid in small amounts, one purchase at a time. Historically, in a nation of farmers, the annual collection of property taxes in the fall after the harvest made sense, because it was the only time most citizens participated in the cash economy in a large way. Flush with cash from sales of their crops, they would pay their taxes and buy their supplies for the following year. However, that pattern of economic activity is a rarity in a post-agricultural, post-industrial society.

This higher visibility may discourage the use of property taxes relative to other kinds of taxes. For homeowners with mortgages, the tax is often paid monthly through an escrow account, which makes their property taxes less highly visible. Local tax collectors have been exploring other methods of collection, such as credit card payments and installment payments, to make property tax payments more similar to the payment of other kinds of taxes.

Narrow base

The use of a limited base that represents only a partial subset of total wealth or assets is the result of the difficulty of locating and valuing many kinds of assets, such as financial assets, commodities, precious metals, and jewelry. In most states, the property tax base consists mainly of land and improvements, vehicles, business equipment, boats, and a few other large, highly visible items that are difficult to conceal from the tax assessor.

As a result, the property tax is not a tax on all wealth, just that part of wealth held in these particular forms. By singling out one form of wealth for taxation, the property tax discourages investment in improving land or purchasing items subject to property tax relative to other kinds of assets. This distortion of investment decisions is an undesirable efficiency consequence of property taxation in its present form.

Market value

The biggest challenge facing property tax administrators is how to establish a credible market value as a basis for taxation. It is easy to establish a value for property that is sold, but there are many parcels of property that rarely change ownership. In rural areas, there are not enough transactions in similar properties to provide a benchmark. Some taxable assets remain in family or corporate ownership for decades or even centuries. The value for those properties has to be established by other methods, which are described below.

Because the value of land and improvements is estimated, taxpayers often challenge the value placed on the property by the tax assessor. Defending these decisions or making a justified change adds to the cost of administering the property tax.

Base erosion

Another challenge to the property tax is a greater than average tendency for this tax to erode its base over time. In the case of the property tax, this tendency can escalate to deterioration of whole neighborhoods or communities, especially in older cities. As property values decline, a higher tax rate is necessary to raise the same amount of revenue. As tax rates rise, middle- and upper-income families move to the suburbs, leaving only the poor and a few wealthy families in enclaves in the city. Costs of social services to an increasingly low-income population rise while the inner city's tax base continues to deteriorate. This pattern was particularly noticeable in the 1960s and 1970s as better highway systems and public transportation made it easier to live in the suburbs while continuing to work in the city.

Some of the older cities of the Northeast and Midwest, however, have experienced a resurgence of development called gentrification. As these inner city properties decline in value, particularly older, well-located and well-constructed buildings, they become attractive for redevelopment, and young professionals are attracted to the convenient location and aesthetic appeal of older buildings. Efforts by older cities to make their downtowns more livable and attractive have also made this kind of "second wave" development financially attractive, rescuing some of the property base of older cities like Baltimore, Portland (both Maine and Oregon), and even parts of New York City.

Defining taxable property

There are three kinds of property that are taxed by at least some jurisdictions. **Real property** is the most universal part of the base, consisting of land (developed or undeveloped) and improvements, mainly buildings. Real property is the mainstay of the property tax in just about every jurisdiction, sometimes separated into categories such as agricultural, owner-occupied residential, rental, commercial, industrial and utility.

Personal property consists of other kinds of tangible property besides land and buildings that has been added to the tax base. Automobiles, boats, airplanes, business equipment, farm equipment, railroad rolling stock, and business inventory are the most common categories of taxable personal property, although which ones are subject to tax vary from one jurisdiction to another. In the past few decades, a number of states have reduced personal property taxes by eliminating taxes on merchants' inventory and by reducing or eliminating property taxes on personal vehicles.

Intangibles are the third major category of taxable property. Intangible assets consist of other assets such as stocks, bonds, jewelry, bank accounts, precious metals, art objects, or other financial or physical assets that offer a way to store wealth. Taxation of intangibles, and to a lesser extent personal property, raises all of the major economic issues about tax design—efficiency, equity, collection and compliance cost.

The efficiency criterion suggests that to tax some forms of wealth and not others will distort consumer decisions about the forms in which they choose to hold wealth, favoring those that are not subject to tax. The equity criterion calls for a broad base of wealth so as not to discriminate against those whose wealth is primarily in the form of real or taxable personal property. Both equity and efficiency, then, would call for a very broad property tax base. Collection and compliance costs, however, can be very high if tax assessors have to track wealth in a large number of forms. Taxes on intangibles and personal property are often easier to evade, and any tax that is easy to evade will eventually erode as more and more taxpayers join the stampede.

Capitalization of property taxes

As we discussed in Chapter 3, the level of and changes in property taxes as well as the quality and variety of local public services are reflected in the market value of taxable property. The formula for calculating the present value of any asset reflects future costs and revenues/benefits according to the formula:

$$PV = \Sigma \, [B_i - C_i] \, / \, [1 + r]^i$$

where i is the particular year in the life of the property (from 1 to n), B is benefits in the ith year (including both the use of the property and any public services), C is the cost in the ith year (including property taxes as well as maintenance, depreciation, etc.), and r is the market rate of discount, or "the" interest rate.

If the property has an extremely long lifetime (land, for example, or a well-constructed building that depreciates very slowly), and if the annual benefits and costs are the same in all future years ($B_1 = B_2 = B_3 = \ldots B_n$) then the formula simplifies to

$$PV = [B–C]/r$$

What does this formula tell us about property taxes? Property taxes are reflected in C. An increase in property taxes that was not matched by increases in services (a part of B) that are equally valued by the present and prospective owners of the property will reduce the present (market) value of the property.

Suppose, for example, that a particular property has a present market value of $100,000, and the market rate of interest is 6 percent. Now increase annual property taxes by $100. What happens to the value of the property? It declines by C/r ($1,667) to $98,333. An enhancement—a sidewalk, a sewer line, regular trash pickup—would likewise increase the value of the property. The quality of a school district often has significant impact on housing prices, not only for parents of school-age children but for other buyers as well, because the value of access to those educational services is reflected in demand for housing in that district.

This process by which changes in taxes and/or public services are incorporated into the value of houses is called **capitalization**. The effect of capitalization is that changes in taxes and services accrue to the current owners of property in terms of the market value of their property. At least one study of property tax differentials found a significant amount of capitalization of property taxes in real estate prices, although capitalization is often less than the full amount that one might expect on the basis of a simple present value calculation (Man 1995).

Efficiency issues in property taxation

There are two important efficiency issues in property taxation. One is the incentive to hold wealth in non-taxable form. The second is the impact on location of households and business firms.

Efficiency issues, or distortions of consumer decisions, are particularly significant for the property tax because the effective tax rate is higher than it may appear. As you learned in Chapter 11, the distortions in decisions and the deadweight loss from a tax rise with the square of the tax rate.

The property tax is levied on wealth, but it is paid each year out of the income flow from the assets subject to the tax. Typical property tax rates (as a percentage of market value) are in the range of 1–2 percent of the value of the property. Nine of the ten cities with the lowest rates in the United States are found in Alabama, where rates are in the 0.3–0.5 percent range. Among the top ten cities, five are in New Hampshire, in the 3.4–4 percent range, along with two cities each in New Jersey and New York and one in Illinois. All of these rates may sound low compared to state income and sales tax rates, but they really aren't.

Consider housing, a major component of the property tax base. The income generated by the housing stock is a flow of housing services, which are paid for in rent. If you own a house, you can be viewed as renting it to yourself, in which case the income flow is implicit rather than explicit—the value of the rent you would have to pay for a place to live if you didn't own a house.

A rule of thumb for rental property is that the rent should be about 1 percent a month, or 12 percent a year. After other nontax expenses, such as insurance and repairs, the pretax rate of return on rental housing is probably comparable to other investments of similar risk— 7–10 percent a year. (The risks faced by owners of rental property include periods of vacancy, unexpected major repairs, or decline in the value of property when they decide to sell.)

If you think of the property tax as a percentage of the income from the property, then the rate is much higher. A net return of 10 percent before property taxes, subject to property at a tax rate of 1.5 percent would mean an effective tax rate on the property income of

15 percent. The same tax with a net return of only 7 percent would mean an effective tax rate of more than 20 percent![2]

Distorting asset patterns

Households and firms will be influenced in their asset acquisition by property tax consider-ations. Smaller homes, smaller lots, and a shift of "amenity" assets toward those that are not taxed (such as furnishings) may be a typical household response. Households are often reluctant to make major improvements in their real property because of the property tax consequences.

Partly offsetting this effect of the property tax, however, is the federal (and often state) deduction for both property taxes and interest on home mortgages, which make houses more attractive relative to other assets. The United States continues to claim one of the highest rates of owner-occupied property in the developed world, so it appears that the federal income tax advantages more than offset the impact of property taxes on investment in owner-occupied housing. The same may not be true for other types of property, such as rental and commercial property and, where taxed, cars and boats.

Business firms, likewise, must take property taxes into consideration in deciding what mix of assets to use, what kinds of plants to construct, what size facility to build, how much land to acquire. Firms have the choice of alternative production processes that may substitute labor and/or equipment for floor space and acreage. If a property tax is imposed (or increased), the balance of the cost/benefit calculations will be altered in ways that might not be optimal from the standpoint of resource use.

Distorting location decisions

Far more significant for most public policy-makers are the effects of property tax differen-tials on location choices by both households and firms. Lower taxes for the same public services, or better public services for the same taxes, will cause decision-makers to opt for one location over another. Many times economic efficiency (transportation costs, for example) might call for a different decision than the one that was induced by fiscal surplus calculations.

A community that has some degree of monopoly power—oceanfront location, spectacular vistas, attractive employment opportunities, good access to highways, or other factors—can levy a higher property tax rate and still be attractive to residents and investors in commercial and industrial firms. Property owners in these communities may be more successful in shifting the burden of the property tax to tenants because they, in turn, have a degree of monopoly power.

There are only so many beachfront locations or so many highway interchanges with choice locations for a truck stop. Owners of property in prime locations can continue to earn rents, or above average returns, because of the very limited supply of such locations. For the average community or the average location, however, property taxes that are higher than in competing locations may induce relocation of residential, commercial and industrial siting to lower tax jurisdictions.

Equity issues in property taxation

Before we can assess the equity effects of property tax, we need to be clear about incidence. There is no problem of determining the incidence of the property tax on owner-occupied property or for personal property such as motor vehicles, because the "buyer" and "seller" of the services of the property are the same. When it comes to other kinds of property, however, the incidence is more complex.

Much residential and commercial property is rented. If you rent an apartment, how much of the property tax falls on you in the form of higher rent and how much is absorbed by the landlord in the form of a lower return on investment? The incidence of property taxes on commercial and industrial property is even more complex. If the commercial or industrial firm owns the property, there are three possible parties who could bear some part of the property tax burden—the owners of the firm (lower profits), the workers (lower wages and benefits), and the customers (higher prices). If the commercial or industrial firm leases the property, the owner of the real property becomes a fourth candidate for bearing some of the burden in the form of lower lease payments received.

The regressive view

Figure 15.1 illustrates the short-run supply and demand for rented apartments in a single city, Metropolis, which has just imposed (or increased) its property tax. In the short run, the supply of apartments is fixed. With demand unchanged, the property tax falls entirely on the owner in the form of lower net rent.

Demand is represented by D, while the impact of a property tax (or an increase in the property tax) can be represented by shadow demand curve D_T, which represents demand net of tax as seen by the owner of the taxed property. The difference between the unchanged rental price P_1 and the net rent received by the owner P_T corresponds to the property tax per rental unit. Revenue from the tax is rectangle P_1P_Tba.

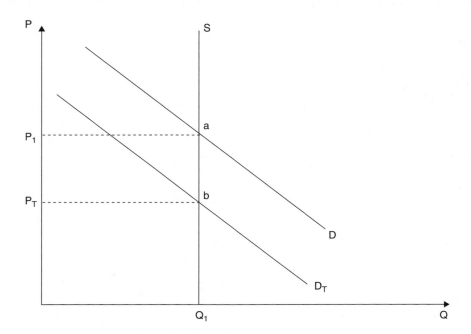

Figure 15.1 The short-run market for apartments.

However, a lower return to rental property will result in a decrease in the supply, since it may no longer be profitable to maintain older apartment buildings. With some supply elasticity (Figure 15.2), the burden of the property tax will eventually be shared between buyer and seller; the rental price for increasingly scarce apartments rises to P_F, while the rental payment net of tax to the owner falls to P_1. In larger cities, where apartments at desirable locations close to work or to public transportation are scarce, the owner of such properties often possesses a degree of monopoly power that may make it possible to shift more of any change in property taxes forward to buyers.

So far, the analysis looks very much like the standard discussion of the effects of an excise tax. Since this tax is levied on housing, which everyone consumes, and since spending on housing declines as a percentage of income as income rises, one might conclude that the property tax is regressive. More generally, the property tax on wealth might be expected to be progressive simply because wealth is even more unevenly distributed than income, with a substantial concentration of wealth in the top 5 percent of households.

The progressive view

However, there is a widely held alternative view that has been supported by at least some empirical studies. This alternative view is based on a broader perspective that looks more carefully at interrelated markets and the flow of resources between them.

People who are in the business of constructing rental property must compete in financial markets for loanable funds with other borrowers who are borrowing for purposes that do not involve a property tax obligation, or involve a smaller property tax obligation. The rate of return on constructing rental property will be lower than could be earned on other uses of the same funds. Resources that would otherwise have been directed toward the production of apartment buildings in Metropolis will now be diverted to other uses, either building

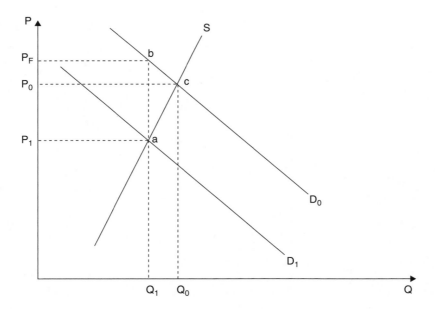

Figure 15.2 The longer-term market for apartments.

apartments where property taxes are lower or acquiring other forms of capital not subject to the property tax. Over time, existing properties will be allowed to deteriorate, and some will eventually be torn down. In other words, the supply of rental property may decline, or at least grow more slowly than other kinds of investments not as heavily impacted by the property tax.

Initially, a lower rate of return on rental property compared to other investments implies that at least part of the property tax falls at least partly on owners of rental property, as the previous analysis suggested. But rental property does not exist in isolation. As investors move funds out of rental property into other kinds of assets with smaller tax burdens, the lower rate of return spreads to owners of all kinds of capital.

In a world with a property tax, there will be less investment in improvements (mostly buildings) to real estate and more investment in other, non-taxed assets than there would otherwise be. Resources will shift between the two groups of investments until their rates of return are equalized; fewer rental units will earn a higher rate of return than they did when the tax was first imposed (lower, however, than before the tax). Other investments, however, will earn a lower rate of return. According to this view, then, the property tax is a tax on capital. Since ownership of capital is much greater at higher income levels, this view suggests that the property tax is progressive.

Other considerations

This theoretical description of the incidence of the property tax must be qualified by some real-world considerations. First, real property receives some other tax breaks, particularly in federal and state income tax treatment of depreciation and mortgage interest, which may mitigate the effects of property taxes. Second, markets may not function perfectly in terms of capital being totally fluid or fungible and flowing to more attractive uses. Capital is usually embedded in sites, in buildings, and in equipment. Finally, other factors besides the property tax may affect the return to building or owning or leasing real property that could offset the negative effect of the property tax.

Empirical evidence may shed some light on this debate. One study, using data from Boston, finds that in the case of rental housing, landlords are only able to shift about 11–16 percent of any increase in property taxes forward to tenants, at least in the short run. A second study, examining the property tax on commercial real estate in the Phoenix area, fins similar results, with 60–70 percent of the burden of the tax falling on property owners rather than on consumers of the products and services offered in those establishments (Carroll and Yinger 1994). Additional studies would be necessary to confirm these results for other areas and other types of property, but these two studies suggest support for the progressive view.

Is there a firm consensus? No. The older view was compatible with a world of little mobility of individuals among locations or of capital among uses, one of imperfect markets with limited information and slow response. Those circumstances have changed in the past few decades. Information spreads faster and capital markets of all kinds are more closely interconnected. However, improvements to real property (buildings) still represent capital embedded in a particular form and place from which it cannot easily be converted into a different form of capital in the short run. Buildings can be torn down or allowed to depreciate by not maintaining them, but the opportunity cost may be very high relative to the property tax burden, delaying the market response. Thus, the short-run burden is likely to be distributed differently from the long-term burden.[3]

Property taxes and education funding

In most states (Hawaii being the primary exception), the property tax plays a significant role in funding education. Property taxes for education are different from property taxes for the support of other local public services in several respects.

First, a property tax for city or county services has a more direct benefit aspect to it for all residents than the property tax for education, because a significant number of residents may not have children in the public schools. The use of property taxes to fund public education has become particularly controversial with the fairly rapid growth of retirement communities, which generate few, if any, school pupils, and with the more modest growth of private and home schooling as alternatives to the public schools.

Second, there is often not as direct a link between the level of property taxes and the quality of the public schools as there is for other local services. In most states (New Hampshire being the chief exception), funding for local school is heavily supplemented with equalizing state aid that reduces the differences in per-pupil resources between wealthier and poorer jurisdictions.

A series of court decisions have forced states to attempt to more nearly equalize per pupil resources among school districts in order to ensure that the quality of a child's education is not held hostage to being located in a district with a limited property tax base. While few states aim for total equality, most do direct more resources to poorer districts than to wealthier districts in order to blunt the impact of differences in local taxable wealth.

When states undertake to more nearly equalize school resources, then local effort becomes a smaller percentage of school funding. Suppose that state aid is 60 percent of school funding. Then increasing the local property tax rate in a given district by 20 percent will only increase total resources available for education by 8 percent (20 percent of the 40 percent local funding), so the increase in relative school quality or school resources is small relative to the size of the tax increase. Some critics of school funding equalization argue that the loss of direct connection between local taxes and school taxes may have been a factor in property tax protests in the 1970s and 1980s.

Finally, school quality is often a significant factor in the price of property, because with a home purchase or a rental lease, a family is buying access to a particular school district or even a particular school. Where school quality is a factor in housing property values, the capitalization process will reflect school quality at least as much as, if not more than, the level of local property taxes. Even households without school children will take current and expected future school quality into account because it will affect the resale value of their property.

Designing and administering property taxes

Some of the anger toward the property tax in the last few decades has been directed at the way it is administered rather than the property tax rate or the size of the property tax bill. Property taxation is a two-step process. The first step is to determine the value of the individual taxable properties and then aggregate them into a tax base. The second step is to establish a tax rate, or **mill rate**, to apply to that base in order to raise the amount of revenue required.

Income tax rates and sales tax rates are stable for years at a time while their bases grow at a steady if sometimes uneven pace. For the property tax, however, with infrequent reassessment, the base grows slowly in many years with jumps in reassessment years, while the tax rate or mill rate is changed frequently in order to yield the amount of revenue needed to balance city, county and school district budgets.

Valuing property for tax purposes

The first step in levying a property tax is to identify all the taxable properties—land, buildings, and taxable personal property—and to determine a market value for each. This process is known as **assessment**. Some properties, such as automobiles, are relatively easy to value because there are many similar properties being bought and sold on a national market and the assessor can determine the values from readily available sales information. The same is true of other kinds of personal property from tractors to office furnishing to railroad rolling stock. Standard rates of depreciation from the Internal Revenue Service code can be applied to the original cost of such properties to determine a taxable value.

For land and improvements—houses, stores, warehouses, factories, professional offices—the assessment process is more complex. Assessors generally use a combination of three methods to assess real property: replacement cost, comparative sales prices, and regression analysis.

The first method is to determine the replacement cost of structures on the basis of current building costs per square foot and the size of the structure. For example, if current building costs per square foot are $150 and the assessor is looking at a 2,000 square foot house, the replacement cost would be $300,000. If the house is not new, depreciation is factored in for age to reduce the value. Land is usually assessed separately based on recent market prices for undeveloped land in the immediate area.

The second method is to look at the sales prices of comparable properties in the neighborhood. For areas with substantial turnover in real property, this market price method is useful, but it is less useful for rural areas, unusual or unique properties, or industrial properties.

The third method, increasingly widely used, is regression analysis. A regression equation for a house might include such variables as land (acreage), square footage, number of bathrooms, basement, garage, and a dummy variable to represent location. The coefficients in the regression equation would be developed by putting in the information for actual property sales in the area. The resulting equation, which represents a combination of the first two methods, would then be applied to valuing property that had not been sold recently.

Most states oversee the assessment process at the local level, providing training and checking to ensure that local valuations are not out of line with actual market values of properties that are sold. The state may require reassessment at regular intervals. Because a complete revaluation of all the taxable property in a jurisdiction is a tedious and expensive process, most local governments reassess less often than annually. Typically from three to seven years elapse between assessments. More frequent reassessment ensures greater equity between property owners, and less of a "sticker shock" effect when the value of property is adjusted, but the administrative cost usually makes annual reassessment impractical.

Assessment rates

To further complicate matters, once the market value of a particular property is determined, it is then added to the tax base at some percentage of that value. Some states practice 100 percent assessment. Others have formally determined fractions of the market value that are used to compute the taxable value, and apply that percentage to all taxable property. Still other states use different percentages for different kinds of property.

If different kinds of property are included in the base at different percentages of their market value, then the state has a **classified property tax**. The aim of a classified system is to distribute the property tax burden in a way that is proportional to market value within a classification but not between classifications. For example, owner-occupied residential property may receive a favorable assessment rate, while commercial or industrial property may be added into the tax base at a higher assessment rate. Seventeen states have classified systems, with as few as two classes and as many as eight. Residential property and agricultural property are the classes most likely to receive favored treatment.

The mil(l) rate

The term mil rate reflects the English origins of the property tax in the United States. The mil, now more commonly spelled mill, was an old English monetary unit that was one-tenth of a cent. A tax rate of 70 mills, then, would be 7 percent of the market value. The use of this antiquated unit of measure further compounds the aura of mystery and confusion that surrounds the property tax.

The mill rate is usually set by local governments. Because the property tax plays such a central role in funding local governments, the mill rate often becomes the piece of elastic that has to stretch between other revenue sources and expenditure demands to balance the local budget. A first cut at a city, county or school district budget would estimate expenditures, subtract other revenues (fees and charges, state and federal aid, etc.) and then determine the balance to be raised through property taxes. Given the size of the property tax base, a mill rate can be determined that would raise the needed amount. If that mill rate represents a large jump over previous years, there may be a need to go back to the drawing boards on the spending side.

Mill rates are not comparable between states because of different assessment methods. A mill rate of 250 on a 6 percent assessment is equivalent to a mill rate of 15 on a 100 percent assessment. In both cases, the tax is 1.5 percent of the value of the property. Because both mill rates and assessment rates enter into determining the tax burden, interstate comparisons are usually made by dividing the dollar tax collections by the market (not assessed) value of the property tax base to calculate property tax burdens as a percentage of property values. Typical values are in the 1–3 percent range for most states, generally lower than average in the Southeast and higher than average in the Northeast.

The French system: taxing rental value

Most Americans and Canadians are familiar with the method of assessing and collecting property tax just described, which is common throughout the English-speaking world. The tax is computed as a percentage of the value of the property asset, as a tax on wealth. Whether the value of the property asset is expressed as 100 percent of market value, as it is in many states, or as some fraction of that value, it is the market value of the asset that is the basis for computing the tax. This system is found wherever the predominant influence has been British.

In other parts of the world, however, there is a different system of property taxation that is based on the income flow rather than the asset value. Because this method of property taxation is used in France, it spread to former French colonies in Africa and is used there as well. This method can be integrated with the income tax, can stand alone where there is not an income tax, or can create a double tax burden on income from real property.

If a real property is leased, there is a flow of rental payments from the lessee to the owner that can be taxed. Suppose, for example, you own an office building that has a market value of $1 million and generates rental income of $120,000. An English-style property tax system would base your tax liability on the asset value of $1 million. A mill rate of 25 (2.5 percent) would generate a tax liability of $25,000. To generate the same tax liability on the gross rental income would require a tax rate of 20.8 percent. (Some systems tax gross rents, while others tax rents net of expenses.)

The nominal rates are higher under a French-style system, but the effects are the same. It is easy to compute a mill rate and a tax rate on rental income that would yield the same revenue from the same tax base, whether the base is defined as the value of assets or the stream of rental income from those assets.

What about property that is owner-occupied and thus generates no income? The French system requires the calculation of a rental equivalent, just as assessors under an English system must estimate a market value for properties that are not sold.

The advantage of the French-type property tax system is that it recognizes that the tax burden must be paid out of the income the property generates, whether that income is explicit (actual rental payments) or implicit (the value of the rental services enjoyed by the owner-occupant). A property with little or no rental value should pay little or no tax.

The value of land and buildings as an asset is simply the capitalized sum of future net income streams. A French-style property tax collects revenue on the basis of the annual flow rather than the capitalized sum, and is therefore more flexible in responding to changes in the rental values of taxable properties.

Behavioral economics: sticker shock and the property tax revolt

The term "property tax revolt" refers to a series of events that began in California in the mid-1970s and spread across the nation through the rest of the twentieth century. Protests against escalating property tax burdens that came with rapidly increasing housing values led to an initiative in California called Proposition 13, which reduced property taxes and sharply curbed their growth. When property values are rising rapidly, and property is reassessed only at intervals, property owners are confronted with sticker shock. The good news to home-owners is that their property has appreciated in value, and in the 1970s, that was especially important with double-digit inflation. The bad news is, their tax bill has also appreciated in value. Service costs were also rising with double digit inflation. So the property tax revolt got started in part as a form of fiscal illusion.

Of course, it's not that simple. Nothing ever is. Families had been speculating in houses, buying them in hopes of appreciated value which could then be turned into cash when it was resold, but in the interim, it was a place to live. They bought the most house they could afford, sometimes more, and they weren't prepared for the added cost of an increased property tax liability on the appreciated value. So a combination of poor planning, short-term thinking, and speculative investments on assets that are not always easy to sell or liquidate caught a lot of homeowners by surprise—and a not very pleasant surprise. It was another case of imperfect information and incomplete processing of information, but the effects have been felt for more than three decades in restraints on assessment growth and property tax limitations.

Proposition 13

In June 1978, voters in California approved of an initiative that radically changed not only property taxes but also state-local fiscal relations dramatically. The Jarvis-Gann Initiative, better known as Proposition 13, was the opening volley in a revolt against the property tax that spread from state to state and continued through the end of the twentieth century. This initiative limited property tax rates to 1 percent of market value, rolled back property taxes to their 1975–76 value, gave the state responsibility for distributing property tax revenues among jurisdictions, and based assessment on the market price at the time of sale.

Prior to Proposition 13, the average property tax was about 2.7 percent of market value, so this initiative resulted in a sweeping reduction in property taxes, estimated at $7 billion in the first year. The impact on cities, counties, and school districts was enormous. Since the local property tax was the primary source of revenue for schools, and the property tax rate and revenue were no longer locally controlled, California's school system became the fiscal responsibility of the state, much like Hawaii but unlike most other states.

Counties much became more heavily dependent on state aid. Schools in California also saw a decline in per pupil spending relative to other states over the next two decades. Cities, which generally are least dependent on property taxes (compared to other local governments), shifted more heavily to fees and charges to cover the drop in property tax revenue. By 1996, California cities saw property taxes decline from more than 16 percent to less than 8 percent of revenues. So one unintended consequence was "reverse devolution," or shifting responsibility for providing county and educational services up to the state level.

Taxpayers frequently complain that assessments are arbitrary and unfair, but so is California's system based only on the value at the time of purchase. That value can be increased to account for inflation by up to 2 percent a year. The result of this system is that there is an actual transaction base for assessment, but it also means that similar properties bear very different tax burdens, depending on how often they are sold.

Observers disagree on the overall effects of Proposition 13. Proponents credit it with helping to fuel the boom in California, along with general economic growth, and to contain the growth of government spending. Critics argue that it has not only gutted local control but also seriously damaged the quality of local public services, especially education. For good or for ill, Proposition 13 changed the face of the property tax not only in California but in the rest of the nation as well.[4]

Other responses: repeal, restraint, relief, and reform

Several states, including Michigan. Arkansas, and Utah, attempted to **repeal** the property tax, that is, to develop some other basis for local government funding, including funding for education. None of these efforts were successful, although in Michigan there was a substantial shift of education funding away from the local property tax toward state funding through a higher sales tax.

The failure to repeal the property tax in any state reflects the fact that there are only a limited number of broad-based taxes to provide an adequate and stable revenue source for any government. The property tax is the one tax that has proved most suitable for local use both because property is immobile and because local governments provide services that benefit property owners.

Restraint refers to any method of tying the hands of local officials in order to limit growth in taxing and spending. Many state governments have constrained themselves and sometimes their local governments in terms of overall growth of revenue or spending, setting a maximum growth rate or tying it to the growth of personal income. Often there are restraints (mostly state-imposed) aimed directly at the unpopular property tax. The forms of property tax restraints have included limits on increases in assessments or the use of reassessment to increase revenues, limits on the percentage value of the property that can be collected in tax, or restrictions on increases in the mill rates.

Restraint is a rather clumsy tool for containing the growth of government. It has encouraged the growing use of fees and charges. For schools, which tend to depend most heavily on the property tax as a local revenue source, it has meant diminished funding and declining educational quality in some areas, particularly California.

Relief is a difficult political issue. Almost every state has made some effort to provide property tax relief either in general or to specific groups in the past 30 years, often by substituting state funds for local funds in paying for public education, or by providing local governments with access to other revenue sources besides the property tax.

Much of the relief, however, has been for designated groups of taxpayers. Groups asking for specific rather than general relief usually represent a category of property (homeowners, new industry, owners of automobiles) or another segment of society that claims injury because of high property tax burdens (the elderly, veterans, etc.). In states with classified systems, the categories and their assessment rates are prime targets for differential relief. Farmers, owners of undeveloped land, and homeowners tend to receive the most favorable treatment in classified systems.

All three of these groups are in a position to make an emotional appeal for special treatment based on the fact that their taxable property may not be yielding much of a cash income stream from which to pay taxes. Legislators are encouraged have a vision of widows and orphans being evicted from their family homes, or farmers being forced to sell the land that has been in their family for generations in order to pay taxes. While some of these hardship stories are genuine, they also supply political cover for many homeowners and landowners who are not genuine hardship cases. The result is, however, that many states offer favorable tax treatment to these two groups of property owners in one form or another.

Property tax relief also comes in a number of other forms in non-classified systems. The most common forms of relief are:

- Exemption of part of all of the value of property for tax purposes, often called a homestead exemption in the case of owner-occupied housing or a business tax incentive in the case of industry. For homeowners, the exemptions are often categorical—over age 65, veterans, disabled, blind, etc. For business firms, the exemption may be across the board or it may be negotiated as part of a package of incentives for locating in a particular state or a particular location within a state.
- Rebating part of the property tax burden to all taxpayers or to selected taxpayers. The rebates may be funded by the state or by another local tax.
- Income tax credits or other direct payments to reduce the property tax burden on housing, usually based on income. The income tax credit is called a **circuit breaker**. At least 30 states have some form of circuit breaker, some of which include renters as well as homeowners.

Reform of the property tax is a slower, more demanding, and more difficult process of rethinking the property tax so as to make it more equitable, less inefficient, and also less costly to administer. A number of reforms have been implemented in administration to improve the assessment process.

California's change in the assessment process was the most radical of all. Residential property is now only reassessed at the time of sale. If it is not sold, its value is increased at a rate of 2 percent a year. This system, called **acquisition value**, results in substantial inequities in tax burdens between properties of similar market value. Properties that are repeatedly sold at escalating prices will have much higher property tax burdens than properties that remain in the same hands and just see their assessed values rise at a slow and steady 2 percent a year.

At least a dozen other states have copied some aspects California's system, most commonly caps on increases in assessments. Others have moved to more frequent assessment. State oversight of local assessors or direct state assessment is often used to improve the accuracy of the assessment process. Other administrative reforms have focused on allowing installment payment of taxes, improving appeals processes, and pooling the property base of smaller jurisdictions to provide more market comparisons. Reform may also involve sweeping rethinking of decisions about the distribution of the tax burden in systems that have either classified assessments or differential rates for different kinds of property.

Other taxes on wealth

The property tax is the primary form of taxation of wealth in the United States as well as the major source of local government revenue, unlike many other nations. There are two other kinds of taxes that can be considered taxes on wealth rather than on income or consumption. One is the **poll tax**. The other is a tax on the transfer of property at death to heirs, known as inheritance or estate taxes.

Poll taxes

A poll tax is a per capita or per household tax that is the same regardless of any measure of ability to pay. It is a specific tax—$10 per head, or per adult, or per household, for example. Because the tax does not vary with income, it is the most regressive of all taxes. Its primary appeal is that it does not distort any decisions, because the only way to avoid the tax is to die or disappear, which are too extreme for most people to consider as a form of tax avoidance!

Its other major attraction is simplicity. While it is still labor-intensive and prone to corruption, it may be easier to count people than to track and measure income and assets in an economy where a significant amount of production and consumption takes place outside market channels.

The poll tax is rarely used in most industrial countries, although there was a brief and disastrous attempt to use it to replace the property tax in the United Kingdom in the 1980s. It is still used in some less developed nations, particularly in Africa. This tax was used in some parts of the United States at modest levels well into the late twentieth century. Its name reflects the fact that proof of payment of the poll tax was sometimes required in order to vote in elections (polls refer to the places where elections are held, or the process of voting).

Estate, inheritance and gift taxes

When the federal government levies a tax on the transfer of property at the time of death, it is called an **estate tax**, which is a tax on the net worth of the deceased. Fifteen states levy a separate **inheritance tax**, which is a tax on the amount that heirs receive from an estate, which can be credited against the federal estate tax.

An estate can avoid tax if it passes to a spouse, but eventually it will come to the attention of the Internal Revenue Service. Prior to 2001, taxes were levied on estates in excess of a threshold level after subtracting expenses, charitable bequests, and payment of debts. The rates were progressive, starting at 18 percent and rising to 55 percent on estates in excess of $3 million.

In 2001, the estate tax was phased out by reducing rates and increasing the threshold, with complete elimination in 2010. However, in order to minimize the projected revenue loss, the legislation ended at 2010. The estate tax has been reinstated, but at a lower rate and a higher threshold ($5 million) than the tax before 2001.

One of the reasons offered for eliminating the estate tax was that wealthy households have invested a great deal of effort in finding ways to avoid or minimize estate and inheritance taxes. Wealthier persons can transfer up to $10,000 per recipient ($20,000 if the donors are a married couple) per year without incurring a gift tax. The gift tax, at the same rates as the estate tax, was instituted to limit this way of avoiding estate taxes. Trusts and other devices take assets out of the estate and reduce the tax burden. The estate and inheritance taxes have also been a major incentive for charitable bequests, which expect to suffer a decline in revenue as the estate tax is phased out.[5]

The estate and inheritance taxes have not been major sources of government revenue, and in practice are paid by only a very small fraction of the population. However, they have been very controversial. One school of thought sees these taxes as an appropriate redistribution of wealth that somewhat levels the economic playing field within generations, as well as a potentially significant source of revenue as estates accumulated during the prosperous years of the twentieth century are passed on to heirs. Critics, who won the debate in Congress in 2001, claim that the estate tax is a confiscation of the result of a lifetime of hard work and wise management of resources, and a disincentive to save and invest in order to pass wealth on to one's heirs.

Summary

- The property tax is a significant source of funding for local governments in the United States. Property taxes are imposed on real property (land and buildings), personal property (tangible assets such as cars, boats, and business equipment), and sometimes intangibles (mostly financial assets).
- The property tax is the primary form of taxation of wealth; other (minor) taxes on wealth are poll taxes, used only in a few countries, and estate and inheritance taxes.
- There are three rationales for a local property tax: (1) property ownership is one indicator of ability to pay; (2) most local public services benefit property owners; and (3) real property is less mobile than other possible local tax bases.
- The disadvantages of using this tax are the limited base of real property and a few kinds of personal property, the difficulty of establishing the market value, and the tendency of this tax to erode its base over time.
- Property taxes are reflected in the market value of property through capitalization. Capitalization means that the value of future benefits (services) and costs (taxes) is discounted and added to or subtracted from the present value of the property.
- The property tax is levied on the value of the asset rather than the annual income stream from the asset and is, in consequence, relatively high if calculated as a percentage of the income stream. Property taxes will influence choices about the forms in which wealth is held and the location of households and firms.
- There is not general agreement about the incidence of the property tax. As an excise tax on rentals, it appears to be regressive. As a tax on capital, it appears to be progressive.

Empirical evidence lends some support to the view of the property tax as a tax on capital.

- Property taxes are a major source of funding for public schools in most states. Both school taxes and the quality of public schools are capitalized into the value of residential property.
- Real property is valued, or assessed, for tax purposes, by a combination of methods, including market comparisons, adjusted replacement cost, and regression analysis.
- Some states value all property at market value or at a uniform percentage of market value. Other states apply different percentages to different classes of property, such as owner occupied, industrial, or commercial.
- The property tax revolt in the past 25 years has resulted in a number of changes in the property tax system. Its role has been reduced in many states by allowing local governments to tap other resources and/or increase the state's share of funding for local services, especially education. Many states have adopted restraints of various kinds on property taxes. Property tax relief targeted at specific groups has also been popular, ranging from homestead exemptions and circuit breakers to tax incentives for industry.
- The poll tax is a tax levied at a flat rate per person or per household. It is non-distorting but highly regressive and is not widely used in industrial countries.
- Estate taxes are levied on the transfer of property at death. States also levy a tax on the inheritance of property.

Key terms

Acquisition value
Assessment
Capitalization
Circuit breaker
Classified property tax system
Estate tax
Inheritance tax
Intangibles
Mill rate
Personal property
Poll tax
Real property

Questions

1   What are the costs and benefits of limiting a property tax to real property (land and buildings) instead of expanding it to include other forms of wealth?
2   Summarize the arguments about the regressivity or progressivity of the property tax. How might you attempt to verify which view is correct? What factors might make either of the two simple models, the excise tax on rentals or the tax on capital, less likely to predict the distribution of the tax burden in the real world?
3   What are the incentive and disincentive effects of an estate and/or inheritance tax on work, saving, consumption, and investment? How, in your view, do those consider-ations weigh against the notion of equality of opportunity discussed in Chapter 5?

4 **By the numbers**. Suppose that a particular piece of property had a market value of $100,000. Now the local government finds that it must increase taxes by $200 a year on this (and other) properties just to maintain the current level of public services. At an interest rate of 6 percent, how would this tax increase affect the market value of this property?

5 **Policy application**. Suppose that your state currently has a uniform assessment rate of 10 percent, but is considering changing to a classified system of property in which owner-occupied property is assessed at 10 percent, farm property and undeveloped land at 5 percent, and all other property (including rental, commercial and industrial) at 15 percent. Evaluate this proposal from an efficiency and equity perspective.

6 **Behavioral economics**. What aspects of the property tax contribute to making it more unpopular than income and sales taxes? (Hint: think about visibility and fiscal illusion, reassessment, and certainty or uncertainty.) How might the administration of the property tax be changed so as to make it more acceptable to taxpayers?

7 **Thinking globally**. Until recently, three East African countries with a shared British colonial heritage had very different property taxes. Tanzania taxed only buildings, as land has been nationalized. Uganda taxed both land and buildings, while Kenya taxed only land. How might these differences (assuming similar levels of taxation across countries on either buildings or land) affect decisions about locating multinational firms in each country? Would certain types of industry be more sensitive to taxes on land as opposed to buildings?

16 Fees and charges as a revenue source

Introduction

Critics of government are fond of saying that government should be run more like a business. By now you have enough familiarity with what government does to understand that some of the techniques used in the private sector are not readily adaptable to situations where there are externalities, public goods, or other issues that mean it is not feasible to supply services on a pure market transaction basis.

However, governments do rely heavily on various kinds of fees and charges to help finances services at all levels of government, from grazing fees on federal lands to dog licenses issued at your local city hall. In many of these cases, a part of government is being run like a business, with signals about demand conveyed through the prices people are willing to pay for services ranging from garbage pickup to airport landing fees.

Fees and charges are a relatively minor source of revenue for the US federal government, but state and local governments collected $374 billion in fees and charges in 2007–08, which accounted for almost 20 percent of all own-source general revenue. State governments have found that fees and charges are a useful supplement to their two primary revenue sources, income and sales taxes. States that do not use one of these major taxes tend to rely even more heavily on fees and charges.

Fees and charges have grown rapidly in the past two decades in response to a number of factors. Expanded use of fees at the federal level was one of the tools used to reduce the budget deficit in the 1980s and 1990s, and again in response to two recessions in the first decade of the twenty-first century. At the local level, fees and charges have proven to be a productive substitute revenue source in response to reduced property tax revenues following the property tax revolt, especially in California.

Fees or taxes?

What is a fee, and what is a tax? Both are sums of money paid by citizens to governments to support services. But there are some important distinctions. First, a tax is involuntary, whereas a fee is paid as a result of a voluntary purchase of services by the payer. Second, a tax normally produces general revenue that can be used for any public purpose, whereas revenue from a fee is supposed to be used to cover the cost of providing a specific service.

In practice, the dividing line between taxes and various kinds of fees and charges is often not that clear-cut. Rather, there is a continuum from a pure tax, not linked to a particular service and just providing general revenue, to a pure fee in which payment is made for services rendered. At the tax end of the spectrum are general sales and income taxes, which are involuntary and are mostly used for support of general government. At the fee end of the spectrum are the operations of government enterprises, such as purchasing stamps from the postal service, buying a token or fare card to ride a public subway, or obtaining a bottle of wine from a state-operated liquor store, all of which are voluntary and related to the provision of specific goods or services.

In between, toward the tax end of the spectrum, are benefit taxes (property, gasoline) and earmarked taxes. **Earmarked taxes** go into special funds or are spent for special purposes. For example, part of the revenue from taxes on alcoholic beverages may be earmarked for alcohol treatment, or taxes on accommodations and admissions (movie theaters, sporting events, concerts) may be earmarked for tourism promotion and/or tourism-related expenses.

Business licenses (usually imposed by local governments) are often assessed on the basis of gross revenue and involve no specific services in return, so that even though they are classed as fees and charges, they are more like a business income tax. Permits, likewise (for hunting, fishing, marriage, building, etc.) and franchise fees are usually sources of general fund revenue, although the permit or franchise fee may or may not be in any way related to provision of particular services. Law enforcement fines and charges, such as speeding fines, also fall into this middle category, and may be considered more like a tax on undesirable behavior. Revenue from fines and law enforcement charges may go into the general fund, or may be used to cover some of the cost of public safety services.

To further complicate the task of distinguishing between taxes and fees, many services in the public sector are funded with a combination of general tax revenue and user fees. A transit system or a recreation program may charge a modest fee but operate at a loss, with the difference made up from general tax revenues.

Types of fees and charges

Fees and charges fall into three different categories with very different structures, efficiency effects, and distributional impact. The first group is licenses and permits, which are government permissions to engage in certain kinds of activities ranging from hunting and fishing to operating a business. The second group, fees for services, are charges incurred by citizens or firms who wish to use a particular publicly provided service such as garbage pickup, tennis courts, highways (tolls), building inspection, health clinics, etc. Both of these revenue sources normally accrue to the general operating fund of the government imposing the charge.

The third type, which exists at all levels of government but is particularly important at the local government level, is payments for the services of government enterprises, or quasi-business entities in governments with separate fund accounting from the general fund. Surpluses may be transferred to the general fund, however, or deficits may have to be made up out of the general fund, so even government enterprises are not entirely autonomous from their sponsoring governments. Table 16.1 lists some of the more common kinds of payments in each category.

Many of the items that fall in the category of licenses and permits are more like excise taxes on certain activities (hunting, fishing, marriage, building). Franchise fees and impact fees are discussed separately in the efficiency section because there are pricing elements in both that are quite different from those involved in setting other kinds of fees and charges— granting monopoly privileges in the case of franchise fees and using fees as a tool to manage growth in the case of impact fees. The discussion that follows concentrates on fees for service and government enterprises.

Table 16.1 Major types of fees and charges

Licenses and permits
Business licenses (primarily local)
Drivers' licenses
Marriage licenses
Hunting, fishing, camping and dog licenses
Building permits
Automobile license/registration
Franchise fees (e.g., cable television, electric and gas service)
Fees for service
Grazing fees (primarily federal)
Landing fees (airports)
Park entry fees
Recreation fees
Highway tolls
Solid waste collection and disposal fees
Government enterprises
Postal service
Water and sewer
State liquor stores
Transit services (bus, subway, etc.)
Electric and gas utilities operated by state or local governments
Difficult to classify
Law enforcement fees and fines
Impact fees

Efficiency issues in fees and charges

The efficiency issues related to fees and charges and the services of government enterprises are different from those that arise from taxation, and more similar to the kinds of questions addressed in the theory of the firm. In taxation, there is a concern about taxes distorting decisions, which is not the case with fees. In fact, an important purpose of fees may be to influence people's decisions about how much to use a particular service such as public parking, public transit, public recreation, or solid waste collection. Taxation is concerned with developing appropriate rules about the distribution of the tax burden, while fees are designed to ensure that the burden falls on the user who can rely on the usual decision rules (is the service worth the price?).

Fees and charges have five purposes that fall under the heading of efficiency: (1) to measure and control demand for certain kinds of services; (2) to implement the benefit principle (user pays); (3) to reduce negative externalities; (4) to reduce the pressure on taxes where feasible; and (5) to capture monopoly profits (in the case of franchise fees or government enterprises). In addition, there are some specialized fees, in conjunction with other tools such as zoning, that enable governments to address growth management issues, which is an aspect of intertemporal efficiency.

Measuring and controlling demand

While funding through taxes is appropriate for pure public goods, a great many goods or services provided through the public sector are not pure public goods. They may be goods or services with substantial positive externalities, or something that the local community has chosen to provide through government rather than the market for reasons such as ensuring access for low-income citizens. Having the government provide services with a strong element of rivalry and excludability in consumption is particularly true of local government, somewhat less for state and central governments. Examples of such local services with strong private good characteristics include street maintenance, solid waste collection, fire and police protection, recreation and parks, and of course, education.

Figure 16.1 presents the demand and supply (marginal cost) for solid waste collection. Because there are positive externalities associated with solid waste collection (most of us would prefer not only to have our garbage collected and disposed of properly but also benefit from our neighbors having the same service!), the "full" demand curve reflecting both private and social demand is D_T, which is the sum of private demand D_P and social benefits D_S. The socially optimal price and level of output is P_0 and Q_0.

If a good or service with strong private good characteristics provided by the public sector is funded through general taxes, such as sales or income taxes, then citizens respond as if it were free, because their personal tax cost for an additional unit is essentially zero. In Figure 16.1, they will opt for a quantity Q_1, because the marginal benefit of the last unit is equal to the price of zero. That is, citizens will demand a quantity of service beyond the social optimum—daily pickups, perhaps, or backyard instead of curbside collection.

On the other hand, if solid waste pickup is left to the private market to provide, there will be too little consumed—Q_2 at a price of P_2. Some consumers will not choose to have their garbage picked up, or picked up as often, creating problems of odor, appearance, and even health risks.

This service is a prime candidate for using a mixture of tax and fee financing. Ideally, the fee would cover the private benefits and the tax funding would cover the social benefits, so the average household should pay a fee of P_3, with the difference $P_0 - P_3$ paid out of general

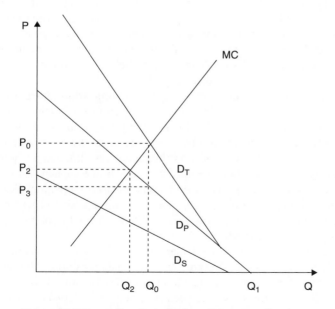

Figure 16.1 Demand and supply for solid waste collection.

tax revenue. This funding mix will set private marginal benefit plus social marginal benefit equal to the marginal cost of providing additional services.

Note that the margin at which additional units of the service are provided can be either extensive or intensive. At the extensive margin, the city can extend the service to more remote or more scattered customers at the fringes of the service, incurring a higher marginal cost for serving these households. These cost considerations are reflected in annexation and other growth-related issues, discussed below. At the intensive margin, the city could increase the quantity of service provided per household by offering backyard pickup, separate recycling pickups, or more frequent pickups.

In either case, however, the city has accomplished two important goals with this pricing scheme. It has reduced the quantity of services demanded from the quantity at a zero price to the socially optimal amount by requiring people to pay something toward the cost of the service.

It has also made a crude measure of demand. If the initial price was too high, people would be likely to opt out, taking their own trash to the landfill or using private providers, as has happened, for example, in Durham, North Carolina. City government could read that signal (or more direct complaints about the high cost!) as an indicator that they had over-estimated the private benefits of solid waste collection. If everyone uses the city service, and there are demands for more service at that price, then the initial price was too low. Like a private firm, the city will learn how much to charge by trial and error with the help of customer feedback.

Addressing positive externalities

A blend of tax and fee financing is common for many services that are judged to have positive externalities. Public higher education is financed partly by tuition fees and partly by state and local governments, reflecting a mix of private benefits and positive externalities. K-12 education is generally believed to have a higher proportion of social benefits than private benefits and is therefore funded much more heavily out of taxes than fees. The use of public transit, which reduces congestion, air pollution, and demand for parking, is generally subsidized so that the fee charged is less than the marginal cost of service. Such a blend of tax and fee financing rather than purely fee-based financing also helps to ensure access to certain services regardless of ability to pay, as was discussed above.

A related use of fees in order to influence demand is the use of **congestion charges** or **peak-load pricing**. For example, tolls on highways or fees on subways, such as the Washington (DC) Metro, may vary by time of day. The intended result is to shift some users from peak-demand to off-peak times. If users can shift between times, then there is less pressure to add extra lanes on highways or extra cars or more frequent runs on the subway to accommodate a peak load during a few rush hour periods, with much idle capacity sitting around unused during the off-peak periods. Many federal agencies offer employees flex-time, coming in very early and leaving early or coming in after morning rush and leaving after evening rush, to reduce the problems of highway congestion and air pollution as well as to reduce stress on Washington's public transit.

Figure 16.2 illustrates congestion pricing. Off-peak demand is represented by D_A and peak (rush hour) demand by D_A''. The marginal cost of serving an additional user during off-peak periods is essentially zero, but once capacity is reached, marginal cost rises quite sharply.

To simplify matters, assume that the subway is free. Then consumers will demand a quantity of service Q_0 at which the marginal benefit is zero, far less than marginal cost. Charging

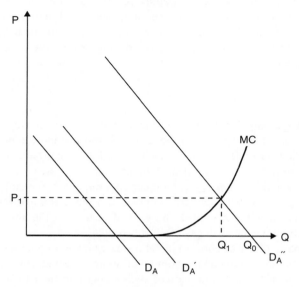

Figure 16.2 Congestion pricing on a subway.

peak-period prices to rush hour customers will reduce quantity demanded to Q_1. Some of those customers may switch to off-peak hours, reducing off-peak demand to D_A', which makes better use of idle equipment during the off-peak hours. In practice, because marginal costs are not exactly zero, the subway will charge a low rate during off-peak periods and a higher rate during peak periods, but the effect is the same.

There are many applications of congestion charges and peak-load pricing in the public sector. Many public recreation areas collect fees only during the season, in part because the costs of hiring a gatekeeper exceed the revenue that it would generate, and the marginal congestion cost of another visitor to a lakefront park in the winter is essentially zero. Only when demand for the service by one user begins to limit the amount available to another or to create additional costs of provision is there any reason to charge a fee.

Addressing negative externalities

Either a fee or a tax is an appropriate way of discouraging the production of negative externalities, such as noise, particulate matter in the air, or effluents into public waters. Such charges fall in the gray area that marks the dividing space between taxes and fees. Such a charge can be regarded as payment for a permit to create negative externalities, much like a building or hunting permit, or as an excise tax on an undesirable activity with the goal of reducing it, like taxes on cigarettes, alcohol or gambling. Charges on the production of negative externalities are sometimes labeled as taxes and other times as fees, but more often are fees. (The term **effluent charge** is used to describe a tax or fee based on the volume of emission of either airborne or waterborne pollutants.[1])

The revenue from such fees may go into the general fund, or may be earmarked for specific environmental uses. From an economic perspective, earmarking either fees or taxes on negative externalities for further reduction in the activity generating the externalities is unnecessary. The important issue is that the tax or fee should be set so as to reduce the level of pollution activity to the socially optimal level, as described in Chapter 7. If the resulting revenue is then used to further reduce emissions, then the level of pollution could be below the optimal level; that is, more resources would be devoted to reducing externalities than is justified by the social costs they create.

Elasticity and fees

Like excise taxes, fees both reduce quantity demanded and generate public revenue. The mix of quantity change and revenue outcomes depends on the height of the fee and the price elasticity of demand. Some publicly provided services, such as parking, may have very inelastic demand because there are no good substitutes. A higher fee in an area without adequate parking can generate substantial revenue without much of a reduction in quantity. Other services, such as recreation, may be very sensitive to price. If a fee is charged for a service with highly elastic demand, it will accomplish the goal of restricting the amount people demand, but it will raise little revenue as they shift to substitutes.

Elasticity and substitution are particularly of concern in solid waste pickup in places that have adopted "pay as you throw" policies based on the volume of waste collected. If the fee is too high, people may resort to less desirable alternatives such as burning their trash or burying it in the backyard. If demand is inelastic, the fee will not be very effective as a way to control demand, but it will have the potential to raise a great deal of revenue.

Fees and the benefit principle

The primary justification offered for the use of fees for publicly provided services is that many services provided in the public sector do not meet either of the criteria for public goods, non-rivalry or non-exclusion. One might question why the service is being provided in the public sector in that case, or whether it should be privatized.

Sometimes privatization is an appropriate answer. In other cases, providing the service through the public sector is justified on some other basis. Perhaps public involvement is the only way to provide access for all citizens regardless of ability to pay. In other cases, there may be a desire to respond to externalities, or the market may be too small to support more than one supplier, which creates a monopoly situation. There may be no private supplier willing and able to provide a service which is not profitable on private grounds but desirable when social benefits are included. In these cases, where the private beneficiaries can be identified and charged, a fee can approximate the goal of Lindahl prices for public goods, which would mean assigning them in proportion to the benefits received cost to the extent possible.

Equity issues in fees and charges

Equity issues in fees and charges are just as contentious as they are in taxation, but they take different forms. It can be argued that equity calls for having users of services pay for them, but it can also be argued that equity implies that citizens should have access to public services regardless of ability to pay. Fees and charges in combination with taxes and other revenue sources have to balance these two conflicting equity criteria.

Until the past few decades, the access argument tended to dominate, and it was common practice to provide a wide range of services through government with little or no payment by users. However, budgetary pressures at all levels of government, changing philosophies about the appropriate role of government, and recognition of some efficiency values in requiring at least partial payment by at least some users have changed the way policy-makers and citizens think about fees and charges for a wide range of public services.

Protecting the poor

Access for low-income households is often used as a justification for any kind of blanket subsidy, whether it is eliminating sales tax on food or providing free tuition at public colleges. However, the revenue loss or expenditure demand can be excessive relative to the amount of the services that actually get to the target low-income population. A sales tax exemption for food not only benefits the 15 percent of the population that might be considered poor, but also the 85 percent who are not, with substantial loss of revenue. Free tuition rains on the rich and poor alike. At a zero price, there will be large and growing demand for services that would be moderated in the face of some fee or charge (see below).

The middle ground between free and unlimited access to protect the poor and ensuring that users pay can be attained by a variety of techniques. One technique is vouchers or other ways of allowing the poor to have access while others pay. Price discrimination based on some easily verifiable characteristic is another technique. One common form of price discrimination in the public sectors is the **cross-subsidy**, in which one group pays a price that exceeds marginal cost in order to help fund the service for another group that pays a price below marginal cost.

Vouchers

Vouchers consist of some kind of coupon redeemable for goods and services. The most familiar kinds of vouchers currently are food stamps, vouchers for housing and for K-12 education, and chits redeemable for child care for working mothers coming off public welfare. In all these cases, government funds allow low-income families to purchase services from private commercial sources. But the same voucher concept appears under other names for services provided in the public sector. Children of low-income parents are eligible for free or reduced-price school lunches, while their classmates pay the full cost. The same children often receive reduced prices or scholarships in local public recreation programs.

The drawback of using such a system, which provides subsidies for the poor but not for the non-poor, is the need to verify eligibility based on family income, size, and assets. However, once a system is in place for one service, it can easily be extended to others. Often proof of eligibility for food stamps or free school lunches is used by other government agencies as sufficient validation for free or reduced fee access to other services.

Price discrimination

Many goods and services are available at reduced prices for senior citizens, with the age minimum ranging from 55 to 65. In the private sector, senior citizen discounts on airline tickets, movie theaters, restaurants, and other places are simply a form of price discrimination based on different elasticities of demand. Senior citizens are assumed to have not only lower incomes but also more time for comparison shopping and consequently to be more sensitive to differences in price.

In the public sector, the rationale for special treatment of elderly citizens in assessing fees for services is not as clear. Historically senior citizens have, on average, had lower incomes than the rest of the population, but poverty among the elderly has dropped dramatically in the past 30 years, and they are now less likely to be poor than younger families. Preferential treatment of senior citizens, from reduced rates on public buses to Golden Eagle passes for access to national parks, monuments, and historic sites, may simply reflect a lag in awareness of the improved income position of most seniors. In public choice terms, one might also consider the greater tendency of older citizens to vote and to participate in public affairs as a reason for favoring this group.

Cross-subsidies are often used in public enterprises such as water, sewer, solid waste collection, and public transit. Different users are charged different prices per unit, or different flat rates, based on easily identified categories such as residential or commercial/industrial, with the latter often subsidizing the former.

In this way, households can be assured access to public services at a subsidized rate, while higher charges for business users reduce the amount of tax financing that needs to be devoted to providing these essential basic services. In public transit, the charge may be the same for all users even when the cost of providing the service may be higher to some areas than others, which means that those in low-cost, easy-to-serve areas are subsidizing others living in places that are more remote, less dense, or in some other way more costly to serve.

Collecting from nonresidents

When public services are available to residents and nonresidents alike, tax financing would put too much of the burden on residents. A museum, park, or library fee will ensure that even people who do not pay local taxes but use the service will contribute to its cost. Fees are generally a better way to internalize these kinds of positive externalities, especially at the local government level. Sometimes the users live in the county while the service is provided by the city. County residents enjoy lower taxes while obtaining the benefits of the nearby city.

The same principle applies to interstate equity, especially in the case of tourists who use state roads and state parks and create burdens on local trash collection and public safety. Tourism taxes are one mechanism for shifting the burden, but so are admission fees to state parks, tolls on state roads, and various kinds of local fees for tourism-related services.

Fees as tax relief

Much of the growth in fees at the local government level in the past two decades, especially in California, is not based on theoretical considerations as much as on a need to find some alternative local revenue source to replace part of property tax revenues. The property tax revolt, discussed in Chapter 15, led to substantial reductions in property tax revenues in a number of states, including California, Michigan, and Massachusetts. State aid filled some of the gap, especially for schools, but cities and counties had to look elsewhere. While there has been an increase in the use of local sales and excise taxes, much of the shortfall in more recent years has been taken up by fees, charges, licenses, and permits. Because fees tend to be more regressive than broad-based taxes, the effect of using fees to provide tax relief has been a redistribution of the cost of public services toward lower-income citizens.

Earmarked taxes and fees

Earmarked revenues are dedicated to a particular use and are not available for general spending purposes. Earmarked revenues are a common practice at all levels of government in the United States. There are three main arguments for earmarking.

The first argument is that there is an element of quid pro quo, or a market-like exchange. For taxes, some earmarking is related to the benefit principle—the gasoline tax being the most obvious case. Some fees and charges are payments for service, much like private sales, and good accounting practice suggests that these enterprise activities should segregate their revenue and spending streams from the general public budget.

Second, there is an equity argument. Many fees are designed to ensure that the cost of additional service, or services to particular groups or areas, falls on those who demanded that service, rather than on taxpayers in general. Impact fees in particular are a way of sharing the cost of public capital among newcomers to the community, rather than imposing additional tax burdens on existing taxpayers in order to accommodate the needs of new arrivals.

Finally, the third and most important argument is political; earmarking may make a tax or other revenue stream more acceptable to the public if they know it will all be spent on some desirable purpose. For example, states that have adopted lotteries almost always have had to have a referendum, because most states had anti-lottery provisions in their constitutions. To make a lottery more attractive, legislators promised to use the revenue for specific desirable purposes, such as education, economic development, local government, or senior citizen programs. If citizens have to vote on any kind of tax or revenue increase, earmarking increases the chances for approval.

Most economists support the limited kinds of earmarking associated with fees for service or a clear benefit principle relationship between the revenue source and the object of the earmarking. However, earmarking usually extends far beyond the fee for service or benefit principle to ensure preferential treatment for certain groups in the budgetary process. Sometimes schools or local governments are guaranteed the proceeds of a particular revenue source regardless of the competing demands on the state budget. Other times supporters of parks, or highways, or some service with a vocal and effective lobbying group within or outside of government succeeds in obtaining an earmarked revenue source. When earmarking is not clearly justified in terms of some kind of "user pays" principle, then it needs to be re-examined.

The arguments against earmarking are powerful because they are grounded in fundamental economic principles about choice, tradeoffs, and equating at the margin (marginal benefit = marginal cost). When revenues are earmarked, they are removed from that process of weighing one expenditure against another that lies at the heart of good budgetary practice.

The amount of revenue going to a particular purpose, such as gasoline taxes for highways, may be too much or too little relative to how much would be spent if highways were funded through the general budgetary process. If it is too much, the surplus is not available for other uses. If it is too little, that spending category may find it difficult to compete for additional funding out of general revenue because it already has preferential access to its "own" funds.

For example, lottery funding for education has made it more difficult for public education to get increased funds from general revenue sources, even though most state lotteries generate only a modest portion of the funding needed to provide for public education. At the other end of the spectrum, tourism destination states have been involved in a costly and escalating advertising war simply because state tourism departments had preferential access to dedicated revenues from accommodations and admissions taxes.

Finally, earmarking can worsen a budget crunch in a revenue downturn. It is often easy to persuade elected officials to earmark certain revenue sources for pet programs when revenue is rising and competition for public resources is not too severe. But with a revenue downturn, legislators may find that a substantial part of their revenue stream has been taken off budget, so that preferred projects cannot be cut because their revenues are protected. The burden of budget cuts then falls disproportionately on those public programs and services that do not have access to earmarked revenues. In the next budget upswing, there will be increased pressure to earmark revenue for some of these programs and services, further reducing the ability of legislators to make the kinds of budgetary tradeoffs that are needed.

Despite its political popularity, the weight of good economic reasoning is against earmarking. The case for earmarking needs to be made carefully on the basis of efficiency and equity considerations, and the bulk of the revenue stream at any level of government needs to remain available to the general fund where the important tradeoffs are made among spending priorities.

Franchise fees

Franchise fees are payments for the privilege of being the exclusive provider of a service for a given area. Heavily used by local governments, these fees determine which cable service, electricity supplier, etc. will serve a given area. States also charge franchise fees that range from the highly general (equivalent to a business license fee) to the highly specific (franchises for service providers or concessions at state parks and/or on major highways and airports). In the latter case, the state is using its power to create a monopoly privilege just like local governments awarding cable TV franchises.

All three levels of governments derive revenue from franchise fees, which are payments in exchange for a grant of exclusive privilege. There are activities or privileges for which franchise fees would be appropriate, such as radio and TV licenses, where they are not used or not used very heavily, but governments have taken advantage of many of the opportunities to generate revenue from this source. Cable TV companies generally pay a franchise fee, which is negotiated, to counties or municipalities in exchange for the exclusive right to serve customers in a given area. The same is often true of telephone, gas, electric, and other utility services. Service areas on some major highways, such as the New Jersey turnpike, are operated by private firms under franchise agreements. Publicly owned airports have the opportunity to grant a variety of privileges ranging from landing slots to restaurants to parking management, for which they normally extract a fee.

Franchise fees are an effort to capture some of the monopoly profits that result from the grant of an exclusive privilege to provide commercial services in a given area. They are also used by private firms; baseball parks, for example, grant franchises (for a price) to vendors of food, drink, souvenirs, and programs. Because it is difficult to determine the exact amount of monopoly profit that will result from a given franchise, the city, county, state, or federal agency has to estimate how much it can charge while still attracting enough competing prospective franchise holders to be able to select for desirable characteristics.

Figure 16.3 illustrates the effect of a flat franchise fee on the profits of a monopolistic firm in the short run. Note that, because the franchise fee increases fixed cost but not variable or marginal cost, it has no effect on price or output. It does, however, reduce profits from $AC_0 P_0 ac$ to $AC_1 P_0 ab$, with the difference transferred to the government as general revenue. Franchise fees can also be based on gross or net revenue, in which case they are more like a business income tax. Since such a fee affects marginal cost, it would raise prices and reduce quantity.

Growth management and impact fees

An increasingly common use of fees by local governments is to attempt to direct the pattern of growth in order to minimize the cost of servicing a growing population. Land

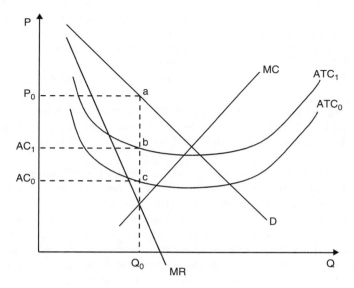

Figure 16.3 Effect of a franchise fee.

development can follow many alternative patterns even in accommodating the same amount of population. One pattern has been described as "ranchette"—large lots with scattered housing. Another pattern is dense development that may or may not be surrounded by open space. A third is a random distribution with patchwork developments on moderate-sized lots separated by undeveloped land. A fourth pattern is infill development, making use of scattered lots within the developed urban and suburban areas. These alternative land use patterns have very different implications not only for the loss of prime lands to other uses but also for local government service costs.

Land use patterns are the result of individual choices, influenced heavily by both market forces and constraints imposed and incentives offered by governments at all levels. Left to the individual buyer and seller, the ownership and use of land would be determined by the highest present value in terms of projected future revenues and costs, discounted at prevailing private market rates of interest. In some instances, leaving land "idle" while awaiting a future more attractive use may be the most attractive alternative, an outcome familiar to those who are aware of the workings of futures markets.

The actual pattern of land use may be different from the socially optimal pattern for several reasons. Among the major sources of distortions in land use choice are imperfect information, over-discounting future costs and benefits where benefits are immediate and costs are delayed, spillover effects (externalities), and public policies that create perverse incentives (such as the tax favoritism for owner-occupied residential property in both income and property taxes).

Established residents and local public officials are persuaded that growth will reduce their tax burdens through sharing the cost of public services among more citizens. That expectation is rarely fulfilled in practice. Residential development in particular tends to add more to the cost than the revenue side of local government budgets. Loudon County, Virginia, just outside Washington, DC, is one example:

In Loudon County, Virginia, officials in 1994 estimated that a new home must sell for at least $400,000 to bring in sufficient property taxes to cover the cost of all the services the county provides. By contrast, the average home sold that year for less than $200,000. The fastest selling properties in 1995 were town homes averaging between $120,000 and $160,000.

(Diamond and Noonan 1996, p. 35)

An earlier study in Culpepper County, Virginia, found that residential development cost $1.25 in county services for every $1 of revenue, while service costs were only 19 cents per dollar of revenue generated for industrial, commercial, or agricultural land (American Farmland Trust 2007).

Another study by the American Farmland Trust found the revenue-to-cost ratio for residential property is 1:1.11, while the ratios are 1:0.29 for commercial and industrial property and 1:0.31 for farmland, forests and open space (ibid.: p. 36.).

Local governments have several nonrevenue tools at their disposal to attempt to direct growth into patterns that are less costly to serve and make better use of existing infrastructure, including zoning and land-use plans. One of the most widely used revenue tools, however, is the development **impact fee**. New development requires additional infrastructure and may increase the average cost of providing certain services, such as police and fire protection. The cost of serving new developments depends on such factors as contiguity (how close they are to existing developments) and density (number of houses or dwelling units per acre). Close-in and dense developments are generally less costly to service per household.

An impact fee assesses a charge against each lot developed to cover some part of the additional costs attributed to the new occupants, which may include building additional water and sewer capacity, police and fire substations, staff and equipment, additional garbage trucks, new landfill capacity, more street maintenance, and construction and operation of additional schools.

The rationale behind an impact fee is, once again, user pays. If established residents are not going to benefit from lower taxes as a result of sharing costs with new neighbors, they can at least be shielded from seeing their tax and fee burdens rise with no increase in services just because the city or county must now extend services to new residents. Impact fees, then, serve both equity and efficiency goals. The equity is between new and established residents. The efficiency goal is to constrain growth to what can be effectively serviced and to make sure that the additional costs created by new development are internalized, i.e., they fall on those who create the costs.

Case study: grazing fees on federal lands

Among the many assets owned by the U.S. government are millions of acres of public lands, most of them in the west. The federal government owns and manages approximately 650 million acres of land, or 28 percent of the land area of the United States. Four federal agencies manage these lands for various purposes, which are the conservation, preservation, and/or development of natural resources. The Bureau of Land Management and the Forest Service are the two agencies that have responsibility for grazing rangelands totaling about 260 million acres.

In the nineteenth century, access to public lands was free, but in 1906 the Forest Service began to charge grazing fees on land under its control, although much other public land was still available for use without regulation or fees until 1934. Even today, the grazing fees on federal lands are substantially lower than the rates charged on comparable private lands. In 1993, the monthly fee on federal lands was $1.86 per head of livestock, while fees on state lands averaged $4.58 and on private lands, $9.80 (Cody 1996).

As a result of this history of free (or subsidized) and largely unregulated access, Western ranchers have come to think of grazing on public lands as a property right, and oppose any restrictions on that perceived right as an action that reduces the value of their assets invested in livestock and equipment. On the other hand, public land is not an unlimited resource. It has competing uses; not only do ranchers compete for a limited supply of grazing land, which will deteriorate in quality over time if overused, but grazing also competes with other uses of the land, such as recreation and fish and wildlife habitats.

There are several reasons why a fee for grazing rights is appropriate. First, private firms are using a scarce resource as a production input to a product to be sold in the marketplace. In the absence of a fee, consumers will pay too little for beef and will consume more of it than they would if they had to pay the full cost, including the value of the input of grazing land. Second, grazing land requires maintenance and controlled grazing to prevent deterioration. A fee is a way of controlling demand to prevent overuse.

Third, public lands are in competition with private lands, on which a fee for grazing is routinely charged. Owners of cattle and sheep are being encouraged to overuse the public resource and underuse the private resource because of the price differential. Livestock owners with federal grazing permits are being subsidized relative to their competitors who must pay full market value for private land grazing rights. The estimated revenue loss is between $20 million and $150 million a year (Cody and Baldwin 1998).

In the 1990s, the battle between the Department of the Interior and Western ranching interests represented in Congress focused on the proposal to more than double grazing fees over a three-year period and to change rangeland rules to allow more public participation in decisions, greater efforts to protect ecosystems, and reductions in the number of livestock allowed to graze. The increase in the fee was deferred after protests from Congress, but the other regulations were put into effect.

There is little dispute among economists that it is appropriate for the government to charge grazing fees for public land that are comparable to those charged by private landowners. Such fees should cover the cost of managing the program (at present, administrative costs exceed revenue by a substantial amount) as well as the environmental impact, and should serve to ration a scarce resource among competing uses.

But, like many programs that benefit a small number of citizens, it's not easy to gather the political will or critical mass to make a change. Arrayed on one side are the ranching interests, wishing to preserve access to a low-cost source of grazing land. On the other side are environmentalist and recreation interests. For the average citizen, who feels little impact from the revenue loss, the loss of wildlife habitat, or even the price of beef, grazing fees are never going to make it to the top of the political agenda.

Pricing for public enterprises

Public enterprises are operations that are run separately from the general fund, with the accounts kept in an enterprise fund, which receives revenues and pays the costs of providing the service. As with any business activity, there is an appropriate price at which marginal revenue equals marginal cost, but since these enterprises are not-for-profit monopolists, they have some discretion in setting prices, since their objective is likely to be other than profit maximization.

A public enterprise may set a price equal to marginal cost rather than marginal revenue equal to marginal cost, or it may operate somewhere in between. Depending on average cost, this pricing strategy could result in a deficit, which will be made up out of the general fund. At this lower price, more use will be made of the service. If the service, such as garbage pickup or public transit, has important positive externalities, then this pricing strategy will move output closer to the socially optimal level at which price (including social benefits) equals marginal cost.

It may be difficult for the public enterprise to determine that price and output level precisely, and the public enterprise may be constrained by the amount of subsidy its parent government is willing to provide out of general revenues. But conceptually such a pricing strategy could increase efficiency in the allocation of resources. Many public transit services operate at an intentional deficit in order to subsidize the use of public transit by citizens for both efficiency and equity reasons.

Other public enterprises may intentionally set prices in order to run a surplus (which would be known as a profit in a private firm), which is then transferred to the general fund to provide tax relief for all citizens, regardless of the extent to which they use the service. These enterprises use their monopoly position in much the same way as a private monopoly, except that the surplus is used for public purposes.

Many municipalities operate as retail electricity service suppliers, and many of these municipalities transfer surplus funds each year to their regular budgets. As a result, their citizens enjoy lower taxes and/or better services at the expense of electricity customers. Many of these people are the same (citizens and electricity customers), but some are not.

Many of these municipalities may have electricity service areas that extend beyond their corporate limits to include households and business firms who enjoy the benefits of convenient access to the municipality and benefit from some of its services but pay no taxes. Higher electric rates are one way of making these "free-riders" contribute to the cost of maintaining the city. There are also non-taxpaying entities inside and outside the city—churches, other nonprofit entities, and state government facilities—that use some city services but are exempt from property taxes. The electric utility enterprise is a way of generating some general revenue from these sources to relieve the burden on taxpaying residents.

Another strategy in pricing public enterprises is to charge a flat rate rather than a fee based on usage, or a combination of a flat fee and a per unit fee. Students on college campuses often find a transportation fee on their tuition bill, which covers part of the cost of shuttle buses. Students pay this fee regardless of whether they never use the shuttle bus, use it occasionally, or use it regularly. The fee has no impact on their decision on how often to ride the shuttle, because the marginal cost is still zero. By encouraging students to make more use of the shuttle buses at a marginal price of zero, school authorities reduce congestion and demand for on-campus parking, and save themselves the cost of collecting from each passenger.

Water is an example of an enterprise that often makes use of a combination of a flat fee and a per unit fee. The flat fee may include a certain amount of "free water," such as 1,000 gallons per household per month, with water beyond that amount charged for by the gallon. The fee per gallon may be flat ($2/thousand gallons) or it may rise with higher usage. What objectives are served by such a pricing structure?

One objective is to ensure access to a certain basic amount of water to all households regardless of ability to pay. A low flat fee will address that objective, while covering some of the infrastructure costs and administrative costs of connecting to the system and measuring usage. (A pure per household flat fee would have the additional advantage of no expenditures for metering usage, but has other drawbacks.)

Lower-income households may find that the amount of water permitted under the flat fee is adequate to their needs. Higher-income households may use more water for cleaning, gardening, etc. and will pay more for their water use, making the payment system more progressive or at least less regressive than a flat fee per household.

The fee for additional use also serves to control demand. Water is not free; it must be pumped, purified, and stored, all of which incur marginal costs. By charging by the unit, marginal units will not be free beyond the basic amount, and households will have an incentive to conserve water, reducing pressures to provide capacity that is based on high peak loads rather than lower average use. Charging per gallon also offers a useful incentive mechanism in times of drought or other water shortage, when rates can be raised to control usage.

Behavioral public finance: taxes versus fees

Behind the rhetoric about running government as a business is a sense that those who use government services should pay for them, an attitude that is more favorable to fees or earmarked taxes and less favorable to general taxes. "Running government like a business" is an example of **framing**. Framing means putting a question or an issue in a particular context with the goal of eliciting a particular kind of response.

That frame or framework in which people are invited to think of their interactions with the government as similar to their purchases at the store or their payment for a haircut, evokes a simple context of a market exchange. But it leaves out vital features such as the way collective choices are made and common pool resources are managed. It also leaves out externalities (both positive and negative), distributional concerns, shared responsibility for public goods, and other reasons why our financial relationship to government is different from our financial relationship to our local bank or hardware store or doctor's office. It also creates a bias toward using more fees and charges to support government activities and to reduce reliance on general taxes.

Everyone hears or processes information and ideas in some kind of framework. People are influenced by their education, their friends and neighbors, the media, and other social interactions. Over time, each of us develops an image or understanding of the world. If new facts are shared with us that do not fit into that framework, it is easier to reject the new facts than to reconstruct our framework. A major goal of political parties and ideological groups is to create frames, encourage people to adopt them, and then to describe issues and policy proposals in ways that their particular position seems to fit better into that framework than any alternatives.

An economic view of the world, *Homo economicus*, is a different kind of framework, but it can have the same effect on people's perceptions of information. A framework that views people's motivations as more complex and their ability to acquire and process information more limited might result in very different responses to the same information. Such a framework, which appears in some limited degree in each chapter in this book, can result in different conclusions about many public policies, including the appropriate balance between fees and charges in financing government.

Summary

- Fees and charges are a large and growing component of government revenue in the United States, particularly at the local level. The major types of fees and charges are licenses and permits, fees for public services, and payments for the output of government enterprises.

- Fees and charges differ from taxes in that fees and charges result from voluntary decisions by individuals to use particular services, and are often (but not always) dedicated to covering the cost of the services for which they are charged. In practice, there is a continuum from a pure tax, charged regardless of the consumption of service and used to generate revenue for the general fund, through earmarked taxes, franchise fees, and permits, to pure exchange of payment for services such as water and sewer utilities.
- Specialized kinds of fees for specific purposes include franchise fees to capture monopoly profits and impact fees to channel growth in desired directions and ensure that those who cause increased service demands bear a proportionate share of the cost.
- Equity in the use of fees and charges must balance the conflicting demands that those who use a service should pay for it with the equally compelling need for citizens to have access to basic public services regardless of ability to pay. Techniques for ensuring access while using fees include vouchers and price discrimination.
- Fees and charges are used to measure and control demand for certain kinds of services, to implement the benefit principle (user pays), to reduce negative externalities, to reduce the pressure on taxes where feasible, and to capture monopoly profits. In the absence of a fee, the price to the consumer for another unit of a public good would be zero, so he or she would consume until the marginal benefit was zero, or less than the marginal cost. Fees make it possible both to measure demand and to restrict demand to the socially optimal level. For goods with positive externalities, the fee should cover the private benefit with the social benefits aspects funded through general taxes.
- Congestion charges can be used not only to restrict demand but also to shift demand from one time period or location to another, making better use of existing facilities and reducing demand to create additional capacity.
- Impact fees are a useful tool for local governments attempting to address the needs for infrastructure and services in response to population growth by ensuring that the additional costs fall on the owners of the newly developed property rather than burdening existing residents with higher costs but no improved levels of public services.
- Public enterprises ranging from the Postal Service to a local municipal water service face many of the same pricing challenges as private firms, with the added complication of having to serve the entire population. Some public enterprises are subsidized out of general tax revenues to provide for social benefits and/or to ensure access to services for low-income households. Others run surpluses that are then transferred to general fund budgets to help pay the cost of other public services
- A preference for fees over taxes is at least in part a result of framing the discussion in terms of government being more similar to business in its operations.

Key terms

Congestion charges
Cross-subsidy
Earmarked taxes
Effluent charges
Framing
Franchise fees
Impact fee
Peak-load pricing
Vouchers

Questions

1   Copy Figure 16.3, but change the franchise fee from a flat fee that shifts average total cost up parallel without changing marginal cost to one that increases with volume (quantity). Demonstrate that not only profits but also quantity will fall. (Hint: MC shifts up and rotates clockwise; ATC shifts up, but by increasing amounts as Q increases.)

2   How should the cost of each of the following services be distributed? What role can fees and charges play in each instance? What part should be played by general tax revenues? Justify your answers in both efficiency and equity terms.

- City streets
- Sewer service
- Solid waste disposal
- Fire protection
- National defense
- City summer recreation for children
- State highways
- Public libraries
- Local bus service
- Public parking
- Higher education
- Street lights

3   You are a Senate committee staff person charged with analyzing the impact of a proposed substantial increase in grazing fees on federal lands, with the proceeds to be used for erosion control and animal health services for owners of livestock. Evaluate this proposal from both efficiency and equity perspectives. How would you decide how much to increase the fee?

4   **By the numbers**. Using data from the Bureau of the Census, look up the amount of revenue derived from current charges (fees) by state and local governments over the most recent available 15-year period. Create a graph showing the change in fees and charges as a percentage share of own-source revenue. The web address is: http://www.census.gov/govs/estimate/historical_data.html.

5   **Policy application**. Suppose that you are in charge of the municipal water system of Smallville. A drought is threatening your water supply just as the city council has asked you to develop a new water fee schedule. In designing the fee schedule, how would you take into account the need to restrict demand, differences in elasticities of demand and ability to pay, and other considerations?

6   **Behavioral economics**. The frame "running government like a business" encourages people to prefer fees and charges over general taxation in funding public services. Can you come up with a similar slogan that might provide a framework that encourages the opposite preference?

7   **Thinking globally**. Choose another country and learn what you can about the role fees and charges may play in funding one or more of the services listed in Question #2. Is that role larger or smaller than the same role of fees and charges in funding that service or those services in the United States?

17 Intergovernmental grants

Introduction

Whether a government is federal or unitary, there are always some fiscal links between levels of government. Many of those fiscal linkages are explored in Chapters 2 and 3 that described the basic structure and fiscal operations of federal, state, and local governments in the United States and elsewhere.

Often these fiscal linkages take the form of shared responsibilities for programs or services. In the United States, for instance, the National Guard is a shared federal and state responsibility, and the provision of K-12 education is shared primarily between state and local governments, with some limited federal role. Usually that sharing involves a transfer of funds from one level of government to another that is primarily responsible for providing the service. Such transfers are called **intergovernmental grants**.

Intergovernmental grants mean that lower levels of government do not have to raise all the revenue to fund their programs and services. From the federal perspective, grants are a significant budgetary outlay. In 2007, $467 billion in grants (mostly to state governments) accounted for about 17 percent of all on-budget outlays and 20 percent of state and local revenue. State aid is also very significant for local governments. In 2007, according to the Census of Governments, states provided $447 billion in aid to local governments, of which 55 percent went to school districts.

A different scenario: collect locally, spend centrally

The notion that the central government has greater revenue-raising power than state or local governments is not universally shared. In many parts of Africa and Asia, it is considered easier to collect most or all the taxes at the local level and send them to the central government, which keeps a large share and sends the rest back with instructions about how to spend it.

A somewhat similar system existed until the 1990s in Eastern and Central Europe prior to the end of communism, and in China. Since that time, revenue collection has become more centralized in both places. But one feature of communism was a high degree of centralization. So even the largest of these countries were not federal in the sense that the United States, Canada, Germany and Australia are federal. Consequently, the concept of intergovernmental grants that take place at "arm's length" between somewhat autonomous governments did not apply to these situations.

Why does it make sense in the United States (and many other Western industrial nations as well) to collect centrally and spend locally through intergovernmental grants, while in large parts of the rest of the world, the opposite has been true? Probably the key differences are mobility and information systems. In a society where workers and firms are highly mobile, which is true of the Western industrial world, it is difficult to collect taxes at the local level because tax differences between cities, school districts or states are likely to induce those mobile taxpayers to relocate to a more kindly jurisdiction. Likewise, in a society where workers and firms are highly mobile, they do not stay put long enough for the local tax collector to get a handle on their income, assets and ability to pay as might be true in a more stable community. Only the property itself, which cannot move, lends itself to local assessment and collection of taxes. The existence of information networks that track that information on income, assets and ability to pay also creates some economies of scale in centralizing collection.

But consider a society of stable rural villages, where people live for many generations. Tax differences would not be a factor in mobility where there is little information about alternatives and a culture in which mobility is discouraged. Without complex computer-based information systems, the local tax collector is in a much better position to determine ability to pay and extract revenue than the distant central government.

Many of the features of our revenue system that we take for granted are culturally conditioned. The logic of intergovernmental grants in a Western, industrial, market-based economy gets turned on its head when transplanted to a very different historical, cultural, and institutional environment.

Purposes of grants

Grants may have a single purpose or serve multiple purposes. Among these purposes are vertical and horizontal equalization, correcting **spatial externalities**, redirecting priorities, and experimenting with new ideas and approaches. Sometimes a grant serves only one of these purposes, while other grants may serve multiple purposes.

Equalizing grants

One important function of grants is to balance revenue with service responsibilities both by levels of government and across governments at the same level. In the 1960s, it was widely believed that the federal government had a greater ability to raise revenue because it had more 'monopoly' power. People might move from city to city or state to state in search of a lower tax burden, but they were unlikely to move to another country just to reduce their taxes. The conclusion that was drawn from this argument was that it would be appropriate for the federal government to raise money for state and local governments to spend, without specifying the uses except in very broad terms.

This line of reasoning led to General Revenue Sharing, unrestricted federal grants to state and local governments, which lasted from the mid-1960s until the mid-1980s. General Revenue Sharing to states ended in 1982 and to local governments in 1986. General Revenue Sharing was an example of **vertical equalization**, which attempts to correct the difference between the amount of revenue that a government can raise and the amount of responsibility that appropriately falls to that level in a multi-level or federal system.

State aid to schools and local governments also falls at least partly in this category, because states have greater ability than local governments to raise revenue without driving away households and firms. Local governments exist in a highly competitive Tiebout situation and must always be mindful of the effect of their tax rates on location decisions. As a consequence, every US state except New Hampshire provides a substantial amount of state aid to local governments, which averaged 33.3 percent of local government revenue in 2007.

There is a horizontal dimension to the imbalance between revenue needs and ability to raise revenue as well. Cities, counties, and school districts vary greatly within and among states in their taxable wealth, the income and property wealth of their residents. The same tax rate will raise very different amounts of revenue per person in different jurisdictions.

The federal government addresses this disparity in some of its grants with formulas that favor states and local governments with greater indexes of "need" (poverty rates, per capita income, etc.). Most state education funding formulas also use some index of need or ability to pay as part of the distribution plan.

Per capita grants also address horizontal equalization, because more revenue per person will be collected from higher-income areas, but each local government will receive back the same amount per resident. All of these grants are designed to promote **horizontal equalization**, or reduction in the disparities in resources among governments of the same level or type (between cities, or counties, or states, or school districts). Many grants incorporate both vertical and horizontal equalization, particularly at the state-to-local level.

Correcting spatial externalities

A second purpose of grants is to offset the spillovers that occur because the service provided by a local or state government may generate benefits to those who live outside that government's boundaries and do not contribute to its support. Washington, DC, provides valued services and a significant employment destination for three adjacent counties in Virginia and two in Maryland. If the social benefits to nonresidents are not taken into account, then the local government in charge will produce less than the socially optimal level of the service. The last few chapters explored the use of exportable taxes and/or fees and charges as mechanisms for correcting such externalities.

Intergovernmental grants can also play a role in correcting spatial externalities. If, for example, having well-paved and well-lit streets benefits not only the residents of Lincoln, Nebraska, but also people who are just visiting or driving through, most of them from other parts of Nebraska, then state aid to street maintenance and lighting will use tax revenues from non-Lincoln residents to improve the quality and quantity of such services. Because the residents of Lincoln are the primary beneficiaries, they should bear most of the cost, but they are not the only beneficiaries.

Recall the analysis of public goods in Chapter 6, reproduced here as Figure 17.1. Now we are reinterpreting that analysis of tax price for two voters by recasting the two demand curves as those of residents (D_B) and nonresidents (D_A). If only the demands of residents are considered, the amount of service provided will be too low. One solution is a subsidy by the state on behalf of nonresident users. The appropriate tax price to be funded by the state is the nonresidents' share of the benefits, or the difference between P_1 and P_B. While such a share may be difficult to pinpoint in practice, it is at least conceptually clear that there are local services with spillover benefits for which a state subsidy through statewide general tax revenue is appropriate.

The same is true of spillovers between states. Charlotte, North Carolina, is an urban center for upstate South Carolina, as Memphis is for northern Mississippi, and New York City is for two adjacent states, providing services ranging from airports to museums to regional health centers. State watershed management creates literal spillovers from the many rivers that serve as state boundaries! The federal government can intervene constructively by providing grants that subsidize activities that also benefit residents of adjacent states.

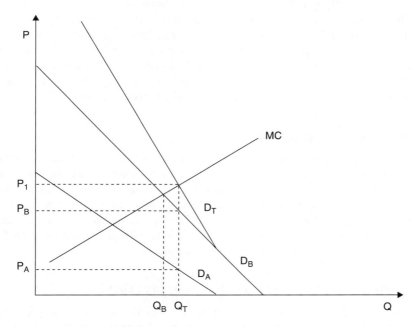

Figure 17.1 Demand by residents and nonresidents.

Redirecting priorities

Each level of government has its own priorities in terms of the variety and quality of public services to be provided and the externalities to be corrected. Sometimes higher levels of government attempt to override those priorities by mandating local governments to provide certain services. The US federal government, for example, mandates certain drinking water standards that local governments must meet. Compliance with both Affirmative Action to reduce education and employment discrimination and the Americans with Disabilities Act that regulates access to buildings has generated major complaints from state and local governments about the cost of compliance. State governments exert considerable control over local public schools, even when schools are nominally controlled by local school boards or city or county governments. States also have a great deal of authority over how the property tax is structured and administered in most states, even though the property tax is primarily a local revenue source.

When the higher level of government simply orders a state or local government to perform certain functions or meet certain standards without offering to pay some of the cost, that order is known as an **unfunded mandate**. Unfunded mandates have been a source of considerable dissension between state governments and the federal government in the United States. Unfunded mandates are usually a bone of contention between local and state public officials as well.

A less contentious and more incentive-based way to impose the preferences of a higher level of government on a lower one is through an intergovernmental grant that is earmarked for a particular service. When the services are largely funded by one level of government and actually provided by a different level, grants can be a tool of persuasion for redirecting priorities.

For example, the federal government in the United States has a cabinet-level Department of Education, but in fact both K-12 education and higher education are largely a function of state and local governments. If the federal government wants to be a 'player' in public education, it must persuade state and local governments to adopt its priorities and values. The federal government may want to see more emphasis on health education, or school readiness for preschoolers, or vocational training, or computers in schools. Grants are a tool for persuading states and school districts to refashion their priorities in order to receive federal aid.

Experimentation: laboratories of federalism

Grants are a particularly useful device in a federal system because new ideas and programs can be tried out in one or more states or local areas on an experimental basis before being spread to other states if they are successful. States and local governments make useful laboratories of federalism to carry out new ideas and test new approaches on a less than national scale. Usually grants for this purpose are project grants that invite proposals and select the most promising ones for funding, those that might offer useful information for designing broader programs or for implementing in other places.

The choice of tools: grants, direct expenditures, or tax relief?

When the central government or a state or provincial government wants to accomplish any of these objectives, a grant is not the only tool and often not the most desirable tool. Direct expenditures are another method. The US federal government made this choice in 1965 when Medicare for those over 65 made health care for most of the nation's elderly a direct federal responsibility. (Some health care costs for the elderly, mostly nursing home care, come under Medicaid, a federal–state shared responsibility.) Federal grants and subsidized student loan programs encourage higher education, which states may choose to supplement; no intergovernmental grants are involved. Instead, federal funds flow directly to individuals rather than to other levels of governments.

Tax expenditures in the form of tax credits, adjustments, or deductions are another tool to promote specific goals, such as encouraging private forms of welfare supported by charitable donations or seeking higher education with the aid of various tuition tax credits.

State governments also have the options of direct spending and tax expenditures as alternatives to grants. Much of the property tax relief in the past two decades funded by state governments has been an indirect form of aid to public schools, a move which has been more politically popular although perhaps less effective than direct grants in improving the quality of public education.

Types of grants

There are two basic kinds of grants in terms of use of funds: **general purpose grants** and **categorical grants**. There are also two different ways of distributing revenue: formula grants and project grants, depending on whether the money is automatically distributed according to some pre-set criteria or whether the recipient government must apply and sometimes compete with other applicants for a limited pool of funds. Other project grants are assigned to particular places by legislative action.

For both types, the revenue may be given as a lump sum or may require matching (e.g., one local dollar for every five federal dollars). Finally, a grant may be closed-ended (a limited pool of available funds) or open-ended (everyone who qualifies or submits an appropriate request is automatically funded). As a rule, general purpose grants are distributed by formula on a lump-sum basis, while categorical grants may be formula, project, or some of each, and may be either lump-sum or matching. Both types can be either closed-ended or open-ended.

General purpose or categorical

The structure or form of a grant is often dictated by its purpose. A pure equalization grant, such as many kinds of state aid to local governments, does not put many constraints on how the funds may be spent. A categorical grant, in contrast, must be spent for a designated use, such as putting more police patrols on the street or providing free or reduced price lunches to school children.

In practice, even categorical grants have the effect of giving recipient governments some flexibility in the use of their funds. If a local government had planned to put additional police patrols on the streets and federal funds became available for that purpose, then that government could redirect some of its own-source revenues to other priorities, such as more frequent garbage pickup or more street lights.

The ability to shift dollars to other purposes in response to grants is called **fungibility**. Higher levels of government are aware of this possibility and often take safeguards to prevent such shifting of funds, because their goal is to ensure more police patrols or more free lunches than there would have been in the absence of the grant money. Many grants contain **maintenance of effort** requirements, which make continuation of the grantee's current level of spending on the designated purpose a condition for funding.

In the 1970s, the US federal government began to use a hybrid type of grant, which has seen even more use in the past three decades, called a block grant. A **block grant** consists of funds that must be used within a broad category, such as law enforcement or secondary education or community development, but the recipient government has a great deal of flexibility about exactly how to spend the funds within that category. Many block grants were used to consolidate proliferating categorical grants, with the tradeoff that state and local governments received less funding but with more flexibility.

Formula or project grants

Another issue in designing intergovernmental grants is how they should be distributed among recipients. A **formula grant** is distributed according to some set of criteria, while a **project grant** is usually received in response to competitive applications (or sometimes competition among legislators to provide for their own districts).

The formula may be as simple as so many dollars per capita, or may include other factors such as the poverty rate, the number of school pupils, the number of miles of highway, the percentage of the population that is elderly, or the relative amount of substandard housing. Much of state aid to local schools is distributed on the basis of complex formulas that are described in Chapter 18. A formula grant can be used for either general-purpose grants or for categorical grants (including block grants) that specify the use to which the funds must be directed.

Project grants invite state or local governments to compete for a limited pool of funds by submitting proposals to the agency dispensing the funds. At both the state and federal levels, project grants are sometimes noncompetitive. Pork-barrel politics (along with "bringing home the bacon") is the colorful term used to describe the political wheeling and dealing by which representatives ensure that their districts receive funds for special purposes ranging from railroad museums to wetlands conservation to highway construction.

Lump sum or matching

A third issue in grant design is whether to provide the funds with or without requiring the recipient government to increase its effort. A **lump sum grant** provides a certain number of dollars to the recipient, which may be available for general use or restricted use, without condition or with a requirement of maintenance of effort. Most of the US federal block grants such as Job Training and Partnership Act (JTPA) grants or community development block grants (CDBG) are lump sum. Medicaid, a joint federal–state program for the medically indigent, requires a state match.

A **matching grant**, which is almost always tied to a specific purpose such as highway construction or increased law enforcement effort, changes the relative price of additional units of that particular kind of service. With a matching grant, an extra dollar's worth of highway or police patrol may only cost 50 cents in local funds, while an extra dollar's worth of any other service will cost an entire locally raised dollar. Matching grants use the persuasion of relative price in the marketplace to induce recipients to change their spending patterns in ways preferred by the donor level of government.

Open-ended or closed-ended

An **open-ended grant** obligates the grantor government to fund as many projects, recipients, or governments as meet the stated qualifications. In contrast, a **closed-ended grant** allocates a specific sum through the budget and that amount cannot be exceeded. Closed-ended grants have a specific budgeted amount which must be rationed among competing claimants through a grant application process, a formula, or some other distribution mechanism.

Open-ended grants create challenges for budget-makers, who must estimate how many recipients will qualify for how much in the way of funds. Until welfare reform in the 1990s, the principal welfare program Aid to Families with Dependent Children (AFDC) was an open-ended program. Since reform, federal aid to states for welfare-type programs, now known as Temporary Assistance to Needy Families (TANF), has become a closed-ended program with specific dollar amounts. Medicaid, which provides funds for the medically indigent, is also an open-ended program which has seen rapid growth in costs in the past 20 years.

Efficiency effects of grants

Efficiency effects of grants are complicated to analyze. Sometimes the purpose of a grant is pure equalization; that is, the higher level of government wants to ensure a minimum amount of publicly funded services available to citizens, regardless of the tax wealth of the place where they live. Lump sum general purpose grants are non-distorting within the public sector in much the same way that a poll tax is non-distorting. A lump sum general purpose grant does not distort decisions by local public officials about how to spend the funds available to them because the amount of revenue they receive is independent of the actions that they take.

As soon as conditions are attached, however—maintenance of effort, management, specification of how the funds must be used—then there is redirection of local decisions. Some of these distortions are intentional, in order to impose the preferences of a higher level of government on a local government that would not spend in the same way without the carrot and stick of conditional grants. Other distortions are not intended. Sometimes the link between condition and grant is tenuous; the federal government has withheld highway funds from states that did not conform to its desires for higher minimum ages for drinking alcohol or mandatory helmet laws for motorcyclists.

The challenge facing the donor government is to ensure that an additional dollar of funds made available to a recipient government results in increased spending on the intended purpose, rather than reduced local tax effort or shifting funds to other purposes. The challenge facing the recipient government is to continue to honor their own priorities and preferences in the spending mix and the level of taxation while taking advantage of the availability of additional funds.

From a larger perspective, these grant funds are not "free." If there are more grant dollars returning to Chicago or Dallas from their state or federal government, some of those extra dollars came from the citizens of Chicago or Dallas. But from the local perspective, each community and even each state is almost a pure competitor. If these recipient governments provided no additional tax revenue from which the state or federal government could make grants, the loss of their contribution would be too small to make a difference in the size of the pot available. Consequently, at the margin, local and even state governments often separate the desirability of having the grant program at all and its cost to their citizens from any decisions about whether to accept or apply for funds and how to use them.

Indifference analysis of grants

Each type of grant presents different challenges of analysis. Three kinds of grants are analyzed here. The first is a simple lump sum grant with no maintenance of effort and no spending restrictions. The second is a lump sum grant that must be used for public safety, broadly defined, with a maintenance-of-effort requirement. The third is a matching grant for additional police patrols in local communities. These three types do not exhaust the possibilities, but they present most of the challenges faced by donor governments in designing grants and by recipient governments in responding to grants.

Note that efficiency is more difficult to define when there are two parties with different objectives. From the standpoint of the donor government, a grant is more efficient if it directs more resources toward the desired objective. From the standpoint of the recipient government, however, efficiency means that they have the freedom to allocate resources in the way that they believe will maximize the well-being of the citizens to whom they are accountable. As the analysis that follows bears out, efficiency from the donor standpoint means lots of "strings" attached, while for recipient governments efficiency means as few strings as possible.

The basic technique of analysis is the same for all kinds of grants. Indifference maps, which were introduced in Chapter 10 on cost-benefit analysis, represent the preferences of decision-makers, who may be elected officials, appointed officials, or voters. The axes represent alternative bundles of goods. Sometimes the choices on the axes are publicly produced goods and private goods, as in Figure 17.2, while other times one axis will represent a particular publicly produced good (such as public safety) and all other publicly produced goods and services.

The shape of the indifference curve reflects diminishing marginal utility of both bundles of services. A higher indifference curve (one above and to the right of another) represents

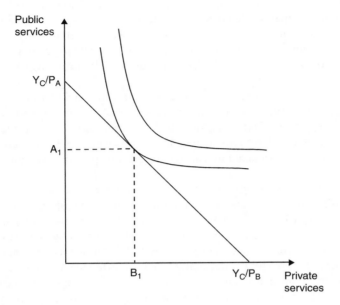

Figure 17.2 Indifference analysis of community choice.

more of one or both bundles of services and therefore a higher level of satisfaction at any point on that curve compared to any point on a lower curve.

The budget constraint (the straight line in Figure 17.2) represents available budgetary resources and the prices of each of the two bundles. If the axes are publicly versus privately produced goods and services, the budgetary resources to be allocated are all the community's income (Y_C). If the axes both represent bundles of publicly produced goods, the budget constraint represents the revenue available to the public sector to allocate.

The budget constraint shows the various combinations of the two bundles of goods and services that can be purchased out of that revenue at the given prices of the two bundles. If the entire budget were spent on public services, with a price of P_A for each unit, then it would be possible to purchase Y_C/P_A units of public services. Likewise, if the entire budget were spent on private services, with a price of P_B for each unit, then it would be possible to purchase Y_C/P_B units of public services.

The budget line is where the effects of the grant are translated into the diagram. An increase in available revenue will shift the budget constraint outward in parallel fashion. A change in the price of one bundle or good but not the other will cause the budget line to rotate. For example, a decrease in the price of a unit of public services means that more of it can be purchased in combination with any given amount of all private services. The budget constraint would rotate upward on the vertical axis while going through the same intercept on the horizontal axis, and the community would be able to attain a higher indifference curve.

Analysis of a lump sum grant

Figure 17.2 represents the choices of a local public sector prior to receiving a lump sum grant. The price for one unit of a bundle of public services is P_A and the price for one unit of a bundle of private services is P_B. Total income in the community is Y_C. If all resources are devoted to public services, the maximum number of units that can be purchased is Y_C/P_A; if all resources are devoted to private services, the maximum number of units that can be purchased is Y_C/P_B. Given the community's (or decision-makers') preferences as expressed in the indifference map, this community has chosen to consume A_1 of publicly produced services and B_1 of privately produced goods and services.

Now the community receives a lump sum grant to be used for any public purpose, illustrated in Figure 17.3. The amount of the grant is measured by the vertical distance between the two budget lines, A_3 minus A_1. The community, or its decision-makers, respond to this increase in income by choosing a new combination of publicly and privately produced goods and services, A_2 and B_2. Citizens have increased their consumption of publicly produced goods and services, but not by the full amount of the grant. Some of the increased revenue has come in the form of a reduction in taxes or other local revenue, leaving consumers more after-tax income to spend on private consumption.

This analysis of even this simplest kind of intergovernmental grant has some profound policy implications. One implication is that donor governments may find it difficult to impose preferences on recipient governments. The other implication comes from empirical research on responses to different kinds of funding, known as the flypaper effect (see p. 293).

Fungibility and maintenance of effort

If the intent of the grant in Figure 17.3 was to increase funds available to the public sector, it was only partially successful. Some of the funds were diverted into private consumption by substituting intergovernmental funds for locally raised revenues. This is a graphic illustration of the notion of fungibility, or the ability to shift funds between uses in

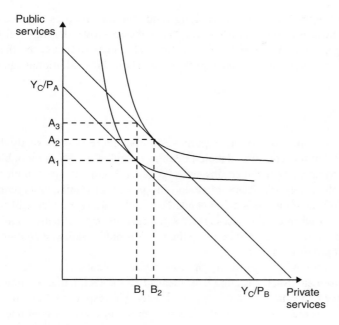

Figure 17.3 A lump sum grant.

response to changing needs and opportunities. Fungibility is generally regarded by those who spend the money as a good thing, because it gives them more flexibility. But the donor government, or sometimes the citizens, may feel differently about giving them that kind of flexibility.

Case study: fungibility and the lottery

Even though a state-run lottery is not a grant, it does offer one of the clearest illustrations of the issue of fungibility. Lotteries are state-sponsored monopolies that generate revenue for public use. In the nineteenth century, most states wrote into their constitutions a prohibition on state-sponsored lotteries in response to widespread scandals. When lotteries again became popular in the United States, a referendum was required in order to change that constitutional prohibition. Today 37 states have state-run lotteries. Lotteries are popular throughout the world, and many of them are publicly run.

In order to increase the likelihood that the lottery would be approved, state governments adopted a practice of earmarking lottery revenues for some designated public purpose. Education has been the most common purpose, but economic development and senior citizen services are also beneficiaries of lottery revenues in some states. However, some states, including Florida, Illinois, and New York, used part of the additional revenue from the lottery to substitute for existing education funding rather than to increase the total pool of funds for that purpose. Many citizens felt misled.

Lotteries adopted more recently have addressed that citizen concern by safeguarding lottery funds from the general budget in a number of ways. Georgia is one of several states that segregates lottery funds from general fund revenue and uses the proceeds for some specific programs that receive all of their funds from the lottery. These programs include a college scholarship program for Georgia high school graduates and newly created programs for early childhood education.

While economists generally are critical of earmarking funds for specific uses because it reduces budget flexibility, citizens often feel differently. When they discover that fungibility offers a way to assert legislators' preferences over voter preferences, it increases their distrust of government as not responding to their preferences about how additional funds should be spent.

Fungibility and block grants

The problem of fungibility is not limited to general purpose grants. Figure 17.4 is exactly the same as Figure 17.3 except that the axes are relabeled "Public safety" and "All other public goods." Suppose that this community received, instead of a general purpose grant, a block grant to use to provide public safety services (police and fire protections, jails, emergency medical services, etc.) All of the grant funds are expended on public safety, but some of the locally raised funds are diverted into other uses, such as recreation or libraries or public health. The intent of the donor government to increase the level of public safety spending is met, but not by the full amount of the grant.

The most common solution to this problem for donor governments is to impose a maintenance of effort requirement. Such a requirement means that the recipient government cannot reduce its own-source expenditures on the specified service in response to a grant. In Figure 17.5, there is a break in the grant line. If the local government does not continue to maintain its prior spending of B_1 on public safety, the grant will be withdrawn. This constraint

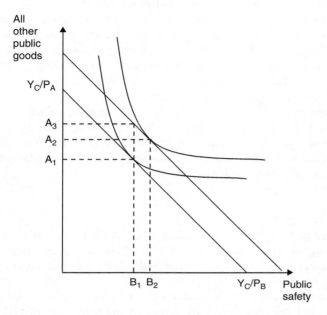

Figure 17.4 Analysis of a specific purpose grant.

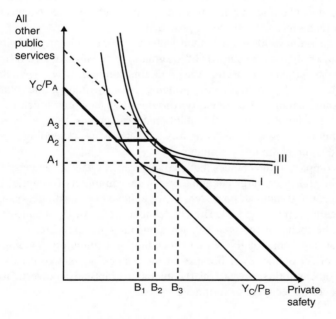

Figure 17.5 A maintenance of effort requirement.

forces the local government to choose a different combination of services than it would otherwise have chosen, so that all the grant funds are expended on increased public safety services.

The highest indifference curve that this community can reach with the maintenance of effort requirement is curve II instead of III. Curve II represents an improvement over the no grant situation, but a lower level of satisfaction with the spending mix compared to what would have been chosen in the absence of a maintenance of effort requirement. Of course, this outcome is much more satisfying for the donor government!

Maintenance of effort is conceptually simple but difficult to administer in practice, particularly for continuous funding rather than a one-time grant. With annual funding, the local effort to be maintained has to be adjusted from year to year by some kind of index or formula. Some of the problems associated with implementing a maintenance of effort requirement are discussed in more detail in Chapter 18 on public education.

Analysis of matching grants

Matching grants are designed to encourage specific kinds of spending. Instead of a maintenance of effort requirement, matching grants require that additional dollars from the donor government must be matched in some proportion by additional local dollars spent for that particular purpose. The match may be as high as 1:1 but more commonly is an 80:20, 90:10, or 70:30 match, which would mean that an additional $80 (or $90, or $70) of federal or state money requires that the local government also spend an additional $20 (or $10, or $30) on the specified purpose as a condition of receiving the grant.

From the standpoint of the recipient government, a match is the equivalent of a price cut for one particular service. While a lump sum grant has only an income effect, a matching grant has both an income and a substitution effect toward that particular service because it becomes relatively cheaper than other services being provided.

One popular grant program in the 1990s in the United States was for community policing. Figure 17.6 shows community policing (the purpose of the grants) on the horizontal axis and all other public services on the vertical axis. Before the grant, this community was spending A_1 on all other public services and B_1 on community policing. Now the budget line rotates to reflect the fact that the same amount of community resources will now buy much more community policing because a large share of the additional cost comes from a federal matching grant. The community changes its spending mix so that it is now spending A_2 on all other public services and B_2 on community policing.

How does this outcome compare to the choices the local government would have made if there were not a match? If the grant were large enough to move the community from indifference curve I to indifference curve II, but had no match, it would have been a parallel budget line that resulted in a choice of combination A_3, B_3. This change from A_1, B_1 is called the income effect of the grant. The change in the spending mix along the same indifference curve to A_2, B_2 a combination that represents relatively more spending on community policing— represents the substitution effect of the grant because of the change in relative prices of community policing versus other public services. Clearly, matching grants are a powerful tool for imposing donor preferences on recipient governments.

Equity effects of grants

Grants have both equity and efficiency purposes. Equity is served by collecting from citizens in both rich and poor jurisdictions (with more usually coming from richer citizens and/or

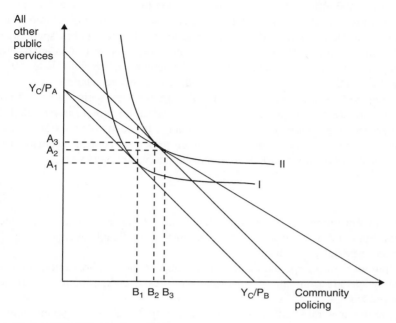

Figure 17.6 Effects of a matching grant.

richer jurisdictions) and redistributing a larger share of the funds to jurisdictions with higher concentrations of low-income citizens. For example, the US federal government collects more income tax per capita from residents of Washington, Michigan, and New York, which are relatively high-income states. Within those states, more of the tax payments come from their wealthier citizens.

When the central government gives grants for school lunches, community development, welfare, or other programs that are targeted at lower-income areas, more of those funds are directed on a per capita basis to South Carolina, Arkansas, and Mississippi, which have lower average incomes and more residents below the poverty line. There are other equity indicators that are factored into this distribution as well, but poverty rates figure strongly in many grants. It should be noted, however, that even if the grants were distributed purely on a per capita basis, there would still be some redistribution, because relatively more of the funds being redistributed were collected from higher-income households.

Behavioral economics: the flypaper effect

The second interesting consequence of this analysis of grants is an empirical finding known by the colorful name of "the **flypaper effect**," which is shorthand for "money sticks where it lands." If Figure 17.3 represented a tax cut to citizens instead of a lump-sum grant to a local government, the analysis implies that the resulting spending mix would be the same, i.e., the same relative increases in spending on public and private goods and services. In other words, a simple application of the theoretical model would predict that public officials would be merely passive translators of the preferences of the median voter expressed in the community indifference map.

In reality, however, the effects are quite different. Even though an increase in private incomes and an intergovernmental lump sum grant represent the same shift in the budget line and the same increase in total community resources, a grant will increase public spending by about 40 percent of the amount of the grant. An increase in private income (including through tax cuts) will only increase public spending by about 10 percent (Hines and Thaler 1995). Clearly, a larger share of the money seems to stick in the sector where it lands!

A number of explanations have been offered, but the simplest one seems to be that both public officials and private citizens have their own preferences for how resources shall be used. Those preferences may not exactly coincide. Change the locus of decision-making, and you change the outcome. The voting process is an imperfect control mechanism for forcing public officials to determine and respond precisely to what voters want.

Summary

- Central government grants can be an important source of revenue to state and local governments. State aid to local governments is also a significant revenue source for most US states, especially for education.
- Among the purposes of intergovernmental grants are vertical and horizontal equalization, correcting spatial externalities, redirecting priorities, and experimenting with new ideas and approaches.
- Equalizing grants can address either vertical equalization (the ability of governments at different levels to raise revenue commensurate with their expenditure demands) or horizontal equalization (redirecting fiscal resources from wealthier to poorer jurisdictions of the same type, e.g., state to state, county to county).
- Spatial externalities can lead to spending less than the optimal amount by a state or local government if a significant part of the benefits spill over to an adjacent jurisdiction. Grants from a higher level of government to encourage the provision of more of such services can correct for this problem.
- Grants can also be used to redirect priorities, which can also be achieved by mandates. A grant can offer an incentive to a state or local government to provide a new service or expand provision of a particular service. Grants for this purpose are usually quite constrained and focus on the ways that funds can be used.
- Grants can be used to try new ideas, approaches, or programs on a limited basis before trying them on a national scale. Other communities or states can learn from these experiments in the laboratories of federalism that grants can encourage.
- Grants are just one way of accomplishing the objectives of a higher level of government through partnership with other governments. Sometimes direct expenditures are a good alternative. Other times the incentives can be offered to individuals instead of other governments through tax expenditures. The best choice of a tool depends on the nature of the objective being sought.
- Grants can be general purpose grants that can be spent on any public purpose, or categorical grants that must be spent on a specific use. The revenue may be distributed automatically according to some pre-set criteria (formula grants, which are about 71 percent of all federal grants) or only to designated recipients based on competitive applications or legislative discretion. Grants may be given as a lump sum or may require matching contributions by the recipient government. Matching grants change relative prices and generally have a stronger incentive effect toward the target objective than a lump sum grant for the same purpose.

- A grant may be closed-ended (a limited pool of available funds) or open-ended (everyone who qualifies or submits an appropriate request is automatically funded). Closed-ended grants provide some budgetary predictability, but at the expense of meeting the needs of all the targeted recipients determined by the grant criteria. Where the grant is directed toward a specific purpose, the donor government may have to attach maintenance of effort requirements to ensure that there is a significant increase in spending on the designated purpose.
- Block grants have been used to reduce the number of categorical grants and provide more flexibility in the use of funds by recipient governments. A block grant is designated toward a broad area of public expenditure, such as community development, but allows recipients broad latitude in adapting the program to local needs and conditions.
- Grants have both equity and efficiency effects. Equity effects can be measured by how well grants meet redistributional goals. Efficiency effects are analyzed with indifference curves and budget constraints.
- A simple lump sum grant will increase spending both on public purposes and on private purposes. Donor governments often impose maintenance of effort requirements to ensure that local spending on the target purpose does not decline. Matching grants change the relative price of different kinds of public services and encourage more spending on the designated purpose.
- The flypaper effect finds that "money sticks where it lands," i.e., funds that are sent to the local public sector are spent there while funds that are sent to private citizens via tax relief are largely spent for private purposes.

Key terms

Categorical grant
Closed-ended grant
Flypaper effect
Formula grant
Fungibility
General purpose grant
Horizontal equalization
Intergovernmental grant
Lump sum grant
Maintenance of effort
Matching grant
Open-ended grant
Project grant
Spatial externalities
Unfunded mandate
Vertical equalization

Questions

1 If you were running the donor government, and wanted to encourage more local spending on immunizations for children, what kind of grant would you devise? Why? How might your answer be different from the perspective of recipient governments?

2   Using the same analytical techniques as those developed in this chapter, develop a diagrammatic analysis of a matching grant with a maximum amount available. (Hint: when the maximum is reached, the rest of the budget line becomes vertical or horizontal.) How are the effects different from those of a simple matching grant? Does it depend on the size of the maximum? The shape/position of the indifference map? Are there circumstances in which the ceiling on available funds might have no effect on the mix of services provided?

3   What role might grants play in correcting negative externalities, such as air pollution? Under what circumstances might they be preferred on equity or efficiency grounds to taxes on emissions or regulatory approaches?

4   **By the numbers**. Using data from the US Bureau of the Census, graph the intergovernmental grants to state and local governments and the grants from state to local governments from 1990 to the most recent available year. What pattern do you see? The web address is http://www.census.gov/govs/estimate/.

5   **Policy application**. Suppose you are in charge of grants from state to local government in order to reduce inequality in the amount of resources that counties have to provide certain basic services such as roads, sheriff's office, emergency medical services, libraries, and health clinics. Your state has a few large urban areas with some poverty but also a lot of taxable commercial and industrial wealth, prosperous suburban areas, and a lot of rural areas with limited job opportunities and low population density. It is your job to come up with a distribution formula for state aid to counties. What factors might you include in your formula? Why?

6   **Behavioral economics**. Project grants, based on competitive applications, implicitly assume that all competing state or local governments have access to the information and resources to make an effective grant application. How might differences in information and resources between potential grant recipients influence the ability of some governments to acquire project grants? How might the grants be designed to level the playing field?

7   **Thinking globally**. Intergovernmental grants at the international level take many forms, including development assistance and military aid. What kinds of challenges exist in this kind of grants that are not a problem for grants within a country?

18 Public education

Introduction

Public education from pre-school through higher education is a major activity of governments at all levels, but in the United States the primary responsibility lies at the state and local levels. The share of public education financing at the federal level has declined over the past two decades. At the same time, in many states, there has been a reallocation of responsibility away from local governments toward the state, partly to provide property tax relief and partly to equalize educational resources between rich and poor school districts.

Few other functions of government touch so many lives so directly. Almost everyone in the country has had some link to a public school or college as a student, teacher, administrator, public official, or community volunteer—not to mention citizen/taxpayer. Public schools are not only expected to educate young people for the basic skills of a modern industrial society, including work and citizenship skills, and to instill in them a desire for lifelong learning, but are also called upon to provide ancillary services, including social services, mental and physical health assistance, and recreation. Public schools provide meeting space for a variety of community activities. At the same time no public function is subjected to greater scrutiny and complaint, with taxpayers and parents demanding better performance for fewer dollars of inputs.

Table 18.1 summarizes the size and scope of elementary and secondary education activities in the United States, including public and private sectors, and federal, state, and local financing. As you can see, elementary and secondary education is a direct and important part of life for more than 50 million Americans as teachers and students, or about 15 percent of the population.

Why public education?

While societies have provided for formal education for children and youth for thousands of years, it is only recently that education has been perceived as a function of government. In ancient Rome and Greece, education was provided by the family, with tutors educating the sons (and sometimes even daughters) of wealthier families. For those who were not wealthy, education was more likely to be an apprenticeship to learn a trade or skill, a pattern that has continued well into modern times. In much of Western society, religion offered another path to education. Judaism laid great stress on learning to read for religious purposes, and monasteries and convents were havens for education and scholarship throughout the Middle Ages.

Even today, private education for the children of the wealthy and church-related schools from pre-school through higher education play an important role in the provision of

Table 18.1 Education in the United States, Kindergarten to Grade 12, 2007

	Schools	Students	Teachers	Public spending ($)
			(1998–99)	*(2010)*
Public	98,793		3.1 million	Federal $84.1 billion
Public schools		49.3 million		State and local $566.9 billion
Private	33,740	5.9 million	456,270	
Home-schooled		1.5 million		
Total		56.7 million	3.6 million	$650 billion
Average revenue per pupil (public schools, 2007)		$11,277		

Sources: Public spending data from U.S. Bureau of the Census. Other data from National Center for Education Statistics.

education. But the important difference between earlier societies and modern industrial economies is that education is expected to be both available to and required of everyone, regardless of ability to pay and even to some extent regardless of ability or willingness to learn. There has been a collective judgment that the costs of ignorance are higher than the price society must pay to provide universal access to education.

Education does not meet the standard tests for a pure public good, because it is neither truly non-rival in consumption nor non-excludable. There is some opportunity for collective consumption (hundreds of people can listen to a lecture) but, particularly at younger ages, consumption of education services is also competitive. More time and attention given to one student means less for another. There are also benefits of shared learning, so that the optimum class size for learning purposes is not necessarily one, but congestion sets in quickly, which is the reason for pressure to reduce class sizes.

Exclusion is easy, as anyone who has been sent away because their name is not on the class roll can testify. So education is excludable and at least somewhat rival in consumption. The justification for public involvement in education, then, must rest on other grounds besides public goods. The efficiency rationale is based on positive externalities, both civic and economic. The equity rationale is equality of opportunity rather than equality of results.

Efficiency issues in public education

In education, as in other public and private goods and services, efficiency means allocating scarce resources to generate the maximum potential benefit. Some of the benefits of education are private—they accrue to the person who gets educated. Others are social—they spill over to the rest of the society, especially those with whom the educated person shares a work environment, a community, or a family. Education is a form of investment that pays future dividends, but capital markets are not necessarily well structured to make that kind of financial capital available for people to invest in themselves without some government intervention. So market failure is another efficiency issue in public education.

Private benefits: returns to investment in human capital

Education, especially beyond high school, is an investment in human capital that pays significant lifetime dividends. Among the developed nations that are part of the Organization for Economic Cooperation and Development, the average earnings differential for those with a bachelor's degree or higher over those with less education is 52 percent. In 2007, the US worker with a bachelor's degree enjoyed a 72 percent earnings advantage, and in the United Kingdom, 57 percent (Education Counts 2010).

Even after allowing for the years of little or no earnings while attending college, the return to higher education is pretty impressive. So it is reasonable to ask why private decisions might result in less than optimal provision of education. For the answer, we turn primarily to externality arguments, secondarily to arguments involving either missing markets or equity.

Social benefits

Suppose that you live in a subdivision, and have no children, but your neighbors do. Why should you contribute to their education? Shouldn't that be the responsibility of their parents, who chose to bring them into the world and thereby assumed the responsibility for providing them with diapers, formula, toys, pets, transportation, braces, and bicycles?

This argument is not just hypothetical. It is one of the reasons why retirement communities sometimes attempt to withdraw from their school districts, arguing that their neighborhood produces no education demands and therefore should not have to contribute to paying for it. Senior citizens have been quoted as saying, "I educated my children, let them educate theirs."

The problem with this argument, of course, is that the now-senior citizens are unlikely to have contributed enough tax dollars over their parenting years to cover the cost of educating even their own children, let alone anyone else's. Since their children's education was subsidized by others, one could argue that intergenerational equity requires them to contribute in turn (based on their ability to pay) to the cost of educating other children—including their own grandchildren. But the primary rationale for asking all taxpayers to contribute to the cost of public education whether or not they now have or ever have had children in the public schools is the argument that the education of all children creates social benefits.

There are at least three benefits that correspond to the three functions of individuals in a market democracy as citizens, consumers, and workers. The first benefit is civic in nature. A democratic society can only function with an educated citizenry that understands their civic duties and can carry them out, watch-dogging the political process so that it does not generate into the purely self-interested morass that public choice theorists warn us about. The ability to locate, absorb, and interpret information is an essential part of civic participation. Beyond that basic skill, students are trained in the arts of citizenship, including participation in civic affairs and learning how the political system works and how to engage it. The rest of us should benefit from their active and informed participation in the political process by enjoying a more responsive and accountable government at all levels.

The same kinds of skills are essential to participating in the marketplace as an informed consumer, the second form of social benefit. Economists assume that information is available and utilized. Rational expectations theory assumes that this process is continuous and rapid, weeding out inferior products and services and ensuring a good match between consumer and product, worker and employer.

But that process of acquiring, disseminating, and acting on information assumes that consumers are educated, that they are literate, that they have basic skills in critical interpretation of information. The same kind of watch-dogging that can keep government more honest and accountable is important in the market for consumer goods and services. Everyone as a consumer is protected and benefited by the presence of other informed, articulate consumers in the marketplace, spreading and acting on information to widen the range of informed choice.

The third way in which individuals participate in a market democracy is as producers—worker or entrepreneur or some combination of the two. As the economy has become more technologically sophisticated, the level of basic skills in reading, math, writing, and analysis required for even entry-level jobs has also increased. While it was once possible to get a few years of education to learn basic writing and arithmetic and then go to work on the farm or in the mill, those options are no longer open.

These benefits are those most often emphasized in promoting and supporting public education, but the person being educated actually captures a larger share of work-related benefits of investing in human capital than civic or consumption effects, because of the gains in lifetime income that may result. However, there are still social benefits for the worker training component of public education. An educated workforce is an essential precondition for economic development and a continuing requirement to sustain a growing and increasingly sophisticated economy.

A more subtle benefit to public schools that is not entirely captured in these three roles is the exposure to diversity and the recognition and acceptance of legitimate differences in values, behavior, attitudes and practices of people from different religious and/or cultural backgrounds. In a culturally heterogeneous society such as the United States, public education that brings people together at a young age can promote an understanding and acceptance of diversity that may contribute significantly to the reduction of social tensions and social conflicts.

One might expect that in well-functioning markets, it would be possible to borrow to pay for education and repay the loan with interest while still having a larger income than one would have had without the education. That strategy has become commonplace in financing higher education, both undergraduate and graduate. There is a well-developed market with both private and public lenders to provide loans to college students. But such a market would be harder to develop for K-12 students because of the longer period of study and the greater difficulty in "picking winners."

By the time students arrive at college, there are already clear indications of their learning and earning potential and thus their ability to repay a loan. College students are also of legal age, so that they can borrow on their own accounts, which is not true of children under the age of 18. The parents of younger children may not be willing to commit themselves to repay and are not legally able to bind their underage children to a loan obligation. While the market works reasonably well at the post-high school level, these market imperfections would lead to underinvestment in human capital at the pre-college level in the absence of public subsidy of some kind.

Equity issues: equality of opportunity

From an equity perspective, education is sometimes classified as a merit good—something to which one is entitled by virtue of membership in society, regardless of ability to pay. Like housing vouchers, food stamps and Medicaid, education can be viewed as an in-kind transfer program designed so that the children of the poor get the benefits rather than giving money to their parents and relying on then to make sure that the children get what they need.

But there is an important difference between education and other services to children in low-income households in the United States. Many other countries provide both universal health insurance and universal children's allowances (cash aid) to children without regard to need, with some of the cash aid recaptured through the income tax system. The United States dispenses both health care for children (Medicaid) and cash support on a need basis, including welfare (TANF), food stamps and housing assistance. Using a need basis means making a careful distinction between those who should be able to pay their own way and those cannot manage without a public subsidy.

K-12 education is one of the few forms of in-kind redistribution in the United States where the same service is offered to all without requiring payment, regardless of ability to pay. Since the public schools are supported by taxes, the wealthy contribute the largest share of the cost and the poor contribute little or nothing, but the only place in school where there is any distinction between rich and poor students is in access to the free and reduced price lunch program.

An important part of the equity rationale for providing education at no cost, and the reason that it is generally provided at no charge or only nominal cost to the child's family, is that education is an investment in human capital that will make these children able to become productive and self-supporting adult members of society. Without such an investment, the children could easily become trapped in an endless cycle of generations of poverty, with families too poor to invest in them even when the return is very high.

Social benefits by themselves justify some degree of subsidy, but because there are private benefits that accrue to the child and his or her family in terms of increased productivity, economic efficiency suggests that the household should pay for those private benefits. It is only when education is seen as a poverty-preventing, productivity-enhancing strategy that it might be possible to justify what is typically a 100 percent subsidy.

Inputs and outputs: the education production function

Economists and educational researchers have devoted considerable attention to measuring the effects of various levels and combinations of educational inputs on student performance both on standardized tests and in the job market (measured by earnings). This relationship is the **education production function**, which shows the amount of "output" (learning or increased productivity) that results from a given mix and/or level of inputs.

It is much easier to define a production function for wheat, or steel, or haircuts in terms of the labor, capital, and raw materials inputs needed to produce a given quantity of output because these products and services have clearly measurable outputs. While we can measure educational inputs, it is harder to get any clear agreement about the appropriate measure of educational output.

Comparing inputs

Because US federal aid is a relatively modest component of K-12 education spending, and because different states have not only difference resources but also different attitudes and values about public education, there is considerable variation not only within states but also between states in educational spending per pupil, educational resources, and educational outcomes. According to the National Center for Education Statistics, spending per pupil in 2008 for current operations ranged from $17,620 in New Jersey to $5,978 in Utah, with an average of $10,927.

In some cases the difference in per pupil spending reflects differences in such factors as regional costs of living or average school or district size. (Rural districts tend to be more costly per student because scattered student populations result in high transportation costs, small schools and small class sizes.) In other cases, the spending per pupil reflects the taxable wealth of the school district or state and/or the value that citizens and political leaders place on education relative to other spending priorities.

Comparing outcomes: the accountability debate

The issue of **accountability** is important because policy-makers face conflicting pressures. Parents and employers are anxious to improve school quality while taxpayers (including many of the same people) want to contain or reduce the amount of tax resources devoted to public education.

Numerous economic studies provide no clear conclusion. Some find a statistically significant link between certain inputs (such as the teacher–student ratio) and test scores, while others find little relationship, and others find that the sign is sometimes negative rather than positive. Studies by Card and Krueger did find a positive relationship between educational inputs, specifically expenditures per pupil and the teacher–pupil ratio, and later earnings across a broad spectrum of age groups (Card and Krueger 1996).

More recent studies by Pogue, Maxey and Lu and by Taylor control for family and community backgrounds and other factors so that they can measure the schools' "value added," i.e., separate the effect of schools from other influences on performance. In both cases, these researchers find strong and positive effects of additional resources on outcomes as measured by student performance (Pogue *et al* 1999 and Taylor 1999). Neither side of the debate can demonstrate conclusively, however, that there is a clear and direct relationship between inputs and outputs in education.

There has been considerable controversy in the past two decades about output measures, particularly excessive reliance on standardized tests. At the height of the controversy, in 2001, the Bush administration persuaded Congress to enact the **No Child Left Behind Act (NCLB)** with bipartisan support. This legislation stressed standards-based education using measurable goals set by individual states with federal funding linked to results.

Critics of No Child Left Behind argue that performance on standardized tests is not necessarily either an adequate measure of learning or a predictor of future success as a worker, consumer, and citizen, which are presumably the primary objectives of education. Heavy reliance on test scores to measure the performance of not only students but teachers and individual schools has created a perverse incentive system that encourages teachers to focus on "teaching to the test," at the expense of developing skills and abilities that take longer to acquire and are not directly reflected on the tests.

Cross-country comparisons

There are two major testing systems that are used across countries to compare student performance. One test, administered by the International Association for the Evaluation of Educational Achievement (IEA), is a multiple choice test called Trends in International Mathematics and Science Study (TIMSS), which is given to fourth and eighth grade students every four years. Fifty-four countries participated in 2007.

The other test, administered by the 30-member Organization for Economic Cooperation and Development (OECD), is the Programme for International Student Assessment (PISA), developed in 1997 that tests a nationally representative sample of 15-year-olds in mathematics, reading, and science every three years. In 2006, 57 nations representing 90 percent of the world's economy participated in the PISA testing. TIMSS tends to emphasize rote learning while PISA is more focused on measuring critical thinking skills. On the 2007 TIMSS test, the United States ranked 9th in eighth grade math and 11th in eighth grade science. On the 2006 PISA test, however, the United States ranked only 21st out of the 30 OECD member countries in science, 25th in math, and 15th in reading.

Measures of both performance and inputs are at best suggestive; they are the stuff of head-lines, not the products of careful development of models of educational production functions that link outcomes to inputs in any systematic way. Critics of the US educational system focus on outcomes, but fail to address the question of whether performance in mathematics and science is an appropriate or adequate measure of what the schools are being asked to do. Supporters of the public school system focus on the inputs, and particular spending per pupil, and suggest that the United States is investing too little in its children. Education, more than any other area of public sector activity, offers a real challenge to measuring and valuing inputs, intermediate outcomes, and final output even within a single country, let alone between countries.

Financing education

Paying for education is a large part of the budgets of state and local governments in the United States, with some limited (and declining) targeted federal aid. Table 18.2 summarizes public expenditures for education for both public and higher education in the United States in 2007.

Several important facts stand out. Education is primarily a state and local responsibility, with only about 8.8 percent of the funding coming from the federal government. Much of that federal aid to public elementary and secondary education is in the form of school lunch funds and other forms of aid to schools or students with special needs, i.e., it is primarily categorical aid.

What Table 18.2 does not indicate is a steady decline in the federal share of funding, from 11.4 percent in 1980 to 8.2 percent in 2008. State and local governments have had to pick up the slack. There has also been a modest shift from local to state funding of public elementary and secondary education in that same 15-year period; states provided 48 percent of the revenue in 2008 compared to 43 percent in 1980. The role of other funding sources—fees, tuition, grants, donations, etc.—is an important component of the total, although most of it is directed at private education at all levels.

The federalism issue in education

The rationale for supporting education in the public sector needs to be more finely tuned in a federal system, because there are decisions to make not only about the overall level of expenditures but also how to allocate responsibility among levels of government. How local-ized are the social benefits of education? To what extent are these benefits, measured in educational quality, captured in housing prices?

To the extent that the major benefits from education, and from quality education, accrue to local residents, they should have primary responsibility for financing and overseeing or

Table 18.2 Public expenditures in the United States for K-12 education, 2007

Level of government	Amount ($ billions)
Federal	47.7
State	282.7
Local	254.4
Total	584.7

providing K-12 education. There may be some spillovers within a state and more limited spillovers across state lines from mobile workers, citizens and consumers that might justify more involvement by higher levels of government.

The principal rationale for a state and national role in financing for K-12 education comes from the equity side. School districts or other local governments responsible for providing education have very different tax resources, and the only way to provide any degree of **equalization** of access to educational resources is through redistribution of school funds at the state and/or federal level.

States play the primary role in equalizing educational funding resources between their school districts or cities and counties. Federal funds target specific programs aimed at children who are disadvantaged in terms of household income or other characteristics—special needs children, feeding programs, and other categorical grant programs that single out schools with a high proportion of students with special needs that may range from a free breakfast to disability access to special education. Only in the past decade, with the No Child Left Behind Act, has the federal government involved itself in assessing outcomes of the educational process.

State formula funding and equalization

A number of court cases over the past few decades have challenged the way schools are funded. One of the most famous cases was a California decision in 1978, *Serrano v. Priest*. In that case, the state Supreme Court agreed with the complaining parent that the quality of a child's education should not depend on the taxable wealth of the district in which the child's family resides.

This case resulted in a significant shifting of responsibility for school funding from the local to the state level in California in order to reduce disparities that resulted from differences in property tax resources. Similar cases in other states have resulted in a variety of responses. The challenge to states is to devise a suitable system of **formula funding** to redistribute funds among school districts that will ensure adequate funds for each child while requiring school districts to maintain their local contribution.

One simple answer is to fund education primarily through the state, as is true of Hawaii, where the state provides more than 90 percent of education funding (most of the rest is federal). Most states are not willing to assume that large a share of education funding or control and prefer to leave a large share of the responsibility for funding and overseeing schools to the local government, who on average bear 43.5 percent of the cost of K-12 education. But a number of states have moved toward assuming a larger share of funding in order to take pressure off the local property tax and provide greater equality in resources among school districts, while still requiring an appropriate local contribution.

In many states, a large share of state aid for education is distributed through some kind of formula that incorporates such factors as the number of students, adjusted for different cost for elementary, secondary, special education, vocational, and other groups; the estimated cost of educating a student; the tax base of the local district, reflecting local ability to pay; and the legislatively determined division of effort between state and local governments.

In most states there is a factor in the formula that reflects differences in cost per student for different levels of education or different special student needs. High school students are more expensive to educate than elementary students. Special education students have much lower student–teacher ratios, and vocational education students require a lot of equipment, so both groups cost more to educate.

In some cases, local governments are required to charge a certain millage or mill rate set by the state to support education, and the state makes up the difference between what that mill rate raises and the state average. This method is called **district power equalization**. School districts (or cities and counties, if they are responsible for education) are usually free to charge a higher school mill rate than the state minimum requirement, but may not charge less.

The diversity of ways of equalizing state aid is almost as great as the number of states. Texas at one time proposed a method of equalization that simply required the wealthiest districts to send funds to the poorest districts, bypassing any direct state funding. Both California and Michigan responded to school funding crises combined with property tax revolts by shifting a substantially larger share of funding to the state in trade for lower residential property taxes. A larger state share of funding should almost always result in greater equalization of resources per pupil among districts, because states tend to distribute a large share of their support on a formula basis that has some similarities to the one described above.

Even in those states with formula-based distribution of revenue, the share of total state aid flowing through that formula may be only a moderate part of total state aid. Formula-driven state aid is usually for operational purposes, not for capital expenditures for school buildings, equipment, and buses, which must be funded separately. Grants for special purposes and funding for various kinds of remedial and enrichment programs are additional components of most state aid programs that are not tied to the formula

The downside of equalization

Equalization of educational inputs is intended to create more equality of opportunity for students so that some of them would not arrive in the labor market significantly disadvantaged by the quality of the public schools they had attended. However, there are some side effects of equalization that have been raised by parents, politicians, and economic researchers, particularly when equalization puts limits on maximum spending rather than concentrating on guaranteeing a minimum.

Critics of equalization argue that leveling of school quality has limited parental choice and encouraged flight from the public schools to private schools as more affluent parents seek higher quality than the public schools offer. With state aid and state requirements resulting in greater uniformity in school quality, households do not face the same array of options in fiscal packages of tax rates, house prices, and the mix of public services offered (including schools). Should households be free to choose a package of lower school quality that comes with lower house prices, lower tax rates, and/or better non-school local public services? Or do the interests of children, which may not be fully expressed in the preferences of their parents, take precedence?

The role of the property tax in school funding

Another group of proposals for school funding reform calls for separating school funding from the property tax. Recall from Chapter 15 that the original purpose and rationale for the property tax was that it paid for services that benefited property owners—roads, street lights, police and fire protection, etc. The value of those benefits is roughly proportional to the value of property.

The benefits of education, however, are not distributed in proportion to property values. As education consumes increasing shares of property tax revenue, citizens who think of property taxes as payments for those non-education services may conclude that their benefits are too low relative to their tax burdens and will demand property tax relief. This attitude has been a significant factor in property tax revolts of the past 35 years, starting with Proposition 13 in California in 1978 (Sexton *et al.* 1999).

Case study: funding school capital in Florida

Areas experiencing rapid growth not only have to fund school operations, they have to build and equip new schools. It is rare for residential property taxes from new housing to cover the cost of educating the community's children. School districts depend on commercial and industrial property to pick up a large share of the cost without generating any extra pupils.

When growth is primarily residential, there is demand for new schools but not much new revenue to pay for them. Some states offer state aid for school construction in areas of rapid growth, but in many states the challenge of providing enough classrooms falls to the city, county, or school district.

Florida has been one of a handful of states attempting to resolve this problem with a school impact fee. Development impact fees are designed to put the burden of paying for additional public infrastructure on the newly developed property that the infrastructure will serve.

For most communities, school buildings, school buses, and other education facilities represent a major part of any community's infrastructure investment. An impact fee, assessed on a per-property basis, is intended to shift the cost of creating new schools to those who created the need. Other states are considering the use of school impact fees as a way to distribute the burden of building new schools more fairly among existing and new residents.

Florida is a major retirement destination, so a significant number of those new homes will not be housing school children. Many of Florida's residential developments are age-restricted, not allowing children under age 18 to live in the housing subdivision, apartment or condo complex, or mobile home park. Developers and residents of these age-restricted developments went to court to demand exemption from the school impact fee on the very reasonable grounds that they do not generate demand for additional schools. Their argument reflects the general perception that fees and charges are intended to make users of services bear the cost, and with no children to put in school, these homeowners (or renters) are not users of public school services.

The issue raises some important questions about equity in paying for public schools. If the spillover benefits from education are concentrated in the local community, then it may be reasonable to expect everyone to contribute, even if they life in an age-restricted development. Supporters of the impact fee argue that exempting these communities and putting the burden on homeowners and renters violates the state constitution's guarantee of free access to public education.

On the other side, there is a non-age-related issue of equity. A school impact fee that is a flat amount per housing unit, regardless of whether it is a mobile home or a mansion, is a highly regressive way of funding school construction, almost like a poll tax. Funding school capital is a challenge with no easy answers.

Public production, public provision, or public subsidy?

The argument that there are important social benefits and equity issues in ensuring that all children have an adequate K-12 education does not necessarily imply that education should be produced in the public sector. Right now, in the United States, the vast majority of children attend public schools. The school buildings are owned by state or local governments, and the teachers are public employees. Decisions about hiring teachers and administrators, class sizes, curriculum, and other matters are made by public officials ranging from state departments of education to local school boards.

At the same time, there are a few places where public schools are run under contract by private for-profit entities, whose earnings depend on the performance of students on standardized tests. There are also children in private schools who receive some degree of public assistance in the form of vouchers to pay their tuition, as well as children whose parents pay both taxes to support the public schools and tuition to send their children to private schools.

Finally, there is a modest but growing number of children educated at home by their parents, usually their mothers—the home schooling movement. The government requires that children receive a basic education, but they are not compelled to attend public schools as long as they are receiving a reasonably comparable and adequate education elsewhere.

Competition and school quality

Critics of the public school system argue that it has all the drawbacks of any monopoly. Without competition from other suppliers of educational services, this tax-supported exclusive provider can be inefficient and unresponsive to consumers without risking a loss of "customers" or revenue. These critics argue that we cannot evaluate the performance of the public school system without the existence of some nonpublic entity to which it can be compared. While there may well be a public interest in ensuring that children receive an education, that goal can be accomplished in other ways.

Defenders of public education disagree, pointing out the competitive effect of residential mobility on school quality. Recall from Chapter 3 that households choose their residential location at least partly on the basis of the package of taxes and services offered by each locality (the Tiebout model). For families with children, schools and school quality are a major factor in that decision.

School quality is incorporated in the price of housing in those places where attendance zones are clearly defined so that each house is associated with the right to attend a particular school or set of schools. School quality is reflected in higher housing prices; buyers are willing to pay for school quality, and even buyers who do not have school-age children are aware that the quality of the schools will affect the resale value of their home.

There is a real tension in public policy between the desire to provide equality of opportunity for all children through education and the advantages of local control, consumer choice, competition within the public sector, and diversity. Inner city schools in particular, with a declining tax base and an increasing number of "challenge" students (students from backgrounds of poverty or abuse, students from other cultures whose primary language is not English) are unable to compete with suburban schools with supportive parents, well-prepared students, and a stronger local tax base. These schools need state equalization in order to meet the basic needs of their students. On the other hand, the recent trend toward increased state funding of education has leveled the playing field in terms of educational quality but has also in some cases limited the ability of a local community to voluntarily tax itself to provide better than average schools.

Vouchers

Critics of public schools want to go beyond the Tiebout-type competition that forces schools to be accountable and allow parents to make choices about where to educate their children.

School **vouchers** allow parents to "buy" education for their children at any accredited school, public or private, up to a certain sum per child.

A voucher for the full amount of the cost of educating the student at some basic level in a private school would be public provision of education. Vouchers that covered less than the full cost of that basic education would be equivalent to a public subsidy. The debate over vouchers has brought to the forefront the question of whether public education requires public production or just public funding with partial or complete private production.

Under a system of vouchers that retained public schools, failing public schools would lose students, while successful schools would attract students, and market forces would force standards of quality upward. Some voucher proponents would limit the use of vouchers to public schools, a program also known as school choice. Most voucher proposals would extend the use of vouchers to private schools as well, although in many cases the voucher is likely to need supplementing by additional payments by the family in order to cover the tuition at a private school.

Supporters of vouchers argue that they are more equitable and more efficient than the present system. They are more equitable because everyone has the same choice and every child receives the same amount of tax support for their education, regardless of which school they attend or which district they live in. They are more efficient because they force schools to compete to attract students, thus mitigating the unresponsiveness of poorly managed schools.

In addition, one researcher has pointed out that vouchers decouple the existing relationship between housing prices, property taxes, and school quality. Higher-income families might be more willing to live in low-income communities when they can use vouchers to send their children to a more satisfactory school than the local tax base would provide, resulting in a more equal distribution of tax resources for non-school purposes (Nechyba 1997).

How does a voucher work in practice? Whether the voucher is used to allow a student to transfer from one public school to another, or from a public to a private school (including religious schools), the principle is the same. A figure that represents the average cost of educating a student is transferred from the school being left to the newly chosen school, coming out of the former school's income from state aid and local taxes. However, the household of the pupil is paying taxes to its district of residence. Equity would require that if the pupil is attending elsewhere, its school taxes should be adjusted upward to reflect those of the receiving district.

So the voucher would consist of revenue from the former school district based on average per-pupil spending there, and revenue from the household (or the state) based on any difference in property tax rates if the student is attending a public school. If the student is attending a private school, the voucher would reflect the average cost of public school education in the district of residence and the parents would have to make up any difference in cost.

Experiments with vouchers

Vouchers have been used by states to support students in private schools in a number of places, including Milwaukee since 1990–91 and Cleveland since 1995. The Milwaukee experience has appealed most to researchers because of the long time period. Vouchers were provided by lottery to low-income applicants to be used in secular private schools. Initially five private schools agreed to accept the students and vouchers, which covered one-half the cost of public education ($2,500). The amount of the voucher was later increased. Of the initial voucher-takers, more than one-third had left the private schools by the end of the fourth year.

Three separate studies were conducted of the Milwaukee experience. The Witte study found no significant difference in math and reading performance between pupils in the private schools and similar students remaining in public schools. The Peterson study found gains in math but not reading. The Rouse study found similar results, but a follow-up study found that gains for low-income public school students in smaller classes were higher than the gains of voucher students in private schools (Canoy and Rothstein 2001).

Cleveland's vouchers included religious schools, an issue that was challenged in court. Again, evaluations of student performance in Cleveland resulted in conflicting evidence. Other voucher experiments in Dayton, New York, Washington, DC, and Charlotte provide mixed results with some scattered gains.

Equity and vouchers

Equity issues in vouchers are not limited to ensuring an adequate education to children of low-income families who are presently trapped in inadequate public schools. A second issue is the perceived inequity of paying taxes to support public schools and then also paying tuition to support one's children in private schools, either because of dissatisfaction with the public schools or because of a preference for a religious or other kind of private school education. If vouchers were universal, rather than targeted at disadvantaged children, a significant amount of public education funding would be diverted to assisting more affluent families with their private school education. The public schools would be left with very limited resources with which to educate remaining students.

Behavioral economics and vouchers: Exit, Voice and Loyalty

In 1970, economist Albert Hirschman wrote a classic book called *Exit, Voice and Loyalty*. In this book, he examined the responses to decline in firms and organizations. Do people switch to another firm or organization? Or do they remain and try to bring about change from within? What role does loyalty—to a brand, to co-workers, to a purpose—play? What kind of people are the first to leave, and who stays until the firm or organization recovers or dies? And what difference does it make for the likelihood of recovery for the firm or organization? These questions are particularly important in the debate over vouchers for private schools for children whose parents are dissatisfied with the public schools.

Exit is the market mechanism. Dissatisfied customers will switch to another supplier, and the firm will either go out of business or respond by improving their product, service, or price. Voice is the political mechanism, to stay with the firm or the organization and try to improve it from within. But, according to Hirschman, it's not just that simple. Sometimes exit makes things better, sometimes worse. If the most concerned parents leave public education in pursuit of a better education for their own children, the public schools are likely to deteriorate further, hurting the quality of education for the remaining students. Exercising voice may help all of the students, but possibly at the expense of one's own children. Loyalty in this case takes the form of loyalty to the community or at least the community's children. The question of whether a particular parent removes his or her children from the public schools is an example of the complexity of people's motives beyond simple self-interest.

Vocational education and training

Vocational education and training take place in a variety of settings from "vo-tech" high schools and "tech-prep" public school programs to community colleges, for-profit training institutes, colleges, short courses and workshops, and on-the-job training. There are three possible sources of funding for such investment in human capital: the worker, the present or future employer, and the public sector. Each of these three groups does contribute to some degree in investing in human capital, but each one by itself will tend to under-invest for different reasons.

Vocational and technical training comes in three forms: general, job-specific, and employer-specific. General skills refer to such knowledge as the ability to communicate, collaborate, and calculate, to operate basic equipment, and to follow and give instructions. This kind of skill is acquired to some degree as part of the general education curriculum in K-12, although some people finish high school lacking in some or all of these skills, which are also emphasized in technical schools, community colleges, and four-year colleges.

Because these skills are highly generalized (applicable to a great variety of jobs), they have a value to the worker, to society as a whole, and to the employer. The employer will simply discriminate in hiring by using tests to evaluate whether a prospective employee has these basic general skills. For this reason, the same arguments that apply to shared responsibility for the individual and the public sector for K-12 and higher education also apply to ensuring that all labor force entrants be equipped with these basic skills.

Other countries invest heavily in job training of various kinds, including a highly regarded apprenticeship program in Germany. In the United States, the **Job Training and Partnership Act (JTPA)** has been a major source of federal funding for such training for unemployed workers, housewives reentering the labor force, and others in need of remedial or expanded skills to become employable. Most of the training takes place at community colleges. Studies that attempt to measure the increase in earnings and other effects of JTPA training indicate a positive return to the individual, along with relatively weak social benefits (Heckman *et al.* 1997).

The second kind of vocational training prepares a worker for a particular kind of skill that would be useful to a number of prospective employers, such as computer skills, auto repair, truck driving, or retail management. Individual employers are hesitant to make such an investment in a particular worker because workers are mobile, and some other future employer, perhaps even a rival firm, may reap the benefits of that training. This investment in vocational training is made in some combination by the present or future worker and the public sector. It is difficult to determine the appropriate balance between public spending and private responsibility in this area, just as it is for higher education.

Finally, there is on-the-job training. Historically this kind of training has been paid for by the employer, because much (but not all) of it is employer-specific and not readily transferable to another employer. Increasingly, however, with greater job mobility of workers and more contingent and temporary employment, workers have had to invest in maintaining, upgrading and expanding their skills in order to remain attractive to future employers.

Higher education

Higher education is quite different from K-12 education in several respects. First, there is general agreement that more of the benefits of higher education accrue to the student and less to society as a whole in the form of higher lifetime earnings, and as a consequence, the appropriate subsidy is a smaller share of the total cost. Second, college students are of a legal age to assume responsibility for loans to pay for their education; the argument of capital market imperfections has been demonstrated to be less relevant to post-secondary education as student loans became an option for paying for college.

Higher education, public and private, is big business in the United States. Table 18.3 summarizes the size of the sector in terms of institutions and enrollment (both public and private) and Table 18.4 shows the sources of funding per student for public institutions. Only about 3.5 percent of the US population is enrolled in higher education, about evenly divided between two-year and four-year institutions.

The dramatic change over the past three decades has been in the division of funding per student between tuition and public support. In 1982, tuition only covered about one-sixth of the cost. By 2007, that share had more than doubled. The dollar amount of public support per student was relatively stable, but because these figures are not adjusted for inflation, public support fell in real terms and in the share of total cost. Student aid has shifted to grants (especially federal Pell grants to low-income students), loans, and in many states, lottery-funded scholarships. While vouchers have made few inroads in the funding of K-12 education, the concept has taken deep root in the financing of higher education as students are encouraged to choose colleges and carry their funding with them.

Scholarships in general have taken on a more important role in higher education as a form of price discrimination as financing packages are tailored to the needs of particular students and driven by the desire of colleges to attract and retain a student body that is both academically talented and culturally diverse (and often athletically gifted as well!). Scholarships are used to lure students with high academic potential, to fill places in low enrollment majors, to support student athletes, and to attract and retain minority students. Many scholarships are funded out of contributions to the university by private donors, some for general purposes and others focused on students from particular areas or in specific majors.

Table 18.3 Higher education in the United States, 2007

	Total	Two year	Four year
Number of institutions	4,352	1,677	2,675
Total enrollment	18.2 million	11.6 million	10.4 million

Source: U.S. Statistical Abstract (2010).

Table 18.4 Sources of funding for public higher education institutions (per student), 2007

	1982	1995	2007
Government expenditures ($)	6,451	6,832	6,773
Tuition revenue ($)	1,226	2,093	3,845
Tuition share of total (%)	16.4	23.5	36.2

Source: Zumeta (2009: 40).

Public funding of higher education

Public support for higher education in the United States dates back to the Land Grant Act of 1863 for the federal government and much earlier for states that chartered institutions of higher education supported with public funds. There are both efficiency and equity arguments for supporting the acquisition of human capital that clearly yields major future income benefits to those who attend these institutions, but they are much weaker than the arguments for K-12 education. In addition, the private sector plays a much larger role in higher education. But publicly supported or publicly assisted institutions still dominate, and as indicated above, the public share is quite large.

Four arguments are offered for publicly supported higher education, although all of them can be challenged. The first is an equity argument. Children of higher-income families historically had much greater access to higher education and the resulting greater earnings and opportunities than children from working- and middle-class families, a pattern that changed sharply with the growth of state-supported universities and later, community colleges. In an increasingly technically sophisticated world, equality of opportunity requires access to higher education.

The second argument relates to the ancillary functions of public colleges in terms of research and public service, especially land-grant colleges. Some of the public funding goes for those functions which benefit the state in terms of quality of life, economic development, or availability of research and knowledge on public issues that must come from a reasonably objective outside source. Some of the public support for higher education pays for these functions, which are closely intermingled with the educational function, especially graduate education where industry, government, and the nonprofit sector offer training grounds for graduate students in exchange for the benefits they receive from their research and public service involvement.

The third argument, somewhat related, is that higher education is an essential component of an economic development strategy to attract industry that is more technologically sophisticated. Research Triangle Park in North Carolina is often cited as an example of the role of colleges (two public, one private) in attracting sophisticated industry because of the benefits of "agglomeration" in locating near the scientific, technical, and intellectual resources and the potential workers and managers that such industry will need. Colleges are also attractions for retirement communities and commercial facilities because of the intellectual and cultural resources they offer to their surrounding communities.

Finally, for a long time, public support for higher education reflected the imperfect capital markets that did not make it feasible for poor but bright students to borrow to pay for their education and repay the loan out of future higher earnings. Such loans are relatively new to the educational financing scene, and may justify less public support of higher education in the future.

In addition, not all degree programs enhance earnings equally; some generate more cultural or consumption benefits than earnings opportunities. Students who have to repay borrowings out of future earnings may be misdirected into career choices that are less suited to their talents and abilities based on current market prospects for those careers, which can change rapidly. Public support for education may deflect some career choices that are based purely on short-term financial calculations.

Summary

• Education does not meet the standard tests of non-rivalry and non-excludability to qualify as a public good. The public role in providing K-12 education is justified in terms of social benefits and equity.

- Social benefits include positive externalities of having better-educated fellow citizens, consumers and workers to make government and producers more responsive and to improve productivity in ways that benefit everyone. Public education is also justified by the argument that imperfect capital markets lead to underinvestment in human capital in the absence of government intervention.
- The equity argument for public funding of education is equality of opportunity.
- Researchers find diverse results about the relationship between educational inputs and outcomes. Some studies find that such factors as teacher–student ratios or per pupil spending have a significant effect on student performance on standardized tests, while others are not able to confirm such results.
- State and local governments share most of the responsibility for paying for K-12 education. States can ensure a basic minimum standard by providing more aid to poorer school districts. Formulas for distributing state aid include such factors as the cost per student, the number of students (adjusted for differences in costs for different ages, curricular, or special needs), and the taxable wealth of the district.
- Critics argue that state equalization aid limits the ability of local communities to choose the level of education support they want to provide, and breaking the link between property taxes and schools may weaken local support for education.
- It is not necessary that education be publicly produced, only that it be publicly provided. Public education has aspects of monopoly. Supporters of vouchers argue that public school performance would improve if schools had to compete to attract and retain students.
- Vouchers allow students to use public funds to purchase education, sometimes from competing public schools or school districts, other times from either public or private schools. Studies of student performance in voucher experiments are inconclusive about whether students actually experience significant gains from shifting to private schools.
- Public support for acquiring vocational skills is based on the same arguments as public support for K-12 education. When the skills are related to a particular job for a particular employer, benefits are largely private, so the costs should be borne by the worker and the employee in some proportion. Firms are unwilling to invest heavily in skill development that can be transferred to another employer because workers are mobile.
- The arguments for public support for higher education are weaker than those for public education because more of the benefits of higher education accrue to the person being educated and because capital markets now function more effectively in making loans available for higher education, a relatively recent development. The rationale for a public role in higher education draws on equity arguments (equality of opportunity), the benefits of research and public service, and the importance of higher education institutions as a factor in economic development.

Key terms

Accountability
District power equalization
Education production function
Equalization
Formula funding
Job Training and Partnership Act (JTPA)
No Child Left Behind Act (NCLB)
Vouchers

Questions

1   What are the advantages and disadvantages of vouchers as a method of improving equity and school quality? In what ways might they enhance or reduce the social benefits of publicly provided K-12 education?

2   Explain how the Tiebout model results in beneficial competition between school districts for higher income residents and how that outcome would be changed by either a larger state funding share or school vouchers.

3   Why is a larger public subsidy justified for K-12 education than for higher education?

4   Colleges engage in price discrimination among students with scholarships and other aid packages. Among the types of discrimination are those based on income (ability to pay or need), ability (SAT scores), and athletic skills. What is the rationale in terms of appropriate public subsidy for each type of student? Consider equity and efficiency issues in your answer.

5   **By the numbers**. If you attend a public college or university, search the web to find out how the funding sources for education at your institution has changed over the past 15 years. If you are at a private institution, do the search for a nearby public college. How has the public subsidy per student changed in current and constant dollars? How much has tuition risen? What are the implications for access to higher education for low-income students?

6   **Policy application**. You are an intern in your State Department of Education, which is revisiting the formula for distribution of state aid to school districts. The goal is to split the cost ($10,000 per student) equally between the state and the average district, with more than 50 percent going to poorer districts and less to districts with more ability to raise their own revenue. What elements go into the formula? How would you take into account the additional costs of educating students with special needs—physical or learning disabilities, poverty background, gifted and talented, vocational education, etc.?

7   **Behavioral economics**. Albert Hirschman's book *Exit, Voice and Loyalty* has applications to many situations beyond vouchers and public education. Suppose you are a regular patron of a discount store that has good prices but poor customer services and does not treat its employees well. Would you look for another place to shop or continue to shop there but voice your dissatisfaction? What factors might influence your decision?

8   **Thinking globally**. What factors other than spending per student might influence the comparative performance of students across countries reported in this chapter? What kinds of changes might influence student performance?

19 Social Security

Introduction

Most developed nations have some kind of system to provide public pensions for retired workers. In the United States, the public pension system is Social Security, which covers almost all working Americans and provides them with a pension when they retire at age 62 or later. This system was created during the depths of the Great Depression, in 1935, awarding the first check in 1939.

Initially Social Security was only a pension system. In 1939, survivor benefits were added to provide income for dependent widows and widowers and children under 18 (or to age 22 if in college, a benefit that has since been eliminated), and the program became OASI (Old Age and Survivors' Insurance). In 1950, benefits for disabled workers with at least 40 quarters (ten years) of covered employment were added, and the program became the Old Age, Survivors, and Disability (OASDI) Program. In 1965, Medicare for those over 65 was added, putting an H for health into the acronym, so that the program today is known as the **Old Age, Survivors, and Disability Health Insurance (OASDHI)** program. Medicare is covered separately in Chapter 20.

Funding Social Security

The benefits for OASDI programs are financed by a tax on wages, up to a maximum ($106,800 in 2010). The tax rate is 12.4 percent of covered wages, and is according to law paid half (6.2 percent) by the employer and half (6.2 percent) by the employee. Self-employed persons pay both halves but receive an income tax deduction for the employer's share.

While this distinction between employer and employee liability is important for federal income tax purposes, the employer's half represents an increase in hourly labor costs. In a competitive market, that increase will usually be passed on to employees in the form of lower hourly wages. As a result, incidence of the Social Security payroll tax in the long run is generally expected to fall almost entirely on the worker. Exactly how the burden of the tax is divided between employer and employee in the short run can vary, depending on the elasticity of labor supply and demand in particular markets or occupations.

According to the 2009 Annual Report of the Board of Trustees of the Federal Old-Age and Survivors Insurance and Federal Disability Insurance Trust Funds, the Social Security system had accumulated assets of $2.2 trillion in 2008. Total income was $805 billion, of which $672 billion came from Social Security taxes, $17 billion from taxing part of Social Security benefits paid to higher income retirees, and the remaining $116 billion from interest.

Total expenditures were $625 billion, mostly benefits. Administrative expenses accounted for less than 1 percent of expenditures. The net increase in assets in 2008 was $180 billion.

In 2008, Social Security covered 162 million workers and served 50.4 million beneficiaries, of whom 41.4 million received retirement and/or survivors' benefits and the remaining nine million received disability benefits. The ratio of workers to beneficiaries has been declining steadily over the years as life expectancy has increased. In 1950, people over age 65 were only about 8 percent of the population. Today they account for about 12 percent of the population. By 2045, people over age 65 are projected to be about 20 percent of the population.

In 2008, there were 3.2 workers per beneficiary. When the large baby boom generation reaches the retirement age of 67, starting in 2013, that ratio is expected to gradually decline to a low of two workers per beneficiary by 2060. Because Social Security is a pay-as-you-go system, the worker/retiree ratio is central to the challenges facing Social Security. Younger workers are uncertain about whether to count on Social Security as part of their retirement plans.

Social Security: insurance, pension, or redistribution?

The "core business" of Social Security is an intergenerational and interpersonal compact, reflecting both individual and communal values. The design of the US system reflects the values and the context of the 1930s when it was created. Those values and circumstances include a high value placed on individual responsibility, the importance of earned benefits rather than a "handout," some redistribution from wealthier retirees to lower-income retirees, and a labor force in which the norm was that married women did not work outside the home. As a result, OASDI is a hybrid of insurance, pension, and redistribution programs. Like most hybrids, it contains some of the best features of each of those three elements as well as some of the drawbacks of each.

Insurance

Insurance of any kind protects people against risks in exchange for a premium or other payments. The **insurance component** of Social Security protects people against outliving their assets, but the parts of the program that are closest to traditional insurance are benefits paid to survivors (1939) and disabled workers (1950).

Disability is relatively new and much more complex than old age and survivor programs.

Retirement and survivor benefits are largely automatic, but disability requires a complicated legal process to establish eligibility. As in any insurance program, all people who are covered by Social Security pay taxes to benefit survivors and disabled people, but only those who leave dependent survivors or become disabled receive benefits.

Pension

The **pension/annuity component** was the earliest program to be established, and the one most people have in mind when they refer to Social Security. Like private pensions, or government pensions, Social Security pensions are contributory. Social Security taxes are paid into the system and pensions are paid to those who meet the eligibility requirement out of the accumulated reserves and current income.

Some of the original discussions when this program was being designed suggest that the system may have been designed at least in part to protect the middle- and upper-income classes from the poor. More prosperous citizens could expect to have to contribute to the support of the elderly poor in their declining years either through charity or through taxes, because this group was not likely to be able or willing to save for their old age out of their meager earnings. Social Security payroll taxes forced the working poor to contribute something while they were working.

Redistribution

An important difference from other insurance and pension programs is that Social Security includes a strong **redistribution component**, which takes the form of a much higher ratio of benefits to earnings for lower income earners. The lowest income Social Security recipients, or those not covered at all, can receive Supplementary Security Income (SSI) from a separate program funded by general tax revenues.

Under the Old Age (OA) part of Social Security, workers whose earnings fell at the bottom end of the wage scale receive benefits that replace 90 percent of preretirement wages. As earnings and Social Insurance taxes paid both rise above the minimum, benefits become a smaller share of the reported earnings base.

For the highest income workers, additional dollars earned generate additional benefits of only 15 percent of the earnings base. For the average low-earner, Social Security provides replacement of 49 percent of earnings at age 65. For the average earner, replacement is 32 percent of earnings, and for the high income worker, 30 percent (U.S. General Accountability Office, 2005, p. 9).

Design elements

An essential feature of the original design of the system was broad coverage, a breadth that has continued to grow as self-employed persons, farm workers and other groups were added to the system over the years.[1] Today there is close to **universal participation** among those employed, a feature that results in two positive benefits—low administrative costs (about 1.5 percent of benefits paid), and no adverse selection.[2] Those who expect to live to a ripe and healthy old age share the system with those who expect to die young or to be disabled before reaching retirement age.

Another important design feature of Social Security is that it is a **defined benefit** rather than **defined contribution** program. At one time, most pension plans, public or private, were of the defined benefit form. A defined benefit means that the pension one received after retirement was based on wages and length of service in some combination, and the retiree could expect that same amount—sometimes adjusted for inflation, sometimes not—until death, possibly with some benefit to survivors as well. Public pensions were more likely to have an inflation adjustment than private ones.

More recently, many private pension systems and some public ones have shifted to the defined contribution system, where the benefits to the retiree depend on how much is in his or her individual account (contributions plus investment earnings) at the time of retirement and how well that portfolio continues to perform.

With a defined benefit program, the risk falls on the employer if the portfolio underperforms, but the employer also gains if the portfolio does well (and many firms have been able to transfer surplus funds from their retirement programs into other uses). With a defined contribution program, the risk of loss and hope of gain are both transferred to the employee/retiree. Many proposals for reforming Social Security would change part or all of the present program from a defined benefit to a defined contribution program.

Another design element is the **wage ceiling** or maximum amount subject to Social Security taxes ($106,400 in 2010). The wage ceiling is adjusted annually, along with benefits, based on the inflation rate. The result of having a wage ceiling, combined with taxing only wages and not other forms of income, is that the Social Security tax is moderately regressive. Figure 19.1 shows the Social Security tax (including the Medicare tax) as a percentage of wages and salaries up to $200,000. Higher earners often also have nonwage income, such as interest and dividends, so that the Social Security tax is an even smaller percentage of their total income.

Since 1984, retirees with incomes over a certain level ($25,000 for single persons, $34,000 for married couples) have had to pay income taxes on their Social Security benefits. Only a small part of Social Security benefits are return of taxes paid. The rest comes from interest and from the insurance element, money in the trust fund that was paid by people who did not live long enough to collect benefits, or at least much in the way of benefits. Income tax is levied on 50 percent of Social Security benefits, depending on income, with the revenue going to the Social Security Trust Fund. Starting in 1993, households with even higher incomes are taxed on 85 percent of their benefits, with the additional revenue going to the Medicare Trust Fund.

A final design feature, spousal benefits, reflects the birth of the system more than 75 years ago, when women were much less likely to work outside the home. The benefit program provides for widows, widowers, and surviving spouses. A widow (or widower) can collect 80 percent of the deceased spouse's benefit. A wife (or husband) who is not eligible for benefits on the basis of her or his own work history or whose benefits would be very small on her or his own account can collect 50 percent of her or his spouse's benefit.

An increasing proportion of married people are eligible for either but not both types of benefits. As a result, working couples pay more into the system relative to the benefits they may receive than one-earner households.

The Social Security Trust Fund

The revenue from the payroll tax (FICA, or Federal Insurance Contributions Act) is deposited directly into the **Social Security Trust Fund**, and payments to beneficiaries are paid out

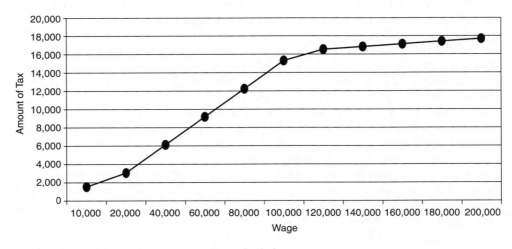

Figure 19.1 Social Security taxes on wages and salaries.

of that trust fund rather than the general operating budget of the federal government. These funds are not part of the budget passed by Congress each year.

There is, of course, a connection between the trust fund and the budget. The Social Security trust fund has been running surpluses of revenue over expenses and benefits for quite some time. Those surplus revenues are invested in federal government bonds, which is the way in which the US government funds its budget deficits. The trust fund earns interest on those bonds, which is added to the balance of the trust fund.

At some point—currently expected to be 2016 or 2017—expenses and benefits are expected to exceed revenues for the Social Security Trust Fund. At that point, Congress will have to redeem some of those government bonds in order to provide the resources for Social Security to continue to pay the promised benefits. Redeeming those bonds may mean higher federal taxes. The last of the bonds are projected to be redeemed in 2041. After that, projected revenue from payroll taxes would be adequate to pay only about 75 percent of projected benefits.

These projections depend on expected employment, wages, interest rates, life expectancy, and retirement rates over very long periods of time, so they are frequently adjusted. Like any economic projections, these figures are based on assumptions about wage growth (1 percent a year adjusted for inflation), fertility, longevity, interest rates, marital stability, immigration, labor force participation (especially by women), and unemployment. Projections for so long a period and so large a system are very sensitive to even minor adjustments in the assumptions.

Congress and the executive branch of the federal government cannot even agree on what economic assumptions should underlie projections of the budget surplus or deficit over periods of up to seven years. For Social Security, projections are much longer, and the projected problems in Social Security come in a period some 23 to 33 years hence. These projected revenue shortfalls in the 2020s and 2030s are crucially dependent on assumptions about wage growth, fertility, labor force participation, and immigration. It only takes very small adjustments in some of these assumptions to make the system viable. Perhaps the cries of disaster are premature.

Interpersonal and intergenerational equity

Many of the concerns about Social Security can be described as equity issues, relating to interpersonal equity and intergenerational equity. **Interpersonal equity** is often measured as the ratio of lifetime taxes to lifetime benefits. These calculations, which appear in the popular press, are not easy to make; there is no typical earner/recipient, and each person's calculation depends on how long that person lives, his/her earnings pattern, and other factors. In making such comparisons it is important to compare apples with apples, considering among other issues the level of risk assumed in the investment mix (it is very low for Social Security Trust Fund investments), and being sure to include administrative costs (also very low for Social Security).

Dean Leimer reviewed and critiqued various "money's worth" studies that looked at such measures as payback period, benefit/tax ratio, lifetime transfer, and internal rate of return (Leimer 1995). Within age cohorts (people born during the same period), it is estimated that the rate of return is better for couples, women, minorities and the poor, because women and couples live longer than men and single persons, respectively, and because those with lower average annual wages (including a disproportionate share of minorities) are entitled to benefits that represent a larger percentage of their past earnings. The present value of taxes less benefits is very positive for the lowest-income decile, remaining positive up to the middle of the income distribution, and is negative for the top half of the income distribution (Pattison 1995).

More attention has been paid to the issue of **intergenerational equity** in publicly funded retirement. Some critics describe the "pay-as-you-go" nature of Social Security as a sort of Ponzi scheme, with the baby bust generation (1965 onward) subsidizing the generations that preceded them in retirement. Again, looking at age cohorts, researchers found that the earliest cohort examined (1895–1903) earned on average a 12.5 percent inflation-adjusted return; the 1917–22 cohort received 5.9 percent, while the babies born in 1995 are projected to receive a 1.5 percent inflation adjusted rate of return. All of these figures compare favorably to a long-term 0.6 percent inflation-adjusted return on government bonds (Pattison 1995).

One important consequence of Social Security has been reduced poverty among the elderly. More than half of those current elderly receive more than half their income from Social Security. Among current workers, about half are covered by a pension plan; the others, apparently, are depending on Social Security to provide for their old age. What will happen to the benefits to the elderly and the rates paid by active workers down the road? Again, there is no simple answer: it depends on fertility, longevity, earnings growth, interest rates, marital stability, immigration, labor force participation, and unemployment.

Proposals for reform

The past 20 years have generated a great variety of proposals to reform Social Security, ranging from modest adjustments in benefits and/or taxes to privatization. Among the proposals are adjusting benefits, capping the cost-of-living adjustment, raising the age for eligibility, reforming or de-linking other components of the system, changing the treatment of working spouses, increasing the wage base, broadening coverage, changing the invest-ment or making the system private and/or voluntary.

Adjusting benefits

The current formula replaces 90 percent of average indexed earnings up to a certain level, then 32 percent, and finally 15 percent of the top share of average indexed earnings. The level and structure of benefits relative to average earnings could be adjusted to reduce payments relative to earnings in order to prolong the life of the trust fund.

Capping the cost of living adjustment (COLA)

There is some evidence that the Consumer Price Index currently used to adjust benefits is overstating inflation, and particularly the impact of inflation on the elderly, because of the strong role of housing and medical costs in the index. Many of the elderly are not affected by rising costs of buying new homes, as they live in homes that are paid for, and much (but not all) of their medical expense is covered by Medicare. Proposals for change include a lower inflation adjustment or linking the annual adjustment to growth in wages rather than in prices.

Raising the age for eligibility

With longer life spans than in the earlier years of Social Security, retirees are collecting much longer. In addition, more workers are opting to collect reduced benefits (75 percent) at age 62 rather than full benefits at age 67. When Social Security began, the average worker was only expected to collect for a few years after retiring at age 65, which was then the standard age for full benefits. Recent changes have adjusted the age of eligibility for full benefits upward, beginning with the 1940 birth cohort, so that workers born from 1940 on must work past age 65 to collect full benefits and will receive only 75 percent of that amount if they retire at age 62. Workers born in 1960 or later are not eligible for full retirement benefits until age 67. Further adjustments have been proposed in both the age for early retirement benefits and the age for full benefits.

Reforming or delinking other components of the system

This means reforming either disability or Medicare or both. Some argue that Social Security is bearing too many unrelated responsibilities, and should be pared back to its "core business"—a form of downsizing or reengineering. Generally, proponents of this reform are not arguing that those other components should be scrapped but rather that they involve other issues and should be separated and treated differently.

Changing the treatment of working spouses

Since the payroll tax covers payments for spousal and survivor benefits, it can be argued that married couples pay twice, but can only collect once. Widows can collect either on their own earnings record or 80 percent of the benefit that would have been received by their deceased husbands; retired wives, likewise, can collect full benefits on their own records or 50 percent of their husbands' benefits. This issue will eventually self-correct as the employment women outside the home becomes the norm rather than the exception. In the interim, it is important not to penalize those traditional homemakers who were caught in a values revolution.

Increasing the wage base

The wage ceiling has gone up, but there is still a ceiling. As a result, the tax is somewhat regressive. In fact, the Social Security payroll tax is the biggest single tax burden for the working poor. Expanding the earnings base would raise more revenue, and make the tax more equitable.

Broadening coverage

A very large share of the labor force is required to participate in Social Security, but there are exceptions. State and local governments are still allowed to opt out, for example. Including all workers would bring in immediate revenue and delayed payments, so it would help the balance sheet, at least in the short run.

Changing the investment mix

Some reformers would like to see at least part of the trust fund's assets invested in equities, for two reasons. First, the fund could experience greater growth, although at some cost in terms of risk and management expense. Second, this change would help to delink the trust fund from any budget deficit, since the Social Security surplus would no longer be invested entirely in Treasury securities. Enthusiasm for investing in equities (stocks) has diminished in recent years as a result of poor stock market performance.

Making the system private and/or voluntary

Republican Presidential candidate Barry Goldwater suggested this idea in 1964, and his campaign never recovered from the backlash! Today, a significant number of public figures support some degree of privatization, although most advocate partial rather than total privatization. Partial privatization proposals range from investing some of the assets in stocks to allowing individuals to own and manage their own accounts.

If people are allowed to have personal accounts but participation in the system remains mandatory, privatization would create a need for monitoring and supervision, in the light of a history of problems with private pensions that did not fulfill their commitment to employees as well as unscrupulous investment advisors. Making the system entirely voluntary would result in many of the poor opting out in order to provide for immediate consumption. Both privatization and voluntarism would reduce or eliminate the insurance and redistribution functions of the system in favor of limiting the role of the pension part of the program to being just another pension provider. None of these problems are insuperable obstacles to making such a change, but they are real problems that would have to be addressed in some way.

What's ahead?

What is the likely future of Social Security? For today's average 30-to-50-year-old worker, it is likely that benefits will be lower in relation to income than they were for older workers. But the program will be there, still financed largely by a dedicated tax on earnings of some kind, still favoring lower income workers over higher income workers. Part of the trust fund may be invested in the private sector of the economy, in equities and corporate bonds, to provide diversity and growth and to unlink Social Security from the broader question of the budget.

The people paying into the system will be different: more women, more minorities, more recent immigrants. Women are more likely to be eligible only on their own accounts, with the few surviving spouses with no earnings of their own shifted to SSI. This change will mean a decline in the survivors' component of the program, in order to focus on the core responsibilities or retirement and disability.

Public pensions in Canada and Europe

One advantage enjoyed by Americans is that their demographic challenge in the social insurance system is hitting later than in other parts of the world, especially Canada and Western Europe. Those countries have already had to address the problem of a declining ratio of workers to retirees, combined with much higher unemployment rates than those experienced in the United States in the last decade. Like the United States, these countries have experienced a demographic crunch in social insurance combined with budgetary pressures, competitive pressures (the social insurance tax adds to labor costs), and conservative, market-oriented critiques of the existing schemes.

All of these challenges have led many countries, not just the United States, Canada, and the nations of Western Europe, to think about how to redesign social insurance schemes developed in the early twentieth century for a new era. Some of these countries have implemented various kinds of changes that are being considered for the United States, so it is possible to learn from their experience.

For many decades, there was a basic similarity in all these retirement systems. Most countries, like the United States, offer lifetime benefits based on past earnings and are pay-as-you-go rather than actuarially funded programs with benefits based on contributions. Most other countries have had a basic benefit level with some means-tested additions (like SSI) and some earnings-related supplements (like Social Security). However, there are important differences as well as similarities between the US social welfare system and those of other industrial countries.

Compared to Canada and Western Europe, the United States has higher retirement ages, lower benefits relative to past earnings, and lower payroll taxes. Some of these other systems also give work credit for military service, or for time spent as an unpaid caregiver to children, disabled persons, and elderly parents. However, the United States is more generous in one respect: unlike some other nations, such as Australia, benefits are an entitlement that is not taken away from the wealthiest citizens, although part of the benefits is taxed for higher-income households.

All of these other social insurance systems have undergone some degree of upheaval in response to demographic and economic changes as well as a shift of policies in general to more private sector, market-based solutions to social problems. Policy analyst R. Kent Weaver sorted the responses into program retrenchment, program refinancing, and program restructuring (Weaver 1998).

Program retrenchment has included reducing the indexing of benefits for inflation, increasing retirement ages, restricting eligibility for early retirement, encouraging delayed retirement, reducing benefits to higher income retirees, and recalculating the wage base to include more working years (which reduces the average wage base). These changes are similar to those made in the United States and represent small adjustments that over time can result in substantial costs savings. In addition, a number of countries have taken steps to encourage more use of voluntary private pensions through favorable tax treatment (France, Canada, Australia) or compulsory contributions to private pension plans by employers (Australia, the UK starting in 2012).

In the area of refinancing, some countries have raised their social insurance tax rates and/or begun to invest part of their social insurance funds in equities in hopes of providing faster growth of assets to provide for future beneficiaries (Sweden, Canada).

A truly significant change is a move toward defined contribution rather than defined benefit plans in countries such as Sweden and Germany. This development is one form of restructuring. More dramatic restructuring is an entirely privatized system, in which each person (voluntarily or under mandate) contributes to his or her own pension account, which is managed for his or her retirement and not commingled with the funds of others. The primary criticism is the very high administrative cost, but there are also concerns over the volatility of investments in private assets, especially equities (stocks).

Chile has had such a privatized system for 15 years, with mixed reviews. The United Kingdom has also moved in that direction, as has Australia. Such plans are generally more politically acceptable as a supplement to a public pension scheme than as a replacement or substitute (Weaver 1998: 225). In addition to citizen resistance, and administrative cost, there is also a transition challenge in funding those currently retired or approaching retirement who have worked under the existing system while also adequately funding a private, individual account-type system for the current generation of workers.

The United Kingdom made some of the most dramatic reforms, with a three-tier system that offers a standard floor benefit to all financed by a payroll tax, a second tier of benefits that is mandatory but can be provided either through the public sector or approved private programs through the employer or individual retirement accounts, and a third tier of tax-favored retirement savings programs.

France and other nations of Western Europe have moved in the same direction with more investment of retirement assets in equities and more emphasis on defined contribution programs. However, recent years of poor stock market performance in many countries have cooled the enthusiasm for both equity investments and defined contribution programs as those near retirement become more concerned about a minimum guarantee rather than the risk-laden potential for higher retirement pensions.

Behavioral public finance: private saving for retirement

One of the areas in which people are unable to make the rational calculations expected of *Homo economicus* is the long-term future. Few 20-year-olds are thinking about retirement before they have even started their first real job. By the time people start planning for retirement, it may be too late to make adequate financial provision. People have preferences—in this case, how they want to divide their income between present and future—but they also have preferences about preferences, which are known as **meta-preferences**.

Meta-preferences may be as simple as wanting to avoid unhealthy foods or driving while intoxicated. Sometimes people can avoid temptation to violate their meta-preferences for the immediate satisfaction of riding a motorcycle without a helmet, eating fried foods, driving home after one too many, or spending now rather than saving for the future by imposing restrictions on themselves, or asking others to do so. They can avoid fast food restaurants, give the car keys to someone else, and have someone (employer or government) require them to wear a helmet and/or save for retirement.

Mandatory pension plans, like motorcycle helmet laws, recognize that we may all give into temptations that are not in our own best interest. The design of universal and mandatory pension plans takes into account not only people's immediate desire to spend but also their long-run meta-preference for a financially secure retirement.

Summary

- Market economies normally provide income support through government for those who are unable to earn an income because of age or disability. Social Security originated in the United States in the 1930s as the federal government took over most of the responsibility from state and local governments. Social Security has significantly reduced poverty among the elderly.
- Social Security provides retirement income for most working Americans as well as survivors' and disability benefits. The benefits for these programs are financed by a payroll tax. The incidence of the Social Security payroll tax is believed to fall almost entirely on the worker in the form of lower net wages.
- Revenue from the payroll tax is deposited in the Social Security Trust Fund and invested in government bonds. Payments to beneficiaries are paid out of that trust fund.
- Annual benefit payments are expected to exceed revenues (including interest) within the next decade. Eventually the trust fund will be exhausted, but current revenue will make it possible to still pay 75 percent of benefits.
- The primary Social Security program, retirement pensions, consists of three elements: insurance for dependent survivors, pension/annuity for retired workers, and redistribution by replacing a larger share of earnings for lower-income workers than higher-income

workers. Nearly universal participation and a simple investment strategy have kept administrative costs very low.

- Important features of the present Social Security program include a defined benefit rather than defined contribution plan, a ceiling on the amount of wages subject to the payroll tax, an annual inflation adjustment in benefits, reduced benefits for early retirement, reduced benefits for retirees who earn over a certain amount in wages, and different treatment for working and non-working spouses.
- Any reform must address questions of intergenerational equity (benefits relative to taxes paid are higher for current retirees than future retirees) and interpersonal equity (benefits relative to taxes paid for men versus women, low versus high wage earners, etc.).
- Proposals for reforming Social Security include adjusting benefits, capping the cost-of-living adjustment, raising the age for eligibility, reforming or de-linking other components of the system, changing the treatment of working spouses, increasing the wage base, broadening coverage, changing the investment or making the system private and/or voluntary.

Key terms

Defined benefit program
Defined contribution program
Insurance component (Social Security)
Intergenerational equity
Interpersonal equity
Meta-preferences
Old Age, Survivors, Disability and Health Insurance (OASDHI)
Pension/annuity component (Social Security)
Redistribution component (Social Security)
Social Security Trust Fund
Universal participation
Wage ceiling

Questions

1 How should the system of old age pensions balance protecting those who are unable to provide for their own retirement and encouraging personal responsibility? Why do you think that the United States, along with most other developed nations, has come to rely so heavily on social insurance for retirement pensions?

2 Do you think the Social Security system as a whole (both taxes and benefits) is progressive, regressive, or proportional in its effect on the lifetime distribution of earnings? Why?

3 **By the numbers**. Using the information on the web site for the Social Security Administration, calculate the monthly benefit for a worker who has 35 years of covered employment at an average wage of (a) $1,500; (b) $3,000; (c) $7,500. What percentage of earnings are replaced in each case?

4 **Policy application**. This chapter identified a number of proposed reforms to the Social Security system in order to ensure that it will be able to continue to pay benefits into the indefinite future. Evaluate each of the following proposed reforms to Social Security in terms of intergenerational equity, cost, risk, freedom of choice, and any other criteria that you think are important:

326 Public Finance in Theory and Practice

    (a) raising the age for eligibility for retirement benefits
    (b) investing the trust fund partially in equities
    (c) adjusting the cost-of-living adjustment

5   **Behavioral economics**. If you were an average employee, would you prefer to have a defined benefit or a defined contribution retirement plan as your primary pension plan? Why? What roles do attitudes toward risk play in your choice? If you were the employer, how might you frame the choice to encourage the defined contribution rather than the defined benefit plan?

6   **Thinking globally**. Some nations of the world have younger populations than the United States, Canada and Europe—more children and young adults and fewer old people. What lessons have been learned from Western countries that might help these nations design social insurance programs for old age pensions that are sustainable?

20 Health care

Introduction

Perhaps no other debate in US public life has gone on so long as discussions over a federal role in guaranteeing access to health care going back to the Roosevelt and Truman administrations in the 1930s and 1940s. While Canada and the nations of Western Europe were creating national health care systems, Americans continued to access health care through a patchwork of public and private hospitals, employer-provided and privately provided health insurance, private physicians and public health clinics.

Many Americans fall through the cracks without either access to adequate health care within reasonable distance or the means to pay for it. A major debate in the early 1990s over the shape and future of health care in the first Clinton administration ended with no significant changes to the system. The United States entered the twenty-first century as the only major industrial nation without some kind of comprehensive health care plan that embraced all citizens.

Finally, in 2010, health care legislation passed that was intended to broaden coverage and contain costs, although the reform did not include a single-payer system like most other countries or even a public option (a default plan provided by the government for those who could not obtain private coverage at reasonable cost). It did, however, require everyone to have health insurance, with government assistance for those who could not afford to pay for coverage and mandates to insurers to offer coverage to everyone regardless of pre-existing conditions.

Health care in international perspective

Canada, Australia, and most of the nations of Western Europe have cradle-to-grave health care funded out of tax revenue and available to all residents at little or no cost. Instead of price rationing, in many countries, health care is rationed either by long waiting periods or by restrictions on the kinds of services that can be offered, although some countries also have doctors and hospitals offering traditional fee-for-service medical care as a supplement or alternative to the public system.

The model for many of these systems was the British National Health Service. Initially, the British government owned all the health care facilities and employed the health care professionals. However, elements of co-payments and private health care systems have been introduced to provide more flexibility and more options for those who are not satisfied with the public program.

Singapore has a somewhat unique system that emphasizes a combination of individual responsibility and community support. Government subsidies are blended with patient co-payments, with higher payments from those who demand a higher level of service. Health care expenditures for Singapore are less than 4 percent of GDP, with 70 percent of spending from private consumers. Singapore ranks fourth in life expectancy and has the lowest infant mortality rate.[1]

The Organization for Economic Cooperation and Development provides periodic comparison of health care in 30 developed nations. Among the dimensions of health care they consider are financing, access to care, health care resources, and outcomes. The United States performs poorly on all of these measures. In 2007, the United States spent $7,290 per capita (public and private) on health care, compared to an OECD 30-country average of only $2,984—so the US spent more than 2.5 times as much. Health care accounts for 16 percent of US GDP, compared to an average of 8.9 percent in all OECD countries.

Yet the United States is the third lowest in percentage of the population with health insurance coverage, followed only by Mexico and Turkey. According to the OECD report, one of the factors contributing to higher per capita spending was the use of more tests and expensive procedures. For example, MRI and CAT scan procedures are both more than twice as common in the United States as in other countries.

Finally, in terms of health outcomes, the United States again fares poorly. Infant mortality there is above average and life expectancy at birth is lower than the OECD average. The United States ranks highest among the 30 nations in obesity (34 percent) and 2nd highest in adult diabetes (10.3 percent of the population) (OECD Health Data 2009).

A report by the Commonwealth Fund makes similar comparisons among just seven countries—the United States and Australia, Canada, Germany, the Netherlands, New Zealand, and the United Kingdom, but with more focus on quality of care and patient outcomes. On 10 measures of quality of coordinated care, the United States ranked sixth, just above Germany. On system performance, which includes quality of care, access, efficiency, equity, and long, healthy and productive lives, the United States ranked seventh (Davis *et al* 2010).

The American health care patchwork

More than any other basic need, health care has been caught in the no man's land of American ambivalence about expanding the role of government. As a consequence, only three programs of publicly provided health care, one purely federal, one jointly provided by the federal and state governments, have evolved since the 1960s to cover only the elderly and the very poor. **Medicare** is a federal program for those over 65, providing hospital and physician care, funded primarily through a payroll tax and to a lesser degree by premiums deducted from Social Security checks. **Medicaid** is a health care program that is means-tested and financed with general revenue, with costs shared between federal and state budgets. The **Children's Health Insurance Program (CHIP)**, created in 1997, extended health care coverage to children in families not poor enough to qualify for Medicaid but unable to afford private insurance. Together, these three programs cost $924 billion in 2008, $677 billion in federal funds and $247 billion provided by states.

The United States is unusual if not unique among modern developed nations in that health care is for the most part produced and to a large degree funded by the private sector. Doctors, hospitals, clinics and pharmacies serve patients in both for-profit and non-profit firms, although some services are provided through publicly owned hospitals and clinics. The largest share of publicly provided medical care is military and veterans' hospitals. Other public programs, primarily Medicare, Medicaid, and CHIP, are financing entities that reimburse private health care providers for some part of services.

Medicaid and Medicare finance health care services directly to specific groups. Indirectly, there is a public subsidy for employer-provided group health insurance to employees. Spending for employer-financed health care is a deductible expense for the firm but is not considered taxable income to employees. Other financing for health care services comes from private insurers and direct consumer payments. This patchwork of funding results in a nearly even split of cost of health care between private and public funds.

Table 20.1 summarizes the sources of spending for health care in the United States in 2008. The health care legislation passed in 2010 is not expected to substantially alter the public-private balance in health care funding. Mandated coverage will increase some private spending, while subsidies for those who cannot afford private insurance will increase public spending.

Efficiency issues in health care

If health care were left entirely to the private sector, access to health care would be subject to price rationing. Those who could not afford to pay for health care would not receive any services. While that picture is appalling to contemplate—babies born without medical attention, heart attack or accident victims left to die—it does serve as a reminder of the positive side of using the market to ration services.

Some health care services are optional. Some conditions have alternative treatments with vastly different costs, and in a private fee-for-service situation, cost would be more carefully considered. If patients do not have third party payments for prescription drugs, for example, doctors are more likely to prescribe or patients to demand generic instead of brand-name drugs. Optional treatments for conditions ranging from baldness to acne to toenail fungus would be postponed, forgone, or treated with over-the-counter products. At the very least, choosing medical care for such conditions would be weighed against other choices about how to spend one's income.

Like Social Security and welfare, health care policy in the United States is the subject of a debate grounded in different views of how certain kinds of personal financial risks are managed and shared in a market economy. These views arise from an understanding of markets and government that stress personal responsibility for earning a living and managing one's income and assets wisely, as opposed to other systems that call for more shared responsibility through government or other cooperative arrangements. Social Security offers protection from outliving one's assets, or earning too little to accumulate any assets for the post-retirement years. Welfare and unemployment insurance together offer a limited guarantee of protection from starvation for those in temporarily distressed circumstances. But for

Table 20.1 Sources of funds for US health care spending, 2008

	$ millions
National health expenditures	2,338,747
Private funds	1,232,030
Public funds	1,106,716
Federal funds	816,936
State and local funds	289,781

Source: US Department of Health and Human Services, Centers for Medicare and Medicaid Services, *National Health Expenditure Data.*

many households, a major threat to their financial well-being is a prolonged illness or a very costly accident or surgery that can rapidly deplete their assets and threaten their standard of living both now and in the future. Despite that serious threat to the financial well-being of all but the wealthiest citizens, a significant part of the population does not have affordable access to health insurance.

Health care, like retirement, appears to be ideally suited for the development of private insurance and payment or prepayment plans. Where does the government come in? Is there a rationale for government production or provision/financing of health care services? Why does it appear that the private sector has failed to deliver socially acceptable outcomes in terms of the quality, cost and availability of health care services?

Health care is not a public good. It is excludable; it can be rationed by price. There is competition for a limited supply of medical resources that must be allocated among competing users. Clearly health care is rival in consumption. The hour Jones takes with the doctor, the bed Jones occupies in the hospital are not available to Smith. As in the case of education, a public role in funding health care must be established primarily on the bases of efficiency (positive externalities) and equity considerations.

Externalities

Some kinds of health care, particularly preventive, have important positive externalities. Your flu shot protects everyone you come in contact with. Vaccinations have almost wiped out many childhood diseases, protecting everyone else in the process. There is now a temptation to be a free-rider and not get shots for measles, smallpox and other diseases on the very great odds of never being exposed! Quick treatment of contagious diseases with antibiotics and other therapies can reduce the spread of the illness to others.

One step removed from these obvious externalities is the effect of health or illness on one's performance as a worker, consumer, and citizen—quite similar to the effects of education. Productivity in the workplace is particularly sensitive to health. In addition, deteriorating health can lead to disability. In a social system where public funds are used to support the disabled and their families, investing in prevention and cure is almost always less expensive than thrusting more households onto Social Security disability or welfare.

Third party payments

Any product or service that is paid for at least in part through insurance or other third parties has some unique challenges in trying to use either market forces or governmental regulations to ration the scarce resources involved. Insurance at its best is a way of paying for the consequences of unpredictable but very expensive events that are largely beyond our control—natural disasters, automobile accidents, death of a breadwinner, or costly surgery or extended illnesses. It is less suitable for more routine, repeated and smaller expenditures, like routine checkups, dental care, or minor auto accidents, although many households have insurance coverage for those kinds of expenses as well.

The original and still primary purpose of insurance is to protect people from the financial consequences of those kinds of risk that are low in probability but very large in amount. Consider a rare disease that might strike one person in a million each year, but if it does, the cost of treating it is $100,000. No one has any way of knowing if he or she will be that one person in a million. In a society of one million people, if each one contributed 10 cents to a fund that provided insurance against that rare disease, then that one person who contracted the disease would at least not suffer major financial injury as well as health injury. The cost per person is small for catastrophic coverage.

In practice, of course, the insurer would have some administrative cost and need to create some reserves against the possibility that two persons in a million rather than one might contract the disease, so the premium for that particular coverage would be more than 10 cents. But even at 50 cents or a dollar, the insurance would provide peace of mind for the 999,999 disease-free policyholders and financial relief to the millionth who contracts the disease.

Scope of coverage

Insurance has been extended in many areas from the catastrophic, as described in the preceding paragraph, to the routine. Dental insurance covers routine checkups, not just crowns and root canals. Homeowners' insurance protects property from minor as well as major disasters. Auto insurance pays for such modest and ordinary costs as replacement of window glass. Deductibles have tended to become smaller over time in all kinds of insurance. In effect, many forms of insurance have become a sort of prepayment plan for routine expenditures.

Health insurance is no different. It is possible to buy only catastrophic health insurance, called major medical, while covering routine expenditures out of household budgets. But the typical policy covers much more in the way of routine medical expenses. The dominant influence in shifting the "norm" for health insurance in the United States toward broad coverage of routine as well as extraordinary expenditures has been employer-provided health insurance. This tax-exempt fringe benefit became a recruiting tool for employers during the tight labor markets of the 1940s (Friedman 2001). Because employer-provided health insurance is not considered taxable income for purposes of either federal income tax or Social Security taxes, it is an attractive form of supplementary compensation.

Consider a worker in a 28 percent federal income tax bracket, a 7 percent state income tax bracket, and subject to 7.6 percent Social Security payroll tax (not to mention the other 7.6 percent paid by the employer). This worker knows that his or her household will incur routine medical expenses of about $1,000 in most years. To pay for those expenses with after tax dollars earned from employment would require a pre-tax income of $1,742. His employer would have to add $108 to pay for the other half of the Social Security tax, for a total cost of $1,850. Clearly it is in the financial interest of the employer and employee to convert some part of salary into prepaid health care benefits.

As a result, most employer-provided health care has low deductibles to cover routine as well as catastrophic health care needs. The definition of what is a risk appropriate to addressing through health insurance has been extended. While health insurance originally focused on major medical insurance—prolonged illnesses and major surgeries—it now commonly covers eye examinations, mental health, routine dental care, some kinds of cosmetic surgery, and other normal and expected or sometimes elective expenditures. Households are more likely to use those services if they do not incur the full cost. Their premiums will be the same whether they use the services or not.

As the breadth of coverage has increased, the issues of cost containment have challenged all of the parties involved in paying for health care. These parties include the government, private insurers, health care providers, employers (who often provide health insurance as a fringe benefit to employees), and of course, households.

Moral hazard

With entirely private health care, competition among suppliers of health care services should put some downward pressure on prices. In fact, even in the current patchwork situation, buyers of employer-provided health insurance for large groups exert some pressure to keep costs and prices down. Certainly the administrators of the Medicare program have attempted to use their leverage as a major purchaser of health services to hold down medical care costs. But the system of third party payments by governments and employers still tends to keep demand high relative to scarce medical service resources. Competition in such a system has not been very effective in constraining either demand or costs.

The biggest challenge in designing any kind of health insurance system, public or private, is controlling costs. If a third party is bearing all the cost, if the premium for insurance is the same regardless of usage, individuals have no incentive to limit their demand for health care. In insurance, this problem of overuse that ultimately drives up premiums is known as **moral hazard**. To economists, it is a simple matter of following the demand curve down to the horizontal axis and determining how much health care people will demand at a price of zero for the marginal unit. Co-payments, typically 20 percent, are a partial solution to this problem of moral hazard. If individuals have to pay part of the cost, even if it is only 20 percent, they may not go to the doctor for routine or minor problems. However, the co-payment can also discourage people, especially low-income people, from obtaining needed medical care.

Behavioral economics: information asymmetry

In health care, moral hazard has an additional dimension. Many of the decisions about a person's health care—whether to have an operation, whether to remain in the hospital, what prescription to take, whether home health care or skilled nursing or hospice is called for— are made by the doctor as the professional expert without a great deal of consideration about cost. Neither the patient nor the insurer is able to adequately evaluate the recommendations of the health care professional, a situation that recurs in many market decisions that is known as **information asymmetry**.

From used cars to financial instruments to over-the-counter drugs, consumer purchases of many kinds depend on the reliability and completeness of information supplied by the seller. For some products where information is difficult to obtain and evaluate, public and private agencies (the Federal Trade Commission or Consumers' Union) attempt to fill the information gap. For example, reading *Consumer Reports* may help a person to avoid buying an unsafe or unreliable car. Required inspections for home loans protect both the home buyer and the lender from buying houses with serious structural defects.

But the amount and variety of information needed for good medical decisions are not always accessible to the patient or the patient's family. The patient is often unable to make a rational choice because of information asysmmetry. With medical professionals in the dual role of service provider and decision-maker but without the responsibility of paying for the services ordered, other entities must provide some oversight to protect consumers and control costs. That role is carried out by both private and public providers of health care payments.

Efforts to contain costs, however, create considerable resistance on the part of both doctors and patients. Employers, who pay part of the cost of employee health insurance, do have an interest in holding down costs, but they have to battle with both the health insurance industry and their own workers in order to do so.

Equity issues in health care

For most people, the argument for a public role in either producing or providing health care services is based not on efficiency but on equity. At least some kind of basic health care is regarded as a merit good in many countries, something to which one is entitled as a member of society along with food, shelter, and some amount of education. Access to such services in the United States depends on a demonstrated ability to pay, either through insurance, Medicare, Medicaid, or personal financial resources. Prior to Medicaid, hospitals took a certain number of "charity" cases among those unable to pay. In fact, many hospitals that were built with federal funds under the Hill-Burton Act were required to provide a certain amount of indigent care services in exchange.

Free medical services are not exactly abundant, but state and local governments do provide some basic services (vaccinations, well-baby and prenatal checkups, routine tests for blood pressure and cholesterol) through public clinics and medical personnel often donate some of their time to privately operated free clinics. Hospitals always have and continue to write off some bills as unpayable, a form of free health care services. The existence of such a loose network of free services for those unable to pay is indicative of some widely held belief that access to basic health services is an entitlement.

With the advent of Medicaid for the poor and Medicare for the elderly, and with the expiration of Hill-Burton obligations for hospitals to provide indigent care, the network of health care access for the poor has become somewhat more spotty.[2] The very poor, those on TANF or those transitioning to work from TANF, are covered by Medicaid. The elderly have either Medicare or Medicaid or sometimes both. Employees of most large firms and public agencies have group health insurance. Individuals not poor enough for Medicaid and not covered by employer-provided health insurance can often pay for routine health care and/or individual health insurance for themselves.

It is the 15 percent of Americans who do not fit into any of those categories who fall through the cracks of this mixed patchwork of public, private for-profit, and private non-profit services that constitutes the major challenge to the American health care system. For many states, the issue of those without any insurance is the most pressing one. Massachusetts, Arizona and Oregon have been leaders among states in attempting to expand the percentage of citizens with health insurance coverage through either private or publicly-funded policies.

Medical catastrophes

The equity rationale for health care is not solely or even primarily directed at the poor. Because the cost of an extended illness or major surgery can threaten the financial stability of even middle-income households, the issue of access to financing for health care cuts across most of the income spectrum. Major medical catastrophes, like earthquakes, tornadoes, and hurricanes, affect a relatively small number of people very intensely, so they are a perfect candidate for insurance.

So many people have the catastrophic part of their insurance (major medical) bundled with coverage for routine medical costs that it is easy to overlook the real insurance content of health care insurance. A major medical or catastrophic policy is less expensive because it processes fewer small claims. It usually offers a very high maximum payment but requires a large deductible in order to exclude routine medical costs.

Much of the debate over health care at both the state and national level has centered on the tradeoffs between providing more adequate services to those already covered and extending the umbrella of health insurance to those who have no protection. As part of that process, health care policy-makers are reconsidering whether the dominant model of employer-provided health insurance with broad coverage of even routine medical costs, low deductibles, and low co-payments is the most appropriate model for publicly funded health insurance.

Community rating

Private health insurers provide two types of health insurance: group and individual. If a group is large enough, it will contain a mix of insured persons of various ages (mostly under 65), states of health and likeliness of illness, and use of health care services. Group insurance typically allows individuals to purchase coverage on their spouse and/or dependent children at a fixed rate. Setting rates on this basis of average cost is called **community rating**.

However, policies for individuals or very small groups often charge different prices to different customers on the basis of how much they are expected to cost in terms of paying for health care services. Age, gender, health history, and risk factors are all taken into account in setting individual premiums. Some insurers simply refuse to sell insurance to customers they expect to be expensive to serve. Like the many prices charged airline customers for the same flight, or the restaurant discount prices for seniors and children, cost-based price discrimination is legal. However, it makes it more difficult for many people to be able to find affordable health insurance.

Price discrimination is not limited to the monthly premium. Co-pays, deductibles, exclusions, time limits, and maximum dollar amounts are all design features of insurance policies that reduce costs instead of raising premiums. Princeton health economist Uwe Reinhardt notes that in virtually all other industrial nations, community rating is the standard practice, whether insurance is provided by a single-payer (government) system or through private insurers (Reinhardt 2010). Switzerland, Germany and the Netherlands all use private insurers but do require community rating. Different insurers can charge different premiums, but any given insurer must charge the same rate for all customers, although they are permitted to change co-pays and deductibles. In the Netherlands and Germany, a payroll tax pay roughly half the cost of health insurance premiums. The payment for any insured person is adjusted for risk, that is, how much that person is likely to cost in health care services. Similar systems are used in other countries.

Adverse selection

When insurance gets expensive, individuals who think their risk of loss is low may choose to go without insurance. Insurance companies lose the least costly group of customers, raising the average cost and forcing the insurers to raise premiums, driving even more low cost customers away. This response is known as **adverse selection**.

Adverse selection is not limited to insurance, but it is probably a more serious problem in that industry than in many others. Adverse selection, or the loss of low-cost customers (usually because of regulatory requirements that prohibit price discrimination), can cause losses to insurers that may drive them out of business. Efforts to avoid adverse selection by charging different premiums to different classes of customers can make insurance unavailable or unaffordable to some people. More commonly, people are refused coverage if they are expected to add more to costs than to revenue.

Health care insurance is particularly noted for a high degree of selectivity by insurers. Many people are rejected for health insurance because of pre-existing conditions or general high risk based on age, weight, or other factors. Others are offered individual insurance policies only at extremely high premiums, or very limited coverage, high deductibles, or other restrictions. Group insurance is always cheaper than individual insurance for the same client because a large group contains a mix of persons with very diverse demands for health care services in a given year.

Prior to the 2010 health care legislation, there were estimated 46 million Americans, almost 15 percent of the population, without any health insurance. Many of them are not poor enough for Medicaid, not old enough for Medicare, not working for an employer who provides health insurance, and/or not able to afford the high premiums for individual health insurance. This issue was the driving force behind legislation that mandated coverage, offered subsidies to those unable to pay, and forbade insurers rejecting applicants with pre-existing conditions.

The 2010 health insurance legislation addressed both ends of the population risk spectrum. All individuals, even the young, healthy, low-risk ones, are required to have health insurance, reducing the adverse selection problem. Companies cannot charge higher premiums for high-risk individuals. For high-risk individuals, there is a commitment to provide access to insurance through other methods such as insurance exchanges. But so far, the United States has not moved in the direction of community rating and public subsidies to high-risk individuals as a policy ensuring equitable access to health care insurance. There are still some questions to be resolved about adverse selection and price discrimination if the system is to continue to rely on private insurers to provide coverage to those not eligible for Medicare, Medicaid, or CHIP.

Health care for the elderly: Medicare

Medicare came into being in 1965 after decades of discussion about universal health insurance dating back to 1916. The decision to offer a more limited program only for those over age 65 was a political compromise. The elderly were selected in part because this age group had so little private health insurance (less than half the elderly at that time). The design of Medicare was modeled on the private insurance plan provided for federal government employees.

For 45 million people over 65 and the disabled, Medicare is the primary source of health insurance, although many of them have supplementary health insurance as well. At $469 billion in 2008, Medicare spent more than $10,000 per beneficiary on average. Spending has grown rapidly in response to cost-increasing changes in medical technology as well as a growing elderly population, although that increased spending has also resulted in improved health and life expectancy among the elderly. The addition of prescription drug coverage in 2006 resulted in a sharp increase in Medicare costs. Prescription drugs now account for about 21 percent of Medicare spending.

Medicare has three parts. About 60 percent of the program is hospital insurance, Part A, which pays for hospital care and some limited alternatives (nursing facilities, home health care, hospices), and is funded by a payroll tax of 2.9 percent, half paid by employers and half by employees. Projections call for a continued increase in both beneficiaries and cost per recipient that will greatly exceed the growth of the payroll contributions for Medicare Part A (hospital insurance). The Medicare trust fund is expected to exhaust its accumulated assets in 2017 and will have to be funded on a year-to-year basis after that.

Part B covers doctors, outpatient care, lab tests, medical equipment, and some other services. Part D is prescription drug coverage. Part B is funded by a combination of general tax revenues (about 75 percent of costs) and premiums paid by beneficiaries (25 percent).

Medicare adopted many features of private employer-financed health insurance. These policies have provisions to control usage by making sure that the patient bears some share of the cost. One such feature is the **deductible**, which the amount the patient must pay out-of-pocket each year before insurance benefits can be tapped. Another feature is **co-payments**, which is the percentage of the bill paid by the patient, typically 20 percent for physicians' services. A third feature of many private policies is an annual and/or lifetime maximum total payment, which is not a part of Medicare. These provisions play an important role in containing the growth of demand for services, essential to any kind of insurance program, public or private.

However, many Medicare clients also have private "Medigap" insurance that covers most of the expenses they would otherwise have to pay, including deductibles and co-payments. Consequently, those over age 65 often have little incentive to restrict their use of health care compared to younger persons, and their demands have contributed to a rise in the cost of health care that is faster than the general rate of inflation. In addition, this age group generally has more health care demands in any payment situation as health begins to deteriorate in the aging process.

Health care for the poor: Medicaid and CHIP

Health care for low-income families with children and low-income elderly is provided through Medicaid, created in 1965, which is funded through general tax revenues with cost-sharing between the federal and state governments. Although ⅔ of the enrollees in Medicaid are under 65 (including many children), the largest share of the spending is for the elderly. Unlike Medicare, Medicaid does pay for long-term nursing home care, and elderly persons who have exhausted their financial resources in long-term care turn to Medicaid. Medicaid also pays for basic health care services such as hospital stays, physicians' care, and medical equipment. Medicaid, like Medicare, sets the amount it will reimburse for various services, usually at rates less than are customarily charged. Some health care service providers refuse to accept patients who will pay through Medicaid or limit the percentage of their services provided to Medicaid patients because of the relatively low reimbursement rates.

Medicaid is administered by the states, with different benefits in different states, although there are federal guidelines about eligible participants and eligible services. Medicaid funds are provided through matching grants, with higher match ratios for lower-income states to encourage them to provide more services. Recall that a matching grant will normally stimulate more spending by the recipient than a flat grant of an equal dollar amount because a matching grant has both income and substitution effects. Medicaid also became the fastest growing item in many states' budgets and the most challenging problem during the last two economic downturns, in 2000–02 and 2007–10.

Originally Medicaid for the nonelderly, nondisabled population was limited to families receiving Aid to Families with Dependent Children (AFDC, the predecessor of the current TANF program). In 1987, Medicaid was expanded to cover prenatal care for women and health services in children with incomes up to 133 percent of the poverty level, and states were allowed to expand that eligibility up to 185 percent of the poverty level and still receive matching federal funds. This change permits states to greatly increase Medicaid eligibility among the low-income population and receive their federal matching funds for such expansion. Not all states adopted the more generous guidelines, however, so eligibility is a continuing bone of contention between the states and the federal government.

At the same time, this legislation created the Children's Health Insurance Program (CHIP). The intent of CHIP was to expand the number of insured children in families previously above the income limits on Medicaid. Congress appropriated about $4 billion a year for approved state programs, which had to be at least as generous in eligibility as the upper limits of existing Medicaid eligibility, but could go higher in the income scale. A state-approved CHIP plan also had to meet at least minimum standards for coverage but also could exceed those limits. This initiative put the responsibility on the states to devise plans in which they would continue to share in the cost, but assisted with additional federal matching grant funds.

Summary

- The debate over the public role in health care is directed primarily at the financing of health care services. The challenge in financing health care is that third-party payments create only limited incentives for the consumer or service provider to restrict their demand.
- The social benefits of health care include the protection to others from contagious diseases as well as more general benefits of a healthy population and the costs of disability resulting from inadequate health care.
- Private employer-provided health insurance combines catastrophic or major medical insurance with payment for routine medical care because of tax advantages, despite the drawbacks in terms of restraining demand and controlling costs.
- Health care costs are affected by information asymmetry since the provider is generally more knowledgeable than the consumer, and by moral hazard because neither the medical professionals nor the patient has an incentive to control costs.
- Public provision of health care services is also an equity issue that cuts across income groups because of the potentially large financial risk from a prolonged illness or other kinds of costly health care needs. A second equity issue is price discrimination among buyers. Community rating requires that everyone be charged the same premium, although some other features of the insurance contract can reflect differences in risk.
- The major public programs to pay for health care are Medicare for the elderly and disabled, Medicaid for poverty-level households, and CHIP for children in households just above the poverty level. Other households rely on private (often employer-provided) health insurance or have no health insurance.

Key terms

Adverse selection
Children's Health Insurance Program (CHIP)
Community rating
Co-payment
Deductible
Information asymmetry
Medicaid
Medicare
Moral hazard

Questions

1   Why is it so difficult to use markets and prices to ration scarce health care resources among consumers compared to other kinds of goods and services?

2   The US health care system has higher per-person costs, higher dissatisfaction, and poorer outcomes than systems in most other industrial countries. What factors contribute to these results? How might the system be changed to get better results at lower costs? What obstacles are there to bringing about such changes?

3   What are the advantages and disadvantages to employers of providing only catastrophic health insurance (major medical) or also including routine care insurance for their employees? How does this choice affect health service providers? sick people?

4   **By the numbers**. Find out how the price index for health care services has performed compared to the overall consumer price index for the past 20 years. Graph both series. What has happed to health care costs compared to other consumer spending? What does this imply for the US debate on health care?

5   **Policy application**. Some states in the United States have experimented with various forms of universal coverage, particularly Oregon and Massachusetts. These states have tried to control costs in various ways. Oregon, for example, attempted to cover all residents but put limits on the kinds of services that might be available in any given year. If you were working for a state legislature that was designing a universal coverage system, how would you attempt to control costs?

6   **Behavioral economics**. Health care costs are affected by information asymmetry since the provider is generally more knowledgeable than the consumer, and by moral hazard because neither the medical professionals nor the patient have an incentive to control costs. What kinds of policy changes might help to address that problem?

7   **Thinking globally**. Employer-provided health insurance, which is the norm in the United States, affects total labor costs differently from health insurance coverage that is financed by general taxation, which is common in other industrial countries. How might this difference affect the competitiveness of American firms in selling exports or competing with imports? What kinds of industries are likely to be most affected?

Afterword

Like any textbook, this one does not say all there is to say about public sector economics. It does provide the basic analytical tools, the institutional and historical context, and the language and practices of this particular branch of economics. The purpose of any textbook is both to provide a foundation of knowledge and skills and to point the student in the direction of his or her continuing self-education in that field.

Armed with the skills developed and knowledge acquired in this course, you should be better able to follow debates in the media and on the web on important public sector policy issues. Your understanding of public sector economics will also spill over into other economics courses, because there is some public role or involvement in all areas of economics. A better understanding of what government is for and what its responsibilities are in a market system may also be helpful in assessing your own values in a political context. This book does not take a particular political stance, but implicit in every chapter is a perspective that government is a potentially useful tool (with some limitations) for improving economic welfare. That view will be disputed by those on the right who find government a useless burden and those on the left who think government should be much more actively involved in income distribution and resource allocation.

I took my first class in public sector economics (then known as public finance) in 1963, during the brief but exciting administration of President John Kennedy. A tax cut was passed to stimulate growth, and a novel proposal for General Revenue Sharing was proposed and passed under his successor, President Lyndon Johnson. At that time, there was a general faith in the ability of the United States to do just about anything and for the government to play a leadership role in making that anything happen. As the dominant world power, we paid little attention to developments in other countries except to try to export our economic model to third world countries and to be a bulwark against the perceived threat of international communism. Economists had enormous faith in the power of their discipline to shape a better world through good economic policy.

Government almost always meant the federal government. Little attention was paid to states, dominated by rural legislators and focused on schools and roads. Local governments existed mainly to provide services to their households and business firms, streets and sidewalks, police and fire protection, and their share of the cost of education, all financed by the property tax.

In the intervening 50 years, the changes in the size and scope of government activity at all levels have been dramatic. That half-century has seen the spread of the property tax revolt, the creation of Medicare and Medicaid, welfare reform, devolution of responsibilities to lower levels of government, the growth of the interstate highway system as a state/federal partnership, more activist and responsive state governments, national debates on Social

Security and health care, ballooning government budget deficits, and a greater awareness of the rest of the world as both a partner and a competitor in the global economy. Our faith in the power of economic analysis has been tempered by a growing awareness of its limitations as well as its strengths.

During your lifetimes, you can expect equally dramatic changes. A textbook and a course can only provide a foundation for encountering and responding to those changes. The rest is up to you.

Glossary

ability to pay A basis for equitable taxation determined by one's income or other measures of resources from which taxes can be paid.

accelerated depreciation Type of depreciation that permits the reduction in the value of an asset to take place more rapidly for tax purposes than the actual rate of decline over the asset's useful lifetime.

accountability Requiring public agencies and governing bodies, including school systems, to provide information about the uses of funds and the value of their work, such as student performance in education.

acquisition value A system of property tax valuation in which properties are only reassessed when sold, and otherwise increase in taxable value by a set percentage each year.

adequacy A property of an individual tax or revenue source, or a revenue system, that means ability to generate sufficient revenues to meet public expenditures requirements.

adjusted gross income (US income tax) Gross income minus certain permitted exclusions and adjustments; an intermediate step toward the determination of taxable income.

ad valorem **tax** A tax that is calculated as a percentage of the price or value of the item subject to tax.

adverse selection In insurance, a tendency to drive away lower-risk/lower-cost customers by rate increases, raising the average cost of the remaining pool of insured persons and putting further upward pressure on cost.

Aid to Families with Dependent Children (AFDC) Former US welfare program that provided public assistance to families with children who did not have sufficient income of their own.

allocation/distribution/stabilization A sorting of the functions of government developed by economist Richard Musgrave into those that affect the mix of output or the use of resources (allocation), the shares of income and wealth among the various groups in the population (distribution), and the macroeconomic impact of government on the level of output, employment, and prices (stabilization).

assessment The process of determining the value of a taxable asset for purposes of imposing property taxes.

average tax rate (income) Total tax liability expressed as a percentage of total income.

base erosion The reduction of the base of a tax either as a result of high rates or as a result of legislative actions to exempt some potential components of the base.

behavioral economics Modifications of traditional economic theory to account for deviations from the model of the rational, self-interested individual in actual behavior, reflecting more complex motivation and less cognitive ability.

benefit principle   The principle that taxes paid should be proportional to benefits received in services.

benefit tax   A tax levied on the users of a particular good or service to finance the provision of that good or service.

bounded rationality   Limiting the scope of choices to be considered to a manageable number rather than exploring all possible options.

budget   A statement of expected revenues and planned expenditures for a future period.

bureaucracy   The collection of agencies and appointed rather than elected leaders and civil servants that carry out the policies of the government.

cap and trade   A method of reducing pollution by issuing permits up to a certain level (the cap) and allowing firms or individuals to buy or sell permits as needed (the trade).

capitalization   The process by which changes in expected future benefits or revenues and expected future costs are incorporated into the market value of an asset.

cascade-type tax   A tax that is imposed at more than one stage of production and/or distribution.

categorical grant   A grant from one government to another, or from a government to a private group, that can only be used for a narrowly specified purpose.

centralization   The degree to which the collection of revenues and/or the provision of services is done at a higher rather than lower level of government.

Children's Health Insurance Program (CHIP)   A federal program created in 1997 to expand the number of children with health insurance in families previously above the income limits for Medicaid eligibility.

circuit breaker   A form of property tax relief in which low-income households receive rebates for part or all of their property tax through the state income tax.

classified property tax system   A property tax system in which different classes of property (such as residential, commercial, industrial, etc.) are assessed for tax purposes at different percentages of their market value, or are taxed at different mill rates.

closed-ended grant   A grant program that has a fixed number of dollars to allocate.

club goods   Quasi-public goods and services that are only available to members of a group.

collection cost(s)   Costs incurred by government in order to collect taxes.

common pool resources   Assets or resources that are held in common rather than in private ownership, such as air, water, and public lands.

community rating   In insurance, charging every insured entity the same rate for the same coverage rather than pricing on the basis of expected risk.

compensation principle   A test for whether a policy change improves economic welfare by determining whether the gainers could compensate the losers for their losses and still have some remaining gain.

compliance cost(s)   Costs incurred by the taxpayer in determining the amount of tax owed and remitting payment.

congestible goods   Goods or services that are non-rival in consumption up to capacity, after which the consumption by one person reduces the availability to another.

congestion charges   Fees charged during periods of peak usage of certain facilities such as roads and parks to reduce congestion.

consumer surplus   The difference between the amount that a consumer pays for a purchase and the total value or utility derived from that purchase.

consumption externalities   Positive or negative spillover effects on third parties that arise from consumption activities.

co-payment   In insurance, the percentage of certain costs that is borne by the policy holder rather than the insurance provider.

corporate income tax   A tax levied on the net income of corporations after all expenses have been subtracted.

cost-benefit analysis   A technique of project evaluation that determines and compares expected future costs and benefits from proposed projects.

cost-effectiveness analysis   A technique of evaluation that compares costs of alternative strategies for situations where outcomes can be measured but not assigned dollar values.

deadweight loss   See **excess burden**.

debt   The total amount owed to lenders by a government or other entity.

debt service   The annual cost for payments of interest and principal on a debt.

deductible (insurance)   The amount of out-of-pocket expense that the policyholder must incur before insurance begins to reimburse.

deficit   The annual excess of expenditures over revenues by a government or other entity.

defined benefit program   A pension program that guarantees certain benefits for life, based on factors such as length of service and average salary.

defined contribution program   A pension program in which benefits are determined by the amount in the pensioner's account resulting from the employee's own contributions, employer contributions, and interest or dividend earnings.

devolution   Assignment of responsibilities to a lower level of government.

distributive justice   Ensuring that access to resources is provided in an acceptable way to all members of the group.

district power equalization   A school funding program in which local governments are required to charge a certain millage or mill rate set by the state to support education, and the state makes up the difference between what that mill rate raises and the state average.

duopoly   A situation with only two suppliers, who will tend to produce similar products, services, and prices.

earmarked taxes   Tax revenues that flow into special funds or are set aside for specific uses rather than being included in the general fund.

Earned Income Tax Credit (EITC)   An income support program administered through the federal income tax that provides income supplements to the working poor.

economic efficiency   Ensuring that resources are used so as to maximize welfare and/or minimize cost for a given level of welfare.

education production function   The relationship between educational resources and educational outcomes or results.

effluent charges   Fees charged for the emission of pollutants based on volume emitted.

enterprise fund(s)   Special accounts outside of the general fund that receive payments and make expenditures to support specific government services, such as water and sewer.

entitlement   A program, service, or funds that one qualifies for by virtue of some characteristic such as age, disability, employment status or other criterion.

equality of opportunity   Programs that attempt to empower individuals to become self-sufficient through education, training, or support services.

equality of results   Programs that attempt to ensure that individuals have equal or at least minimally adequate resources on which to live regardless of how much they themselves contribute through earnings.

equalization   The process of redistributing resources by collecting more from wealthier individuals, communities, states or regions and sending proportionally more to poorer individuals, communities, states or regions.

equity   Fairness in the distribution of income, wealth, and economic opportunity.

estate tax   A federal tax in the United States on the transfer of accumulated wealth to one's heirs at death.

excess burden   The amount of consumer or producer surplus lost as a result of a tax; difference between revenue to the government and change in consumer/producer surplus.

excise tax   Tax imposed on a specific item or service, such as gasoline, tobacco, or alcohol.

exclusions (federal income tax)   Sources of household income that are not counted in adjusted gross income for tax purposes.

exemptions (federal income tax)   An amount per person, including dependents, that is subtracted from adjusted gross income before calculating tax liability.

expenditure forecasting   The process of anticipating expenditures for the upcoming budget based on cost changes, existing programs, population growth, newly authorized programs, and other factors.

externality   A spillover effect to a nonparticipant as a result of economic activity by another.

Fair Tax   A proposal to adopt a form of sales taxation at the federal level in the United States.

federalism   A form of government that includes at least three levels of government and some degree of sovereignty or independent authority at least at the middle level.

fiscal capitalization   The process by which the present and expected future taxes and the value of public services are reflected in the price of housing.

fiscal federalism   The aspects of organization of a federal state that relate to the assignment of revenue sources and expenditure responsibilities among the levels of government.

fiscal illusion   Misperception of the costs of government that leads people to demand more government services because they underestimate the tax cost of those services.

fiscal impact   The effect of a particular change on the government's revenue and costs of providing services.

fiscal surplus (deficit)   The difference between the level of taxes paid or collected and the cost or value of the services provided by the government to a particular household. If taxes paid exceed the value of services, the household has a fiscal deficit. If taxes paid are less than the cost of services provided, the household has a fiscal surplus.

fiscal year   The period covered by a particular government budget, indicated by the year in which that budget ended and the next one began. The US federal fiscal year ends on September 30th.

fiscal zoning   Use of zoning regulations to prevent the in-migration of lower-income households and the increase in construction of lower-value homes from reducing the fiscal surplus experienced by existing residents.

Flat Tax   An income tax reform proposal in the United States that would eliminate many of the complexities of the federal income tax and charge a single flat rate, making the tax less progressive.

flypaper effect   The tendency of intergovernmental aid to "stick where it lands;" funds given to the state or local public sector tend to increase spending for public purposes while funds given directly to households tend to primarily increase spending for private purposes.

formula funding   A method of distributing state aid to local school districts based on a formula that usually includes the number of students, the local tax base, and other factors.

formula grant   A grant based on one or more objective criteria such as population, poverty rate, or miles of highway.

franchise fee   A charge made by a government for the exclusive privilege of operating a private enterprise in a given area.

free-rider   A person who takes advantage of non-excludability by consuming a public good or quasi-public good without contributing to its cost.

fungibility   The ability to shift funds from one use to another in response to a grant for a specific purpose.

general obligation bonds   State or local government debt instruments that are backed by the full faith and credit of the issuing government and are payable out of general revenue.

general purpose grant   A grant from one government to another that may be used for any acceptable public purpose.

general revenue   Funds available for general budgetary purposes, excluding earmarked or off-budget fund and enterprise fund revenue.

General Revenue Sharing   A US federal government program of unrestricted grants to state and local governments in the 1970s and 1980s.

government failure   Outcomes of government activity that are less than optimal, including but not limited to the combination of goods and services produced and the distribution of income as they are influenced by government.

home rule   Independent authority enjoyed by local governments in raising revenue and providing services.

horizontal equalization   Actions by a higher level of government (federal to state, state to local) to ensure that resources are distributed more equally among governments at the same rate in order to compensate for differences in taxable resources in different localities.

horizontal equity   Fairness in the distribution of resources to people or communities in similar economic circumstances.

impact fee   A fee charged to developers or builders for construction on vacant lots to cover the additional cost of providing infrastructure and services to new residents or businesses.

incidence   The determination of who actually bears the burden of a tax in terms of paying higher prices or receiving less income or a reduction in the value of assets.

individual income tax   Income taxes levied on individual persons and households, including unincorporated businesses (proprietorships and partnerships).

information asymmetry   The disparity between the seller and buyer in information about quality, reliability, and other aspects of a product or service.

infrastructure   Physical and other capital assets, usually public, that provide the supporting backdrop for a market system; includes transportation, parks, waterways, public buildings, and water and sewer systems.

inheritance tax   A tax imposed by US states on the receipt of wealth from a deceased person.

initiative   The practice of allowing citizens to legislate by putting proposals on the ballot for a binding referendum.

insurance component (Social Security)   That part of Social Security that protects participants from the risk of disability or loss of a breadwinner.

intangibles   In property tax, taxable assets other than real property or tangible personal property such as cars and business equipment; includes financial assets.

intergenerational equity   Justice or fairness in the distribution of income, assets, or opportunities between individuals of different generations or cohorts.

intergovernmental grant   A sum of money transferred from one government to another, usually from the central government to state or local governments or from state to local governments, with the purpose for which it is to be expended being specified by the granting government.

internalizing externalities   Actions to make individuals bear the external costs or receive the external benefits of their own actions so that they will make decisions that are both socially and privately optimal.

interpersonal equity   Justice or fairness in the distribution of income, assets or opportunities among individuals.

Job Training and Partnership Act (JTPA)   A federal program to provide funds for training for unemployed workers, housewives re-entering the labor force, and others in need of remedial or expanded skills in order to become employable.

Laffer curve   A diagram showing the relationship between tax rate and tax revenue that implies that higher rates may reduce rather than increase revenue beyond some point.

Leviathan   The idea that government is an uncontrollable monster that devours resources; named for a mythical Babylonian sea monster.

Lindahl prices   Individual contributions to the cost of a public good that reflect the intensity of demand for each beneficiary; equal to marginal benefit for each user.

line-item budget   A budget that lists planned expenditures according to items purchased (labor, supplies, etc.) rather than according to the service provided or the agency.

local public goods   Public goods or services for which most of the benefits accrue to residents of a particular local area.

lump sum grant   A grant for which the amount is not dependent on any matching effort by the recipient.

maintenance of effort   A condition of a grant that requires the grantee to continue to expend at least the same amount of own funds on the purpose of the grant.

marginal social benefit   The increase in positive externalities that results from producing or consuming one more unit of a good or service.

marginal social cost   The increase in negative externalities that results from producing or consuming one more unit of a good or service.

marginal tax price   The additional tax cost to a particular individual for providing some additional public good or service.

marginal tax rate   The additional percentage of tax on an additional dollar of income or expenditure in a system with graduated rates.

market failure   Outcomes from private sector activity that are deemed unsatisfactory or less than optimal in terms of the combination of goods and services produced and consumed and/or the distribution of income.

matching grant   A grant that requires the grantee to contribute to the purpose of the grant in some fixed ratio for each dollar received.

means testing   Basing eligibility for programs, services, tax credits, etc. on the individual's or household's income.

median voter model   A model of political behavior based on the assumption that politicians respond to the preferences of the majority, those lying within one standard deviation of the mean in each direction in a normal distribution.

Medicaid   A US health care program that is means-tested and paid for out of general revenue, with costs shared between federal and state governments.

Medicare   A US federal health care program for those over age 65 or eligible for Social Security disability payments, providing hospital and physician care and funded through a combination of payroll taxes and premiums paid by participants.

meta-preferences   Preferences about preferences: rules that individuals make for themselves to constrain their own choices.

mill rate   The property tax rate stated as tenths of a cent per $100 of assessed valuation.

moral hazard   The risk that people who are insured will become careless or overuse services because they know that they will be reimbursed.

municipal bonds   Debt instruments issued by state and local governments. The interest is exempt from federal income taxes.

No Child Left Behind Act (NCLB)   Legislation passed during the Bush administration that stressed standards-based education using measurable goals set by individual states with federal funding linked to results.

non-excludability   Property of a public good that means it is difficult or impossible to keep nonpayers from consuming the good or service.

non-rivalry   Property of a public good that means its consumption by one person is not diminished by the consumption of others.

off-budget accounts   Part of a government's revenue and spending that is not included in the general budget, such as trust funds and enterprise funds.

Old Age, Survivors, Disability and Health Insurance (OASDHI)   The US social insurance program for retiree pensions and health care, surviving dependents of workers, and disabled workers; also known as Social Security.

open-ended grant   Grant program that does not have a fixed dollar ceiling but awards funds to all eligible recipients who meet the criteria.

option demand   Demand for a service to be available in case it is needed; for example, a fire station.

own-source revenue   Revenue raised by the government that spends it; excludes revenue received from other levels of government.

Pareto optimality   A state of production and/or consumption that cannot be improved without making at least one person worse off.

payroll tax   A tax levied on wages and salaries, usually collected by the employer.

peak-load pricing   Setting higher prices for periods of peak demand so as to encourage some users to shift to off-peak periods.

pension/annuity component (Social Security)   The part of Social Security that provides retirement income to workers and their dependents who have accumulated enough quarters of coverage and meet the age requirement.

performance budgeting   Budgeting based on desired outcomes, with budget allocations set so as to try to attain those outcomes.

personal property   Items other than land and buildings that may also be subject to property taxes, such as cars or business inventories.

poll tax   A per capita or per household tax of a flat amount; simple to administer but very regressive.

production externalities   Positive or negative spillover effects on third parties that arise from production activities.

program budget   A budget that defines a group of related governmental activities and specifies the funds to be allocated to those activities.

progressive (tax)   A tax that takes a higher percentage of income from higher-income taxpayers and a lower percentage from lower-income taxpayers.

project grant   Intergovernmental grant distributed on the basis of invited proposals for specific purposes.

proportional (tax)   A tax that takes the same percentage of income regardless of the level of income.

public choice   That branch of economics that deals with the process of decision-making in the public sector, based on the assumption that public officials act as self-interested individuals.

public finance, public sector economics   That branch of economics that deals with the interaction between private and public sectors in the provision and financing of goods and services, including taxation, public goods, redistribution of income, and correcting externalities.

public goods   Goods or services that are both non-rival in consumption and non-excludable of those who do not contribute to its support.

rational ignorance   The choice by citizens to not make the effort to be informed about candidates or issues because the costs of obtaining the information are greater than the personal benefits.

real property   Assets in the form of land or improvements, mainly buildings.

redistribution component (Social Security)   The aspect of Social Security that gives relatively higher benefits to low-wage workers than to higher-wage workers in comparison to their pre-retirement income.

referendum   Direct citizen voting on issues that arise through a legislative process or from citizen initiatives. Referenda can be advisory or binding in nature.

regressive (tax)   A tax that takes a lower percentage of income from higher-income taxpayers and a higher percentage from lower-income taxpayers.

residual claimant   The individual or group that is entitled to the remainder (surplus or profit) after all other claimants have been paid, including workers, suppliers, and bondholders or creditors.

restorative justice   Compensating for losses with some equivalent in resources or circumstances so as to restore those who lost to a position roughly equivalent to their original situation.

retail sales tax   A broad-based consumption tax collected only on final sales of goods and services.

revenue bonds   Debt instruments issued by state and local governments to finance income-generating facilities. Revenue from the facilities is pledged to repay the debt.

revenue forecasting   Predicting the flow of government income in future budget years based on past experience, current conditions, and the revenue structure.

shadow demand (supply) curve   A second demand or supply curve that reflects the differences in the perceptions of supply or demand by buyer or seller. In the case of a tax, the difference is the amount of the tax.

shadow prices   Imputed prices or estimated values for sources of benefit or cost that do not pass through the market; used in cost-benefit analysis.

shifting   Passing the burden of the tax from the person who is initially required to remit the tax to a customer, worker, supplier or owner.

Social Security tax   Tax on wage and salary earnings that is paid into the Social Security Trust Fund.

Social Security Trust Fund   Off-budget federal accounts that receive payroll and Medicare taxes and premiums and make payments to beneficiaries.

spatial externalities   Spillover effects that are experienced by people in proximity to the activity creating the effect.

specific tax   A tax that is expressed as a function of some physical measure rather than as a percentage of the price.

standard/itemized deductions   Reductions of income subject to federal income tax based on designated expenses such as charitable contributions, state and local taxes, and mortgage interest.

subsidy   A government payment to encourage a particular activity or expenditure by reducing the cost.

sumptuary tax   A tax intended to discourage consumption of the item subject to the tax.

Supplementary Security Income (SSI)   A program of public assistance funded out of general tax revenues for those who do not qualify for other programs such as Social Security or TANF.

taxable equivalent yield   The percentage return on a municipal (tax-free) bond that would be equal to the after-tax return on a taxable bond of the same maturity and degree of risk.

taxable income   In US income tax, the amount of income that is the basis for computing tax liability after subtracting exclusions, adjustments, exemptions and deductions.

tax and spending limitations   Ceilings on the growth of taxes, government revenue, or government spending enacted by statute or constitutional amendment in order to limit the growth of government.

tax avoidance   Legal spending, investment or other activities undertaken specifically to reduce one's tax liability.

tax credit   Reductions in tax liability for specific kinds of spending or circumstances; subtracted from taxes rather than from income.

tax evasion   Illegal activities undertaken to reduce one's tax liability, such as misrepresenting income, exemptions, or deductions.

Temporary Assistance to Needy Families (TANF)   Current US welfare program that provides income and support services to families with the goal of helping them to become financially self-sufficient.

Tiebout hypothesis   The argument that people's choices of location will respond to differences in tax-service packages offered by local governments, putting competitive pressure on local governments to provide better services at lower cost.

total revenue   Government income from all sources, including off-budget and enterprise funds.

transfer payments   Government payments to individuals by government for which nothing is required in exchange, including Social Security benefits, veterans' benefits, and welfare payments.

two-part tariff   A charge for a good or service that consists of two parts, a flat charge to cover fixed costs and a per-use payment that reflects variable or marginal cost.

unemployment insurance   A program to provide income support for people who are out of work through no fault of their own, funded by employer payments.

unfunded mandate   A requirement imposed by a higher level of government on a lower one to carry out some specific action, without any provision for the higher level of government to pay part or all of the cost.

unified budget   A government budget that combines all accounts, including off-budget funds and enterprise funds.

unitary state   A country with a central government and local governments but no intermediate level of government.

universal participation   A program requirement that requires everyone who is eligible to participate.

value-added tax   A consumption tax collected at every stage of production and distribution (sometimes exempting retail), with a credit for taxes paid at earlier states so that no accumulation or cascading of taxes occurs.

veil of ignorance   In Rawls' concept of justice, a method of deciding the rules of society's distribution of assets, opportunities and rewards that is made by people who do not know what will be their own position in society in terms of such characteristics as age, gender, abilities, etc.

vertical equalization   Grants from higher to lower levels of government to compensate for the more limited ability of lower levels of government to raise revenue.

vertical equity   A fair distribution of resources or tax liabilities among people at different income levels or different levels of government with different capacities to raise revenue.

voting paradox   A situation in which preferences are not transitive: A is preferred to B, B to C, and C to A, because the voting system does not allow voters to express intensity of preferences.

vouchers   A certificate given to an individual or household to purchase specific kinds of goods or services, such as food (food stamps), housing, or education.

wage ceiling (Social Security)   the maximum amount of wage and salary earnings on which Social Security taxes are collected.

zero-based budgeting   A budgetary process that starts at a base of zero and requires justification of every expenditure instead of making incremental adjustments from the previous budget.

Notes

1 Government in a market system

1 For an extended discussion of the development of the field of public economics or public sector economics, see Dreze (1995).
2 Dan Ariely, a professor of both psychology and behavioral economics, has explained some of the understanding of choice behavior in a recent book called *Predictably Irrational* (2009).

3 The structure of governments

1 The word fiscal describes anything that relates to the treasury or finances of government. Fisc, or the public treasury, is the English form of the Latin word *fiscus*, which was originally a woven basket or money basket used by tax collectors.
2 Economist Alfred Hirschman wrote a classic and often-cited book, *Exit, Voice and Loyalty: Responses to Decline in Firms, Organizations, and States* (Cambridge, MA: Harvard University Press, 1970) that describes the role of leaving (exit) or complaining (voices) in bringing about desirable change or correcting undesirable changes and also offers a rich description of competition in quality that is especially relevant to local governments.
3 Counties are the most common form of general purpose local governments that include all citizens, as opposed to school districts (which are special purpose, providing only one service) or cities/towns, which only include those residents who choose to live inside the corporate limits of the city. In Louisiana, the equivalent of a county is a parish. In New England and some other states, the township is roughly equivalent to the county in terms of functions performed for all citizens, urban or rural.
4 Mathematically, the fiscal surplus for the ith individual in the jth location is given by:

$$FS_{ij} = \Sigma SV_{ij} - \Sigma T_{ij}$$

where FS = fiscal surplus, SV = the value of services received from governments, and T = taxes, including fees and other forms of nontax obligations. More formally, the calculation would include not only current taxes and services but also the present value of expected future taxes and services, appropriately discounted.
5 The mathematical formula is quite similar, with fiscal surplus (FS) replaced by fiscal impact (FI) and the value of services (SV) replaced by the estimated additional service costs (SC):

$$FI_{ij} = \Sigma T_{ij} - \Sigma SC_{ij}$$

6 The assessment rate is the percentage of the market value of taxable property that is used as the base for calculating the tax. The mill rate is the tax rate expressed as one thousandth of a dollar. The mill (or mil) is an old English coin worth 1/10 of a cent. The details of property tax administration are spelled out in Chapter 15.
7 While much more current data is available for the federal government, and for state governments, local government data trickle into the aggregate data system much more slowly, usually with a lag of four to five years from the end of the fiscal year (June 30th) to collection, processing and distribution through state and federal channels.

5 Equity, income distribution, and the social safety net

1 Alternatively, efficiency can be defined as getting the most (output, value, utility, satisfaction) out of available resources.
2 Also known as the Kaldor–Hicks criterion after the British economists who formulated this concept.
3 Think of the high-risk group and the low-risk group in terms of the bimodal distribution described in Chapter 4, with the median insurable person falling in between the two peaks in terms of risk or probability.
4 The disability part of Social Security is another matter altogether, because eligibility rests on a complex screening system to verify the nature and extent of the disability.

6 Public goods

1 There is an extensive literature on the theory of clubs, or private voluntary associations for the production of shared goods, such as churches, tennis and sailing clubs, neighborhood associations, etc. Most of what has been written on this subject draws inspiration from the classic article by James Buchanan, "An Economic Theory of Clubs," *Economica*, 32(5) (February 1965): 1–14. Local governments, especially cities, have many characteristics in common with such clubs. For a thorough summary of some of the earlier literature on local public goods, see David King, *Fiscal Tiers* (London: George Allen and Unwin, 1984).

7 Externalities: dealing with spillover effects

1 US Environmental Protection Agency, "2008 Emission, Compliance, and Market Analyses," available at: http://www.epa.gov/progress/ARP_2.html (accessed June 11, 2010).

8 Budgeting in the public sector

1 I am indebted to a former student, Alfred Bundrick, for providing information on the TABOR experience in Colorado. Additional information came from Iris J. Lav and Erica Williams, *A Formula for Decline: Lessons from Colorado for States Considering TABOR* (Washington, DC: Center on Budget and Policy Priorities, March 15, 2010).

10 Cost-benefit analysis

1 Total welfare could also be minimized if it is the point where the excess of cost over benefit is greatest. However, it's pretty easy to tell which is the case. If the difference between benefit and cost is a negative number, then you are at a minimum rather than a maximum.

11 Principles of taxation I: efficiency and equity issues

1 Unincorporated businesses also pay these taxes, but because their income taxes are paid as individuals, the only issue for these firms is compounding of sales taxes.

12 Principles of taxation II: applied issues

1 The best measure of what is happening to growth of costs/prices for public sector inputs is the GDP deflator for the government sector of Gross Domestic Product (there are separate ones for federal and for state/local). Many state and local governments use the Consumer Price Index, but that does not accurately reflect the cost of what state and local governments purchase. In particular, because so many households have employer-provided health insurance, that cost is not reflected in the Consumer Price Index, but it has been an important source of rising expenses for state and local governments who have a lot of employees to insure.
2 For a thorough analysis of the pros and cons of tax expenditures, see Christopher Howard, "Testing the Tools Approach: Tax Expenditures Versus Direct Expenditures," *Public Administration Review*, 55(5) (September/October 1995), 439–447.

3 For a discussion of this issue, see William F. Fox and David Mayes, "Are Economic Development Incentives Too Large?" (pp. 203–209) in *Proceedings of the 86th Annual Conference* (New York: National Tax Association, 1994), and Douglas Woodward, "Assessing Economic Development Incentives: Lessons from BMW," in *Proceedings of the 86th Annual Conference* (New York: National Tax Association, 1994).

4 Comparison data is available from the Tax Foundation, available at: www.taxfoundation.org.

13 Taxes on income

1 Income from unincorporated businesses, both proprietorships and partnerships, is treated as individual income for tax purposes in the United States.

2 Taxes on wealth, chiefly property taxes, are covered in Chapter 15.

14 Taxes on sales and consumption

1 An alternative representation is to draw a long-run demand curve that is more price-elastic than the short-run demand curve through the initial, pre-tax price and quantity combination Q_0, P_0. That curve would, of course, be flatter. Determining the amount of tax revenue raised in the short run versus long run is left as an exercise for the student.

2 Zero-rating means that the rate at the final stage of distribution is zero, so the tax accumulated to that point is rebated to the seller and not passed forward to the buyer.

15 Taxes on property and wealth

1 Data is from the US Bureau of the Census, *Census of Governments, 2008* (Washington, DC: US Government Printing Office, 2008). Local own-source revenues include fees, charges, licenses, permits and miscellaneous in addition to tax revenue. General revenue includes intergovernmental aid. The largest figure total, revenue, also includes income from local government enterprises such as water and sewer service, transit, electric power, and in some places, liquor stores.

2 This calculation is prior to income taxes. The effective tax rate after adjusting for income tax deductibility of property taxes is somewhat lower. For a person in a 35 percent combined federal and state tax bracket, a 1.25 percent effective property tax rate is only a 0.81 percent rate after deducting property taxes for income tax purposes. The after-tax effective rate is then 8–11 percent rather than 12.5–18 percent.

3 The various views of property tax incidence were summarized in a now-classic work by Henry J. Aaron, *Who Pays the Property Tax?* (Washington, DC: Brookings Institution, 1975).

4 See Terri A. Sexton, Steven M. Shiffrin and Arthur O'Sullivan,"Proposition13: Unintended Effects and Feasible Reforms," *National Tax Journal* LII(1) (March 1999): 99–111 for a good summary of the aftereffects of Proposition 13, including inequities in burden distribution, declining public services, shift to nontax revenue sources, and the impact on support for public education.

5 A useful discussion of the equity and efficiency issues surrounding the estate and gift taxes can be found in William G. Gale and Joel Slemrod, "Life and Death Questions about the Estate and Gift Tax," *National Tax Journal*, LIII(4) (December 2000): 889–912.

16 Fees and charges as a revenue source

1 Fees and charges are only one of many tools for regulating externalities. Other approaches range from the regulatory approach to the creation of markets in pollution rights.

19 Social Security

1 State and local governments have had the option not to include their employees in the Social Security system, although most states have chosen to do so. Some states that had opted out are now reconsidering that decision because of the poor performance of state retirement system funds in recent years.

2 Adverse selection occurs when the people who "buy" a particular insurance policy are the ones most likely to have claims. As insurance becomes more expensive, people "self-insure"—they take

precautions and do without auto insurance or certain kinds of homeowners' insurance unless required to do so by the state or by mortgage lenders. As these lower-cost customers drop out, the average cost rises, making insurance even more expensive for those who remain. Health insurance is particularly careful to avoid adverse selection by refusing to cover pre-existing conditions and by emphasizing sales to large groups such as employees of large firms, which are usually a broad mix of low-claims and high-claims clients.

20 Health care

1 Information provided by Peter Staples, a doctoral student at Clemson University.
2 Some hospitals have paid the government to be released from their Hill–Burton obligations so that they can be sold to private, for-profit hospital conglomerates like Humana or Health Corporation of America.

Bibliography

Aaron, Henry J. (1975) *Who Pays the Property Tax?*, Washington, DC: Brookings Institution.

Alliance for Excellent Education Policy Brief (2009) *Short Sighted: How America's Lack of Attention to International Education Studies Impedes Improvement*, available at: www.all4ed.org (accessed July 16, 2010).

American Farmland Trust, Farmland Information Center (2007) *Fact Sheet: Cost of Community Services Studies*. August, available at: www.farmland.org.

Ariely, Dan (2009) *Predictably Irrational: The Hidden Forces that Shape Our Decisions*, New York: HarperCollins.

Arnold, R. Douglas, Graetz, Michael J. and Munnell, Alicia H. (eds.) (1998) *Framing the Social Security Debate: Values, Politics, and Economics*, Washington, DC: National Academy of Social Insurance.

Barzel, Yoram (1997) *Economic Analysis of Property Rights*, 2nd edn, Cambridge: Cambridge University Press.

Blum, Walter J. and Calven, Harold (1953) *The Uneasy Case for Progressive Taxation*, Chicago: University of Chicago Press.

Board of Trustees of the Federal Old-Age and Survivors Insurance and Federal Disability Insurance Trust Funds (2009) *Annual Report*, Washington, DC: U.S. Government Printing Office.

Buchanan, James (1965) "An Economic Theory of Clubs," *Economica*, 32(5): 1–14.

Buchanan, James and Tullock, Gordon (1962) *The Calculus of Consent*, Ann Arbor, MI: University of Michigan Press.

Canoy, Martin and Rothstein, Richard (2001) "Do School Vouchers Improve Student Performance?" *The American Prospect*, 12(1): 42–46.

Card, David and Krueger, Alan B. (1996) "School Resources and Student Outcomes: An Overview of the Literature and New Evidence from North and South Carolina," *Journal of Economic Perspectives*, 10(4): 31–40.

Carroll, Robert J. and Yinger, John (1994) "Is the Property Tax a Benefit Tax? The Case of Rental Housing," *National Tax Journal*, XLVII(2): 295–316.

Center for Budget and Policy Priorities (2010) *The Earned Income Tax Credit*, available at: http://www.cbpp.org. (accessed June 1, 2010).

Coase, Ronald (1960) "The Problem of Social Cost," *Journal of Law and Economics*, 3: 1–44.

Cody, Betsy A. (1996) *Grazing Fees: An Overview*, Washington, DC: Congressional Research Service.

Cody, Betsy and Baldwin, Pamela (1998) *Grazing Fees and Rangeland Management*, Washington, DC: Congressional Research Service.

Davis, Karen, Schoen, Cathy, and Stremikis, Kristof (2010) *Mirror, Mirror on the Wall: How the Performance of the U.S. Health Care System Compares Internationally, 2010 Update*, New York: Commonwealth Fund.

Diamond, Henry L. and Noonan, Patrick F. (1996) *Land Use in America*, Cambridge, MA: Lincoln Institute of Land Policy.

Dreze, Jacques (1995) "Forty Years of Public Economics: A Personal Perspective," *Journal of Economic Perspectives*, 9(2): 111–130.

Dunbar, Amy and Pogue, Thomas (1998) "Estimating Flat Tax Incidence and Yield: A Sensitivity Analysis," *National Tax Journal*, 51(2): 303–324.

Education Counts (2010) "Impact of Education on Income." Available at: http://www.educationcounts. govt.nz/indicators/education_and_learning/ (accessed July 16, 2010).

Ellwood, David T. (2000) "The Impact of the Earned Income Tax Credit and Social Policy Reforms on Work, Marriage, and Living Arrangements," *National Tax Journal*, LIII, 4(Part 2): 1063–1105.

Felix, R. Alison (2008) "The Growth and Volatility of State Tax Revenue Sources in the Tenth District," *Federal Reserve Bank of Kansas City Economic Review*, 93(3): 63–88.

Fougere, Maxime and Ruggeri, Guiseppe C. (1998) "Flat Taxes and Distributional Justice," *Review of Social Economy*, 56(3): 277–286.

Fox, William F. and Mayes, David (1994) "Are Economic Development Incentives Too Large?" in *Proceedings of the 86th Annual Conference*, New York: National Tax Association, pp. 203–209.

Friedman, Milton (2001) "How to Cure Health Care," *The Public Interest*, Winter: 3–30.

Galbraith, John Kenneth (1958) *The Affluent Society*, Boston: Houghton Mifflin.

Gale, William G. and Slemrod, Joel (2000) "Life and Death Questions about the Estate and Gift Tax," *National Tax Journal*, LIII(4): 889–912.

General Accountability Office (2000) *Sales Taxes: Electronic Commerce Growth Presents Challenges; Revenue Losses Are Uncertain*, Washington, DC: Government Printing Office.

Godschalk, David R., Rose, Adam, Mittler, Elliott, Porter, Keith and Taylor West, Carol (2009) "Estimating the Value of Foresight: Aggregate Analysis of Natural Hazard Mitigation Benefits and Costs," *Journal of Environmental Planning and Management*, 52(6): 739–756.

Greenstein, Robert and Shapiro, Isaac (1998) *New Research Findings on the Effects of the Earned Income Tax Credit*, Washington, DC: Center on Budget and Policy Priorities.

Hahn, Robert W. (1989) "Economic Prescriptions for Environmental Problems: How the Patient Followed the Doctor's Orders," *Journal of Economic Perspectives*, 3(2): 95–114.

Hardin, Garrett (1968) "The Tragedy of the Commons," *Science*, 162(38): 1243–1248.

Heckman, James *et al.* (1997) "Substitution and Drop Out Bias in Social Experiments: A Study of an Influential Social Experiment," University of Chicago Working Paper, August 1997, cited in Thomas J. Kane and Cecilia Elena Rice (1999) "The Community College; Educating Students at the Margins between College and Work," *Journal of Economic Perspectives*, 13(1): 63–84.

Hines, James R. and Thaler, Richard H. (1995) "Anomalies: The Flypaper Effect," *Journal of Economic Perspectives*, 9: 217–226.

Hirschman, Alfred (1970) *Exit, Voice and Loyalty: Responses to Decline in Firms, Organizations, and States*, Cambridge, MA: Harvard University Press.

Howard, Christopher (1995) "Testing the Tools Approach: Tax Expenditures Versus Direct Expenditures," *Public Administration Review*, 55(5): 439–447.

Kaldor, Nicholas (1955) *An Expenditure Tax*, London: George Allen and Unwin.

King, David (1984) *Fiscal Tiers*, London: George Allen and Unwin.

Lav, Iris J. and Williams, Erica (2010) *A Formula for Decline: Lessons from Colorado for States Considering TABOR*, Washington, DC: Center on Budget and Policy Priorities.

Lavee, Doron and Becker, Nir (2009) "Cost-Benefit Analysis of an Accelerated Vehicle-Retirement Program," *Journal of Environmental Planning and Management*, 52(6): 777–795.

Leimer, Dean R. (1995) "A Guide to Social Security's Money's Worth Issues," *Social Security Bulletin*, 58(2).

McCullough, J. R. (1863) *A Treatise on the Principles and Practical Influence of Taxation and the Funding System.*

Man, Joyce, Y. "The Incidence of Differential Commercial Property Taxes: Empirical Evidence," *National Tax Journal*, 48(4): 479–496.

Marwell, Gerald and Ames, Ruth, E. (1981) "Economists Free Ride, Does Anyone Else?" *Journal of Public Economics*, 15: 295–310.

National Center for Education Statistics (2010) *Revenues and Expenditures for Public Elementary and Secondary Education: School Year 2007–08 (Fiscal Year 2008)*, Washington, DC: NCES.

Nechyba, Thomas J. (1997) "Public School Finance and Vouchers in a General Equilibrium Tiebout World," *National Tax Association Proceedings*, pp. 119–125.

Niskanan, William (1971) *Bureaucracy and Representative Government*, Chicago: Aldine.

Noll, Roger G. and Zimbalist, Andrew (eds.) (1997) *Sports, Jobs and Taxes: The Economic Impact of Sports Teams and Stadiums*, Washington, DC: Brookings Institution.

Organization for Economic Cooperation and Development (OECD) (2008) *Statistical Extracts for 2008*, Paris: OECD.

Organization for Economic Cooperation and Development (2009) *OECD Health Data 2009*, available at: http://www.oecd.org/health/healthdata (accessed July 24, 2010).

Ostrom, Elinor (1990) *Governing the Commons: The Evolution of Institutions for Collective Action*, Cambridge: Cambridge University Press.

Pattison, David (1995) "The Distribution of OASDI Taxes and Benefits by Income Decile," *Social Security Bulletin*, Spring: 21–32.

Pogue, Thomas F., Maxey, James and Chia-Hsing, Lu (1999) "Outcomes of Public Education: Weighing the Effects of Dollars, Family, Peers, and Community," *National Tax Association Proceedings*, pp. 222–230.

Rawls, John (1971) *A Theory of Justice*, Cambridge, MA: Harvard University Press.

Rawls, John (1993) *Political Liberalism*, New York: Columbia University Press.

Reinhardt, Uwe E. (2010) "How the World Balances Health Care Risk," *The New York Times*, January 8.

Ring, Raymond J. Jr. (1999) "Consumers' Share and Producers' Share of the General Sales Tax," *National Tax Journal*, 52: 79–92.

Sexton, Terri A., Shiffrin, Steven M. and O'Sullivan, Arthur (1999) "Proposition 13: Unintended Effects and Feasible Reforms," *National Tax Journal*, LII(1): 99–111.

Simon, Herbert (1957) "A Behavioral Model of Rational Choice," in *Models of Man: Social and Rational: Mathematical Essays on Rational Human Behavior in a Social Setting*, New York: Wiley.

Smith, Adam (1776) *An Inquiry into the Nature and Causes of the Wealth of Nations*.

Sobel, Russell S. and Holcombe, Randall G. (1996) "Measuring the Growth and Variability of Tax Bases over the Business Cycle," *National Tax Journal*, XLIX(4): 535–552.

Stiglitz, Joseph (1998) "Distinguished Lecture on Economics in Government: The Private Uses of Public Interests: Incentives and Institutions," *Journal of Economic Perspectives*, 12(2): 3–22.

Taylor, Corinne (1999) "Challenges in Linking Student Outcomes and School Expenditures," *National Tax Association Proceedings*, pp. 231–235.

Tiebout, Charles M. (1956) "A Pure Theory of Local Expenditures," *Journal of Political Economy*, 64: 416–424.

U.S. Bureau of the Census (2008) *Current Population Reports: Income, Poverty and Health Insurance Coverage in the United States: 2008*, Washington, DC: U.S. Government Printing Office.

U.S. Environmental Protection Agency (2009) *2008 Emission, Compliance, and Market Analyses*, available at: http:///www.epa.gov/progress/ARP_2.html (accessed June 11, 2010).

U.S. General Accountability Office (2005) *Social Security Reform*, GAO-05-193SP, Washington, DC: Government Printing Office.

Weaver, R. Kent (1998) "The Politics of Pension Reform: Lessons from Abroad," in R. Douglas Arnold, Michael Graetz, and Alicia Munnell (eds.) *Framing the Social Security Debate: Values, Politics and Economics*, Washington, DC: Brookings Institution Press, pp. 183–229.

Woodward, Douglas (1994) "Assessing Economic Development Incentives: Lessons from BMW," in *Proceedings of the 86th Annual Conference*, New York: National Tax Association.

Yilmaz, Yesim, Hoo, Sonya, Nagowski, Matthew, Rueben, Kim and Tannewald, Robert (2007) *Fiscal Disparities across States, FY2002*, Urban-Brookings Tax Policy Center, No. 16, January.

Zumeta, William (2009) "State Support of Higher Education: The Roller Coaster Plunges Downward Yet Again," *The NEA Almanac of Higher Education*, 2009: 29–43.*Table 8.1* Elasticity relationship between personal income and tax bases.

Index

Page numbers in **bold** denote figures